P9-AFQ-731

Fodor's 2010

MAUI

WITH MOLOKA'I AND LĀNA'I

Fodor's Travel Publications   New York, Toronto, London, Sydney, Auckland
www.fodors.com

Be a Fodor's Correspondent

Your opinion matters. It matters to us. It matters to your fellow Fodor's travelers, too. And we'd like to hear it. In fact, we need to hear it.

When you share your experiences and opinions, you become an active member of the Fodor's community. That means we'll not only use your feedback to make our books better, but we'll publish your names and comments whenever possible. Throughout our guides, look for "Word of Mouth," excerpts of your unvarnished feedback.

Here's how you can help improve Fodor's for all of us.

Tell us when we're right. We rely on local writers to give you an insider's perspective. But our writers and staff editors—who are the best in the business—depend on you. Your positive feedback is a vote to renew our recommendations for the next edition.

Tell us when we're wrong. We're proud that we update most of our guides every year. But we're not perfect. Things change. Hotels cut services. Museums change hours. Charming cafés lose charm. If our writer didn't quite capture the essence of a place, tell us how you'd do it differently. If any of our descriptions are inaccurate or inadequate, we'll incorporate your changes in the next edition and will correct factual errors at fodors.com immediately.

Tell us what to include. You probably have had fantastic travel experiences that aren't yet in Fodor's. Why not share them with a community of like-minded travelers? Maybe you chanced upon a beach or bistro or B&B that you don't want to keep to yourself. Tell us why we should include it. And share your discoveries and experiences with everyone directly at fodors.com. Your input may lead us to add a new listing or highlight a place we cover with a "Highly Recommended" star or with our highest rating, "Fodor's Choice."

Give us your opinion instantly at our feedback center at www.fodors.com/feedback. You may also e-mail editors@fodors.com with the subject line "Maui Editor." Or send your nominations, comments, and complaints by mail to Maui Editor, Fodor's, 1745 Broadway, New York, NY 10019.

You and travelers like you are the heart of the Fodor's community. Make our community richer by sharing your experiences. Be a Fodor's correspondent.

Aloha!

Tim Jarrell

Tim Jarrell, Publisher

FODOR'S MAUI 2010

Editors: Linda Cabasin, Jess Moss, Amanda Theunissen

Writers: Eliza Escaño-Vasquez, Bonnie Friedman, Heidi Pool, Cathy Sharpe, Carla Tracy, Joana Varawa

Production Editor: Evangelos Vasilakis

Maps & Illustrations: Henry Colomb and Mark Stroud, Moon Street Cartography; David Lindroth; *cartographers*; Bob Blake, Rebecca Baer, *map editors*; William Wu, *information graphics*

Design: Fabrizio La Rocca, *creative director*; Guido Caroti, Siobhan O'Hare, *art directors*; Tina Malaney, Chie Ushio, Ann McBride, Jessica Walsh, *designers*; Melanie Marin, *senior picture editor*

Cover Photo: (La Pérouse, Wailea): Pacific Stock/Photolibrary

Production Manager: Angela L. McLean

ISBN 978-1-4000-0835-3

ISSN 1559-0798

SPECIAL SALES

This book is available at special discounts for bulk purchases for sales promotions or premiums. Special editions, including personalized covers, excerpts of existing books, and corporate imprints, can be created in large quantities for special needs. For more information, write to Special Markets/Premium Sales, 1745 Broadway, MD 6-2, New York, New York 10019, or e-mail specialmarkets@randomhouse.com.

AN IMPORTANT TIP & AN INVITATION

Although all prices, opening times, and other details in this book are based on information supplied to us at press time, changes occur all the time in the travel world, and Fodor's cannot accept responsibility for facts that become outdated or for inadvertent errors or omissions. So **always confirm information when it matters,** especially if you're making a detour to visit a specific place. Your experiences—positive and negative— matter to us. If we have missed or misstated something, **please write to us.** We follow up on all suggestions. Contact the Maui editor at editors@fodors.com or c/o Fodor's at 1745 Broadway, New York, NY 10019.

PRINTED IN SINGAPORE

10 9 8 7 6 5 4 3 2 1

CONTENTS

Fodor's Features

CONTENTS

ABOUT THIS BOOK

Our Ratings

Sometimes you find terrific travel experiences and sometimes they just find you. But usually the burden is on you to select. That's where our ratings come in.

As travelers we've all discovered a place so wonderful that its worthiness is obvious. And sometimes that place is so unique that superlatives don't do it justice. These sights, properties, and experiences get our highest rating, **Fodor's Choice**, indicated by orange stars throughout this book. Black stars highlight sights and properties we deem **Highly Recommended**, places that our writers, editors, and readers praise for consistency and excellence.

By default, there's another category: any place we include in this book is by definition worth your time, unless we say otherwise. And we will.

Disagree with any of our choices? Care to nominate a place or suggest that we rate one more highly? Visit our feedback center at www.fodors.com/feedback.

Budget Well

Hotel and restaurant price categories from ¢ to $$$$ are defined in the opening pages of each chapter. For attractions, we always give standard adult admission fees; reductions are usually available for children, students, and senior citizens. Want to pay with plastic? **AE, D, DC, MC, V** following restaurant and hotel listings indicate whether American Express, Discover, Diners Club, MasterCard, and Visa are accepted.

Restaurants

Unless we state otherwise, restaurants are open for lunch and dinner daily. We mention dress only when there's a specific requirement and reservations only when they're essential or not accepted—it's always best to book ahead.

Hotels

Hotels have private bath, phone, TV, and air-conditioning and operate on the European Plan, meaning without meals, unless we specify that they use the Continental Plan (CP, with a Continental breakfast), Breakfast Plan (BP, with a full breakfast), or Modified American Plan (MAP, with breakfast and dinner), or are all-inclusive (AI, including all meals and most activities). We always list facilities but not whether you'll be charged an extra fee to use them, so when pricing accommodations, find out what's included.

Many Listings
- ★ Fodor's Choice
- ★ Highly recommended
- ✉ Physical address
- ↔ Directions
- 🏛 Mailing address
- ☎ Telephone
- 🖷 Fax
- ⊕ On the Web
- ✍ E-mail
- 🖅 Admission fee
- ⊙ Open/closed times
- ▭ Credit cards

Hotels & Restaurants
- 🏠 Hotel
- ⬎ Number of rooms
- ⌂ Facilities
- ⑩ Meal plans
- ✕ Restaurant
- ⬐ Reservations
- ⬎ Smoking
- ⑨ BYOB

Outdoors
- ⛳ Golf
- ⛺ Camping

Other
- ⏱ Family-friendly
- ⇨ See also
- ✉ Branch address
- ☞ Take note

Experience Maui

WELCOME TO MAUI

GETTING ORIENTED

When you experience Maui firsthand, it's hard not to gush about the long, perfect beaches, dramatic cliffs, greener-than-green rain forests, and the fragrance of plumeria that hangs over it all. Add to that the amazing marine life and the culture and history of the Hawaiian people, and it's easy to see why Maui is so popular. Today the threat of overdevelopment is a concern, which may help protect this special place. The island has very different areas, from the resorts of sunny West Maui and the South Shore to the funky small towns of the North Shore, the ranches and farms of Upcountry, and the remote village of Hāna in unspoiled East Maui. ■TIP➜Directions on the island are often given as mauka (toward the mountains) and makai (toward the ocean).

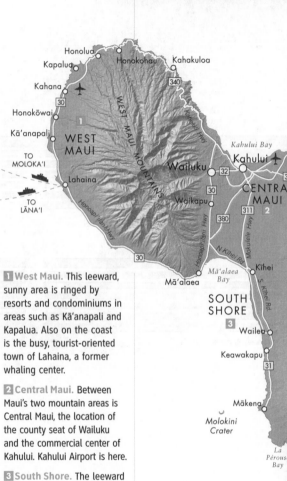

1 West Maui. This leeward, sunny area is ringed by resorts and condominiums in areas such as Kā'anapali and Kapalua. Also on the coast is the busy, tourist-oriented town of Lahaina, a former whaling center.

2 Central Maui. Between Maui's two mountain areas is Central Maui, the location of the county seat of Wailuku and the commercial center of Kahului. Kahului Airport is here.

3 South Shore. The leeward side of Maui's eastern half is what most people mean when they say South Shore. This popular area is sunny and warm year-round and is home to Wailea, an upscale resort area.

4 North Shore. The North Shore has no large resorts, just plenty of picturesque small towns like Pā'ia and Ha'ikū—and great surfing action at Ho'okipa Beach.

5 East Maui. The island's northeastern, windward side is largely one great rain forest, traversed by the stunning Road to Hāna. The town of Hāna preserves the slow pace of the past.

6 Upcountry. Island residents affectionately call the regions climbing up the slope of Haleakalā Crater Upcountry. This is farm and ranch country.

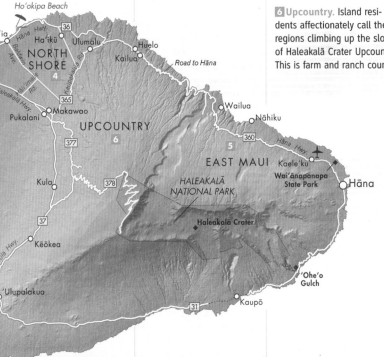

Ho'okipa Beach

'ia

36

Ha'ikū   Ulumalu

NORTH   Kailua   Huelo

SHORE   Road to Hāna

4

365

Makawao

Pukalani

UPCOUNTRY   Wailua

377   6   Nāhiku

360

5   Hāna Hwy

Kula   EAST MAUI   Kaele'ku

378   Wai'ānapanapa

State Park

HALEAKALĀ   Hāna

NATIONAL PARK

37

Kēōkea   Haleakalā Crater

'Ohe'o

Gulch

'Ulupalakua

31   Kaupō

MAUI PLANNER

When You Arrive

Most visitors arrive at Kahului Airport in Central Maui. A rental car is the best way to get from the airport to your destination. The major car-rental companies have desks at the airport and can provide a map and directions to your hotel. ■TIP➡ Flights in Maui tend to land around the same time, leading to long lines at car-rental windows. If possible, send one person to pick up the car while the others wait for the baggage.

Timing Is Everything

In winter, Maui is *the* spot for whale-watching. The humpback whales start arriving in December, are in full force by February, and are gone by early May. The biggest North Shore waves show up in winter, whereas kiteboarders and windsurfers enjoy the windy, late summer months. Jacarandas shower Upcountry roads in blossoms in spring, and silverswords bloom in summer. In high season—June through August and Christmas through spring break—the island is jampacked with visitors. The best months for bargain hunters are May, September, and October. ⇨ *See When to Go for weather advice.*

Renting a Car

A rental car is a must on Maui. It's also one of your biggest trip expenses, especially given the price of gasoline— higher on Maui than on Oʻahu or the Mainland. *See Travel Smart Maui for details of renting a car and driving.*

If you need to ask for directions, try your best to pronounce the multivowel road names. Locals don't use (or know) highway route numbers and will respond with looks as lost as yours. Also, they will give you directions by the time it takes to get somewhere instead of by the mileage.

■TIP➡ Soft-top jeeps are a popular option, but they don't have much space for baggage and it's impossible to lock anything into them. Four-wheel-drive vehicles are the most expensive options and not really necessary.

■TIP➡ Don't be surprised if there is an additional fee for parking at your hotel or resort; parking is not always included in your room rate or resort fee.

■TIP➡ Booking a car-hotel or airfare package can save you money, so always ask if anything is available.

Dining and Lodging on Maui

Hawaiʻi is a melting pot of cultures, and nowhere is this more apparent than in its cuisines. From lūʻau and "plate lunches" to sushi and steak, there's no shortage of interesting flavors and presentations.

Whether you're looking for a quick snack or a multicourse meal, we'll help you find the best eating experiences the island has to offer. Jump in, and enjoy!

Choosing lodging is a tough decision, but fret not—our expert writers and editors have done most of the legwork.

To help narrow your choices, consider what type of property you'd like to stay at (big resort, quiet bed-and-breakfast) and what type of island climate you're looking for (beachfront strand or remote rain forest). We give you all the details you need to book a place that suits your style.

■TIP➡ Reserve your room well in advance, and ask about discounts and packages. Hotel Web sites often have Internet-only deals.

Island Hopping

If you have a week or more on Maui, you may want to set aside a day or two for a trip to Moloka'i or Lāna'i. Tour operators such as Trilogy offer day-trip packages to Lāna'i, which include snorkeling and a van tour of the island. Ferries are available to both islands and have room for your golf clubs and mountain bike. (The Moloka'i channel can be rough, so avoid ferry travel on a blustery day.)

If you prefer to travel to Moloka'i or Lāna'i by air, and you're not averse to flying on 4- to 12-seaters, your best bet is a small air taxi. Book with Pacific Wings (⇨ see Air Travel in Getting Here and Around in Travel Smart Maui) for flights to Hāna, Maui, or Kalaupapa and Moloka'i, as well as the main airports.

If you're considering a visit to Kaua'i, Oahu, or the Big Island, ⇨ see Travel Smart, which includes the details of ferry service as well as information about interisland air carriers.

Island Driving Times

Maui may seem like a small island, but driving from one point to another can take longer than the mileage indicates. It's only 52 mi from Kahului Airport to Hāna, but the drive will take you about three hours. As for driving to Haleakalā, the 38-mi drive from sea level to the summit will take you about two hours. The roads are narrow and winding; you must go at a slow pace.

Kahului is the transportation hub—the main airport and largest harbor are here. Traffic on Maui's roads can be heavy, especially during the rush hours of 6 AM to 8:30 AM and 3:30 PM to 6:30 PM; this will add time to your drive. Here are average driving times to key destinations.

Kahului to Wailea	17 mi/30 mins
Kahului to Kā'anapali	25 mi/45 mins
Kahului to Kapalua	36 mi/1 hr, 15 mins
Kahului to Wailuku	6 mi/15 mins
Kahului to Makawao	13 mi/25 mins
Kapalua to Haleakalā	73 mi/3 hr
Kā'anapali to Haleakalā	62 mi/2 hr, 30 mins
Wailea to Haleakalā	54 mi/2 hr, 30 mins
Kapalua to Hāna	88 mi/5 hr
Kā'anapali to Hāna	77 mi/5 hr
Wailea to Hāna	69 mi/4 hr, 30 mins
Wailea to Lahaina	20 mi/45 mins
Kā'anapali to Lahaina	4 mi/15 mins
Kapalua to Lahaina	12 mi/25 mins

Money Savers

Maui has deals these days, and there are ways to travel to Paradise even on a budget.

Accommodations: No matter what the season, ask about deals—a free night after three or four or five paid nights, kids stay free, meal credits. Condos are less expensive and bigger than hotel rooms and are perfect for families or groups of friends. If you pass up the ocean view, you'll save money on your hotel or condo. September, October, and May are off-peak months with many hotels offering reduced rates.

Food: Eat a big breakfast and skip lunch. You'll probably be sightseeing or at the beach anyway. It's easy to get by with a smoothie or fruit and yogurt. If you eat lunch out, go to that high-end restaurant. Lunch will be less expensive. If you're staying in a condo, eat in or pack a picnic as often as you can.

Activities: Pick up free publications at the airport and at racks all over the island; many of them are filled with money-saving coupons; also check newspapers. Activity desks—there are dozens around Kā'anapali and Wailea as well as in Lahaina and Kīhei—are good places to check on deals and discounts if you're not booking in advance. However, advance booking will ensure you get the activity you want; sometimes you can save 10% or more if you book on outfitters' Web sites.

TOP MAUI EXPERIENCES

Hike Haleakalā

(A) Take time to trek down into Haleakalā National Park's massive bowl and see proof, at this dormant volcano, of how very powerful the earth's exhalations can be. The cinder cones have beautiful swirls of subtle colors that can sparkle in the sunlight. You won't see landscape like this anywhere, outside of visiting the moon. The barren terrain is deceptive, however—many of the world's rarest plants, birds, and insects live here.

Take the Road to Hāna

(B) Spectacular views of waterfalls, lush forests, and the sparkling ocean are part of the pleasure of the twisting drive along the North Shore to tiny, timeless Hāna in East Maui. The journey is the destination, but once you arrive, kick back and enjoy. Wave to pedestrians, "talk story" with locals in line at Hasegawa store, and explore the multicolor beaches. An overnight stay here allows for the most relaxed experience, though; a day trip here is a big push. You may decide to drive just part of the way as an alternative.

Discover the joy of snorkeling

(C) Snorkeling is a must, either on your own with a buddy or on a snorkel cruise. Maui has snorkel boats of all sizes. Wherever you duck under, you'll be inducted into a mesmerizing world underwater. Slow down and keep your eyes open: even fish dressed in camouflage can be spotted when they snatch at food passing by. Some great spots to try right near the shore are Honolua Bay and Kekaʻa (also known as Black Rock; it's in front of the Sheraton Maui) in West Maui; there are also good spots on the rocky fringes of Wailea's beaches on the South Shore.

Stretch out on Mākena (Big Beach)

(D) This South Shore beauty is the sand dreams are made of: deep, golden, and pillowy. Don't be discouraged by the crammed parking lots; there's more than

enough room. Mākena (Oneloa in Hawaiian) is still wild. There are no hotels, minimarts, or even public restrooms nearby—instead there's crystal-clear water, the occasional pod of dolphins, and drop-dead gorgeous scenery (including the sunbathers). You can grab a fish taco and a drink at a nearby truck.

Buy tropical fruit at a roadside stand

(E) Your first taste of ripe guava or mango is something to remember. Delicious lychees, mangoes, star fruit, bananas, passion fruit, and papaya can be bought on the side of the road with the change in your pocket. Go on, let the juice run down your chin. No one's looking!

Try the resorts and spas

(F) Indulge your inner rock star at the posh, pampering resorts and spas around the island. Sip a "Tommy Girl" in the hot tub at the Four Seasons or get massaged poolside at the Grand Wailea. Even if you don't stay the night, you can enjoy the opulent gardens, restaurants, art collections, and perfectly cordial staff. For pure relaxation, set up a spa treatment such as a lavender scrub.

Escape to a bed-and-breakfast

(G) Being a shut-in isn't so bad at a secluded B&B. It's a sure way to get a taste of what it's like to live in Paradise: ripe fruit trees outside your door, late-night tropical rainstorms, a wild chicken or two. Rather than blasting the air-conditioning in a hotel room, relax with the windows open in a plantation house designed to capture sea breezes.

Whale-watch

(H) Maui is the cradle for hundreds of humpback whales that return every year to frolic in the warm waters and give birth. Watch a mama whale teach her 1-ton calf how to tail-wave. You can eavesdrop on them, too: book a tour boat with a hydrophone or just plunk your head underwater

TOP MAUI EXPERIENCES

to hear the strange squeaks, groans, and chortles of the cetaceans.

Listen to Hawaiian music

(I) Before his untimely death in 1997, Israel Kamakawiwoʻole, or "IZ," woke the world to the sound of modern Hawaiian music. Don't leave without hearing it live. The Maui Arts & Cultural Center in Kahului has top Hawaiian entertainers regularly, and so do many island bars and restaurants. The Wednesday-night Masters of Hawaiian Slack Key Guitar concert series at the Napili Kai Beach Resort in West Maui is excellent. The Slack Key Guitar Festival (check ⊕ www.slackkeyfestival.com) features guest performers who play Hawaiʻi's signature style.

Go surfing on West Maui

(J) Feel the thrill of a wave rushing beneath your feet at any one of the beginner's breaks along Honoapiʻilani Highway. Ask local surf schools about the best locations for beginners. You can bring surf wax home as a souvenir.

Attend the Old Lahaina Lūʻau

(K) The Old Lahaina Lūʻau has a warm heart—and seriously good *poke* (chopped, raw tuna tossed with herbs and other seasonings). Tuck a flower behind your ear, mix a dab of *poi* (paste made from pounded taro root) with your *lomilomi* (rubbed with onions and herbs) salmon, and you'll be living like a local. Different styles of hula are part of the performance; the fire dancers may not be traditional, but they are fun. Reserve well in advance of your trip.

Tee off in paradise

(L) Spectacular views, great weather year-round, and awesome, challenging courses created by the game's top designers make Maui an inspiring place to play golf. The Kapulua Resort on West Maui and the Wailea and Mākena resort courses on the South Shore, among others, offer

memorable rounds. Check about twilight fees to save some money. A number of professional golf tournaments held on Maui are worth watching, too.

Tour Upcountry

(M) Die-hard beach lovers might need some arm-twisting to head up the mountain for a day, but the 360-degree views and the fresh-smelling countryside are ample reward. On the roads winding through ranchlands, crisp, high-altitude air is scented with eucalyptus and lavender. Stop for an agricultural tour and learn about where the island's bounty comes from; you can sample it, too.

Dig into 'ono kine grinds

(N) "'Ono kine grinds" is local slang for delicious food you'll find at dozens of restaurants island-wide. Maui chefs take their work seriously, and they have good material to start with: sun-ripened produce (don't pass up sweet Maui Gold pineapples) and seafood caught the very

same morning. Try a plate lunch, that reminder of the state's cultural mix, at a casual spot. Sample as many types of fish as you can and don't be shy: try it raw.

Windsurf at Kanaha or Ho'okipa

(O) You might not be a water-sports legend, but that doesn't mean you can't get out on the water and give it a try. In the early morning, some of windsurfing's big-wave spots are safe for beginners. Don't settle for the pond in front of your hotel—book a lesson on the North Shore and impress yourself by hanging tough where the action is.

WHEN TO GO

Long days of sunshine and fairly mild year-round temperatures make Hawai'i, including Maui, an all-season destination. Most resort areas are at sea level, with average afternoon temperatures of 75°F to 80°F during the coldest months of December and January; during the hottest months of August and September the temperature often reaches 90°F. Higher "Upcountry" elevations have cooler and often misty conditions. Only at mountain summits does it reach freezing.

Moist trade winds drop their precipitation on the north and east sides of all the Islands, creating tropical climates, whereas the south and west sides remain hot and dry with desertlike conditions. Rainfall can be high in winter, particularly on the North and East shores.

Many travelers head to the Islands in winter, especially during Christmas and spring break. This means that fewer travel bargains are available; room rates average 10% to 15% higher during these times than the rest of the year.

Typically the weather on Maui is drier in summer (more guaranteed beach days) and rainier in winter (greener foliage, better waterfalls). Throughout the year, West Maui and the South Shore (the leeward areas) are the driest, sunniest areas on the island—that's why the resorts are there. The North Shore and East Maui and Hāna (the windward areas) get the most rain, are densely forested, and abound with waterfalls and rainbows.

Only in Hawai'i Holidays

Hawaiians appreciate any occasion to celebrate; not only are indigenous Hawaiian holidays honored, so are those of the state's early immigrant cultures. If you happen to be in the Islands on March 26 or June 11, you'll notice light traffic and busy beaches—these are state holidays. March 26 recognizes the birthday of Prince Jonah Kūhio Kalaniana'ole, a member of the royal line who served as a delegate to Congress and spearheaded the effort to set aside homelands for Hawaiian people. June 11 honors the first island-wide monarch, Kamehameha I; locals drape his statues with lei and stage elaborate parades. May 1 isn't an official holiday, but it's Lei Day in Hawai'i, when schools and civic groups celebrate the flower lei with lei-making contests and pageants. Statehood Day is celebrated on the third Friday in August (Admission Day was August 21, 1959). Most Japanese and Chinese holidays are widely observed. On Chinese New Year, in winter, homes and businesses sprout red good-luck mottoes, lions dance in the streets, and everybody eats *gau* (steamed pudding) and *jai* (vegetarian stew). Good Friday is a state holiday in spring, a favorite for picnics. Summertime is for Obon festivals and the July 4 Rodeo; the Maui County Fair and Aloha Festivals are in fall.

Climate

The following are average maximum and minimum temperatures for Lahaina in West Maui; the temperatures throughout the Hawaiian Islands are similar.

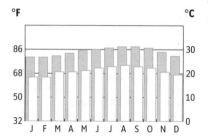

GREAT ITINERARIES

Maui's landscape is incredibly diverse, offering everything from underwater encounters with eagle rays to treks across moonlike terrain. Although daydreaming at the pool or on the beach may fulfill your initial island fantasy, Maui has much more to offer. The following one-day itineraries will take you to our favorite spots on the island.

Beach Day in West Maui

West Maui has some of the island's most beautiful beaches, though many of them are hidden by megaresorts. If you get an early start, you can begin your day snorkeling at Slaughterhouse Beach (in winter, D.T. Fleming Beach is a better option as it's less rough). Then spend the day beach-hopping through Kapalua, Nāpili, and Kā'anapali as you make your way south. You'll want to get to Lahaina before dark so you can spend some time exploring the historic whaling town before choosing a restaurant for a sunset dinner.

Focus on Marine Life on the South Shore

Start your South Shore trip early in the morning, and head out past Mākena into the rough lava fields of rugged La Pérouse Bay. At the road's end, there are areas of the 'Āhihi-Kīna'u Marine Preserve (some are closed at this writing) open to the public which offer good snorkeling. If that's a bit too far afield for you, there's excellent snorkeling at Polo Beach. Head to the right (your right while facing the ocean) for plenty of fish and beautiful coral. Head back north to Kīhei for lunch, and then enjoy the afternoon learning more about Maui's marine life at the outstanding Maui Ocean Center at Mā'alaea.

Haleakalā National Park, Upcountry and the North Shore

If you don't plan to spend an entire day hiking in the crater at Haleakalā National Park, this itinerary will at least allow you to take a peek at it. Get up early and head straight for the summit of Haleakalā (if you're jet-lagged and waking up in the middle of the night, you may want to get there in time for sunrise). Bring water, sunscreen, and warm clothing; it's freezing at sunrise. Plan to spend a couple of hours exploring the various lookout points in the park. On your way down the mountain, turn right on Makawao Avenue, and head into the little town of Makawao. You can have lunch here, or make a left on Baldwin Avenue and head downhill to the North Shore town of Pā'ia, which has a number of great lunch spots and shops to explore. Spend the rest of your afternoon at Pā'ia's main strip of sand, Ho'okipa Beach.

The Road to Hāna

This cliff-side driving tour through rainforest canopy reveals Maui's most lush and tropical terrain. It will take a very full day to explore this part of the North Shore and East Maui, especially if you plan to make it all the way to 'Oheo Gulch. You'll pass through communities where old Hawai'i still thrives, and where the forest runs unchecked from the sea to the summit. You'll want to make frequent exploratory stops. To really soak in the magic of this place, consider staying overnight in Hāna town. That way you can spend a full day winding toward Hāna, hiking and exploring along the way, and the next day traveling leisurely back to civilization.

WEDDINGS AND HONEYMOONS

There's no question that Hawai'i is one of the country's foremost honeymoon destinations. Romance is in the air here, and the white, sandy beaches and turquoise water and swaying palm trees and balmy tropical breezes and perpetual summer sunshine put people in the mood for love. It's easy to understand why Hawai'i is fast becoming a popular wedding destination as well, especially as the cost of airfare has gone down, and new resorts and hotels entice visitors. A destination wedding is no longer exclusive to celebrities and the super rich. You can plan a traditional ceremony in a place of worship followed by a reception at an elegant resort, or you can go barefoot on the beach and celebrate at a lū'au. There are almost as many wedding planners in the Islands as real-estate agents, which makes it oh-so-easy to wed in paradise, and then, once the knot is tied, stay and honeymoon as well.

The Big Day

Choosing the Perfect Place. When choosing a location, remember that you really have two choices to make: the ceremony location and where to have the reception, if you're having one. For the former, there are beaches, bluffs overlooking beaches, gardens, private residences, resort lawns, and, of course, places of worship. It really depends on you. As for the reception, there are these same choices, as well as restaurants and even lū'au. If you decide to go outdoors, remember the seasons— yes, Hawai'i has seasons. If you're planning a winter wedding outdoors, be sure you have a backup plan (such as a tent), in case it rains. Also, if you're planning an outdoor wedding at sunset—which is very popular—be sure you match the time of your ceremony to the time the sun sets at that time of year. If you choose indoors, be sure to ask for pictures of the environs

when you're planning. You don't want to plan a pink wedding, say, and wind up in a room that's predominantly red. Or maybe you do. The point is, it should be your choice.

Finding a Wedding Planner. If you're planning to invite more than a minister and your loved one to your wedding ceremony, seriously consider an on-island wedding planner who can help select a location, help design the floral scheme and recommend a florist as well as a photographer, help plan the menu and choose a restaurant, caterer, or resort, and suggest any Hawaiian traditions to incorporate into your ceremony. And more: Will you need tents, a cake, music? Maybe transportation and lodging. Many planners have relationships with vendors, providing packages—which mean savings.

If you're planning a resort wedding, most have on-site wedding coordinators; however, there are many independents around the island and even those who specialize in certain types of ceremonies—by locale, size, religious affiliation, and so on. A simple "Hawaii weddings" Google search will reveal dozens. What's important is that you feel comfortable with your coordinator. Ask for references— and call them. Share your budget. Get a proposal—in writing. Ask how long they've been in business, how much they charge, how often you'll meet with them, and how they select vendors. Request a detailed list of the exact services they'll provide. If your idea of your wedding doesn't match their services, try someone else. If you can afford it, you might want to meet the planner in person.

Getting Your License. The good news about marrying in Hawai'i is that no waiting period, no residency or citizenship

requirements, and no blood tests or shots are required. However, both the bride and groom must appear together in person before a marriage license agent to apply for a marriage license. You'll need proof of age—the legal age to marry is 18. (If you're 19 or older, a valid driver's license will suffice; if you're 18, a certified birth certificate is required.) Upon approval, a marriage license is immediately issued and costs $60, cash only. After the ceremony, your officiant will mail the marriage license to the state. Approximately 120 days later, you will receive a copy in the mail. (For $10 extra, you can expedite this process. Ask your marriage-license agent when you apply for your license.) For more detailed information, visit ⊕*www. hawaii.gov* or call ☎*808/241-3498*.

Also—this is important—the person performing your wedding must be licensed by the Hawai'i Department of Health, even if he or she is a licensed minister. Be sure to ask.

Wedding Attire. In Hawai'i, basically anything goes, from long, formal dresses with trains to white bikinis. Floral sundresses are fine, too. For the men, tuxedos are not the norm; a pair of solid-color slacks with a nice aloha shirt is. In fact, tradition in Hawai'i for the groom is a plain white aloha shirt (they do exist) with slacks or long shorts and a colored sash around the waist. If you're planning a wedding on the beach, barefoot is the way to go.

If you decide to marry in a formal dress and tuxedo, you're better off making your selections on the mainland and hand-carrying them aboard the plane. Yes, it can be a pain, but ask your wedding-gown retailer to provide a special carrying bag. After all, you don't want to chance losing your wedding dress in a wayward piece of luggage. And when it comes to fittings, again, that's something to take care of before you arrive in Hawai'i.

Local Customs. When it comes to traditional Hawaiian wedding customs, the most obvious is the lei exchange in which the bride and groom take turns placing a lei around the neck of the other—with a kiss. Bridal lei are usually floral, whereas the groom's is typically made of maile, a green leafy garland that drapes around the neck and is open at the ends. Brides often also wear a haku lei—a circular floral headpiece. Other Hawaiian customs include the blowing of the conch shell, hula, chanting, and Hawaiian music.

The Honeymoon

Do you want champagne and strawberries delivered to your room each morning? A maze of a swimming pool in which to float? A five-star restaurant in which to dine? Then a resort is the way to go. If, however, you prefer the comforts of a home, try a bed-and-breakfast. A B&B is also good if you're on a tight budget or don't plan to spend much time in your room. On the other hand, maybe you want your own private home in which to romp naked—or just laze around recovering from the wedding planning. Maybe you want your own kitchen in which to whip up a gourmet meal for your loved one. In that case, a private vacation-rental home is the answer. Or maybe a condominium resort. That's another beautiful thing about Hawai'i: the lodging accommodations are almost as plentiful as the beaches, and there's one to match your tastes and your budget.

KIDS AND FAMILIES

With dozens of adventures, discoveries, and fun-filled beach days, Maui is a blast with kids. The entire family, parents included, will enjoy surfing, discovering a waterfall in the rain forest, and snorkeling with sea turtles. And there are organized activities for kids that will free parents' time for a few romantic beach strolls.

Choosing a Place to Stay

Resorts. All of the big resorts make kids' programs a priority, and it shows. When you are booking your room, ask about "kids eat free" deals and the number of kids' pools at the resort. Also check out the ages and size of the groups in the children's programs, and find out whether the cost of the programs includes lunch, equipment, and activities.

On the South Shore, the best bet for families is the Fairmont Kea Lani Maui where the accommodations are spacious suites. Kids will love the beach right in front of the Mana Kai Maui on the island's south side. The Westin Maui Resort & Spa, with its long list of activity programs for kids and adults, is a good choice in the Kāʻanapali Resort. Also in West Maui, Nāpili Kai Beach Resort sits on a crescent of white-sand beach that is perfect for boogie boarding and sunbathing.

Condos. Condo and vacation rentals are a fantastic value for families vacationing in Hawaiʻi. You can cook your own food, which is cheaper than eating out and sometimes easier, and you'll get twice the space of a hotel room for about a quarter of the price. If you decide to go the condo route, be sure to ask about the size of the complex's pool (some try to pawn off a tiny soaking tub as a pool) and whether barbecues are available. One of the best parts of staying in your own place is

having a sunset family barbecue by the pool or overlooking the ocean.

On West Maui, all the Aston Hotels & Resorts properties, such as those at the Papakea Resort, offer children's packages such as "Kids Stay, Play and Eat Free" and have a *keiki* (child) activity program that ranges from sandcastle building to sightseeing excursions. On the South Shore, Kamaʻole Sands is a family favorite, with an excellent location right across from three beach parks that are good for swimming and have grassy fields good for games and picnics.

Ocean Activities

Hawaiʻi is all about getting your kids outside—away from video games. And who could resist the turquoise water, the promise of spotting dolphins or whales, and the fun of boogie boarding or surfing?

On the Beach. Most people like being in the water, but toddlers and school-age kids tend to be enamored of it. The swimming pool at your condo or hotel is always an option, but don't be afraid to hit the beach with a little one in tow. Several beaches in Hawaiʻi are nearly as safe as a pool—completely protected bays with pleasant white-sand beaches. As always, use your judgment, and heed all posted signs and lifeguard warnings.

The leeward side of Maui has many calm beaches to try; good ones include Wailea Beach in front of the Grand Wailea and Four Seasons resorts and Kamaʻole beach parks on the South Shore. Nāpili Bay in West Maui is great for kids and boogie boarding. On the North Shore, at the Kahului end of Baldwin Beach Park, check out the shallow pool known as Baby Beach.

On the Waves. Surf lessons are a great idea for older kids, especially if mom and dad want a little quiet time. Beginner lessons are always on safe and easy waves and last anywhere from two to four hours.

The world-class waves of Maui's North Shore are best left to the pros. The gentle swells off West Maui are where the Nancy Emerson School of Surfing provides lessons designed for beginners. Big Kahuna Adventures will also show you how to ride the waves in the calm mornings off Kalama Beach Park in Kīhei on the South Shore.

The Underwater World. If your kids are ready to try snorkeling, Hawai'i is a great place to introduce them to the underwater world. Even without the mask and snorkel, they'll be able to see colorful fish, and they may also spot turtles and dolphins at many of the island beaches.

It's easy to learn the basics and see sea life right away at Kā'anapali Beach in front of the Sheraton Maui on the island's West Side. For guided snorkel tours that offer beginner instruction, try Trilogy Excursions, a family-oriented day trip from Lahaina to Lāna'i, or Maui Classic Charters out of Mā'alaea Harbor.

Land Activities

In addition to beach experiences, Hawai'i has rain forests, botanical gardens (the Big Island and Maui have the best), numerous aquariums (O'ahu and Maui take the cake), and even petting zoos and hands-on children's museums that will keep your kids entertained and out of the sun for a day.

Central Maui abounds with activities for children, including the Alexander & Baldwin Sugar Museum with its interactive displays, and the hands-on Hawai'i Nature Center next to Kepaniwai Park & Heritage Gardens. If the weather's not great for seeing marine life in the ocean, see it at the excellent Maui Ocean Center in Mā'alaea on the South Shore, where all manner of live marine creatures including reef fish, sea turtles, manta rays, and sharks swim behind glass.

To discover all there is to know about Maui's biggest annual visitor, the humpback whale, children will enjoy the Hawaiian Islands Humpback Whale National Marine Sanctuary on the South Shore and the free museum at Whalers Village in Kā'anapali on West Maui.

For a moving experience, hop aboard the Sugar Cane Train that chugs between Lahaina and Kā'anapali and features a singing conductor; yup, it's corny, but the train is a favorite with kids of all ages.

After Dark

At nighttime, younger kids get a kick out of lū'aus, and many of the shows incorporate young audience members, adding to the fun. Older kids might find it all a bit lame, but there are a handful of new shows in the Islands that are more modern, incorporating acrobatics and lively music.

We think the best lū'au is the Old Lahaina Lū'au, which takes place nightly on the oceanfront at the north end of Lahaina. The show is traditional, lively, and colorful; it will keep the whole family entertained. Book in advance to avoid disappointment; this is extremely popular. An alternative is Ho'omana'o, at Old Lahaina Lū'au; the three-hour morning program (perhaps too long for toddlers) includes hula, a breakfast buffet, and interactive presentations about Hawaiian culture.

CRUISING THE HAWAIIAN ISLANDS

Cruising has become extremely popular in Hawai'i. For first-time visitors, it's an excellent way to get a taste of all the Islands; and if you fall in love with one or even two islands, you know how to plan your next trip. It's also a comparatively inexpensive way to see Hawai'i. The limited amount of time in each port can be an argument against cruising—there's enough to do on any island to keep you busy for a week, so some folks feel short-changed by cruise itineraries.

Cruising to Hawai'i

Until 2001 it was illegal for any cruise ships to stop in Hawai'i unless they originated from a foreign port, or were including a foreign port in their itinerary. The law has changed, but most cruises still include a stop in the Fanning Islands, Ensenada, Mexico, or Vancouver, British Columbia, in Canada. Gambling is legal on the open seas, and your winnings are tax-free; most cruise ships offer designated smoking areas and now enforce the U.S. legal drinking age (21) on Hawai'i itineraries.

Carnival Cruises. They call them "fun ships" for a reason—Carnival is all about keeping you busy and showing you a good time, both on board and on shore. Great for families, Carnival always plans plenty of kid-friendly activities, and their children's program rates high with the little critics. Carnival offers itineraries starting in Ensenada, Vancouver, and Honolulu. Their ships stop on Maui (Kahului and Lahaina), the Big Island (Kailua-Kona and Hilo), O'ahu, and Kaua'i. ☎888/227-6482 ⊕www.carnival.com.

Celebrity Cruises. Celebrity's focus is on service, and it shows. From their waitstaff to their activity directors and their fantastic Hawaiian cultural experts, every aspect of

your trip has been well thought out. They cater more to adults than children, so this may not be the best line for families. Celebrity's Hawai'i cruises depart from San Diego and stop in Maui (Lahaina), O'ahu, the Big Island (Hilo and Kailua-Kona), and Kaua'i. ☎800/647-2251 ⊕www.celebrity.com.

Holland America. The grande dame of cruise lines, Holland America has a reputation for service and elegance. Holland America's Hawai'i cruises leave and return to San Diego, California, and Seattle, Washington, with either a brief stop at Ensenada or British Columbia. In Hawai'i, the ship ties up at port in Maui (Lahaina), the Big Island (Kailua-Kona and Hilo), O'ahu, and for half a day on Kaua'i. Holland America also offers longer itineraries (30-plus days) that include Hawai'i, Tahiti, and the Marquesas. ☎877/724-5425 ⊕www.hollandamerica.com.

Norwegian Cruise Lines. Norwegian has traditionally been one of the more casual cruise lines and offers a variety of service, activity, and excursion options; the company calls this freestyle cruising. The Pride of America embarks and disembarks in Honolulu and stops on Maui (Kahului), the Big Island (Hilo and Kailua-Kona), and Kaua'i. There are dozens of sailings year-round. It's a family-friendly ship (there are no casinos) and boasts extensive on-board Hawaiian culture programs. ☎800/327-7030 ⊕www.ncl.com.

Princess Cruises. Princess strives to offer affordable luxury. Their prices start out a little higher, but you get more bells and whistles (more affordable balcony rooms, nice decor, more restaurants to choose from, personalized service). They're not fantastic for kids, but they do a great job of keeping teenagers occupied. Princess's

Hawaiian cruise is 14 days, round-trip from Los Angeles, with a service call in Ensenada. The *Golden Princess* stops in Maui (Lahaina), the Big Island (Hilo and Kailua-Kona), O'ahu, and Kaua'i. For the cruise goer looking for the epic voyage, Princess Cruises offers a Sydney, Australia, to Los Angeles route, which includes stops in Hawai'i and Tahiti. ☎ *800/774–6237* ⊕ *www.princess.com.*

Royal Caribbean. Royal Caribbean offers two itineraries onboard Rhapsody of the Seas: a 10-night cruise that originates in Honolulu and disembarks in Vancouver; and a 12-night cruise that starts in Vancouver and ends in Honolulu. Both stop in Maui (Lahaina), Kaua'i, and the Big Island (both Hilo and Kailua-Kona). In keeping with its reputation for being all things to all people, Royal Caribbean offers a huge variety of activities and services on board and more excursions on land than any other cruise line. ☎ *800/521–8611* ⊕ *www.royalcaribbean.com.*

TIPS

■ On all but the *Pride of America* cruises (operated by Norwegian Cruise Lines), you must bring a passport, as you will be entering foreign ports of call.

■ Think about booking your own excursions directly (except on Maui). You'll often pay less for greater value. For example, if you want to take a surfing lesson on O'ahu, visit one of the beachside shacks to find excellent instructors who offer better deals to individuals than they do to the cruise lines. The downside, though, is that whereas cruise-booked tours guarantee the ship will wait for you should your tour run late, if you make your own plans and miss the "all aboard," you'll have to find your own way to the ship at the next port.

■ Tendering in Maui can be a tedious process—if you want to avoid a little bit of the headache (and hours waiting in the sun), be sure to book an excursion there through the ship and you'll have smooth sailing.

■ Most mainland cell phones will work without a hitch on board between the Islands and at all Hawaiian ports of call.

A SNAPSHOT OF HAWAI'I

The Neighbor Islands

O'ahu. The state's capital, Honolulu, is on O'ahu; this is the center of Hawai'i's economy and by far the most populated island in the chain—900,000 residents adds up to 71% of the state's population. At 597 square mi O'ahu is the third-largest island in the chain; the majority of residents live in or around Honolulu, so the rest of the island still fits neatly into the tropical, untouched vision of Hawai'i. Situated southeast of Kaua'i and northwest of Maui, O'ahu is a central location for island hopping. Surfing contests on the legendary North Shore, Pearl Harbor, and iconic Waikīkī Beach are all here.

Maui. The second-largest island in the chain, Maui encompasses 729 square mi and is home to only 119,000 people, but it hosts approximately 2.5 million tourists every year. Known as the Valley Isle, Maui is northwest of the Big Island, and close enough to be visible from its beaches on a clear day. With its restaurants and lively nightlife, Maui is the only island that competes with O'ahu in terms of entertainment. The island's charm lies in the fact that although entertainment is available, Maui's towns still feel like island villages compared to the modern city of Honolulu.

Hawai'i (The Big Island). The Big Island has the second-largest population of the Islands (167,000) but feels sparsely settled due to its size. It's 4,038 square mi and growing—all of the other islands could fit onto the Big Island and there would still be room left over. The southernmost island in the chain (slightly southeast of Maui), the Big Island is home to Kīlauea, the most active volcano on the planet. It percolates within Volcanoes National Park, which draws 2.5 million visitors every year.

Kaua'i. The northernmost island in the chain (northwest of O'ahu), Kaua'i is, at approximately 540 square mi, the fourth largest of all the Islands and the least populated of the larger islands, with just under 63,000 residents. Known as the Garden Isle, Kaua'i claims the title "wettest spot on Earth" with an annual average rainfall of 460 inches. Kaua'i is a favorite with honeymooners and others wanting to get away from it all—lush and peaceful, it's the perfect escape from the modern world.

Moloka'i. North of Lāna'i and Maui, and east of O'ahu, Moloka'i is Hawai'i's fifth-largest island, encompassing 260 square mi. On a clear night, the lights of Honolulu are visible from Moloka'i's western shore. Moloka'i is sparsely populated, with just under 7,400 residents, the majority of whom are native Hawaiians. Most of Moloka'i's 85,000 annual visitors travel from Maui or O'ahu to spend the day exploring its beaches, cliffs, and former leper colony on Kalaupapa Peninsula.

Lāna'i. Lying just off Maui's western coast, Lāna'i looks nothing like its sister islands, with pine trees and deserts in place of palm trees and beaches. Still, the tiny 140-square-mi island is home to nearly 3,000 residents and draws an average of 90,000 visitors each year to two resorts, both operated by Four Seasons.

Geology

The Hawaiian Islands comprise more than just the islands inhabited and visited by humans. A total of 19 islands and atolls constitutes the State of Hawai'i, with a landmass of 6,423.4 square mi. The Islands are actually exposed peaks of a submersed mountain range called

DID YOU KNOW?

Maui is famous for water-falls, and Wailua Falls is both accessible and exquisite, particularly on a sunny morning. It's south of Hāna, just past mile marker 45 on the road to 'Ohe'o Gulch.

A SNAPSHOT OF HAWAI'I

the Hawaiian-Emperor seamount chain. The range was formed as the Pacific plate moved slowly (around 32 mi every million years) over a "hot spot" in Earth's mantle. Because the plate moved northwestwardly, the Islands in the northwest portion of the archipelago (chain) are older, which is also why they're smaller— they have been eroding longer.

The Big Island is the youngest, and thus the largest, island in the chain. It is built from seven different volcanoes, including Mauna Loa, which is the largest shield volcano on the planet. Mauna Loa and Kīlauea are the only Hawaiian volcanoes still erupting with any sort of frequency. Mauna Loa last erupted in 1984. Kīlauea has been continuously erupting since 1983. Mauna Kea (Big Island), Hualālai (Big Island), and Haleakalā (Maui) are all in what's called the Post Shield stage of volcanic development—eruptions decrease steadily for up to 250,000 years before ceasing entirely. Kohala (Big Island), Lāna'i (Lāna'i), and Wai'anae (O'ahu) are considered extinct volcanoes, in the erosional stage of development; Ko'olau (O'ahu) and West Maui (Maui) volcanoes are extinct volcanoes in the rejuvenation stage—after lying dormant for hundreds of thousands of years, they began erupting again, but only once every several thousand years.

There is currently an active undersea volcano called Lo'ihi that has been erupting regularly. If it continues its current pattern, it should breach the ocean's surface in tens of thousands of years.

Flora and Fauna

Though much of the plant life associated with Hawai'i today (pineapple, hibiscus, orchid, plumeria) was brought by Tahitian, Samoan, or European visitors,

Hawai'i is also home to several endemic species, like the koa tree and the yellow hibiscus. Long-dormant volcanic craters are hiding places for rare plants (like the silversword, a rare cousin of the sunflower, which grows on Hawai'i's three tallest peaks: Haleakalā, Mauna Kea, and Mauna Loa, and nowhere else on Earth). Many of these endemic species are now threatened by the encroachment of introduced plants and animals. Hawai'i is also home to a handful of plants that have evolved into uniquely Hawaiian versions of their original selves. Mint, for example, develops its unique taste to keep would-be predators from eating its leaves. As there were no such predators in Hawai'i for hundreds of years, a mintless mint evolved; similar stories exist for the Islands' nettle-less nettles, thorn-less briars.

Hawai'i's climate is well suited to growing several types of flowers, most of which are introduced species. Plumeria creeps over all of the Islands; orchids run rampant on the Big Island; bright orange 'ilima light up the mountains of O'ahu. These flowers give the Hawaiian lei their color and fragrance.

As with the plant life, the majority of the animals in Hawai'i today were brought here by visitors. Axis deer from India roam the mountains of Lāna'i. The Islands are home to dozens of rat species, all stowaways on long boat rides over from Tahiti, England, and Samoa; the mongoose was brought to keep the rats out of the sugar plantations—a failed effort as the mongoose hunts by day, the rat by night. Many of Hawai'i's birds, like the nēnē (Hawai'i's state bird) and the pu'eo (Hawaiian owl) are endemic; unfortunately, about 80% are also endangered.

The ocean surrounding the Islands teems with animal life. Once scarce manta rays have made their way back to the Big Island; spinner dolphins and sea turtles can be found off the coast of all the Islands; and every year from December to May, the humpback whales migrate past Hawai'i in droves.

History

Long before both Christopher Columbus and the Vikings, Polynesian seafarers set out to explore the vast stretches of open ocean in double-hulled canoes. Now regarded as some of the world's greatest navigators, the ancestors of the Hawaiian people sailed across the Pacific Ocean using the stars, birds, and sea life as their guides. From Western Polynesia they traveled back and forth between Samoa, Fiji, Tahiti, the Marquesas, and the Society Isles, settling the outer reaches of the Pacific, Hawai'i, and Easter Island, as early as AD 300. The golden era of Polynesian voyaging peaked around AD 1200, after which the distant Hawaiian Islands were left to develop their own unique cultural practices in relative isolation.

When the British explorer Captain James Cook arrived in 1778, he found a deeply religious, agrarian society governed by numerous ali'i, or chiefs. Revered as a god upon his arrival, Cook was later killed in a skirmish over a stolen boat. With guns and ammunition purchased from Cook, the Big Island chief, Kamehameha, gained a significant advantage over the other Hawaiian ali'i. He united Hawai'i into one kingdom in 1810, bringing an end to the frequent interisland battles that had previously dominated Hawaiian life.

Tragically, the new kingdom was beset with troubles. The local religion was abandoned. European explorers brought foreign diseases with them; within a few short years the Hawaiian population was cut in half. It was further weakened by the onset of the sandalwood trade in the mid-1800s. All able-bodied men were sent into the forest to harvest the fragrant tree, so that Kamehameha's successor, Liholiho, could pay off debts incurred to American merchants. Onto this stage came foreign whalers, ambitious entrepreneurs, and well-intentioned but perhaps misguided missionaries. New laws regarding land ownership and religious practices eroded the cultural underpinnings of precontact Hawai'i. Each successor to the Hawaiian throne sacrificed more control over the island kingdom.

In 1893, the last Hawaiian monarch, Queen Lili'uokalani, was overthrown by a group of American and European businessmen and government officials, aided by an armed militia. This led to the creation of the Republic of Hawai'i, which quickly became a territory of the United States through resolutions passed by Congress (rather than through treaties). Hawai'i remained a territory for 60 years; Pearl Harbor was attacked as part of the United States in 1941 during World War II. It wasn't until 1959, however, that Hawai'i was officially admitted as the 50th State.

Legends and Mythology

Ancient deities play a huge role in Hawaiian life today—not just in daily rituals, but in the Hawaiians' reverence for their land. Gods and goddesses tend to be associated with particular parts of the land, and most of them are connected with many places thanks to the body of stories built up around each.

The goddess Pele lives in Kīlauea Volcano and rules over the Big Island. She is a feisty

A SNAPSHOT OF HAWAI'I

goddess known for turning enemies into trees or destroying the homes of adversaries with fire. The Valley Isle's namesake, the demigod Maui, is a well-known Polynesian trickster. When his mother Hina complained that there were too few hours in the day, Maui promised to slow the sun. Upon hearing this, the god Moemoe teased Maui for boasting, but undeterred, the demigod wove a strong cord and lassoed the sun. Angry, the sun scorched the fields until an agreement was reached: in summer, the sun would travel more slowly. In winter, it would return to its quick pace. For ridiculing Maui, Moemoe was turned into a large rock that still juts from the water near Kahakualoa.

One of the most important ways the ancient Hawaiians showed respect for their gods and goddesses was through the hula. Various forms of the hula were performed as prayers to the gods and as praise to the chiefs. Performances were taken very seriously, as a mistake was thought to invalidate the prayer, or even to offend the god or chief in question. Hula is still performed both as entertainment and as prayer; it is not uncommon for a hula performance to be included in an official government ceremony.

Hawai'i Today

After a long period of suppression, Hawaiian culture and traditions have experienced a renaissance over the last few decades. There is a real effort to revive traditions and to respect history as the Islands go through major changes and welcome more newcomers. New hotels and resort properties often have a Hawaiian cultural expert on staff to ensure cultural sensitivity and to educate newcomers. Nonetheless, development remains a huge issue for all Islanders—land prices

are skyrocketing, putting many areas out of reach for the native population. Traffic is becoming a problem on roads that were not designed to accommodate all the new drivers, and the Islands' limited natural resources are being seriously tapped. The government, though sluggish to respond at first, is trying to make development in Hawai'i as sustainable as possible. Rules for new developments protect natural as well as cultural resources, and local governments have set ambitious conservation goals (Honolulu's mayor is actively pursuing mass transit and light-rail options for the city's commuters). Despite all efforts to ease its effect on the land and its people, large-scale, rapid development is not anyone's ideal, and Islanders are understandably less than thrilled with the prospect of a million more tourists visiting every year or buying up property that residents themselves can't afford.

That said, the central Hawaiian value of "aloha" is alive and well. Though you may encounter a bit of resentment from a local or two, the majority of Islanders are warm, a welcoming people who are eager to share their culture with those who respect it.

Exploring Maui

WORD OF MOUTH

"We went to Maui for our honeymoon. We saw the sunrise at Haleakalā, did the Old Lahaina Luau, sailed to and snorkeled at Molokini with Trilogy, and did the Road to Hāna. Maui was a great island—pretty pricey though . . . We also spent a lot of time just relaxing on the beach and snorkeling. Enjoy your trip!"

—volcanogirl

Updated
by Bonnie
Friedman

"Maui nō ka 'oi" is what locals say—it's the best, the most, the top of the heap. To those who know Maui well, there's good reason for the superlatives. The island's miles of perfect-tan beaches, lush green valleys, historic villages, top-notch windsurfing and diving, stellar restaurants and high-end hotels, and variety of art and cultural activities have made it an international favorite.

Maui is more than sandy beaches and palm trees: the natural bounty of this place is impressive. Pu'u Kukui, the 5,788-foot interior of the West Maui Mountains, also known as Mauna Kahalawai, is one of Earth's wettest spots—annual rainfall of 400 inches has sculpted the land into impassable gorges and razor-sharp ridges. On the opposite side of the island, the blistering lava fields at 'Ahihi-Kīna'u receive scant rain. Just above this desertlike landscape, *paniolo*, Hawaiian cowboys, herd cattle on rolling, fertile ranchlands reminiscent of northern California. On the island's rugged east side is the lush, tropical Hawai'i of travel posters.

Nature isn't all Maui has to offer—it's also home to a rich culture and stunning ethnic diversity. In small towns like Pā'ia and Hāna you can see remnants of the past mingling with modern-day life. Ancient *heiau* (Hawaiian stone platforms once used as places of worship) line busy roadways. Old coral and brick missionary homes now house broadcasting networks. The antique smokestacks of sugar mills tower above communities where the children blend English, Hawaiian, Japanese, Chinese, Portuguese, Filipino, and more into one colorful language. Hawai'i is a melting pot like no other. Visiting an eclectic mom-and-pop shop (like Makawao's Komoda Store & Bakery in Upcountry) can feel like stepping into another country, or back in time. The more you look here, the more you will find.

At 729 square mi, Maui is the second-largest Hawaiian island, but offers more miles of swimmable beaches than any of the other islands. Despite growth over the past few decades, the local population is still fairly small, totaling only 119,000.

GEOLOGY

Maui is made up of two volcanoes, one now extinct and the other dormant, which erupted long ago and joined into one island. The resulting depression between the two is what gives the island its nickname, the Valley Isle. West Maui's 5,788-foot Pu'u Kukui was the first volcano to form, a distinction that gives that area's mountainous topography a more weathered look. Rainbows seem to grow wild over this terrain as gentle mists fill the deeply eroded canyons. The Valley Isle's second volcano is the 10,023-foot Haleakalā, where desertlike terrain butts up against tropical forests.

FLORA AND FAUNA

Haleakalā is one of few homes to the rare *'ahinahina* (silversword plant). The plant's brilliant silver leaves are stunning against the red lava rock that blankets the walls of Haleakalā's caldera—particularly during blooming season from July to September. A distant cousin of the sunflower, the silversword blooms just once before it dies—producing a single towering stalk awash in tiny fragrant blossoms. Also calling Haleakalā home are a few hundred *nēnē*—the Hawaiian state bird (related to the Canada goose), currently fighting its way back from near extinction. Maui is the best Hawaiian Island for whale-watching, and migrating humpbacks can be seen off the island's coast from December to April, and sometimes into May.

HISTORY

Maui's history is full of firsts—Lahaina was the first capital of Hawai'i and the first destination of the whaling industry (early 1800s), which explains why the town still has that fishing-village vibe. Lahaina was also the first stop for missionaries (1823). Although they suppressed aspects of Hawaiian culture, the missionaries did help invent the Hawaiian alphabet and built a printing press in Lahaina (the first west of the Rockies), which rolled out the news in Hawaiian. Maui also boasts the first sugar plantation in Hawai'i (1849) and the first Hawaiian luxury resort (Hotel Hāna-Maui, 1946).

ON MAUI TODAY

In the mid-1970s, savvy marketers saw a way to improve Maui's economy by promoting the Valley Isle to golfers and luxury travelers. The ploy worked all too well; Maui's visitor count continues to swell. Impatient traffic now threatens to overtake the ubiquitous aloha spirit, development encroaches on agricultural lands, and county planners struggle to meet the needs of a burgeoning population. But Maui is still carpeted with an eyeful of green, and for every tailgater, there's a carefree local on "Maui time" who stops for each pedestrian, whale spout, and sunset.

WEST MAUI

Separated from the remainder of the island by steep *pali* (cliffs), West Maui has a reputation for attitude and action. Once upon a time, this was the haunt of whalers, missionaries, and the kings and queens of Hawai'i; now it's one of Maui's main resort areas. Lahaina Town was not only once the kingdom's capital but also the ali'i's (royalty's) playground. Today the main drag, Front Street, is crowded with T-shirt and trinket shops, art exhibits, and restaurants where tourists stroll day and night. Farther north is Kā'anapali, Maui's first planned resort area. Its first hotel, the Sheraton, was opened in 1963. Since then, resorts, luxury condominiums, and a shopping center have sprung up along the white-sand beaches, with championship golf courses across the road. A few miles farther up the coast is the ultimate in West Maui luxury, the resort area of Kapalua. In between, dozens of condominiums and strip malls line both the *makai* (toward the sea) and *mauka* (toward

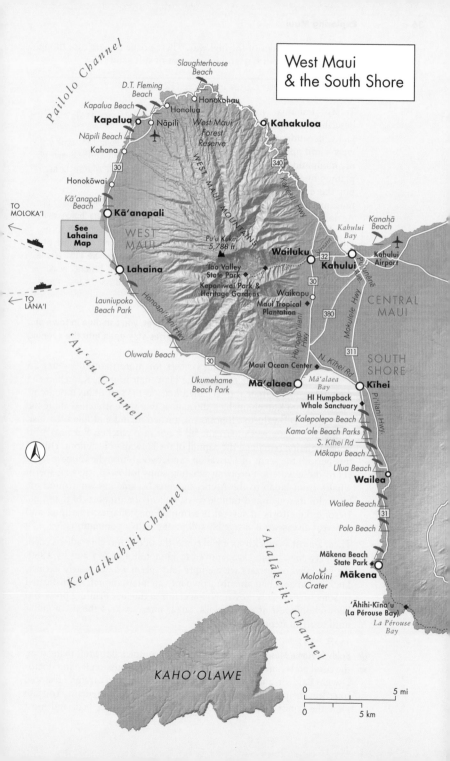

West Maui
& the South Shore

Pailolo Channel

Slaughterhouse Beach

D.T. Fleming Beach

Kapalua Beach

Honokōhau

Honolua

Kapalua

Nāpili

Kahakuloa

Nāpili Beach

West Maui Forest Reserve

Kahana

30

Honokōwai

Kā'anapali Beach

Kā'anapali

WEST MAUI

WEST MAUI MOUNTAINS

Pu'u Kukui 5,788 ft.

TO MOLOKA'I

See Lahaina Map

340

Kahakuloa Hwy

Kahului Bay

Kanahā Beach

Kahului Airport

Wailuku

32

Kahului

Pu'unēnē Ave

Lahaina

'Īao Valley State Park

Kepaniwai Park & Heritage Gardens

Waikapū

Honoapi'ilani Hwy

30

CENTRAL MAUI

TO LĀNA'I

Launiupoko Beach Park

Maui Tropical Plantation

380

Mokulele Hwy

'Au'au Channel

Oluwalu Beach

30

Honoapi'ilani Hwy

Maui Ocean Center

N. Kīhei Rd

311

SOUTH SHORE

Ukumehame Beach Park

Mā'alaea

Mā'alaea Bay

Kīhei

HI Humpback Whale Sanctuary

Kalepolepo Beach

Kama'ole Beach Parks

Pi'ilani Hwy

Kealaikahiki Channel

S. Kīhei Rd

Mōkapu Beach

Ulua Beach

Wailea

Wailea Beach

31

'Alalākeiki Channel

Polo Beach

Mākena Beach State Park

Mākena

Molokini Crater

'Āhihi-Kīna'u (La Pérouse Bay)

La Pérouse Bay

KAHO'OLAWE

0   5 mi

0   5 km

the mountains) sides of the highway. There are gems here too, though, like stunning Nāpili Bay and its crescent of soft sand.

LAHAINA

Today Lahaina may best be described as either charming or tacky, depending on your point of view—and opinions do differ. Ethnic mom-and-pops have been supplanted by too many T-shirt shops, but there are some excellent restaurants and interesting galleries. At dusk, when the lights first come on, the town looks vaguely like a Disney theme park. Sunset cruises and other excursions depart from Lahaina Harbor. Happily, at the far south end of town an important ancient site—Mokuʻula—is being restored. ■TIP➔ **If you arrange to spend a Friday afternoon exploring Front Street, you can dine in town and hang around for Art Night, when the galleries stay open into the evening and entertainment fills the streets.**

> ### WORD OF MOUTH
>
> "Lahaina may appeal to some visitors, but it has no worthy beach; it's famous for kitsch, trinkets, a lūʻau, and a banyan tree." –Lex1
>
> "Lahaina IS busy! That's what I like about it. It has a very 'honky-tonk,' end-of-the-line feel about it. It's historically interesting, and I love that I can walk everywhere. I like all the shops, galleries, historic walking tour, restaurants, and bars." –suze

The town has been welcoming visitors for more than 200 years. In 1798, after waging war to unite the Hawaiian Islands, Kamehameha the Great chose Lahaina, then called *Lele,* as the seat of his monarchy. Warriors from Kamehameha's 800 canoes that were stretched along the coast from Olowalu to Honokōwai, turned inland and filled the lush valleys with networks of stream-fed *loi* or taro patches. For nearly 50 years, Lahaina remained the capital of the Hawaiian Kingdom. During this period, the scent of Hawaiian sandalwood brought Chinese traders to these waters. European whaling ships followed, chasing sperm whales from Japan to the Arctic. Lahaina became known around the world for its rough-and-tumble ways, typical of most ports of that time. Despite the efforts of several determined missionaries, smallpox and venereal disease took a terrible toll on the native population.

Then, almost as quickly as it had come, the tide of foreign trade receded. The Hawaiian capital was moved to Honolulu in 1845 and by 1860, the sandalwood forests were empty and sperm whales nearly extinct. Luckily, Lahaina had already grown into an international, sophisticated (if sometimes rowdy) town, laying claim to the first printing press and high school west of the Rockies. Sugar interests kept the town afloat until tourism stepped in.

TOP ATTRACTIONS

❼ ★ **Baldwin Home Museum.** Begun in 1834 and completed the following year, the coral and stone house was originally home to missionary and doctor Dwight Baldwin and his family. The building has been carefully restored to reflect the period; many of the original furnishings remain. You can view the family's grand piano, the carved four-poster bed, and most interestingly, Dr. Baldwin's dispensary. During a brief tour conducted by Lahaina Restoration Foundation volunteers, you'll be shown the "thunderpot" and told how the doctor single-handedly inoculated 10,000 Maui residents for smallpox. ⊠*696 Front St., Lahaina* ☎*808/661–3262* ⊕*www.lahaina restoration.org* ⊠*$3 per person, $5 per couple* ⊗*Daily 10–4.*

WALKING TOURS

Lahaina's side streets are best explored on foot. Both the Baldwin Home and the Lahaina Court House offer free self-guided walking tour brochures and maps. The Court House booklet is often recommended and includes more than 50 sites. The Baldwin Home brochure is less well known but, in our opinion, easier to follow. It details a short but enjoyable loop tour of the town.

NEED A BREAK? The sandwiches have real Gruyère and Emmentaler cheese at **Maui Swiss Cafe** (⊠*640 Front St.*)—expensive ingredients with affordable results. The friendly owner scoops the best and cheapest locally made ice cream in Lahaina. Daily lunch specials are less than $6.

⑩ Banyan Tree. This massive tree was planted in 1873. It's the largest of its kind in the state and provides a welcome retreat for the weary who come to sit under its awesome branches. ■TIP→The Banyan Tree is a popular and hard-to-miss meeting place if your party splits up for independent exploring. It's also a terrific spot to be when the sun sets—mynah birds settle in here for a screeching symphony, which can be an event in itself. ⊠*Front St. between Hotel and Canal Sts., Lahaina.*

⑫ Hale Pa'ahao (Old Prison). Lahaina's jailhouse dates to rowdy whaling days. Its name literally means "stuck-in-irons house," referring to the wall shackles and ball-and-chain restraints. The compound was built in the 1850s by convict laborers out of blocks of coral that had been salvaged from the demolished waterfront fort. Most prisoners were sent here for desertion, drunkenness, or reckless horse riding. Today, a wax figure representing an imprisoned old sailor tells his recorded tale of woe. ⊠*Waine'e and Prison Sts., Lahaina* ☎*Free* ⊗*Weekdays 10–4.*

⑬ Holy Innocents' Episcopal Church. Built in 1927, this beautiful open-air church is decorated with paintings depicting Hawaiian versions of Christian symbols, including a Hawaiian Madonna and child, rare or extinct birds, and native plants. The congregation is beautiful, typically dressed in traditional clothing from Samoa and Tonga. Anyone is welcome to slip into one of the pews, carved from native woods. Queen Liliu'okalani, Hawai'i's last reigning monarch, lived in a large grass house on this site as a child. ⊠*South end of Front St. near Mokuhina St., Lahaina* ☎*808/661–4202.*

⑨ Lahaina Court House. The Lahaina Town Action Committee and Lahaina Heritage Museum occupy this charming old government building in the center of town. Pump the knowledgeable staff for interesting trivia and ask for their walking-tour brochure, a comprehensive map to historic Lahaina sites. Erected in 1859 and restored in 1999, the building has served as a customs and court house, governor's office, post office, vault and collector's office, and police court. On August 12, 1898, its

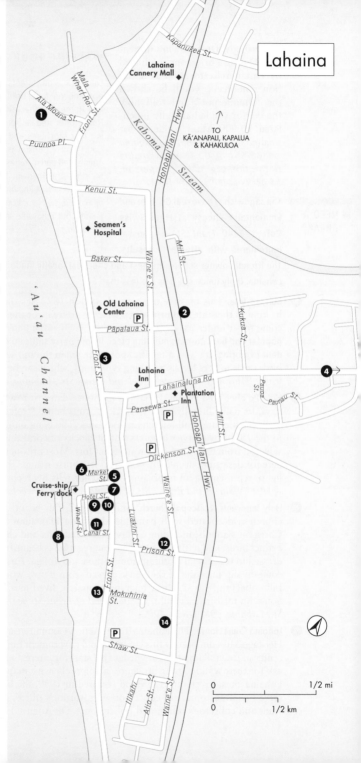

Lahaina

postmaster witnessed the lowering of the Hawaiian flag when Hawai'i became a U.S. territory. The flag now hangs above the stairway. You'll find terrific museum displays, the active Lahaina Arts Society, and an art gallery. ■TIP→There's also a public restroom. ✉649 Wharf St., Lahaina ☎808/661–0111 for the Arts Society, 808/667–9175 for the Lahaina Town Action Committee ✇Free ☉Daily 9–5.

FUN THINGS TO DO IN WEST MAUI

■ Get into the Hawaiian swing of things at the Old Lahaina Lū'au.

■ Take a late afternoon stroll on the beach fronting the Jodo Mission.

■ Make an offering at the Taoist altar in the Wo Hing Museum.

■ Sail into the sunset from Lahaina Harbor.

■ Attend the mynah birds' symphony beneath the Banyan Tree.

⑭ **Waiola Church and Waine'e Cemetery.** Better known as Waine'e Church and immortalized in James Michener's *Hawai'i*, the original building from the early 1800s was destroyed once by fire and twice by fierce windstorms. Repositioned and rebuilt in 1951, it was renamed Waiola ("water of life") and has been standing proudly ever since. The adjacent cemetery was the first Christian cemetery in the Islands and is the final resting place of many of Hawai'i's most important monarchs, including Kamehameha the Great's sacred wife, Queen Keōpūolani. ✉535 Waine'e St., Lahaina ☎808/661–4349.

❸ **Wo Hing Museum.** Smack-dab in the center of Front Street, this eye-catching Chinese temple reflects the importance of early Chinese immigrants to Lahaina. Built by the Wo Hing Society in 1912, the museum now contains beautiful artifacts, historic photos of old Lahaina, and a Taoist altar. Don't miss the films playing in the rustic theater next door—some of Thomas Edison's first films, shot in Hawai'i circa 1898, show Hawaiian wranglers herding steer onto ships. Ask the docent for some star fruit from the tree outside, for the altar or for yourself. ✉858 Front St., Lahaina ☎808/661–5553 ✇$1 ☉Daily 10–4.

WORTH NOTING

⑪ **Fort.** Stone ruins are all that remain at the site that used to be used mostly as a prison. It was built from 1831 to 1832 after sailors, angered by a law forbidding local women from swimming out to ships, lobbed cannonballs into town the previous year. The fort was finally torn down in the 1850s and the stones used to construct the new prison. Cannons raised from the wreck of a warship in Honolulu Harbor were brought to Lahaina and placed in front of the fort, where they still sit today. ✉Canal and Wharf Sts., Lahaina.

❹ **Hale Pa'i.** Protestant missionaries established Lahainaluna Seminary as a center of learning and enlightenment in 1831. Six years later, they built this printing shop. Here at the press, they and their young Hawaiian scholars created a written Hawaiian language and used it to produce a Bible, history texts, and a newspaper. An exhibit displays a replica of the original Rampage press and facsimiles of early printing. The oldest U.S. educational institution west of the Rockies, the seminary

Fodor'sChoice ★

Once a whaling center, Lahaina Harbor bustles with tour boats, fishing vessels, and pleasure craft.

now serves as Lahaina's public high school. ⊠ *980 Lahainaluna Rd., Lahaina* ☎ *808/661–3262* 💲 *Donations accepted* ⊙ *Weekdays 10–4.*

6 Hauola Stone. Just visible above the tide is a gigantic stone, perfectly molded into the shape of a low-backed chair and believed by Hawaiians to hold healing powers. It sits in the harbor where the sea and the underground freshwater meet. ⊠ *In water behind public library on Front St., Lahaina* 💲 *Free.*

7 Jodo Mission. This mission, established at the turn of the 20th century by Japanese contract workers, is one of Lahaina's most popular sites, thanks to its idyllic setting and spectacular views across the channel. Although the buildings are not open to the public, you can stroll all of the grounds and enjoy glimpses of the 90-foot-high pagoda, as well as a great, 3.5-ton copper and bronze statue of the Amida Buddha. It's a relaxing and contemplative spot just outside the tumult of Lahaina Town. If you're nearby at 8 any evening, listen for the temple bell to toll 11 times; each peal has a specific significance. ⊠ *12 Ala Moana St., just before Lahaina Cannery Mall, Lahaina* ☎ *808/661–4304* ⊕ *www.lahainajodomission.org* 💲 *Free.*

8 Lahaina Harbor. For centuries, Lahaina has drawn ships of all sizes to its calm harbor. King Kamehameha's conquering fleet of 800 carved *koa* canoes gave way to Chinese trading ships, Boston whalers, United States Navy frigates, and finally, a slew of cruise ships, catamarans, and deep-sea fishing operators. During World War II, "a white tide" of Navy seamen flooded the town. Stroll past the various tour boats to see who's had the best luck fishing. If they're filleting their catch, you might glimpse eagle rays underwater snapping up the trimmings. ⊠ *Wharf St., Lahaina* ⊡ *Free.*

❷ Lahaina–Kā'anapali and Pacific Railroad. Affectionately called the Sugarcane Train, this is Maui's only passenger train. It's an 1890s-vintage railway that once shuttled sugar but now moves sightseers between Kā'anapali and Lahaina. This quaint little attraction with its singing conductor is a big deal for Hawai'i but probably not much of a thrill for those more accustomed to trains (though children like it no matter where they grew up). ⊠ *1½ blocks north of Lahainaluna Rd. stoplight, at Hinau St., on Honoapi'ilani Hwy., Lahaina* ☎ *808/667–6851 or 800/499–2307* ⊡ *Round-trip $22.50* ☉ *Daily 10:15–4.*

❺ Master's Reading Room. Generally acknowledged as Maui's oldest residential building, the Master's Reading Room was constructed in 1834. In those days the ground floor was a storeroom; the room upstairs was a comfortable place from which naval officers could escape the heat and dust of Lahaina. Today, it houses the Lahaina Restoration Foundation, and is not open to the public. ⊠ *Front and Dickenson Sts., Lahaina* ☎ *808/661–3262.*

NORTH OF LAHAINA

As you drive north from Lahaina, the first resort community you come to is Kā'anapali, a cluster of high-rise hotels framing a beautiful white-sand beach. A little farther up the road lie the condo-filled beach towns of Honokōwai, Kahana, and Nāpili, followed by the stunning resort area, Kapalua. At the very end of the Honoapi'ilani Highway you'll find the remote village of Kahakuloa.

KĀ'ANAPALI

In ancient times, this area was known for its bountiful fishing (especially lobster) and its seaside cliffs. Pu'u Keka'a, today incorrectly referred to as "Black Rock," was a *lele*, a place in ancient Hawai'i from which souls leaped into the afterlife. But times changed and the sleepy fishing village was washed away by the wave of Hawai'i's new economy: tourism. Clever marketers built this sunny shoreline into a playground for the world's vacationers. The theatrical look of Hawai'i tourism—planned resort communities where luxury homes mix with high-rise hotels, fantasy swimming pools, and a theme-park landscape—all began right here in the 1960s. Three miles of uninterrupted white-sand beach and placid water form the front yard for this artificial utopia, with its 40 tennis courts and two championship golf courses. The six major hotels here are all worth visiting, if only for a look around, especially the Hyatt Regency Maui, which has a multimillion-dollar art collection and plenty of exotic birds in the lobby.

Whalers Village. While the kids hit Honolua Surf Company, mom can peruse Versace, Prada, Coach, and several fine jewelry stores at this casual, classy mall fronting Kā'anapali Beach. Pizza and Häagen-Dazs ice cream are available in the center courtyard. At the beach entrance, you'll find a wonderful restaurant, Hula Grill. ⊠ *2435 Kā'anapali Pkwy.* ☎ *808/661–4567* ⊕ *www.whalersvillage.com.*

On the north end of West Maui, remote Kahakuloa is a reminder of old Hawai'i.

🕙 **Whalers Village Museum.** A giant bony whale greets shoppers to Whalers Village. The massive skeleton is the herald of the Whale Center of the Pacific museum on the second floor where you'll hear stories of the 19th-century *Moby-Dick* era. Baleen, ambergris, and other mysterious artifacts are on display. A short film features Hawaiian turtles and the folklore surrounding them. ✉ *2435 Kā'anapali Pkwy., Suite H16* ☎ *808/661–5992* ✉ *Free* 🕙 *Daily 9:30 AM–10 PM.*

KAPALUA

Beautiful and secluded, Kapalua is West Maui's northernmost resort community. The area got its first big boost in 1978, when the Maui Land & Pineapple Company (ML&P) built the luxurious Kapalua Bay Hotel. ML&P owns the entire area known as "Kapalua Resort," which includes the Ritz-Carlton, three golf courses, and the surrounding fields of Maui Gold pineapple. The quaint Kapalua Bay Hotel has been replaced by extremely upscale residences with a spa and a golf club. The area's shopping and freestanding restaurants cater to dedicated golfers, celebrities who want to be left alone, and some of the world's richest folks. Mists regularly envelop Kapalua, which is cooler and quieter than its southern neighbors.

> **CHEAP EATS**
>
> In contrast to Kapalua's high-end glitz, the old **Honolua Store**, just above the Ritz-Carlton, still plies the groceries, fishnets, and household wares it did in plantation times. Hefty plates of 'ono (delicious) local foods are served at the deli until 8:30 PM. The plate lunches are the quintessential local meal and are very popular. ✉ *504 Office Rd., Kapalua* ☎ *808/669–6128* 🕙 *Daily 6 AM–9 PM.*

The landscape of tall Cook pines and rolling fairways is reminiscent of Lāna'i, and the beaches and dining are among Maui's finest.

KAHAKULOA

This is the wild side of West Maui. Untouched by progress, this tiny village at the north end of Honoapi'ilani Highway is a relic of pre–jet travel Maui. Remote villages similar to Kahakuloa were once tucked away in several valleys of this area. Many residents still grow taro and live in the old Hawaiian way. The unimproved road weaves along coastal cliffs. Watch out for stray cattle, roosters, and falling rocks. True adventurers will find terrific snorkeling and swimming along this drive, as well as some good hiking trails. *See Chapters 4 and 5, Water Sports and Tours and Golf, Hiking, and Outdoor Activities.*

THE SOUTH SHORE

Blessed by more than its fair share of sun, the southern shore of Haleakalā was an undeveloped wilderness until the 1970s. Then the sun-worshippers found it; now restaurants, condos, and luxury resorts line the coast from the world-class aquarium at Mā'alaea Harbor, through working-class Kīhei, to lovely Wailea, a resort community rivaling its counterpart, Kā'anapali, on West Maui. Farther south, the road disappears and unspoiled wilderness still has its way.

Because the South Shore includes so many fine beach choices, a trip here (if you're staying elsewhere on the island) is an all-day excursion—especially if you include a visit to the aquarium. Get active in the morning with exploring and snorkeling, then shower in a beach park, dress up a little, and enjoy the cool luxury of the Wailea resorts. At sunset, settle in for dinner at one of the area's many fine restaurants.

MĀ'ALAEA

Mā'alaea, pronounced Mah-*ah*-lye-*ah,* is not much more than a few condos, an aquarium, and a wind-blasted harbor—but that's more than enough for some visitors. Humpback whales seem to think Mā'alaea is tops for meeting mates. Green sea turtles treat it like their own personal spa, regularly seeking appointments with cleaner wrasses in the harbor. Surfers revere this spot for "freight train," reportedly the world's fastest wave.

A small Shinto shrine stands at the shore here, dedicated to the fishing god Ebisu Sama. Across the street, a giant hook often swings heavy with the sea's bounty, proving the worth of the shrine. Down Hau'oli Street (Hawaiian for *happy*) the Waterfront restaurant has benefited from its close proximity to the harbor. At the end of Hau'oli Street (the town's single road), a small community garden is sometimes privy to traditional Hawaiian ceremonies. That's all; there's not much else. But the few residents here like it that way.

Mā'alaea Small Boat Harbor. With only 89 slips and so many good reasons to take people out on the water, this active little harbor needs to be expanded. The Army Corps of Engineers has a plan to do so, but harbor users are fighting it—particularly the surfers, who say the plan would destroy their surf breaks. In fact, the surf here is world-renowned. The elusive spot to the left of the harbor called "freight train" rarely breaks, but when it does, it's said to be the fastest anywhere. ⊠*Off Honoapiʻilani Hwy., Rte. 30.*

FodorsChoice ★ **Maui Ocean Center.** You'll feel as though you're walking from the seashore down to the bottom of the reef, and then through an acrylic tunnel in the middle of the sea at this aquarium, which focuses on Hawaiʻi and the Pacific. Special tanks get you up close with turtles, rays, sharks, and the unusual creatures of the tide pools. The center is part of a complex of retail shops and restaurants overlooking the harbor. ⊠*Enter from Honoapiʻilani Hwy., Rte. 30, as it curves past Māʻalaea Harbor, Māʻalaea* ☎*808/270–7000* ⊕*www.mauioceancenter. com* ⊠*$25* ⊙*Daily 9–5.*

> ## FUN THINGS TO DO ON THE SOUTH SHORE
>
> ■ Observe the green sea turtles while snorkeling at ʻUlua beach.
>
> ■ Spike a volleyball at Kalama Park.
>
> ■ Witness the hammerheads feeding at the excellent Maui Ocean Center.
>
> ■ Follow the Hoapili Trail through an ancient Hawaiian village.
>
> ■ Sink into Mākena's endless soft sand.
>
> ■ Decipher whale song at the Hawaiʻi Humpback Whale Sanctuary.

KĪHEI

Thirty years ago, Kīhei was a dusty, dry nondestination. Now about one-third of the Maui population lives here in one of the fastest-growing towns in America. Development is still under way: a greenway for bikers and pedestrians is under construction, as is a multitude of new homes and properties.

Traffic lights and mini-malls may not fit your notion of paradise, but Kīhei offers dependably warm sun, excellent beaches, and a front-row seat to marine life of all sorts. The county beach parks such as Kamaʻole I, II, and III have lawns, showers, and picnic tables. ■TIP➔**Remember: beach park or no beach park, the public has a right to the entire coastal strand but not to cross private property to get to it.** Besides all the sun and sand, the town's relatively inexpensive condos and excellent restaurants make this a home base for many Maui visitors.

ⓒ ★ **Hawaiian Island Humpback Whale National Marine Sanctuary.** The sanctuary itself includes virtually all the waters surrounding the archipelago; the Education Center is located beside a restored ancient Hawaiian fishpond, in prime humpback-viewing territory. Whether the whales are here or not, the center is a great stop for youngsters curious to know how things work underwater. Interactive displays and informative naturalists will explain it all. Throughout the year, the center hosts intriguing activities, ranging from moonlight tidal-pool explorations to "Two Ton Talks." ⊠*726 S. Kīhei Rd., Kīhei* ☎*808/879–2818 or 800/831–4888* ⊕*www.hawaiihumpbackwhale.noaa.gov* ⊠*Free* ⊙*Weekdays 10–3.*

DID YOU KNOW?

Snorkel cruises are popular on Maui, but you can find great snorkeling on your own. Try the rocky borders of beaches on the South Shore in places such as Kīhei (shown here) or Wailea.

2

🕐 ★ **Keālia Pond National Wildlife Reserve.** Long-legged stilts casually dip their beaks in the shallow waters of this wildlife reserve as traffic shuttles by. If you take time to read the interpretive signs on the boardwalk, you'll learn that endangered hawksbill turtles return to the sandy dunes here year after year. Sharp-eyed birders may catch sight of occasional migratory visitors, such as a falcon or osprey. ⊠*N. Kīhei Rd., Kīhei* 🖃*Free* 🕐 *Weekdays 7:30–4.*

WAILEA AND FARTHER SOUTH

Wailea, the South Shore's resort community, is slightly quieter and drier than its West Maui sister, Kāʻanapali. Many visitors cannot pick a favorite, so they stay at both. The first two resorts were built here in the late 1970s. Soon a cluster of upscale properties sprung up, including the Four Seasons and the Fairmont Kea Lani. Check out the Grand Wailea Resort's chapel, which tells a Hawaiian love story in stained glass. The luxury of the resorts (edging on the excessive) and the simple grandeur of the coastal views make the otherwise stark landscape an outstanding destination. A handful of perfect little beaches, all with public access, front the resorts.

★ **Coastal Nature Trail.** A paved beach walk allows you to stroll among Wailea's prettiest properties, restaurants, and rocky coves. The trail teems with joggers in the morning hours. The *makai,* or ocean, side is landscaped with exceptionally rare native plants. Look for the silvery *hinahina,* named after the Hawaiian moon goddess because of its color. In winter this is a great place to watch whales. ⊠*Accessible from Polo or Wailea Beach parks.*

The Shops at Wailea. Louis Vuitton, Tiffany & Co., and the sumptuous Cos Bar lure shoppers to this elegant mall. Honolulu Coffee brews perfect shots of espresso to fuel those "shop-'til-you-drop" types. The kids can buy logo shirts in Pacific Sun while mom and dad ponder vacation ownership upstairs. Tommy Bahama's, Ruth's Chris, and Longhi's are all good dining options. ⊠*3750 Wailea Alanui Dr.* 🕾*808/891–6770* 🌐*www.shopsatwailea.com.*

Fodor'sChoice **Mākena Beach State Park.** Although it's commonly known as "Big Beach,"
★ its correct name is Oneloa ("long sand"), and that's exactly what it is—a huge stretch of heavenly golden sand without a house or hotel in sight. More than a decade ago, Maui citizens campaigned successfully to preserve this beloved beach from development. It's still wild, lacking in modern amenities (such as plumbing) but frequented by dolphins and turtles; sunsets are glorious. At the end of the beach farthest from Wailea, skim-boarders catch air. On the opposite end rises the beautiful hill called Puʻu Ōlaʻi, a perfect cinder cone. A climb over the steep rocks at this end leads to "Little Beach," which, although technically it's illegal, is clothing-optional. On Sunday, it's a mecca for drummers and island gypsies. On any day of the week watch out for the mean shore break—those crisp, aquamarine waves are responsible for more than one broken arm.

ʻAhihi-Kīnaʻu (La Pérouse Bay). Beyond Mākena Beach, the road fades away into a vast territory of black-lava flows, the result of Haleakalā's last eruption. Also known as La Pérouse Bay, this is where Maui received its first official visit by a European explorer—the French admiral Jean-François de Galaup, Comte de La Pérouse, in 1786. Before it ends, the road passes through the ʻAhihi-Kīnaʻu Marine Preserve, an excellent place for morning snorkel adventures *(see Chapter 4, Water Sports and Tours)*. However, visitors should note that until August 2010 at the earliest, most of the area will be closed to the public, including unofficial trails to Kalua o Lapa, Kalaeloa (popularly known as "the Aquarium"), and Mokuha (also known as "the Fishbowl"). Access to northern portions of the reserve most used by the public will remain open during visiting hours. Some of these open areas are Waiala Cove and the coastal area along ʻAhihi Bay including the "Dumps" surf break. This is also the start of the Hoapili Trail, or "the King's Trail," where you can hike through the remains of one of Maui's ancient villages. For more information, you can visit the State Department of Land and Resources Web site at ⊕*hawaii.gov/dlnr*. ■TIP→**Bring water and a hat, as there are no public facilities and little shade, and tread carefully over this culturally important landscape.**

CENTRAL MAUI

Kahului, where you most likely landed when you arrived on Maui, is the industrial and commercial center of the island. The area was developed in the early 1950s to meet the housing needs of the large sugarcane interests here, specifically those of Alexander & Baldwin. The company was tired of playing landlord to its many plantation workers and sold land to a developer who promised to create affordable housing. The scheme worked, and "Dream City," the first planned city in Hawaiʻi, was born.

West of Kahului is Wailuku. The county seat since 1950, it is the most charming town in Central Maui—

> **FUN THINGS TO DO IN CENTRAL MAUI**
>
> ■ Unwind to slack-key guitar at a Maui Arts & Cultural Center concert.
>
> ■ Marvel at the indigenous plant life at Maui Nui Botanical Gardens.
>
> ■ Pick your way through ʻIao Valley's guava and ginger forest.
>
> ■ Imagine mastering the ancient weapons at the Bailey House.
>
> ■ Boost your fortune with a pair of foo dogs bought on Market Street.

though it wasn't always so. Its name means "Water of Destruction," after the fateful battle in ʻIao Valley that pitted King Kamehameha the Great against Maui warriors. Wailuku was a politically important town until the sugar industry began to decline in the 1960s and tourism took hold. Businesses left the cradle of the West Maui Mountains and followed the new market to the shore, where tourists arrived by the boatload. Wailuku still houses the county government but has the feel of a town that's been asleep for several decades. The shops and offices now inhabiting Main Street's plantation-style buildings serve as reminders of a bygone era, and continued attempts at "gentrification," at the very least, open the way for unique eateries, shops, and galleries.

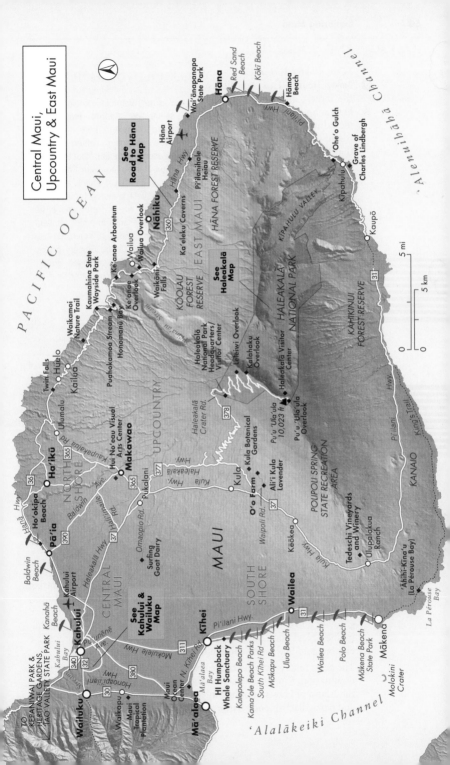

Central Maui, Upcountry & East Maui

PACIFIC OCEAN

'Alenuihāhā Channel

See Road to Hāna Map

See Haleakalā Map

See Kahului & Wailuku Map

HĀNA FOREST RESERVE

EAST MAUI

HALEAKALĀ NATIONAL PARK

KĪPAHULU VALLEY

KOOLAU FOREST RESERVE

KAHIKINUI FOREST RESERVE

UPCOUNTRY

NORTH SHORE

CENTRAL MAUI

MAUI

SOUTH SHORE

KANAIO

POLIPOLI SPRING STATE RECREATION AREA

Hāna
Red Sand Beach
Kōki Beach
Hāmoa Beach
Wai'ānapanapa State Park
Hāna Airport
Ka'eleku Caverns
Pi'ilanihale Heiau
'Ohe'o Gulch
Grave of Charles Lindbergh
Kīpahulu
Kaupō

Pi'ilani Hwy

Hāna Hwy
360

Nāhiku
Wailua
Wailua Overlook
Ke'anae Arboretum
Kaumahina State Wayside Park
Honomanū Bay
Ke'anae Overlook
Waikāni Falls
Pua'aka'a State Park
Puohokamoa Stream
Waikamoi Nature Trail
Twin Falls
Huelo
'Ula'ula
Kailua
Haleakalā National Park Headquarters/Visitor Center
Leleiwi Overlook
Kalahaku Overlook
Haleakalā Visitor Center
Pu'u 'Ula'ula 10,023 ft
Pu'u 'Ula'ula Overlook

Haleakalā Crater Rd.

378

Kula Botanical Gardens
Ali'i Kula Lavender
Kula
O'o Farm
Keōkea
Tedeschi Vineyards and Winery
'Ulupalakua Ranch

Kula Hwy

Kula Hwy

Waipoli Rd.

377

Makawao
Hui No'eou Visual Arts Center
Ha'ikū
Pukalani
365
Haleakalā Hwy

Baldwin Ave.

Kaupakalua Rd.

Olinda Rd.

Haliimaile Rd.

'Ulumalu
36
Ho'okipa Beach
Pā'ia
390
Surfing Goat Dairy
Omaopio Rd.

Haleakalā Hwy
37

Baldwin Beach
Kahului Beach
Kahului
Kanahā Beach
Kahului Airport
Kahului Bay
340
32

Wailuku
Maui Tropical Plantation
Waikapu
30
380
Honoapi'ilani Hwy

TO KEPANIWAI PARK & HERITAGE GARDENS; 'IAO VALLEY STATE PARK

Mā'alaea
Mā'alaea Bay
Maui Ocean Center
HI Humpback Whale Sanctuary
Kalepolepo Beach
Kama'ole Beach Parks
South Kīhei Rd.
311
Pi'ilani Hwy
Kīhei
Mōkapu Beach
Ulua Beach
Wailea Beach
Polo Beach
Wailea
31
Mākena Beach State Park
Mākena
'Āhihi-Kīna'u (La Pérouse Bay)
La Pérouse Bay
Molokini Crater

Mokulele Hwy
Pu'unēnē Ave.
Maui Veterans Hwy

'Alalākeiki Channel

King's Trail

Pi'ilani Hwy

311

Honoapi'ilani Hwy

Kīhei
N. Kīhei Rd.

0   5 mi
0   5 km

KAHULUI AND WAILUKU

TOP ATTRACTIONS

❸ Bailey House. This repository of

Fodor'sChoice the largest and best collection of

★ Hawaiian artifacts on Maui—including objects from the sacred island of Kahoʻolawe—was first the Wailuku Seminary for Girls and then the home of missionary teachers Edward and Caroline Bailey. Built in 1833 on the site of the compound of Kahekili (the last ruling chief of Maui), the building was occupied by the Bailey family until 1888. Edward Bailey was something of a Renaissance man: beyond being a missionary, he was also a surveyor, a naturalist, and an excellent artist. In addition to the fantastic Hawaiian collection,

WHILE YOU'RE HERE

You may want to combine sightseeing in Central Maui with some shopping. There are three large shopping centers—Queen Kaʻahumanu Center, Maui Mall, and Maui Marketplace *(see Chapter 6, Shops and Spas)*. This is also one of the best areas on the island to stock up on groceries and basic supplies, thanks to major retailers including Wal-Mart, Kmart, Costco, and Home Depot. Grocery prices, particularly for packaged goods, on Maui are much higher than on the mainland.

the museum displays a number of Bailey's landscape paintings, which provide a snapshot of the island during his time. There is missionary-period furniture, and the grounds include gardens with native Hawaiian plants and a fine example of a traditional canoe. The gift shop is one of the best sources on Maui for items that are actually made in Hawaiʻi. ⊠ *2375A Main St., Wailuku* ☏ *808/244–3326* ⊕ *www.mauimuseum. org* ⊠ *$5* ☉ *Mon.–Sat. 10–4.*

❷ ʻĪao Valley State Park. When Mark Twain saw this park, he dubbed it

Fodor'sChoice the Yosemite of the Pacific. Yosemite it's not, but it is a lovely deep

★ valley with the curious ʻĪao Needle, a spire that rises more than 2,000 feet from the valley floor. You can walk from the parking lot across ʻĪao Stream and explore the thick, jungle-like topography. This park has some lovely short strolls on paved paths, where you can stop and meditate by the edge of a stream or marvel at the native plants and flowers. Locals come to jump from the rocks or bridge into the stream—this isn't recommended. Mist often rises if there has been a rain, which makes being here even more magical. ⊠ *Western end of Rte. 32* ⊠ *Free* ☉ *Daily 7–7.*

❶ Kepaniwai Park & Heritage Gardens. This county park is a memorial to

☾ Maui's cultural roots, with picnic facilities and ethnic displays dotting the landscape. Among the displays are an early-Hawaiian hale (meetinghouse), a New England–style saltbox, a Portuguese-style villa with gardens, and dwellings from such other cultures as China and the Philippines. Next door, the Hawaiʻi Nature Center has excellent interactive exhibits and hikes easy enough for children.

The peacefulness here belies the history of the area. During his quest for domination, King Kamehameha the Great brought his troops from the Big Island of Hawaiʻi to the Valley Isle in 1790 and waged a successful and particularly bloody battle against the son of Maui's chief, Kahekili,

MAUI SIGHTSEEING TOURS

Maui is really too big to see all in one day, so tour companies offer specialized tours, visiting either Haleakalā or Hāna and its environs. A tour of Haleakalā and Upcountry is usually a half-day excursion and is offered in several versions by different companies for about $60 and up. The trip often includes stops at a protea farm and at Tedeschi Vineyards, Maui's only winery.

A Haleakalā sunrise tour starts before dawn so that you can get to the top of the dormant volcano before the sun peeks over the horizon. Because they offer island-wide hotel pickup, many sunrise trips leave around 2:30 AM.

A tour of Hāna is almost always done in a van, since the winding Road to Hāna just isn't built for bigger buses. Of late, Hāna has so many of these one-day tours that it seems as if there are more vans than cars on the road. Still, to many it's a more relaxing way to do the drive than behind the wheel of a car. Guides decide where you stop for photos. Tours run from $80 to $120.

The key is to ask how many stops you get and how many other passengers will be on board—otherwise you could end up on a packed bus, sightseeing through a window.

Most of the tour guides have been in the business for years and some have taken special classes to learn more about the culture and lore. They expect a tip ($1 per person at least), but they're just as cordial without one.

Maui Pineapple Plantation Tour. Explore one of Maui's pineapple plantations by going right into the fields in a company van. The 2¼-hour, $39.95 trip gives you firsthand experience of the operation and its history, some incredible views of the island, and the chance to pick a fresh pineapple for yourself. Two tours depart each weekday morning from the Kapalua Logo Shop. Reservations are required. ✉ *Maui Gold, Kapalua* ☎ *808/665-5491.*

Polynesian Adventure Tours. This company uses large buses with floor-to-ceiling windows. The drivers are fun and really know the island. ☎ *808/ 877-4242 or 800/622-3011* ⊕ *www. polyad.com.*

Roberts Hawai'i Tours. This is one of the state's largest tour companies, and its staff can arrange tours with bilingual guides if asked ahead of time. Eleven-hour trips venture out to Kaupo, the wild area past Hāna. ☎ *808/871-6226 or 866/898-2519 www.robertsha waii.com.*

Temptation Tours. Temptation Tours has targeted members of the affluent older crowd (though almost anyone would enjoy these tours) who don't want to be herded onto a crowded bus. Tours in plush six-passenger limovans explore Haleakalā and Hāna, and range from $110 to $249 per person. The "Hāna Sky-Trek" includes a return trip via helicopter. ☎ *808/877-8888 or 800/817-1234* ⊕ *www.temptation tours.com.*

Tour da Food Maui. Maui resident Bonnie Friedman (a Fodor's contributor) guides small, customized food tours that include a couple of holes-in-the-wall some locals don't even know about. Tours leave Tuesday, Wednesday, and Thursday mornings and cost from $105 to $130 per person. ✉ *Wailuku96793* ☎ *808/242-8383* ⊕ *www.tourdafoodmaui.com.*

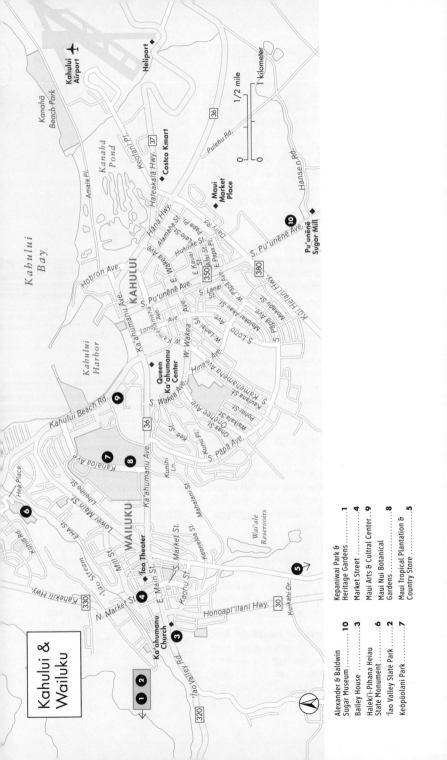

Kahului & Wailuku

Alexander & Baldwin
Sugar Museum **10**
Bailey House **3**
Haleki'i-Pihana Heiau
State Monument **6**
'Iao Valley State Park **2**
Keōpūolani Park **7**

Kepaniwai Park &
Heritage Gardens **1**
Market Street **4**
Maui Arts & Cultral Center ..**9**
Maui Nui Botanical
Gardens **8**
Maui Tropical Plantation &
Country Store **5**

2

near Kepaniwai Park. An earlier battle at the site had pitted Kahekili himself against an older Big Island chief, Kalaniʻōpuʻu. Kahekili prevailed, but the carnage was so great that the nearby stream became known as Wailuku (water of destruction) and the place where fallen warriors choked the stream's flow was called Kepaniwai (the water dam). ⊠ʻĪao Valley Rd., Wailuku ☎Free ⊙Daily 7–7.

❹ Market Street. An idiosyncratic assortment of shops makes Wailuku's Market Street (affectionately known as "Antiques Row") a delightful place for a stroll. Brown-Kobayashi and the Bird of Paradise Unique Antiques are the best for interesting collectibles and furnishings. Cafe Marc Aurel started out as a great espresso spot and has expanded to become a popular gathering place serving food and offering an excellent wine list. ⊠Wailuku96793.

WORTH NOTING

❿ Alexander & Baldwin Sugar Museum. "A&B," Maui's largest landowner,
★ was one of the "Big Five" companies that spearheaded the planting, harvesting, and processing of sugarcane. Although Hawaiian cane sugar is now being supplanted by cheaper foreign versions—as well as by sugar derived from inexpensive sugar beets—the crop was for many years the mainstay of the Hawaiian economy. You can find the museum in a small, restored plantation manager's house next to the post office and the still-operating sugar refinery (black smoke billows up when cane is burning). Historic photos, artifacts, and documents explain the introduction of sugarcane to Hawaiʻi and how plantation managers brought in laborers from other countries, thereby changing the Islands' ethnic mix. Exhibits also describe the sugar-making process. ⊠3957 Hansen Rd., Puʻunēnē ☎808/871–8058 ⊕www.sugarmuseum.com ☎$ 7 ⊙Mon.–Sat. 9:30–4.

❻ Halekiʻi-Pihana Heiau State Monument. Stand here at either of the two heiau (ancient Hawaiian stone platforms once used as places of worship) and imagine the king of Maui surveying his domain. That's what Kahekili, Maui's last king, did, and so did Kamehameha the Great after he defeated Kahekili's soldiers. Today the view is most instructive. Below, the once-powerful ʻĪao Stream has been sucked dry and boxed in by concrete. Before you is the urban heart of the island. The suburban community behind you is all Hawaiian Homelands—property owned solely by native Hawaiians. ⊠End of Hea Pl., off Kuhio Pl. from Waiehu Beach Rd., Rte. 340, Kahului ☎Free ⊙Daily 7–7.

❼ Keōpūolani Park. Covering 101 acres in Central Maui, this park reflects
☾ island residents' traditional love of sports. It was originally named "Maui Central Park," but schoolchildren argued before the County Council that it be named for Hawaiʻi's most sacred queen, who was born near here and was later forced to flee across the mountains when Kamehameha the Great's army arrived. The park includes seven playing fields, a running path, skate ramp, and grass amphitheater. ⊠Kanaloa Ave. next to YMCA.

❾ Maui Arts & Cultural Center. An epic fund drive by the citizens of Maui
★ led to the creation of this $32 million facility. The top-of-the-line Castle Theater seats 1,200 people on orchestra, mezzanine, and balcony

levels; rock stars play the A&B Amphitheater. The MACC (as it's called) also includes a small black-box theater, an art gallery with interesting exhibits, and classrooms. The building itself is worth a visit: it incorporates work by Maui artists, and its signature lava-rock wall pays tribute to the skills of the Hawaiians. But the real draw is the Schaeffer International Gallery, which houses superb rotating exhibits. ⊠*Above harbor on Kahului Beach Rd.* ☎*808/242–2787, 808/242–7469 box office* ⊕*www.mauiarts.org* ⊙ *Weekdays 9–5.*

❽ Maui Nui Botanical Gardens. The fascinating plants grown on these 7 ☼ acres are representative of precontact Hawai'i. Both native and Polynesian-introduced species are cultivated—including ice-cream bananas, varieties of sweet potatoes and sugarcane, native poppies, hibiscus, and *anapanapa,* a plant that makes a natural shampoo when rubbed between your hands. Ethnobotany tours and presentations are offered on occasion. ⊠*150 Kanaloa Ave.* ☎*808/249–2798* ⊕*www.mnbg.org* ☜*Free* ⊙*Mon.–Sat. 8–4.*

❺ Maui Tropical Plantation & Country Store. When Maui's once-paramount ☼ crop declined in importance, a group of visionaries decided to open an agricultural theme park on the site of this former sugarcane field. The 60-acre preserve, on Route 30 just outside Wailuku, offers a 30-minute tram ride through its fields with an informative narration covering growing processes and plant types. Children will probably enjoy the historical-characters exhibit as well as fruit-tasting, coconut-husking, and lei-making demonstrations, not to mention some entertaining spider monkeys. There's a restaurant on the property and a "country store" specializing in "Made in Maui" products. ⊠*Honoapi'ilani Hwy., Rte. 30, Waikapu* ☎*808/244–7643* ☜*Free; $11 for a tram ride with narrated tour* ⊙*Daily 9–5.*

UPCOUNTRY MAUI

The west-facing upper slopes of Haleakalā are locally called "Upcountry." This region is responsible for much of Hawai'i's produce—lettuce, tomatoes, strawberries, sweet Maui onions, and much, much more. You'll notice cactus thickets mingled with purple jacaranda, wild hibiscus, and towering eucalyptus trees. Keep an eye out for *pueo,* Hawai'i's native owl, which hunts these fields during daylight hours.

Upcountry is also fertile ranch land; cowboys still work the fields of the historic 20,000-acre 'Ulupalakua Ranch and the 32,000-acre Haleakalā Ranch. ■TIP→**This is a great area in which to take an**

FUN THINGS TO DO UPCOUNTRY

■ Swig a cup of joe with a *paniolo* (Hawaiian cowboy) at Grandma's Coffee Shop in Kēōkea.

■ Nibble lavender scones with a view of the Valley Isle at Ali'i Kula Lavender farm.

■ Open the car windows wide and breathe in the fresh, cool country air.

■ Taste pineapple wine at Tedeschi Vineyards and Winery.

■ Watch a plein-air painter work on the grounds of the Hui.

agricultural tour and learn more about the island's bounty. Lavender, veg-etables, cheese, and wine are among your choices.

A drive to Upcountry Maui from Wailea (South Shore) or Kā'anapali (West Maui) can be an all-day outing if you take the time to visit Tedeschi Vineyards and the tiny town of Makawao. You may want to cut these side trips short and combine your Upcountry tour with a visit to Haleakalā National Park *(see Haleakalā National Park feature)*. It's a Maui must-see. If you leave early enough to catch the sunrise from the summit of Haleakalā, you'll have plenty of time to explore the mountain, have lunch in Kula or at 'Ulupalakua Ranch, and end your day with dinner in Makawao.

THE KULA HIGHWAY

Kula . . . most Mauians say it with a hint of a sigh. Why? It's just that much closer to heaven. On the broad shoulder of Haleakalā, this is blessed country. From the Kula Highway most of Central Maui is visible—from the lava-scarred plains of Kenaio to the cruise-ship-lighted waters of Kahului Harbor. Beyond the central valley's sugarcane fields, the plunging profile of the West Maui Mountains can be seen in its entirety, wreathed in ethereal mist. If this sounds too prosaic a description, you haven't been here yet. These views, coveted by many, continue to drive real-estate prices further skyward. Luckily, you can still have them for free—just pull over on the roadside and drink them in.

★ **Ali'i Kula Lavender.** Reserve a spot for tea or lunch at this lavender farm with a falcon's view. It's *the* relaxing remedy for those suffering from too much sun, shopping, or golf. Owners Ali'i and Lani lead tours through winding paths of therapeutic lavender varieties, proteas, succulents, and rare Maui wormwood. Their logo, a larger-than-life dragonfly, darts above chefs who are cooking up lavender-infused shrimp appetizers out on the lānai. The gift shop abounds with the farm's own innovative lavender products. ⊠*1100 Waipoli Rd., Kula* ☎*808/878–3004* ⊕*www.aliikulalavender.com* ☜*$12 for walking tours; combine with a lunch basket for $37 per person* ⚲*Reservations essential for group tours* ☉*Daily 9–4, walking tours leave 5 times a day.*

Kēōkea. More of a friendly gesture than a town, this tiny outpost is the last bit of civilization before Kula Highway becomes the winding backside road, heading east around to Hāna. A coffee tree pushes through the sunny deck at Grandma's Coffee Shop, the morning watering hole for Maui's cowboys who work at 'Ulupalakua or Kaupō ranch. Kēōkea Gallery next door sells some of the most original artwork on the island. ■TIP➔**The only restroom for miles is across the street at the public park, and the view makes stretching your legs worth it.**

Kula Botanical Gardens. This well-kept garden has assimilated itself naturally into its craggy 6-acre habitat. There are beautiful trees here, including native koa (prized by woodworkers) and *kukui* (the state tree, a symbol of enlightenment). There's also a good selection of proteas, the flowering shrubs that have become a signature flower crop of Upcountry Maui. A natural stream feeds into a koi pond, which is also home to a pair of African cranes. ⊠*638 Kekaulike Hwy., Kula* ☎*808/878–1715*

⊕ *www.kulabotanicalgarden.com*
⊠ *$7.50* ⊙ *Daily 9–4.*

O'o Farm. About a mile down Waipoli Road from Ali'i Kula Lavender are 8 acres of salad greens, herbs, vegetables, and stone and citrus fruits—all of it headed directly to the Pacific'O and I'o restaurants in Lahaina. Owned and operated by the restaurateurs, more than 300 pounds of fresh O'o Farm produce ends up on diners' plates every week. Tours include an informational walk around the gorgeous Kula property and a pick-your-own lunch, supervised by a chef. Reservations are necessary. ⊠ *Waipoli Rd., Kula* ☎ *808/667–4341* ⊕ *www.oofarm.com* ⊠ *$50* ⊙ *Wed. and Thurs. 10:30–1.*

Surfing Goat Dairy. It takes goats to make goat cheese, and they've got plenty of both at this 42-acre farm. Tours range from "casual" to "grand" and particularly delight children. If you have the time, both the two-hour grand tour (twice a month) and the "Evening Chores & Milking Tour" are educational and fun. The owners make more than two dozen kinds of goat cheese, from the plain, creamy "Udderly Delicious" to more-exotic cheeses that include other, sometimes tropical, ingredients. All varieties are available for purchase in the dairy store, along with gift baskets and even goat milk soaps. ⊠ *3651 Ōmaopio Rd., Kula* ☎ *808/878–2870* ⊕ *www.surfinggoatdairy.com* ⊠ *$7–$25* ⊙ *Mon.–Sat. 10–5, Sun. 10–2; check ahead for tour schedule.*

Tedeschi Vineyards and Winery. You can tour the winery and its historic grounds, the former Rose Ranch, and sample the island's only wines: a pleasant Maui Blush, Maui Champagne, and Tedeschi's annual Maui Nouveau. The top-seller, naturally, is the pineapple wine. The tasting room is a cottage built in the late 1800s for the frequent visits of King Kalākaua. The cottage also contains the **'Ulupalakua Ranch History Room,** which tells colorful stories of the ranch's owners, the *paniolo* (Hawaiian cowboy) tradition that developed here, and Maui's polo teams. The old General Store may look like a museum, but in fact it's an excellent pit stop. ⊠ *Kula Hwy., 'Ulupalakua Ranch* ☎ *808/878–6058* ⊕ *www. mauiwine.com* ⊠ *Free* ⊙ *Daily 9–5; tours at 10:30, 1:30, and 3.*

MAKAWAO

This once-tiny town, at the intersection of Baldwin and Makawao avenues, has managed to hang on to its country charm (and eccentricity) as it has grown in popularity. The district was originally settled by Portuguese and Japanese immigrants who came to Maui to work the sugar plantations and then moved Upcountry to establish small farms, ranches, and stores. Descendants now work the neighboring Haleakalā

Continued on page 63

HALEAKALĀ NATIONAL PARK

HALEAKALA CRATER

From the Tropics to the Moon! Two hours, 38 mi, 10,023 feet—those are the unlikely numbers involved in reaching Maui's highest point, the summit of the volcano Haleakalā. Nowhere else on earth can you drive from sea level (Kahului) to 10,023 feet (the summit) in only 38 mi. And what's more shocking—in that short vertical ascent, you'll journey from lush, tropical-island landscape to the stark, moonlike basin of the volcano's enormous, otherworldly crater.

Established in 1916, Haleakalā National Park covers an astonishing 27,284 acres. Haleakalā "Crater" is the centerpiece of the park though it's not actually a crater. Technically, it's an erosional valley, flushed out by water pouring from the summit through two enormous gaps. The mountain has terrific camping and hiking, including a trail that loops through the crater, but the chance to witness this unearthly landscape is reason enough for a visit.

THE CLIMB TO THE SUMMIT

To reach Haleakalā National Park and the mountain's breathtaking summit, take Route 36 east of Kahului to the Haleakalā Highway (Route 37). Head east, up the mountain to the unlikely intersection of Haleakalā Highway and Haleakalā Highway. If you continue straight the road's name changes to Kula Highway (still Route 37). Instead, turn left onto Haleakalā Highway—this is now Route 377. After about 6 mi, make a left onto

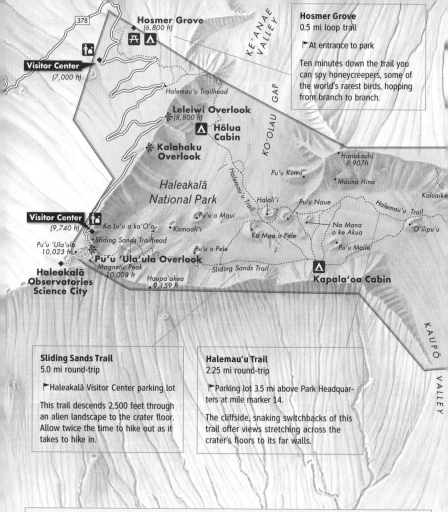

378

Hosmer Grove
(6,800 ft)

Visitor Center
(7,000 ft)

KE'ANAE VALLEY

Hosmer Grove
0.5 mi loop trail

▶At entrance to park

Ten minutes down the trail you can spy honeycreepers, some of the world's rarest birds, hopping from branch to branch.

Halemau'u Trailhead

KO'OLAU GAP

Leleiwi Overlook
(8,800 ft)

Hōlua Cabin

Kalahaku Overlook

Haleakalā National Park

Hanakauhi 8,907 ft

Pu'u Kumu

Mauna Hina

Halali'i

Pu'u Naue

Halemau'u Trail

Kaluaik

Ka Lu'u o ka'O'o

Pu'u o Maui

Kamoali'i

Na Mana o ke Akua

'O'ilipu'u

Visitor Center
(9,740 ft)

Sliding Sands Trailhead

Ka Moa o Pele

Pu'u Maile

Pu'u 'Ula'ula
10,023 ft

Pu'u o Pele

Sliding Sands Trail

Pu'u 'Ula'ula Overlook
Magnetic Peak 10,008 ft

Haupa'akea 9,159 ft

Haleakalā Observatories Science City

Kapala'oa Cabin

KAUPŌ VALLEY

Sliding Sands Trail
5.0 mi round-trip

▶Haleakalā Visitor Center parking lot

This trail descends 2,500 feet through an alien landscape to the crater floor. Allow twice the time to hike out as it takes to hike in.

Halemau'u Trail
2.25 mi round-trip

▶Parking lot 3.5 mi above Park Headquarters at mile marker 14.

The cliffside, snaking switchbacks of this trail offer views stretching across the crater's floors to its far walls.

Crater Road (Route 378). After several long switchbacks (look out for downhill bikers!) you'll come to the park entrance.

■TIP→Before you head up Haleakalā, call for the latest park weather conditions (☎866/944–5025). Extreme gusty winds, heavy rain, and even snow in winter are not uncommon. Because of the high altitude, the mountaintop temperature is often as much as 30 degrees cooler than that at sea level. Be sure to bring a jacket. Also make sure you have a full tank of gas. No service stations exist beyond Kula.

There's a $10 per car fee to enter the park; but it's good for three days and can be used at 'Ohe'o Gulch (Seven Sacred Pools), so save your receipt.

6,800 feet, Hosmer Grove. Just as you enter the park, Hosmer Grove has campsites and interpretive trails (*see* Hiking & Camping *on the following pages*). Park rangers maintain a changing schedule of talks and hikes both here and at the top of the mountain. Call the park for current schedules.

7,000 feet, Park Headquarters/Visitor Center. Not far from Hosmer Grove, the Park Headquarters/Visitor Center (open daily from 8 to 4) has trail maps and displays about the volcano's origins

KALAPAWILI RIDGE

▲ **Palikū Cabin**

*Kīpahulu Valley
Biological Reserve
(no public access)*

KĪPAHULU VALLEY

Kaupō Trail

SUNRISE AT THE SUMMIT

Sunrise at the summit has become the thing to do. You need an hour and a half from the bottom of **Haleakalā Highway** (Route 37) to Pu'u 'Ula'ula Overlook. Add to that the time of travel to the highway—at least 45 minutes from Lahaina or Kīhei. *The Maui News* posts the hour of sunrise every day. Remember the Alpine-Aeolian summit is *freezing* at dawn (Alpine indicates cold, Aeolian indicates windy). Bring hotel towels, blankets—anything you can find to stay warm. Also keep in mind, the highly touted colors of sunrise are weather-dependent. Sometimes they're spectacular and sometimes the sun just comes up without the fanfare.

Waimoku Falls

31

Makahiku Falls

Kuloa Point

Visitor Center

'Ohe'o Gulch

PACIFIC OCEAN

KEY
⚐ *Start of trail*

0 ——————— ½ mi

0 ——————— ½ km

and eruption history. Hikers and campers should check-in here before heading up the mountain. Maps, posters, and other memorabilia are available at the gift shop.

8,800 feet, Leleiwi Overlook. Continuing up the mountain, you come to Leleiwi Overlook. A short walk to the end of the parking lot reveals your first awe-inspiring view of the crater. The small hills in the basin are volcanic cinder cones (called *pu'u* in Hawaiian), each with a small crater at its top, and each the site of a former eruption.

WHERE TO EAT

KULA LODGE (✉ Haleakalā Hwy., Kula ☎ 808/878–2517) serves hearty breakfasts from 7 to 11 AM, a favorite with hikers coming down from a sunrise visit to Haleakalā's summit, as well as those on their way up for a late-morning tramp in the crater. Spectacular ocean views fill the windows of this mountainside lodge.

If you're here in the late afternoon, it's possible you'll experience a phenomenon called the Brocken Specter. Named after a similar occurrence in East Germany's

Silversword

10,023 feet, Pu'u 'Ula'ula Overlook.
The highest point on Maui is the Pu'u
'Ula'ula Overlook, at the 10,023-foot
summit. Here you find a glass-enclosed
lookout with a 360-degree view. The
building is open 24 hours a day, and
this is where visitors gather for the best
sunrise view. Dawn begins between 5:45
and 7, depending on the time of year.
On a clear day you can see the islands
of Moloka'i, Lāna'i, Kaho'olawe, and
Hawai'i (the Big Island). On a *really*
clear day you can even spot O'ahu glim-
mering in the distance.

■TIP→The air is very thin at 10,000 feet.
Don't be surprised if you feel a little breath-
less while walking around the summit.
Take it easy and drink lots of water. Anyone who has been scuba diving within the
last 24 hours should not make the trip up
Haleakalā.

On a small hill nearby, you can see **Science
City**, an off-limits research and communications center straight out of an es-
pionage thriller. The University of Hawai'i
maintains an observatory here, and the
Department of Defense tracks satellites.

For more information about Haleakalā National Park, contact the **National Park Service**
(☎808/572–4400, ⊕www.nps.gov/hale).

HIKING & CAMPING

Exploring Haleakalā Crater is one of
the best hiking experiences on Maui.
The volcanic terrain offers an impressive diversity of colors, textures, and
shapes—almost as if the lava has been
artfully sculpted. The barren landscape is
home to many plants, insects, and birds
that exist nowhere else on earth and have
developed intriguing survival mecha-
nisms, such as the sun-reflecting, hairy
leaves of the silversword, which allow it
to survive the intense climate.

Stop at park headquarters to register
and pick up trail maps on your way
into the park.

Harz Mountains, the "specter" allows you
to see yourself reflected on the clouds and
encircled by a rainbow. Don't wait all day
for this because it's not a daily occurrence.

9,000 feet, Kalahaku Overlook. The
next stopping point is Kalahaku Overlook. The view here offers a different
perspective of the crater, and at this elevation the famous silversword plant grows
amid the cinders. This odd, endangered
beauty grows only here and at the same
elevation on the Big Island's two peaks.
It begins life as a silver, spiny-leaf rosette
and is the sole home of a variety of native
insects (it's the only shelter around). The
silversword reaches maturity between 7
and 17 years, when it sends forth a 3- to
8-foot-tall stalk with several hundred tiny
sunflowers. It blooms once, then dies.

9,740 feet, Haleakalā Visitor Center.
Another mile up is the Haleakalā Visitor Center (open daily from sunrise to
3 PM). There are exhibits inside, and a
trail from here leads to White Hill—a
short easy walk that will give you an
even better view of the valley.

1-Hour Hike. Just as you enter Haleakalā National Park, **Hosmer Grove** offers a short 10-minute hike, and an hour-long, $^1/_2$-mi loop trail into the Waikamoi Cloud Forest that will give you insight into Hawai'i's fragile ecology. Anyone can go on the short hike, whereas the longer trail through the cloud forest is accessible only with park ranger–guided hikes. Call park headquarters for the schedule. Facilities here include six campsites (no permit needed, available on a first-come, first-served basis), pit toilets, drinking water, and cooking shelters.

4-Hour Hikes. Two half-day hikes involve descending into the crater and returning the way you came. The first, **Halemau'u Trail** (trailhead is between mile markers 14 and 15), is 2.25 mi round-trip. The cliffside, snaking switchbacks of this trail offer views stretching across the crater's pu'u-speckled floor to its far walls. On clear days you can peer through the Ko'olau Gap to Hāna. Native flowers and shrubs grow along the trail, which is typically misty and cool (though still exposed to the sun). When you reach the gate at the bottom, head back up.

The other hike, which is 5 mi round-trip, descends down **Sliding Sands Trail** (trailhead is at the Haleakalā Visitor Center) into an alien landscape of reddish black cinders, lava bombs, and silverswords. It's easy to imagine life before humans in the solitude and silence of this place. Turn back when you hit the crater floor.

■TIP→ **Bring water, sunscreen, and a reliable jacket. These can be demanding hikes if you're unused to the altitude. Take it slowly to acclimate, and give yourself additional time for the uphill return trip.**

8-Hour Hike. The recommended way to explore the crater in a single, but full day is to go in two cars and ferry yourselves back and forth between the head of **Halemau'u Trail** and the summit. This way, you can hike from the summit down **Sliding Sands Trail**, cross the crater's floor, investigate the **Bottomless Pit** and **Pele's Paint Pot**, then climb out on the **switchback trail** (Halemau'u). When you emerge, the shelter of your waiting car will be very welcome (this is an 11.2-mi hike). If you don't have two cars, hitching a ride from Halemau'u back to the summit should be relatively safe and easy.

■TIP→Take a backpack with lunch, water, sunscreen, and a reliable jacket for the beginning and end of the 8-hour hike. This is a demanding trip, but you will never regret or forget it.

Overnight Hike. Staying overnight in one of Haleakalā's three cabins or two wilderness campgrounds is an experience like no other. You'll feel like the only person on earth when you wake up inside this enchanted, strange landscape. Nēnē and 'u'au (endangered storm petrels) make charming neighbors. The cabins, each tucked in a different corner of the crater's floor, are equipped with 12 bunk beds, wood-burning stoves, fake logs, and kitchen gear.

Hōlua cabin is the shortest hike, less than 4 hours (3.7 mi) from Halemau'u Trail. **Kapala'oa** is about 5 hours (5.5 mi) down Sliding Sands Trail. The most cherished cabin is **Palikū**, a solid eight-hour (9.3-mi) hike starting from either trail. It's nestled against the rain-forested cliffs above the Kaupō Gap. To reserve a cabin you have to apply to the National Park Service at least 60 days in advance and hope the lottery system is kind to you. Tent campsites at Hōlua and Palikū are free and easy to reserve on a first-come, first-served basis.

■TIP→ Toilets and nonpotable water are available—bring iodine tablets to purify the water. Open fires are not allowed and packing out your trash is mandatory.

For more information on hiking or camping, or to reserve a cabin, contact the National Park Service (⊠Box 369, Makawao 96768 ☎808/572–4459 ⊕www.nps.gov/hale).

OPTIONS FOR EXPLORING

If you're short on time you can drive to the summit, take a peek inside, and drive back down. But the "House of the Sun" is really worth a day, whether you explore by foot, horseback, or helicopter.

BIKING

At this writing, all guided bike tours inside park boundaries were suspended indefinitely while park officials study the safety of this activity. However, the tours continue but now start outside the boundary of the park. The park is still open to individual bikes for a $5 fee. There are no bike paths, however—just the same road that is used by vehicular traffic.

HELICOPTER TOURS

Viewing Haleakalā from above can be a mind-altering experience, if you don't mind dropping $200+ per person for a few blissful moments above the crater. Most tours buzz Haleakalā, where airspace is regulated, then head over to Hanā in search of waterfalls.

HORSEBACK RIDING

Several companies offer half-day, full-day, and even overnight rides into the crater. On one half-day ride you descend into the crater on Sliding Sands Trail and have lunch before you head back.

For complete information on any of these activities, ⇨ see Golf, Hiking and Outdoor Activities.

and 'Ulupalakua ranches. Every July 4 the *paniolo* (Hawaiian cowboy) set comes out in force for the Makawao Rodeo. The crossroads of town—lined with chic shops and down-home eateries—reflects a growing population of people who came here just because they liked it. For those seeking lush greenery rather than beachside accommodations, there are great, secluded little bed-and-breakfasts in and around the town.

Hui No'eau Visual Arts Center. The main house of this nonprofit cultural center on the old Baldwin estate, just outside the town of Makawao, is an elegant two-story Mediterranean-style villa designed in the 1920s by the defining Hawai'i architect C. W. Dickey. "The Hui" is the grande dame of Maui's well-known arts scene. The exhibits are always satisfying, and the grounds might as well be a botanical garden. The Hui also offers classes and maintains artists' studios. ✉ *2841 Baldwin Ave., Makawao* 🕾 *808/572–6560* 🖂 *Free* 🕙 *Mon.–Sat. 10–4.*

> **WORD OF MOUTH**
>
> "In addition to solitude (at night, anyway), Hāna has one of the best beaches on the island, Hāmoa, and one visited by the most interesting crowd, Red Sand. It's also a stone's throw from Wai'nāpanapa black sand beach and park, which features blowholes and lava tubes. It gives you a head start to getting to the 'Ohe'o Gulch pools, where the crowds can be suffocating, even in low season."   –Lex1

NEED A BREAK?

One of Makawao's most famous landmarks is **Komoda Store & Bakery** (✉ *3674 Baldwin Ave. 96768* 🕾 *808/572–7261*), a classic mom-and-pop store that has changed little in three-quarters of a century, where you can get a delicious cream puff if you arrive early enough. They make hundreds but sell out each day.

THE NORTH SHORE

Blasted by winter swells and wind, Maui's North Shore draws watersports thrill-seekers from around the world. But there's much more to this area of Maui than coastline. Inland, a lush, waterfall-fed garden of Eden beckons. In forested pockets, wealthy hermits have carved out a little piece of paradise for themselves.

North Shore action centers around the colorful town of Pā'ia and the windsurfing mecca, Ho'okipa Beach. It's a far cry from the more developed resort areas of West Maui and the South Shore. Pā'ia is also a starting point for the one of the most popular excursions in Maui, the Road to Hāna *(see Road to Hāna feature in this chapter)*. Waterfalls, phenomenal views of the coast and ocean, and lush rain forest are all part of the spectacular 55-mi drive into East Maui.

PĀ'IA

★ This little town on Maui's North Shore (at the intersection of Hāna Highway [Highway 36] and Baldwin Avenue) was once a sugarcane enclave, with a mill, plantation camps, and shops. The town boomed during World War II when the marines set up camp in nearby Ha'ikū. The old HC&S sugar mill finally closed and no sign of the military remains, but the town continues to thrive. In the 1970s, Pā'ia became a hippie town as dropouts headed for Maui to open boutiques, galleries, and unusual eateries. In the 1980s windsurfers—many of them European—discovered nearby Ho'okipa Beach and brought an international flavor to Pā'ia.

> ### FUN THINGS TO DO ON THE NORTH SHORE
>
> ■ Buy a teeny-weenie Maui Girl bikini in Pā'ia.
>
> ■ Watch windsurfers somersault over waves at Ho'okipa.
>
> ■ Load up on provisions at the wildly popular Mana Foods.
>
> ■ Rub elbows with yogis and tow-in surfers at Anthony's Coffee.
>
> ■ Dig into a fish sandwich and fries at the Pā'ia Fishmarket.
>
> ■ Head out on the awesome Road to Hāna, ending up in the tiny East Maui town.

At the intersection of Hāna Highway and Baldwin Avenue, eclectic boutiques supply everything from high fashion to hemp-oil candles. Some of Maui's best shops for surf trunks, Brazilian bikinis, and other beachwear are here. The restaurants provide excellent people-watching and an array of dining options. A French-Caribbean bistro with a sushi bar in back, a French-Indian creperie, a neo-Mexican gourmet restaurant, and a fish market all compete for your patronage. This abundance is helpful because Pā'ia is the last place to snack before the pilgrimage to Hāna and the first stop for the famished on the return trip.

Fodor'sChoice **Ho'okipa Beach.** There's no better place on this or any other island to
★ watch the world's finest windsurfers in action. The surfers know the five different surf breaks here by name. Unless it's a rare day without wind or waves, you're sure to get a show. ■ TIP➔ **It's not safe to park on the shoulder. Use the ample parking lot at the county park entrance.** ⌂ *2 mi past Pā'ia on Rte. 36.*

■ **NEED A BREAK?** **Anthony's Coffee** (⌂ *90 Hāna Hwy.* ☎ *808/579–8340*) roasts its own beans, sells Maui's own Roselani ice cream and picnic lunches, and is a great place to eavesdrop on the windsurfing crowd. **Charley's Restaurant** (⌂ *Hāna Hwy.* ☎ *808/579–9453*) is an easygoing saloon-type hangout with pool tables. Breakfasts are big and delicious. **Mana Foods** (⌂ *49 Baldwin Ave.* ☎ *808/579–8078*), the North Shore's natural-foods store, has an inspired deli with wholesome hot and cold items. The long line at **Pā'ia Fishmarket Restaurant** (⌂ *2A Baldwin Ave.* ☎ *808/579–8030*) attests to the popularity of the tasty mahimahi sandwiches. Pā'ia has an excellent wine store, the **Wine Corner** (⌂ *149 Hāna Hwy.* ☎ *808/579–8904*), helpful because two good eateries nearby are BYOB.

Continued on page 74

ROAD TO HĀNA

As you round the impossibly tight turn, a one-lane bridge comes into view. Beneath its worn surface, a lush forested gulch plummets toward the coast. The sound of rushing water fills the air, compelling you to search the overgrown hillside for waterfalls. This is the Road to Hāna, a 55-mi journey into the unspoiled heart of Maui. Tracing a centuries-old path, the road begins as a well-paved highway in Kahului and ends in the tiny town of Hāna on the island's rain-gouged windward side.

★ Fodor's Choice Despite the twists and turns, the road to Hāna is not as frightening as it may sound. You're bound to be a little nervous approaching it the first time; but afterwards you'll wonder if somebody out there is making it sound tough just to keep out the hordes. The challenging part of the road takes only an hour and a half, but you'll want to stop often and let the driver enjoy the view, too. Don't expect a booming city when you get to Hāna. Its lure is its quiet timelessness. As the adage says, the journey *is* the destination.

During high season, the road to Hāna tends to clog—well, not clog exactly, but develop little choo-choo trains of cars, with everyone in a line of six or a dozen driving as slowly as the first car. The solution: leave early (dawn) and return late (dusk). And if you find yourself playing the role of locomotive, pull over and let the other drivers pass. You can also let someone else take the turns for you—several companies offer van tours, which make stops all along the way (*see Maui Sightseeing Tours box in this chapter*).

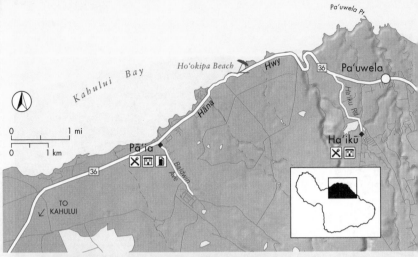

DRIVING THE ROAD TO HĀNA

Begin your journey in Pāʻia, the little town on Maui's North Shore. Be sure to fill up your gas tank here. There are no gas stations along Hāna Highway, and the station in Hāna closes by 6 PM. You should also pick up a picnic lunch. Lunch and snack choices along the way are limited to rustic fruit stands.

About 10 mi past Pāʻia, at the bottom of Kaupakalua Road, the roadside mileposts begin measuring the 36 mi to Hāna town. The road's trademark noodling starts about 3 mi after that. Once the road gets twisty, remember that many residents make this trip frequently. You'll recognize them because they're the ones zipping around every curve. They've seen this so many times before they don't care to linger. Pull over to let them pass.

All along this stretch of road, waterfalls are abundant. Roll down your windows. Breathe in the scent of guava and ginger. You can almost hear the bamboo growing. There are plenty of places to pull completely off the road and park safely. Do this often, since the road's curves make driving without a break difficult. ■ TIP→ If you're prone to carsickness, be sure to take medication before you start this drive. You may also want to stop periodicially.

❶ **Twin Falls.** Keep an eye out for the fruit stand just after mile marker 2. Stop here and treat yourself to some fresh sugar-cane juice. If you're feeling adventurous, follow the path beyond the stand to the paradisiacal waterfalls known as Twin Falls. Once a rough trail plastered with "no trespassing" signs, this treasured spot is now easily accessible. In fact, there's usually a mass of cars surrounding the fruit stand at the trail head. Several deep, emerald pools sparkle beneath waterfalls and offer excellent swimming and photo opportunities.

While this is still private property, the "no trespassing" signs have been replaced by colorfully painted arrows pointing away from residences and toward the falls. ■ TIP→ Bring water shoes for crossing streams along the way. Swim at your own risk and beware: flash floods here and in all East Maui stream areas can be sudden and deadly. Check the weather before you go.

❷ **Huelo & Kailua.** Dry off and drive on past the sleepy country villages of Huelo (near mile marker 5) and Kailua (near mile marker 6). The little farm town of Huelo has two quaint churches. If you linger awhile, you could meet local residents and learn about a rural lifestyle you might not expect to find on the Islands.

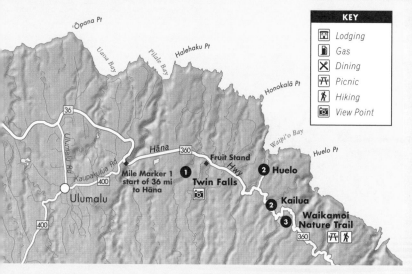

The same can be said for nearby Kailua, home to Alexander & Baldwin's irrigation employees.

❸ **Waikamoi Nature Trail.** Between mile markers 9 and 10, the Waikamoi Nature Trail sign beckons you to stretch your car-weary limbs. A short (if muddy) trail leads through tall eucalyptus trees to a coastal vantage point with a picnic table and barbecue. Signage reminds visitors QUIET, TREES AT WORK and BAMBOO PICKING PERMIT REQUIRED. Awapuhi, or Hawaiian shampoo ginger, sends up fragrant shoots along the trail.

❹ **Puohokamoa Stream.** About a mile farther, near mile marker 11, you can stop at the bridge over Puohokamoa Stream. This is one of many bridges you cross en route from Pā'ia to Hāna. It spans pools and waterfalls. Picnic tables are available, but there are no restrooms.

❺ **Kaumahina State Wayside Park.** If you'd rather stretch your legs and use a flush toilet, continue another mile to Kaumahina State Wayside Park (at mile marker 12). The park has a picnic area, restrooms, and a lovely overlook to the Ke'anae Peninsula. The park is open from 8 AM to 4 PM and admission is free. ☎ *808/984–8109.*

🕐 **TIMING TIPS**

With short stops, the drive from Pā'ia to Hāna should take you between two and three hours one-way. Lunching in Hāna, hiking, and swimming can easily turn the round-trip into a full-day outing, especially if you continue past Hāna to the seven pools and Kīpahulu. If you go that far, you might consider continuing around the "back side" for the return trip. The scenery is completely different and you'll end up in beautiful Upcountry Maui. Since there's so much scenery to take in, we recommend staying overnight in Hāna. It's worth taking time to enjoy the waterfalls and beaches without being in a hurry. Try to plan your trip for a day that promises fair, sunny weather—though the drive can be even more beautiful when it's raining.

Ke'anae Peninsula

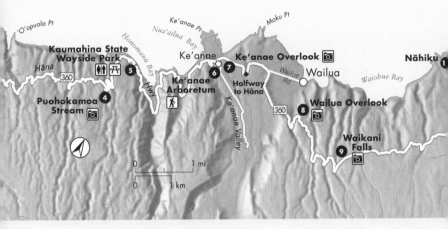

Near mile marker 14, before Keʻanae, you find yourself driving along a cliff side down into deep, lush Honomanū Bay, an enormous valley, with a rocky black-sand beach.

The Honomanū Valley was carved by erosion during Haleakalā's first dormant period. At the canyon's head there are 3,000-foot cliffs and a 1,000-foot waterfall, but don't try to reach them. There's not much of a trail, and what does exist is practically impassable.

6 Keʻanae Arboretum. Another 4 mi brings you to mile marker 17 and the Keʻanae Arboretum where you can add to your botanical education or enjoy a challenging hike into a forest. Signs help you learn the names of the many plants and trees now considered native to Hawaiʻi. The meandering Piʻinaʻau Stream adds a graceful touch to the arboretum and provides a swimming pond.

You can take a fairly rigorous hike from the arboretum if you can find the trail at one side of the large taro patch. Be careful not to lose the trail once you're on it. A lovely forest waits at the end of the 25-minute hike. Access to the arboretum is free.

7 Keʻanae Overlook. A half mile farther down Hāna Highway you can stop at the Keʻanae Overlook. From this observation point, you can take in the quilt-like effect the taro patches create below. The people of Keʻanae are working hard to revive this Hawaiian agricultural art and the traditional cultural values that the crop represents. The ocean provides a dramatic backdrop for the patches. In the other direction there are awesome views of Haleakalā through the foliage. This is a great spot for photos. ■ TIP→ Coming up is the halfway mark to Hāna. If you've had enough scenery, this is as good a time as any to turn around and head back to civilization.

8 Wailua Overlook. Between mile markers 20 and 21 you find Wailua Overlook. From the parking lot you can see Wailua Canyon, but you have to walk up steps to get a view of Wailua Village. The landmark in Wailua Village is a church made of coral, built in 1860.

Taro patch viewed from Hāna Highway

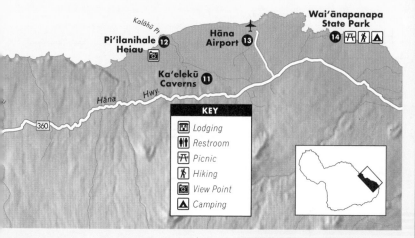

KEY

🏠 *Lodging*
🚻 *Restroom*
🌲 *Picnic*
🚶 *Hiking*
📷 *View Point*
⛺ *Camping*

Once called St. Gabriel's Catholic Church, the current Our Lady of Fatima Shrine has an interesting legend surrounding it. As the story goes, a storm washed enough coral up onto shore to build the church and then took any extra coral back to sea.

❾ Waikani Falls. After another ½ mi, past mile marker 21, you hit the best falls on the entire drive to Hāna, Waikani Falls. Though not necessarily bigger or taller than the other falls, these are the most dramatic falls you'll find in East Maui. That's partly because the water is not diverted for sugar irrigation; the taro farmers in Wailua need all the runoff. This is a particularly good spot for photos.

❿ Nāhiku. At about mile marker 25 you see a road that heads down toward the ocean and the village of Nāhiku. In ancient times this was a busy settlement with hundreds of residents. Now only about 80 people live in Nāhiku, mostly native Hawaiians and some back-to-the-land types. A rubber grower planted trees here in the early 1900s, but the experiment didn't work out, and Nāhiku was essentially abandoned. The road ends at the sea in a pretty landing. This is the rainiest, densest part of the East Maui rain forest.

Coffee Break. Back on the Hāna Highway, about 10 minutes before Hāna town, you

can stop for—of all things—espresso. The tiny, colorful **Nāhiku Ti Gallery and Coffee Shop** (between mile markers 27 and 28) sells local coffee, dried fruits and candies, and delicious (if pricey) banana bread. Sometimes the barbecue is fired up and you can try fish skewers or baked breadfruit (an island favorite nearly impossible to find elsewhere). The Ti Gallery sells Hawaiian crafts.

⓫ Ka'elekū Caverns. If you're interested in exploring underground, turn left onto 'Ula'ino Road, just after mile marker 31, and follow the signs to Ka'elekū Caverns. **Maui Cave Adventures** points amateur spelunkers into a system of gigantic lava tubes, accentuated by colorful underworld formations.

You can take a self-guided, 30- to 45-min tour daily, from 10:30 to 4 PM for $11.95 per person. Flashlights are provided. Children under five are free with a paid adult. ☎808/248–7308 ⊕*www.mauicave.com*

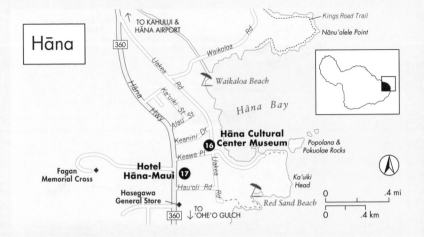

★ **⑫ Pi'ilanihale Heiau.** Continue on 'Ula'ino Road, which doubles back for a mile, loses its pavement, and even crosses a stream before reaching Kahanu Garden and Pi'ilanihale Heiau, the largest prehistoric monument in Hawai'i. This temple platform was built for a great 16th-century Maui king named Pi'ilani and his heirs. This king also supervised the construction of a 10-foot-wide road that completely encircled the island. (That's why his name is part of most of Maui's highway titles.)

Hawaiian families continue to maintain and protect this sacred site as they have for centuries, and they have not been eager to turn it into a tourist attraction. However, they now offer a brochure so you can tour the property yourself for $10 per person. Tours include the 122-acre **Kahanu Garden**, a federally funded research center focusing on the ethno-botany of the Pacific. The heiau and garden are open weekdays from 10 AM to 2 PM. ☎ 808/248–8912

⑬ Hāna Airport. Back on the Hāna Highway, and less than ½ mi farther, is the turnoff for the Hāna Airport. Think of Amelia Earhart. Think of Waldo Pepper. If these picket-fence runways don't turn your thoughts to the derring-do of barnstorming pilots, you haven't seen enough

old movies. Only the smallest planes can land and depart here, and when none of them happens to be around, the lonely wind sock is the only evidence that this is a working airfield. ☎ 808/248–8208

★ **⑭ Wai'ānapanapa State Park.** Just beyond mile marker 32 you reach Wai'ānapanapa State Park, home to one of Maui's only volcanic-sand beaches and some freshwater caves for adventurous swimmers to explore. The park is right on the ocean, and it's a lovely spot in which to picnic, camp, hike, or swim. To the left you'll find the black-sand beach, picnic tables, and cave pools. To the right you'll find cabins and an ancient trail which snakes along the ocean past blowholes, sea arches, and archaeological sites.

The tide pools here turn red several times a year. Scientists say it's explained by the arrival of small shrimp, but legend claims the color represents the blood of Popo'alaea, a princess said to have been murdered in one of the caves by her husband, Chief Ka'akea. Whichever you choose to believe, the drama of the landscape itself—black sand, green beach vines, azure water—is bound to leave a lasting impression.

With a permit you can stay in state-run cabins here for less than $45 a night—the price varies depending on the number of people—but reserve early. They often book up a year in advance. ☎ 808/984–8109

⑮ Hāna. By now the relaxed pace of life that Hāna residents enjoy should have you in its grasp, so you won't be discouraged to learn that "town" is little more than a gas station, a post office, and a ramshackle grocery.

Hāna, in many ways, is the heart of Maui. It's one of the few places where the slow pulse of island life is still strong. The town centers on its lovely circular bay, dominated on the right-hand shore by a pu'u called Ka'uiki. A short trail here leads to a cave, the birthplace of Queen Ka'ahumanu. This area is rich in Hawaiian history and legend. Two miles beyond town another pu'u presides over a loop road that passes two of Hāna's best beaches—Kōkī and Hāmoa. The hill is called Ka Iwi O Pele (Pele's Bone). Offshore here, at tiny 'Ālau Island, the de-migod Maui supposedly fished up the Hawaiian islands.

Sugar was once the mainstay of Hāna's economy; the last plantation shut down in the '40s. In 1946 rancher Paul Fagan built the **Hotel Hāna-Maui** and stocked the surrounding pastureland with cattle. The cross you see on the hill above the hotel was put there in memory of Fagan. Now it's the ranch and

hotel that put food on most tables, though many families still farm, fish, and hunt as in the old days. Houses around town are decorated with glass balls and nets, which indicate a fisherman's lodging.

⑯ Hāna Cultural Center Museum. If you're determined to spend some time and money in Hāna after the long drive, a single turn off the highway onto Uakea Street, in the center of town, will take you to the Hāna Cultural Center Museum. Besides operating a well-stocked gift shop, it displays artifacts, quilts, a replica of an authentic *kauhale* (an ancient Hawaiian living complex, with thatch huts and food gardens), and other Hawaiiana. The knowledgeable staff can explain it all to you. The center is open 10 to 4 daily. ☎808/248–8622 ⊕*www.hookele.com/hccm*

⑰ Hotel Hāna-Maui. With its surrounding ranch, the upscale hotel is the mainstay of Hāna's economy. It's pleasant to stroll around this beautifully rustic property. The library houses interesting, authentic Hawaiian artifacts. In the evening, while local musicians play in the casual lobby bar, their friends jump up to dance hula. The Sea Ranch cottages across the road, built to look like authentic plantation housing from the outside, are also part of the hotel. *See Where to Stay for more information.*

Hala Trees, Wai'ānapanapa State Park

Hāna

Don't be suprised if the mile markers suddenly start descending as you head past Hāna. Technically, Hāna Highway (Route 360) ends at the Hāna Bay. The road that continues south is Pi'ilani Highway (Route 31)—though everyone still refers to it as the Hāna Highway.

18 Hāmoa Beach. Just outside Hāna, take a left on Haneo'o Loop to explore lovely Hāmoa. Indulge in swimming or bodysurfing at this beautiful salt-and-pepper beach. Picnic tables, restrooms, and showers beneath the idyllic shade of coconut trees offer a more than comfortable rest stop.

The road leading to Hāmoa also takes you to **Koki Beach**, where you can watch the Hāna surfers mastering the swells and strong currents, and the seabirds darting over **'Ālau**, the palm-fringed islet off the coast. The swimming is safer at Hāmoa.

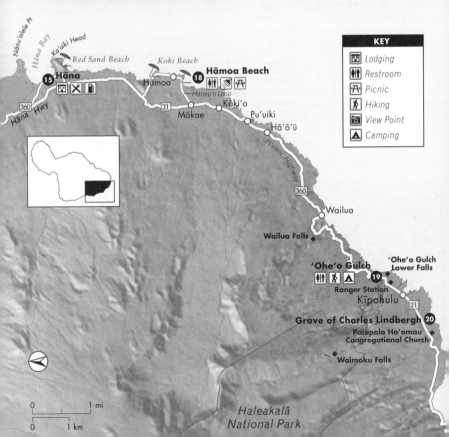

★ ⑲ 'Ohe'o Gulch. Ten miles past town, at mile marker 42, you'll find the pools at 'Ohe'o Gulch. One branch of Haleakalā National Park runs down the mountain from the crater and reaches the sea here, where a basalt-lined stream cascades from one pool to the next. Some tour guides still call this area Seven Sacred Pools, but in truth there are more than seven, and they've never been considered sacred. You can park here—for a $10 fee—and walk to the lowest pools for a cool swim. The place gets crowded, since most people who drive the Hāna Highway make this their last stop.

If you enjoy hiking, go up the stream on the 2-mi hike to **Waimoku Falls.** The trail crosses a spectacular gorge, then turns into a boardwalk that takes you through an amazing bamboo forest. You can pitch a tent in the grassy campground down by the sea. *See Hiking in Golf, Hiking & Outdoor Activities.*

⑳ **Grave of Charles Lindbergh.** Many people travel the mile past 'Ohe'o Gulch to see the Grave of Charles Lindbergh. You see a ruined sugar mill with a big chimney on the right side of the road and then, on the left, a rutted track leading to Palapala Ho'omau Congregational Church. The simple one-room church sits on a bluff over the sea, with the small graveyard on the ocean side. The world-renowned aviator chose to be buried here because he and his wife, writer Anne Morrow Lindbergh, spent a lot of time living in the area. He was buried here in 1974. Since this is a churchyard, be considerate and leave everything exactly as you found it. Next to the churchyard on the ocean side is a small county park, good for a picnic.

Kaupō Road. The road to Hāna continues all the way around Haleakalā's "back side" through 'Ulupalakua Ranch and into Kula. The desert-like topography, with its grand vistas, is unlike anything else on the island, but the road itself is bad, sometimes impassable in winter, and parts of it are unpaved. Car-rental agencies call it off-limits to their passenger cars and there

TROPICAL DELIGHTS

The drive to Hāna wouldn't be as enchanting without a stop or two at one of the countless fruit and flower stands alongside the highway. Every 1/2 mi or so a thatched hut tempts passersby with apple bananas (a smaller firmer variety), liliko'i (passion fruit), avocados, or starfruit just plucked from the tree. Leave a few dollars in the can for the folks who live off the land. Huge bouquets of tropical flowers are available for a handful of change, and some farms will ship.

is no emergency assistance available. The danger and dust from increasing numbers of speeding jeep drivers are making life tough for the residents, especially in Kaupō, with its 4 mi of unpaved road. The small communities around East Maui cling tenuously to the old ways. Please keep that in mind if you do pass this way. If you can't resist the adventure, try to make the drive just before sunset. The light slanting across the mountain is incredible. At night, giant potholes, owls, and loose cattle can make for some difficult driving. The bridge that was damaged in a 2006 earthquake has been repaired, allowing visitors to once again drive all the way around East Maui. Please note, however, that the condition of the road remains rough.

HA'IKŪ

At one time this area vibrated around a couple of enormous pineapple canneries. Both have been transformed into rustic warehouse malls. Because of the post office next door, Old Ha'ikū Cannery earned the title of town center. Here you can snack on pizza at Colleen's or get massaged by the students at Spa Luna. Follow windy Ha'ikū Road to Pauwela Cannery, the other defunct factory-turned-hangout. Don't fret if you get lost. This jungle hillside is a maze of flower-decked roads that seem to double back upon themselves. Up Kokomo Road is a large pu'u (volcanic cinder cone) capped with a grove of columnar pines, and the 4th Marine Division Memorial Park. During World War II, American GIs trained here for battles on Iwo Jima and Saipan. Locals nicknamed the cinder cone "Giggle Hill" because it was a popular hangout for Maui women and their favorite servicemen.

3

Beaches

WORD OF MOUTH

"We went through Hāna and found ourselves at beautiful Hāmoa Beach. It's hard to get a good picture of this beach, but it is the prettiest beach on Maui. Just gorgeous. We found a tree and had our lunch, enjoying the sounds of the waves and the color of the water."

—mer

Updated
by Bonnie
Friedman

Of all the beaches on the Hawaiian Islands, Maui's are some of the most diverse. You'll find the pristine, palm-lined shores you expect with clear and inviting waters the color of sea-green glass, but you'll also discover rich red- and black-sand beaches, craggy cliffs with surging whitecaps, and year-round sunsets that quiet the soul.

As on the other islands, all Maui's beaches are public—but that doesn't mean it's not possible to find a secluded cove where you can truly get away from the world.

The island's leeward shores (the South Shore and West Maui) have the calmest, sunniest beaches. Hit the beach early, when the aquamarine waters are as accommodating as bathwater. In summer, afternoon winds can be a sandblasting force, which can chase even the most dedicated sun worshippers away. From November through May, the South and West beaches are also great spots to watch the humpback whales that spend winter and early spring in Maui's waters.

Windward shores (the North Shore and East Maui) offer more adventurous beach-going. Beaches face the open ocean (rather than other islands) and tend to be rockier and more prone to powerful swells. This is particularly true in winter, when the North Shore becomes a playground for experienced big-wave riders and windsurfers. Don't let this keep you away completely, however; some of the island's best beaches are those remote slivers of volcanic sand found on the wild windward shore.

WEST MAUI

West Maui beaches are legendary for their glittering aquamarine waters banked by long stretches of golden sand. Reef fronts much of the western shore, making the underwater panorama something to behold. The beaches listed here start in the north at Kapalua and head south past Kā'anapali and Lahaina. Note that there are a dozen roadside beaches to choose from on Route 30; here are the ones we like best.

"Slaughterhouse" (Mokulē'ia) Beach. The island's northernmost beach is part of the Honolua-Mokulē'ia Marine Life Conservation District. "Slaughterhouse" is the surfers' nickname for what is officially Mokulē'ia. When the weather permits, this is a great place for body-surfing and sunbathing. Concrete steps and a green railing help you get down the sheer cliff to the sand. The next bay over, Honolua, has no beach but offers one of the best surf breaks in Hawai'i. Often you can see competitions happening there; look for cars pulled off the road and parked in the pineapple field. ⊠ *Mile marker 32 on Rte. 30 past Kapalua* ⚲ *No facilities.*

D.T. Fleming Beach. Because the current can be quite strong, this charming, mile-long sandy cove is better for sunbathing than for swimming

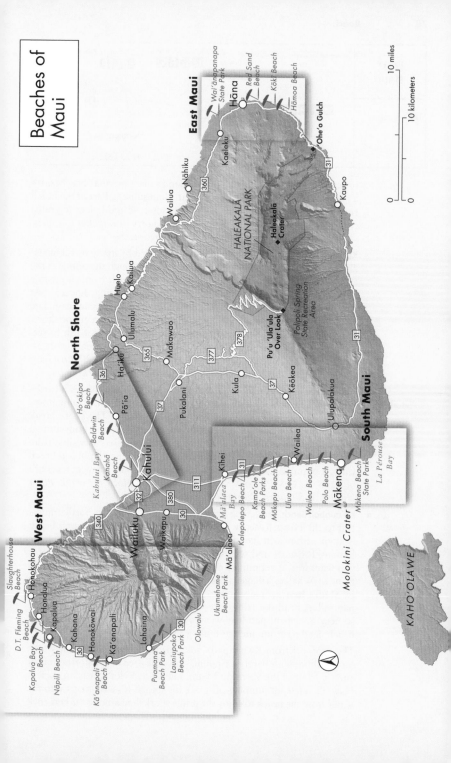

Beaches of Maui

West Maui

Slaughterhouse Beach
D. T. Fleming Beach
Honokohau
Honolua
Kapalua Bay Beach
Kapalua
Nāpili Beach
Kahana
Honokōwai
Kāʻanapali Beach
Kāʻanapali
Lahaina
Puamana Beach Park
Launiupoko Beach Park
Olowalu
Ukumehame Beach Park
Māʻalaea

North Shore

Hoʻokipa Beach
Baldwin Beach
Kahului Bay
Kanahā Beach

East Maui

Waiʻānapanapa State Park
Hāna
Red Sand Beach
Kōkī Beach
Hāmoa Beach
Oheʻo Gulch
Kaupo

South Maui

Māʻalaea Bay
Kalepolepo Beach
Kihei
Kamaʻole Beach Parks
Mōkapu Beach
Ulua Beach
Wailea Beach
Wailea
Polo Beach
Mākena Beach State Park
Mākena
La Pérouse Bay

HALEAKALĀ NATIONAL PARK
Haleakalā Crater
Polipoli Spring State Recreation Area
Puʻu ʻUlaʻula Over Look

Molokini Crater

KAHOʻOLAWE

Wailua
Nāhiku
Kaeleku
Huelo
Kailua
Ulumalu
Haʻikū
Makawao
Pāʻia
Pukalani
Kula
Keōkea
Ulupalakua
Waiheʻe
Wailuku
Waikapu

Kahului

340
36
365
37
32
380
30
311
31
378
377
31

10 miles
10 kilometers

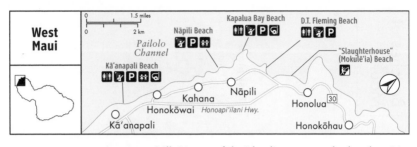

or water sports. Still, it's one of the island's most popular beaches. It's a perfect place to watch the spectacular Maui sunsets. Part of the beach runs along the front of the Ritz-Carlton Hotel—a good place to grab a cocktail and enjoy the view. ⊠ *Rte. 30, 1 mi north of Kapalua* ⚐ *Toilets, showers, picnic tables, grills/firepits, parking lot.*

Kapalua Bay Beach. Kapalua has been recognized by many travel magazines as one of the world's best beaches. Walk through the tunnel at the end of Kapalua Place and you'll see why—the beach fronts a pristine bay good for snorkeling, swimming, and general lazing. Located just north of Nāpili Bay, this lovely, sheltered shore often remains calm late into the afternoon, although there may be strong currents offshore. Snorkeling is easy here and there are lots of colorful reef fish to see. This area is quite popular and is bordered by the Kapalua Resort, so don't expect to have the beach to yourself. ⊠ *From Rte. 30, turn onto Kapalua Pl., walk through tunnel* ⚐ *Toilets, showers, parking lot.*

☺ **Nāpili Beach.** Surrounded by sleepy condos, this round bay is a turtle-filled pool lined with a sparkling white crescent of sand. Sunbathers love this beach, which is also a terrific sunset spot. The shore break is steep but gentle, so it's great for boogie boarding and bodysurfing. It's easy to keep an eye on kids here as the entire bay is visible from any point in the water. The beach is right outside the Nāpili Kai Beach Club, a popular little resort for honeymooners, only a few miles south of Kapalua. ⊠ *5900 Lower Honoapi'ilani Hwy., look for Nāpili Pl. or Hui Dr.* ⚐ *Showers, parking lot.*

Fodor's Choice
★

☺ ★ **Kā'anapali Beach.** Stretching from the Sheraton Maui at its northernmost end to the Hyatt Regency Maui at its southern tip, Kā'anapali Beach is lined with resorts, condominiums, restaurants, and shops. If you're looking for quiet and seclusion, this is not the beach for you. But if you want lots of action, lay out your towel here. The center section in front of Whalers Village is also called "Dig Me Beach," and it is one of Maui's best people-watching spots: catamarans, windsurfers, and parasailers head out from here while the beautiful people take in the scenery. A cement pathway weaves along the length of this 3-mi-long beach, leading from one astounding resort to the next.

The drop-off from Kā'anapali's soft, sugary sand is steep, but waves hit the shore with barely a rippling slap. The area at the northernmost end (in front of the Sheraton Maui), known as Keka'a, was, in ancient Hawai'i, a *lele,* or jumping-off place for spirits. It's easy to get into the water from the beach to enjoy the prime snorkeling among the lava rock

The sandy crescent of Nāpili Beach on West Maui is a lovely place to wait for sunset.

outcroppings. ✉ *Follow any of 3 Kāʻanapali exits from Honoapiʻilani Hwy. and park at any hotel* ♿ *Toilets, showers, parking lot.*

Puamana Beach Park. Puamana is both a friendly beach park and a surf spot for mellow, longboard rides. With a narrow, sandy beach and grassy area providing plenty of shade, Puamana offers mostly calm swimming conditions and a good view of neighboring Lānaʻi. Smaller than Launiupoko, this beach park tends to attract locals looking to surf and barbecue. ✉ *On Rte. 30, ¼ mi south of Lahaina* ♿ *Toilets, showers, picnic tables, grills/firepits.*

Launiupoko State Wayside Park. Launiupoko is the beach park of all beach parks. Both a surf break and a beach, it offers a little something for everyone with its inviting stretch of lawn, soft white sand, and gentle waves. The shoreline reef creates a protected wading pool, perfect for small children. Outside the reef, beginner surfers will find good longboard rides. From the long sliver of beach (good for walking), you'll enjoy superb views of neighbor islands, and landside, of deep valleys cutting through the West Maui Mountains. Because of its endless sunshine and serenity—not to mention its many amenities— Launiupoko draws a crowd on the weekends, but there's space for

DON'T FORGET

All of the island's beaches are free and open to the public—even those that grace the front yards of fancy hotels—so you can make yourself at home on any one of them. Some of the prettiest beaches are often hidden by buildings; look for the blue BEACH ACCESS signs that indicate public rights-of-way through condominiums, resorts, and other private properties.

everyone (and overflow parking across the street). ⊠ *On Rte. 30, just south of Lahaina at mile marker 18* ♿ *Toilets, showers, picnic tables, grills/firepits.*

Olowalu. Olowalu is more an offshore snorkel spot than a beach, but it's a great place to watch for turtles and whales in-season. The beach is literally a pullover from the road, which can make for some unwelcome noise if you're looking for quiet. The entrance can be rocky (reef shoes help), but if you've got your snorkel gear it's just a swim away to an extensive and diverse reef (200 yards). Shoreline visibility can vary depending on the swell and time of day (late morning is best). Except for during a south swell, the waters are usually calm. A half mile north of mile marker 14 you'll find the rocky surf break, also called Olowalu. Snorkeling here is along pathways that wind among coral heads. This is a local hangout and can be unfriendly at times. ⊠ *South of Olowalu General Store, on Rte. 30 at mile marker 14* ♿ *No facilities.*

Ukumeheme Beach Park. This popular park is also known as "Thousand Peaks," because the waves just keep coming. Beginning to intermediate wave riders will enjoy this as a good spot to longboard or boogie board. It's easy entry into the water and you don't have to paddle out very far. The beach itself leaves something to be desired, as it's more dead grass than sand, but there are plenty of barbecues, picnic tables, and some shade mostly from thorny kiawe trees, so footwear is a good idea at this beach. Portable toilets are available. ⊠ *On Rte. 30, near mile marker 12* ♿ *Toilets, picnic tables, grills/firepits.*

THE SOUTH SHORE

Sandy beach fronts nearly the entire southern coastline of Maui, from Kīhei at the northern end to Mākena at the southern tip. The farther south you go, the better the beaches get. Kīhei has excellent beach parks right in town, with white sand, showers, restrooms, picnic tables, and barbecues. Good snorkeling can be found along the beaches' rocky borders. As good as Kīhei is, Wailea is even better. Wailea's beaches are cleaner, facilities tidier, and views even more impressive. ⚠ **Note that break-ins have been reported at many of these beach parking lots**. As you head out to Mākena, the terrain gets wilder. Bring lunch, water, and sunscreen with you.

The following South Shore beaches are listed from north Kīhei southeast to Mākena.

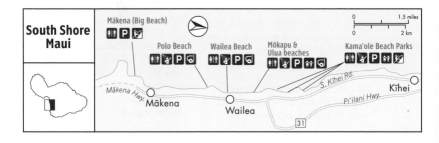

Kalepolepo Beach Park. This tiny spit of beach and rock is the site of the ancient Kalepolepo Village, a large settlement and the prized property of Maui's King Kamehameha in the 1850s. Here the *makaʻāinana* (commoners) tended the man-made pond, farmed, fished, and raised taro. Today the park has lots of shady trees and stays pretty quiet, making it a good getaway from the crowd and sun. However, the beach (if you can call it that) is only a small sprinkling of sand, and swimming in the often-murky waters isn't recommended. Toilets are portable. ⊠ *726 S. Kīhei Rd., just south of Hawaiian Islands Humpback Whale National Marine Sanctuary* ⟠ *Toilets, picnic tables, grills/firepits, parking lot.*

GEAR UP!

Forget your beach gear? No need to fear, Maui is the land-of-plenty when it comes to stores just waiting to pawn off their boogie boards and beach mats. Look for Long's Drugs (in Kīhei and Kahului) or the ABC Stores (in Kāʻanapali, Lahaina, Kīhei, and more) for extra sunscreen, shades, towels, and umbrellas. If you want better deals and don't mind the drive into town, look for Kmart (424 Dairy Rd.) or Wal-Mart (101 Pakaula St.) in Kahului. For more extensive gear, check out Sports Authority (270 Dairy Rd.) in Kahului. Equipment rentals are available at shops and resorts, too.

Waipuʻilani Park. Fronting the Maui Sunset Resort, Waipuʻilani Park is a spectacular place to lay out or picnic on golf-course-quality grass. A small beach hides behind the dunes, although it's usually speckled with seaweed and shells; swimming isn't recommended, as the park is not far from a water-treatment plant. This park often hosts local activities, such as volleyball and croquet, and it attracts many dog lovers. Although it has a resort feel and can be crowded, it's still a perfect place to watch the sunset. ⊠ *From S. Kīhei Rd., turn at Star Market onto W. Waipuʻilani Rd.* ⟠ *Toilets, grills/firepits.*

Kalama Park. This 36-acre beach park is great for families and sports-lovers. With its extensive lawns and sports fields, the park has volleyball, baseball, tennis, and even a skateboard park. Stocked with grills, picnic pavilions, and plenty of shade, it's a recreational mecca. The beach itself is all but nonexistent, but swimming is fair—though you must brave the rocky steps down to the water. If you aren't completely comfortable with the rocky entrance, you're better off sticking to the burgers and boccie ball than venturing into the ocean. ⊠ *On S. Kīhei Rd. across from Kīhei Kalama Village* ⟠ *Toilets, showers, picnic tables, grills/firepits, playground.*

Cove Beach Park. Go to the Cove if you want to learn to surf. All of the surf schools are here in the morning, pushing longboard beginners onto the bunny-slope beginners. For spectators there's a grassy area with some shade, and a tiny blink of a beach. If you aren't here to learn to surf, don't bother swimming. The water is sketchy at best, and there are plenty of better beaches. ⊠ *On S. Kīhei Rd., turn onto ʻIli ʻIli Rd.* ⟠ *No facilities.*

Charley Young Beach. This secluded 3-acre park sits off the main drag in a residential area. The sand is soft and smooth, with a gentle slope

BEACH SAFETY ON MAUI

Hawai'i's beautiful beaches can be dangerous at times due to large waves and strong currents—so much so that the state rates wave hazards using three signs: a yellow square (caution), a red stop sign (high hazard), and a black diamond (extreme hazard). Signs are posted and updated three times daily or as conditions change.

Visiting beaches with lifeguards is recommended, and you should swim only when there's a normal caution rating. Never swim alone or dive into unknown water or shallow breaking waves. If you're unable to swim out of a rip current, tread water and wave your arms in the air to signal for help.

Even in calm conditions, there are other dangerous things in the water to be aware of, including razor-sharp coral, jellyfish, eels, and sharks. Jellyfish cause the most ocean injuries, and signs are posted along beaches when they're present. Box jellyfish swarm to Hawai'i's leeward shores 9 to 10 days after a full moon. Portuguese man-of-wars are usually found when winds blow from the ocean onto land. Reactions to a sting are usually mild (burning sensation, redness, welts); however, in some cases they can be severe (breathing difficulties). If you are stung by a jellyfish, pick off the tentacles, rinse the affected area with water, and apply ice. Seek first aid from a lifeguard if you experience severe reactions.

According to state sources, the chances of getting bitten by a shark in Hawaiian waters are very low; sharks attack swimmers or surfers three or four times per year. Of the 40 species of sharks found near Hawai'i, tiger sharks are considered the most dangerous. They are recognized by their blunt snouts and vertical bars on their sides. To reduce your shark-attack risk:

■ Swim, surf, or dive with others at beaches patrolled by lifeguards.

■ Avoid swimming at dawn, dusk, and night, when some shark species may move inshore to feed.

■ Don't enter the water if you have open wounds or are bleeding.

■ Avoid murky waters, harbor entrances, areas near stream mouths, channels, or steep drop-offs.

■ Don't wear high-contrast swimwear or shiny jewelry.

■ Don't swim near dolphins, which are often prey for large sharks.

■ If you spot a shark, leave the water quickly and calmly.

The Web site ⊕ *http://oceansafety. soest.hawaii.edu/index.asp* provides beach hazard maps for O'ahu, Maui, Kaua'i, and the Big Island, as well as weather and surf advisories, listings of closed beaches, and safety tips.

into the ocean. A cloister of lava rocks shelters the beach from heavy afternoon winds, making this a mellow spot to laze around. The usually gentle waves make for good swimming, and you'll find good snorkeling along the rocks on the north end. Portable toilets are on-site. ⊠ *From S. Kīhei Rd.,* turn onto Kaia'u St., just north of Kama'ole I ⟨ Toilets, shower.

Catching a wave close to shore can give you an exciting ride.

Kamaʻole I, II, and III. Three steps from South Kīhei Road are three golden stretches of sand separated by outcroppings of dark, jagged lava rocks. You can walk the length of all three beaches if you're willing to get your feet wet. The northernmost of the trio, Kamaʻole I (across from the ABC Store, in case you forgot your sunscreen), offers perfect swimming with a sandy bottom a long way out and an active volleyball court. If you're one of those people who like your beach sans sand, there's also a great lawn for you to spread out on at the south end of the beach. Kamaʻole II is nearly identical minus the lawn. The last beach, the one with all the people on it, is Kamaʻole III, perfect for throwing a disk or throwing down a blanket. This is a great family beach, complete with a playground, volleyball net, barbecues, kite flying, and frequently, rented inflatable castles—a birthday-party must for every cool kid living on the island.

Locally—and quite disrespectfully, according to native Hawaiians—known as "Kam" I, II, and III, all three beaches have great swimming and lifeguards. In the morning the water can be as still as a lap pool. Kamaʻole III offers terrific breaks for beginning bodysurfers. ■TIP→**The public restrooms have seen better days; decent facilities are found at convenience stores and eateries across the street.** ⊠*S. Kīhei Rd. between Ke Aliʻi Alanui and Keonekai Rds.* ⚐*Lifeguard, toilets, showers, picnic tables, grills/firepits, playground, parking lot.*

Keawakapu Beach. Who wouldn't love Keawakapu with its long stretch of golden sand, near-perfect swimming, and stunning views of the crater and Kahoʻolawe? It's great fun to walk or jog this beach south into Wailea as the path is lined with over-the-top residences. It's best here

SUN SAFETY ON MAUI

Hawai'i's weather—seemingly never-ending warm, sunny days with gentle trade winds—can be enjoyed year-round with good sun sense. Because of Hawai'i's subtropical location, the length of daylight here changes little throughout the year. The sun is particularly strong, with a daily UV average of 14.

The Hawai'i Dermatological Society recommends these sun safety tips:

■ Plan your beach, golf, hiking, and other outdoor activities for the early morning or late afternoon, avoiding the sun between 10 AM and 4 PM.

■ Apply a broad-spectrum sunscreen with a sun protection factor (SPF) of at least 15. Hawai'i lifeguards use sunscreens with an SPF of 30. Cover areas that are most prone to burning like your nose, shoulders, tops of feet and ears. And don't forget your lips.

■ Apply sunscreen at least 30 minutes before you plan to be outdoors and reapply every two hours, even on cloudy days.

■ Wear light, protective clothing, such as a long-sleeve shirt and pants, broad-brimmed hat and sunglasses.

■ Stay in the shade whenever possible—especially on the beach—by using an umbrella.

■ Children need extra protection from the sun. Apply sunscreen frequently and liberally on children and minimize their time in the sun. Sunscreen is not recommended for children under six months.

in the morning as the winds pick up in the afternoon (beware of irritating sandstorms). Keawakapu has two entrances: one at the Mana Kai Maui Resort (look for the blue SHORELINE ACCESS sign and the parking at Kilohana Street), and the second at the dead end of Kīhei Road. Toilets are portable. ⊠ *S. Kīhei Rd. at Kilohana St. 96753* ⚒ *Toilets, showers, parking lot.*

☾ **Mōkapu and Ulua.** Look for a little road and public parking lot next to the Wailea Marriott. This gets you to Mōkapu and Ulua beaches. Though there are no lifeguards, families love this place. Reef formations create tons of tide pools for kids to explore and the beaches are protected from major swells. Snorkeling is excellent at Ulua, the beach to the left of the entrance. Mōkapu, to the right, tends to be less crowded. The Renaissance Wailea fronting this beach is scheduled to be demolished and construction of a new resort property is planned at some point in the future. ⊠ *Wailea Alanui Dr. north of Wailea Marriott resort* ⚒ *Toilets, showers, parking lot.*

Wailea Beach. A road just after the Grand Wailea Resort takes you to Wailea Beach, a wide, sandy stretch with snorkeling, swimming, and, if you're a guest of the Four Seasons Resort, Evian spritzes! If you're not a guest at the Grand Wailea or Four Seasons, the private cabanas and chaise longues can be a little annoying, but any complaint is more than made up for by the calm, unclouded waters and soft, white sand. ⊠ *Wailea Alanui Dr. south of Grand Wailea Resort entrance* ⚒ *Toilets, showers, parking lot.*

DID YOU KNOW?

You won't find plumbing at stunning Mākena Beach State Park on the South Shore, but the undeveloped, golden-sand, 3,000-foot-long "Big Beach" is home to dolphins and turtles. Sunsets here are glorious.

BEST BEACHES

Maui has miles and miles of great beaches, so how do you choose where to park your towel? Here are some that are sure to satisfy.

BEST FOR FAMILIES

Baldwin Beach, the North Shore. The long, shallow, calm end closest to Kahului is safe even for toddlers—with adult supervision, of course.

Kama'ole III, the South Shore. There's sand, gentle surf, a playground, volleyball net, and barbecues—what more could a family want?

BEST OFFSHORE SNORKELING

Olowalu, West Maui. The beach remains shallow far offshore and there's plenty to see.

Ulua, the South Shore. It's beautiful and the kids can enjoy the tide pools while the adults experience the excellent snorkeling.

BEST SURFING

Ho'okipa, the North Shore. This is a great surfing spot, and one of the best windsurfing beaches in the world, though it's not for beginners.

Honolua Bay, West Maui. One bay over from Mokulē'ia Beach (north of Kapalua) you'll find one of the best surf breaks in Hawai'i.

BEST SUNSETS

Kapalua Bay, West Maui. The ambience here is as stunning as the sunset.

Keawakapu, the South Shore. Since most active beachgoers enjoy this gorgeous spot before mid-afternoon when the wind picks up, it's never crowded at sunset. ■ TIP→ **Bring a picnic.**

BEST FOR SEEING AND BEING SEEN

Kā'anapali Beach, West Maui. The portion of this popular beach that fronts Whalers Village is called "Dig Me"—need we say more?

Wailea Beach, the South Shore. At this beach fronting the ultraluxurious Four Seasons and Grand Wailea resorts, you never know who might be "hiding" in that private cabana!

Polo Beach. From Wailea Beach you can walk to this small, uncrowded crescent fronting the Fairmont Kea Lani resort. Swimming and snorkeling are great here and it's a good place to whale-watch. As at Wailea Beach, private cabanas occupy prime sandy real estate, but there's plenty of room for you and your towel, and even a nice grass picnic area. The pathway connecting the two beaches is a great spot to jog or leisurely take in awesome views of nearby Molokini and Kaho'olawe. Rare native plants grow along the ocean, or *makai*, side of the path; the honey-sweet-smelling one is *naio*, or false sandalwood. ⊠ *Wailea Alanui Dr. south of Fairmont Kea Lani resort entrance* ⌖ *Toilets, showers, picnic tables, grills/firepits, parking lot.*

FodorśChoice
★ **Mākena (Big Beach).** Locals successfully fought to give Mākena—one of Hawai'i's most breathtaking beaches—state-park protection. It's often mistakenly referred to as "Big Beach," but natives prefer its Hawaiian name, Oneloa. This stretch of deep-golden sand abutting sparkling aqua water is 3,000-feet-long and 100-feet-wide. It's never crowded, no matter how many cars cram into the lots. The water is fine for

swimming, but use caution. △The shore drop-off is steep and swells can get deceptively big. Despite the infamous "Mākena cloud," a blanket that rolls in during the early afternoon and obscures the sun, it rarely rains here. For a dramatic view of the beach, climb Puʻu Ōlaʻi, the steep cinder cone near the first entrance. Continue over the cinder cone's side to discover "Little Beach"—clothing-optional

WORD OF MOUTH

"Beaches are nice and sunny on the South Shore. Also, Hoʻokipa beach near Pāʻia on the North Shore is very pretty—watch the wind surfers. There's a blowhole on the west end. The road near there is narrow and curvy!

–trippinkpj

by popular practice, although this is technically illegal. On Sunday, free spirits of all kinds crowd Little Beach's tiny shoreline for a drumming circle and bonfire. Little Beach has the island's best bodysurfing (no pun intended). Skim-boarders catch air at Mākena's third entrance. Each of the three paved entrances has portable toilets. ⊠ *Off Wailea Alanui Dr.* ♿ *Toilets, parking lot.*

THE NORTH SHORE

Many of the folks you see jaywalking in Pāʻia sold everything they owned to come to Maui and live a beach-bum's life. Beach culture abounds on the North Shore. But these folks aren't sunbathers; they're big-wave riders, windsurfers, or kiteboarders. The North Shore is their challenging sports arena. Beaches here face the open ocean and tend to be rougher and windier than beaches elsewhere on Maui—but don't let that scare you off. On calm days, the reef-speckled waters are truly beautiful and offer a quieter and less commercial beach-going experience than the leeward shore. Beaches below are listed from Kahului (near the airport) eastward to Hoʻokipa.

Kanahā Beach. Windsurfers, kiteboarders, joggers, and picnicking families like this long, golden strip of sand bordered by a wide grassy area with lots of shade. The winds pick up in the early afternoon, making for the best kiteboarding and windsurfing conditions—if you know what you're doing, that is. The best spot for watching kiteboarders is at the far left end of the beach. ⊠ *Drive through airport and make right onto car-rental road (Koeheke); turn right onto Amala Pl. and take any left (there are 3 entrances) into Kanahā* ♿ *Lifeguard, toilets, showers, picnic tables, grills/firepits, parking lot.*

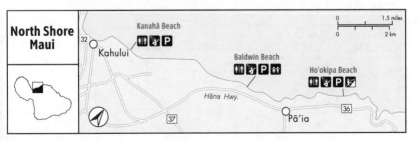

☺ ★ **Baldwin Beach.** A local favorite, right off the highway and just west of Pāʻia town, Baldwin Beach is a big stretch of comfortable white sand. This is a good place to lie out, jog, or swim, though the waves can sometimes be choppy and the undertow strong. Don't be afraid of those big brown blobs floating beneath the surface; they're just pieces of seaweed awash in the surf. You can find shade along the beach beneath the ironwood trees, or in the large pavilion, a spot regularly overtaken by local parties and community events.

The long, shallow pool at the Kahului end of the beach is known as "Baby Beach." Separated from the surf by a flat reef wall, this is where ocean-loving families bring their kids (and sometimes puppies) to practice a few laps. Take a relaxing stroll along the water's edge from the one end of Baldwin Beach to Baby Beach and enjoy the scenery. The view of the West Maui Mountains is hauntingly beautiful from here. ⊠*Hāna Hwy., 1 mi west of Baldwin Ave.* ⚐*Lifeguard, toilets, showers, picnic tables, grills/firepits, parking lot.*

★ **Hoʻokipa Beach.** If you want to see some of the world's finest windsurfers in action, hit this beach along the Hāna Highway. The sport was largely developed right at Hoʻokipa and has become an art and a career to some. This beach is also one of Maui's hottest surfing spots, with waves that can be as high as 20 feet. This is not a good swimming beach, nor the place to learn windsurfing, but it's great for hanging out and watching the pros. Bust out your telephoto lens at the cliff-side lookout to capture the aerial acrobatics of board-sailors and kiteboarders. ⊠*2 mi past Pāʻia on Rte. 36* ⚐*Lifeguard, toilets, showers, picnic tables, grills/firepits, parking lot.*

EAST MAUI AND HĀNA

Hāna's beaches will literally stop you in your tracks—they're that beautiful. Black-and-red sands stand out against pewter skies and lush tropical foliage creating picture-perfect scenes, which seem too breathtaking to be real. Rough conditions often preclude swimming, but that doesn't mean you can't explore the shoreline. Beaches below are listed in order from the west end of Hāna town eastward.

Fodor'sChoice   **Waiʻānapanapa State Park.** Small but rarely crowded, this beach will
★ remain in your memory long after visiting. Fingers of white foam rush onto a black volcanic-pebble beach fringed with green beach vines and palms. Swimming here is both relaxing and invigorating: strong currents bump smooth stones up against your ankles while seabirds flit above

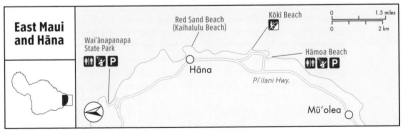

a black, jagged sea arch draped with vines. At the edge of the parking lot, a sign tells you the sad story of a doomed Hawaiian princess. Stairs lead through a tunnel of interlocking Polynesian *hau* (a native tree) branches to an icy cave pool—the secret hiding place of the ancient princess. ⚠ **You can swim in this pool, but be wary of mosquitoes!** In the other direction, a 3-mi, dramatic coastal path continues beyond the campground, past sea arches, blowholes, and cultural sites all the way to Hāna town. Grassy tent sites and rustic cabins that accommodate up to six people are available by reservation only; call ahead for information. ✉ *Hāna Hwy. near mile marker 32* ☎ *808/984–8109* ⚐ *Toilets, showers, picnic tables, grills/firepits, parking lot.*

★ **Red Sand Beach (Kaihalulu Beach).** Kaihalulu Beach, better known as Red Sand Beach, is unmatched in its raw and remote beauty. It's not simple to find, but when you round the last corner of the trail and are confronted with the sight of it, your jaw is bound to drop. Earthy red cliffs tower above the deep maroon–sand beach and swimmers bob about in a turquoise blue lagoon formed by volcanic boulders just offshore (it's like floating around in a giant natural bathtub). It's worth spending a night in Hāna just to make sure you can get here early and have some time to enjoy it before anyone else shows up.

Keep in mind that getting here is not easy and you have to pass through private property along the way—do so at your own risk. You need to tread carefully up and around Ka'uiki (the red-cinder hill); the cliffside cinder path is slippery and constantly eroding. Hiking is not recommended in shoes without traction, or in bad weather. By popular practice, clothing on the beach is optional. ✉ *At end of Uakea Rd. past baseball field. Park near community center, walk through grass lot to trail below cemetery* ⚐ *No facilities.*

Kōkī Beach. You can tell from the trucks parked alongside the road that this is a favorite local surf spot. ■ TIP➔**Watch conditions before swimming or bodysurfing; the riptides here can be mean.** Look for awesome views of the rugged coastline and a sea arch on the left end. *Iwa*, or white-throated frigate birds, dart like pterodactyls over 'Alau islet offshore. ✉ *Haneo'o Loop Rd., 2 mi east of Hāna town* ⚐ *No facilities.*

Hāmoa Beach. Why did James Michener describe this stretch of salt-and-pepper sand as the most "South Pacific" beach he'd come across, even though it's located in the North Pacific? Maybe it was the perfect half-moon shape, speckled with the shade of palm trees. Perhaps he was intrigued by the jutting black coastline, often outlined by rain showers out at sea, or the pervasive lack of hurry he felt once settled in here. Whatever it was, many still feel the lure. The beach can be crowded but nonetheless relaxing. Expect to see a few chaise longues and a guest-only picnic area set up by the Hotel Hāna-Maui. Early mornings and late afternoons are best for swimming. At times, the churning surf might intimidate beginning swimmers, but bodysurfing can be great here. ✉ *½ mi past Kōkī Beach on Haneo'o Loop Rd., 2 mi east of Hāna town* ⚐ *Toilets, showers, picnic tables, parking lot.*

Water Sports and Tours

WORD OF MOUTH

"One piece of advice for your Molokini snorkeling cruise is to plan it for one of the first days you are on Maui . . . You probably will be waking up really early Maui time for the first couple of days due to the time change. Most of the snorkel trips leave early in the AM."

—mollmatt

Updated by
Eliza Escaño-
Vasquez

Getting into (or onto) the water will be the highlight of your Maui trip. On the Valley Isle, you can learn to surf, snorkel, or scuba dive, or board a boat for deep-sea fishing, parasailing, and sunset cocktail cruises. From December into May, whale-watching adventures become a top attraction as humpbacks escaping Alaska's frigid winter arrive in Maui's warm waters to frolic, mate, and birth.

Along Maui's leeward coastline, from Kā'anapali on the West Shore all the way down to Waiala Cove on the South Shore, you can discover great snorkeling and swimming. If you're a thrill-seeker, head out to the North Shore and Ho'okipa, where surfers, kiteboarders, and windsurfers catch big waves and big air.

Treat Mother Nature with respect and, for your safety, choose activities that suit your skill level and health condition. The ocean might be beautiful but it can be quite unpredictable, and your experience can only be as good as the weather. For easy reference, activities are listed in alphabetical order.

BOOGIE BOARDING AND BODYSURFING

Bodysurfing and "sponging" (as boogie boarding is called by the regulars) are great ways to catch some waves without having to master surfing—and there's no balance or coordination required. A boogie board (or "sponge") is softer than a hard, fiberglass surfboard, which means you can ride safely in the rough-and-tumble surf zone. If you get tossed around (which is half the fun), you don't have a heavy surfboard nearby to bang your head on, but you do have something to hang onto. Serious spongers invest in a single short-clipped fin to help propel them into the wave.

BEST SPOTS

D.T. Fleming Beach (⊠*Honoapi'ilani Hwy., below the Ritz-Carlton, Kapalua*) in West Maui, offers great surf almost daily along with some nice amenities: ample parking, restrooms, a shower, grills, picnic tables, and a daily lifeguard. However, caution is advised, especially during winter months when the current and undertow can get rough.

Kama'ole III (⊠*S. Kīhei Rd.*), between Kīhei and Wailea, is another good spot for bodysurfing and boogie boarding. It has a sandy floor, with 1- to 3-foot waves breaking not too far out. It's often crowded late into the day, especially on weekends when local kids are out of school. Don't let that chase you away; the waves are wide enough for everyone.

If you don't mind nudity (officially illegal, but practiced nonetheless), **Little Beach** (⊠*On Mākena Rd., first entrance to Mākena State Beach Park; climb rock wall at north end of beach*) on the South Shore is the best break on the island for boogie boarding and bodysurfing. The

DID YOU KNOW?

Surfing at Māʻalaea and on the rest of the South Shore can be a lively or gentle ride. There are lessons for every skill level, so grab a board and jump on.

HOW TO CATCH A WAVE

The technique for catching waves is the same with or without a board. Swim out to where the swell is just beginning to break, and position yourself toward shore. When the next wave comes, lie on your board (if you have one), kick like crazy, and catch it! You'll feel the push of the wave as you glide in front of the gurgling, foamy surf. When bodysurfing, put your arms over your head, bring your index fingers together (so you look like the letter "A"), and stiffen your body like a board to achieve the same effect.

If you don't like to swim too far out, stick with boogie boarding and body-surfing close to shore. Shorebreak (if it isn't too steep) can be exhilarating to ride. You'll know it's too steep if you hear the sound of slapping when the waves hit the sand. You're looking for waves that curl over and break farther out, then roll, not slap onto the sand. Always watch first to make sure the conditions aren't too strong.

shape of the sandy shoreline creates waves that break a ways out and tumble on into shore. Because it's sandy, you only risk stubbing a toe on the few submerged rocks, not a reef floor. Don't even think about boogie boarding at neighboring Big Beach—you'll be slapped like a flapjack onto the steep shore.

On the North Shore, **Pā'ia Bay** (⊠ *Just before Pā'ia town, beyond large community building and grass field*) has waves suitable for spongers and bodysurfers. ■TIP➔Park in the public lot across the street and leave your valuables at home, as this beach is known for break-ins.

EQUIPMENT

Most condos and hotels have boogie boards available to guests—some in better condition than others (but beat-up boogies work just as well for beginners). You can also pick up a boogie board from any discount shop, such as Kmart or Long's Drugs, for upward of $30.

Auntie Snorkel. You can rent decent boogie boards here for $5 a day, or $15 a week. ⊠ *2439 S. Kīhei Rd., Kīhei* ☏ *808/879–6263.*

Honolua Surf. "Waverider" boogie boards with smooth undersides (better than the bumpy kind) can be rented from this surf shop for $8 a day, or $35 a week (with a $100 deposit). ⊠ *2411 S. Kīhei Rd., Kīhei* ☏ *808/874–0999* ⊠ *845 Front St., Lahaina* ☏ *808/661–8848.*

West Maui Sports and Fishing Supply. This old country store has been around for more than 20 years and has possibly the best prices on the west side. Boogie boards go for $2.50 a day or $15 a week. ⊠ *1287 Front St., Lahaina* ☏ *808/661–6252* ⊕ *www.westmauisports.com.*

DEEP-SEA FISHING

If fishing is your sport, Maui is your island. In these waters you'll find 'ahi, *aku* (skipjack tuna), barracuda, bonefish, *kawakawa* (bonito), mahimahi, Pacific blue marlin, ono, and *ulua* (jack crevalle). You can fish year-round and you don't need a license. ■TIP➔Because boats fill up fast during busy seasons (Christmas, spring break, tournament weeks), consider making reservations before coming to Maui.

Plenty of fishing boats run out of Lahaina and Mā'alaea harbors. If you charter a private boat, expect to spend in the neighborhood of $700 to $1,000 for a thrilling half-day in the swivel seat. You can share a boat for much less if you don't mind close quarters with a stranger who may get seasick, drunk, or worse . . . lucky! Before you sign up, you should know that some boats keep the catch. Most will, however, fillet a nice piece for you to take home. And if you catch a real beauty, you might even be able to have it professionally mounted.

You're expected to bring your own lunch and nonglass beverages. (Shop the night before; it's hard to find snacks at 6 AM.) Boats supply coolers, ice, and bait. A 10% to 20% tip is suggested.

CANOE RACES

Polynesians first traveled to Hawai'i by outrigger canoe, and racing the traditional craft is a favorite pastime on the Islands. Canoes were revered in old Hawai'i, and no voyage began without a blessing, ceremonial chanting, and a hula performance to ensure a safe journey. In Lahaina in mid-May, the two-week **Festival of Canoes** (☎808/667–9193 ⊕ www.visitlahaina.com) includes a torch-lighting ceremony, arts-and-crafts demonstrations, a chance for canoe enthusiasts to observe how Polynesian vessels are rigged, and the launching of a "Parade of Canoes."

4

BOATS AND CHARTERS

★ **Finest Kind Inc.** A record 1,118-pound blue marlin was reeled in by the crew aboard *Finest Kind,* a lovely 37-foot Merritt kept so clean you'd never guess the action it's seen. Ask Captain Dave about his pet frigate bird—he's been around these waters long enough to befriend other expert fishers. This family-run company operates four boats and specializes in live bait. Shared charters start at $139 for four hours and up to $199 for a full day. All-day private trips go from $599 to $1,000. Add 7% for tax and harbor fees. Check for any specials before booking. ⊠*Lahaina Harbor, Slip 7* ☎*808/661–0338* ⊕*www.finestkindsportfishing.com.*

Hinatea Sportfishing. This company is well established and has an excellent reputation. The active crew aboard the first-class, 41-foot *Hatteras* has the motto, "No boat rides here—we go to catch fish!" Charters go from $150 to $210 for a shared boat and from $850 to $1,100 for a private boat. A 7% tax will be included. ⊠*Lahaina Harbor, Slip 27* ☎*808/667–7548.*

Kai Palena Sportfishing. Captain Fuzzy Alboro runs a serious and highly recommended operation on the 32-foot *Die Hard.* Check-in is at 2:45 AM, and he takes a maximum of six people per trip. The cost is from $200 for a shared boat to $1,100 for a private charter; add 7% tax. ⊠*511 Pikanele St., Lahaina Harbor, Slip 10* ☎*808/878–2362.*

Start Me Up Sportfishing. These 42-foot Bertram *Sportfishers* will give you one of the most comfortable fishing trips around. With more than 20 years in business, Start Me Up has a fleet of five boats, all relatively new and impeccably maintained, complete with all the amenities:

TV, VCR, refrigerator, microwave, and ice chest. They provide the tackle and equipment. Six-person max. ✉ *Lahaina Harbor, Slip 12* ☎ *808/667–2774* ⊕ *www.startmeupsportfishing.com.*

Strike Zone. This is one of the few charters to offer morning bottom-fishing trips (for smaller fish such as snapper), as well as deep-sea trips (for the big ones—ono, 'ahi, mahimahi, and marlin). *Strike Zone* is a 43-foot Delta that offers plenty of room (16-person max). Lunch and soft drinks are included. The catch is shared with the entire boat. The cost is $168 per adult and $148 per child for a pole; spectators can ride for $78, plus 7% tax. The four- and six-hour bottom-fishing trips run Monday, Wednesday, Friday, and Saturday; the six-hour deep-sea trips run Tuesday, Thursday, and Sunday, all weather-permitting. All trips leave at 6:30 AM. ✉ *Mā'alaea Harbor, Slip 64* ☎ *808/879–4485* ⊕ *www.strikezonemaui.com.*

KAYAKING

Kayaking is a fantastic way to experience Maui's coast up close. Floating aboard a "plastic popsicle stick" is easier than you might think, and allows you to cruise out to vibrant, living coral reefs and waters where dolphins and even whales roam. Kayaking can be a leisurely paddle or a challenge of heroic proportions, depending on your ability, the location, and the weather. ■ TIP➡ **Though you can rent kayaks independently, we recommend taking a guide.** An apparently calm surface can hide extremely strong ocean currents—and you *really* don't want to take an unplanned trip to Tahiti. Most guides are naturalists who will steer you away from surging surf, lead you to pristine reefs, and point out camouflaged fish, like the stalking hawkfish. Not having to schlep your gear on top of your rental car is a bonus. A half-day tour runs around $75. Custom tours can be arranged.

If you decide to strike out on your own, tour companies will rent kayaks for the day with paddles, life vests, and roof racks, and many will meet you near your chosen location. Ask for a map of good entries and plan to avoid paddling back to shore against the wind (schedule extra time for the return trip regardless). Read weather conditions, bring binoculars, and take a careful look from the bay before heading in. For beginners, get there early before the trade wind kicks in, and try sticking close to the shore. When you're ready to snorkel, secure your belongings in a dry pack on board and drag your boat by its bowline behind you. (This isn't as bad as it sounds.) ■ TIP➡ **The 'Āhihi-Kīna'u Natural Area Reserve, at the southernmost point of South Maui, is closed to all activities until July 31, 2010. You may not kayak, dive, or snorkel in the reserve before this date. Closure is to allow the coral reef system in the area to recover from overuse.**

BEST SPOTS

In West Maui, past the steep cliffs on the Honoapi'ilani Highway and before you hit Lahaina, there's a long stretch of inviting coastline, including **Ukumehame** (✉ *Between mile markers 12 and 14 on Rte. 30*) and Olowalu beaches. This is a good spot for beginners; entry is easy and there's much to see in every direction. If you want to snorkel, the best visibility is farther out at Olowalu, at a depth of about 25 feet. ⚠ Watch for sharp kiawe thorns buried in the sand on the way into the water.

Mākena Landing (✉ *Off Mākena Rd.*) is an excellent taking-off point for a South Shore adventure. Enter from the paved parking lot or the small sandy beach a little south. The bay itself is virtually empty, but the right edge is flanked with brilliant coral heads and juvenile turtles. If you round the point on the right, you come across Five Caves, a system of enticing underwater arches. In the morning you may see dolphins, and the arches are havens for lobsters, eels, and spectacularly hued butterfly fish. Check out the million-dollar mansions lining the shoreline and guess which celebrity lives where. ■ TIP→ Regulators, activity operators, and the public are immersed in a hot debate about shore access to this area due to concerns over conservation, safety, and economic issues. At press time, commercial kayaking was prohibited at Mākena Landing; if you want to kayak here, you'll need to rent equipment and come on your own.

EQUIPMENT, LESSONS, AND TOURS

Kelii's Kayak Tours. One of the highest-rated kayak outfitters on the island, Kelii's offers combo trips where one can paddle, surf, snorkel, or hike to a waterfall. They can take up to eight people per guide. Trips are available on the island's North, South, and West shores, and range from $54 to $149, plus 4.4% tax. ✉ *Kīhei* ☎ *888/874–8652 or 808/874–7652* ⊕ *www.keliiskayak.com.*

Fodor's Choice
★   **South Pacific Kayaks.** These guys pioneered recreational kayaking on Maui—they know their stuff. Guides are friendly, informative, and eager to help you get the most out of your experience; we're talking true, fun-loving, kayak geeks. Some activity companies show a strange lack of care for the marine environment; South Pacific stands out as adventurous *and* responsible. They offer a variety of trips leaving from both West Maui and South Shore locations, including an advanced four-hour "Molokini Challenge." Trips range from $54 to $99. ☎ *800/776–2326 or 808/875–4848* ⊕ *www.southpacifickayaks.com.*

KITEBOARDING

Catapulting up to 40 feet in the air above the breaking surf, kiteboarders hardly seem of this world. Silken kites hold the athletes aloft for precious seconds—long enough for the execution of mind-boggling tricks—then deposit them back in the sea. This new sport is not for the weak-kneed. No matter what people might tell you, it's harder to learn than windsurfing. The unskilled (or unlucky) can be caught in an upwind and carried far out in the ocean, or worse—dropped smack on the shore. Because of insurance (or the lack thereof), companies are not allowed to rent equipment. Beginners must take lessons, and then purchase their own gear. Devotees swear that after your first few lessons, committing to buying your kite is easy.

BEST SPOTS

While Ho'okipa Beach provides awesome spectating, the steady tracks on **Kanahā Beach** (✉ *Amala Pl., Kahului*) make it the premiere spot for learning. Specific areas are set aside for different water activities, so launch and land only in kite-boarding zones, and kindly give way to swimmers, divers, fishermen, and paddlers.

LESSONS

Aqua Sports Maui. "To air is human," or so they say at Aqua Sports, which calls itself the local favorite of kiteboarding schools. They've got a great location right near Kite Beach, at the west (left) end of Kanahā Beach, and offer basic through advanced kiteboarding lessons. Rates start at $210 for a three-hour basics course taught by certified instructors. ✉ *Amala Pl., near Kite Beach, Kahului* ☎ *808/242–8015* ⊕ *www. mauikiteboardinglessons.com.*

Hawaiian Sailboarding Techniques. Pro kiteboarder and legendary windsurfer Alan Cadiz will have you safely ripping in no time at lower Kanahā Beach Park. A "Learn to Kitesurf" package starts at $225 for a three-hour private lesson, which includes all equipment. As opposed to observing from the shore, instructors paddle after students on a chaseboard to give immediate feedback. HST is in the highly regarded Hi-Tech Surf Sports store, located in the Triangle Square shopping center. ✉ *425 Koloa St., Kahului* ☎ *808/871–5423 or 800/968–5423* ⊕ *www. hstwindsurfing.com.*

Kiteboarding School of Maui. Call KSM, one of the first kiteboarding schools in the United States and the first on Maui, for one-on-one "flight lessons." Pro kiteboarders will induct you at Kite Beach, at the west (left) end of Kanahā Beach, providing instruction, equipment, snacks, and FAA guidelines. (Seriously, there are rules about avoiding airplanes at nearby Kahului Airport.) Rates start at $290 for four hours or $490 for two-day private lessons. KSM is the only school that offers retail gear as well as instruction. Thirty percent of your lesson cost can be applied to gear purchase. ✉ *22 Hāna Hwy., Kahului* ☎ *808/873–0015* ⊕ *www.ksmaui.com.*

ON THE SIDELINES

If you're not inclined to go kite-boarding yourself, live vicariously by attending **Red Bull's King of the Air** (✉ *Ho'okipa Beach Park* ☎ *808/573-3222* ⊕ *www.redbull kingoftheair.com*) showcase contest each fall. Contenders travel from as far as Poland and Norway to compete in this world-class big air and freestyle kiteboarding contest.

PARASAILING

Parasailing is an easy, exhilarating way to earn your wings: just strap on a harness attached to a parachute, and a powerboat pulls you up and over the ocean from a launching dock or a boat's platform. ■ TIP→**Parasailing is limited to West Maui, and "thrill craft"—including parasails—are prohibited in Maui waters during humpback whale–calving season, December 15 to May 15.**

LESSONS AND TOURS

UFO Parasail. UFO offers the standard 7-minute ride at 400 feet ($65), or 10-minute ride at 800 feet ($70). Observers are welcome aboard. Be prepared for lots of jokes about alien abduction. ☎*808/661–7836* ⊕*www.ufoparasail.net.*

West Maui Parasail. Launch 400 feet above the ocean for a bird's-eye view of Lahaina, or be daring at 800 feet for smoother rides and better views. The captain will be glad to let you experience a "toe dip" or "freefall" if you request it. For safety reasons, passengers weighing less than 100 pounds must be strapped together in tandem. Hour-long trips departing from Lahaina Harbor, Slip 15, and Kā'anapali Beach include 8- to 10-minute flights and run from $65 for the 400-foot ride to $75 for the 800-foot ride. Observers must pay $30 each. ☎*808/661–4060* ⊕*www.westmauiparasail.com.*

RAFTING

The high-speed, inflatable rafts you find on Maui are nothing like the raft that Huck Finn used to drift down the Mississippi. While passengers grip straps, these rafts fly, skimming and bouncing across the sea. Because they're so maneuverable, they go where the big boats can't—secret coves, sea caves, and remote beaches. Two-hour trips run around $50, half-day trips upward of $100. ■ TIP→**Although safe, these trips are not for the faint of heart. If you have back or neck problems or are pregnant, you should reconsider this activity.**

TOURS

Blue Water Rafting. One of the few ways to get to the stunning Kanaio Coast (the roadless southern coastline beyond 'Āhihi-Kīna'u), this rafting tour begins trips conveniently at the Kīhei boat ramp. Dolphins, turtles, and other marine life are the highlight of this adventure, along with sea caves, lava arches, and views of Haleakalā. Two-hour trips start at $49 plus tax; longer trips cost $90 to $115 and include a deli lunch. ⊠*2777 S. Kīhei Rd., Kīhei* ☎*808/879–7238* ⊕*www.bluewater rafting.com.*

Ocean Riders. This West Maui tour crosses the 'Au'Au Channel to Lāna'i's Shipwreck Beach, then circles the island for 70 mi of remote coast. For snorkeling, the "back side" of Lāna'i is one of Hawai'i's unsung marvels. Tours—$129 plus tax per person—depart from Mala Wharf, at the northern end of Front Street and include snorkel gear, a fruit breakfast, and a deli lunch. ⊠*Lahaina* ☎*808/661–3586* ⊕*www. mauioceanriders.com.*

MAUI'S TOP FOUR WATER ACTIVITIES

TOUR COMPANY/ OUTFITTER	Length	AM/PM	Departure Point	Adult/Kid Price	Kids' Ages	Snack vs. meal	Alcoholic beverages included	Boat type	Capacity	Worth Noting
Kayaking										
Keli'i's Kayak Tours	2.5–4.5 hours	AM	Mākena Landing, Olowalu, D.T. Fleming Beach	$54–$149	minimum age 5 (no kids' prices)	snack/ meal	no	kayak	16	Combo trips include snorkeling, hiking, or surfing.
South Pacific Kayaks	2.5–5 hours	AM	Various locations	$54–$99/ $49–$67	5–11	snack/ meal	no	kayak	16	Maximum of 8 people per guide.
Sunset Sailing										
Paragon	2 hours	PM	Lahaina and Mā'alaea Harbor	$54/$27	12 and under	snack/ meal	yes	47' power/sail catamaran	24 to 38	Vessels are some of the fastest in the state. Sunset sails include champagne.
Scotch Mist	2 hours	PM	Lahaina Harbor	$60/$32	5–12	snack	yes	50' Santa Cruz single-hull sail boat	25	Sail times depend on season.
Trilogy Excursions	2 hours	PM	Kā'anapali Beach Hotel	$63/$32	3–15	snack	no	54' power/sail catamaran	32	Offers an all-day Lāna'i charter. Guests can bring alcohol.
Scuba										
Ed Robinson's Diving Adventure	4.5–6.5 hours	AM/PM	Kīhei Boat Ramp	$135–$178	minimum age 12	snack/ meal	no	30'–32' aluminum dive boat	12	10% discount if you book at least 3 charters, 15% for five.
Lahaina Divers	3.5–10 hours	AM/PM	Lahaina Harbor	$109–$209	minimum age 10	snack	no	46' Newton dive boat	30	Nondiving passengers or snorkelers might accompany a certified diver for $69.

Name	Duration	AM/PM	Location	Price	Age	Meal	Restroom	Boat	Capacity	Notes
Maui Dive Shop	2-8 hours	AM/PM	Kīhei Boat Ramp and Māʻalaea Harbor	$90-$180	minimum age 12	snack/meal	no	48' Pro dive boat	24	Molokini Backwall is the most advanced dive and requires a minimum of 25-dive experience.
Mike Severns Diving	5.5-6.5 hours	AM	Kīhei Boat Ramp	from $145	minimum age 12	snack/meal	no	38' dive boat	12	Dive sites depend on weather and water conditions.
Shaka Divers	2-4 hours	AM/PM	Call for exact location	$59-$89	minimum age 10	snack	no	n/a	8	Offers Torpedo scooter dives and twilight dives.
Snorkeling										
Ann Fielding's Snorkel	5 hours	AM	Call for location	$95	minimum age 7 (no kids' prices)	snack	no	n/a	6	Marine biologist Ann Fielding meets guests by car at the day's most ideal location.
Maui Classic Charters	4-5 hours	AM/PM	Māʻalaea Harbor	$98-$109 /$67-$88	3-12	meal	yes	54' and 55' power catamaran	45 to 120	Offers snuba and waterslide, ideal for children.
Maui-Molokaʻi Sea Cruises	5 hours	AM	Māʻalaea Harbor	$94/$59	5-12	meal	yes	92' power catamaran	149	5 years old and under free. Teen prices (13-18) available.
Paragon	3-7 hours	AM/PM	Lahaina and Māʻalaea Harbor	$53-$155 /$27-$103	4-12	meal	yes	47' power catamaran	24 to 38	3 years old and under free, except for the Lānaʻi trip ($21).
Teralani Sailing Charter	4-5 hours	AM/PM	Whaler's Village	$95-$119/$59-69	3-12	meal	yes	65' power sail/catamaran	49	3 years old and under are free
Trilogy Excursions	6-8 hours	AM	Lahaina and Māʻalaea Harbor	$115-$197	3-15	meal	no	50'-64' power/sail catamaran	40-54	Kids ages 3-15 are half-price. Offers Lānaʻi trip.

4

SAILING

With the islands of Moloka'i, Lāna'i, Kaho'olawe, and Molokini a stone's throw away, Maui waters offer visually arresting backdrops for sailing adventures. Sailing conditions can be fickle, so some operations throw in snorkeling or whale-watching, and others offer sunset cruises. *(For more sunset cruises, see Chapter 7, Entertainment and Nightlife.)* Winds are consistent in summer, but variable in winter, and afternoons are generally windier all throughout the year. Prices range from around $40 for two-hour trips to $80 for half-day excursions. ■TIP→You won't be sheltered from the elements on the trim racing boats, so be sure to bring a hat (one that won't blow away), a light jacket or cover-up, sunglasses, and extra sunscreen.

> ### PRIVATE CHARTERS
>
> Hiring a private charter for a sail will cost you more, but it's one way to avoid crowds. Although almost all sailing vessels (including those in this section) offer private charters, a few cater to them specifically. Among the top three, *Shangri-La* (☎888/855–9977 ⊕www.sailing maui.com) is the largest and most luxurious 65-foot catamaran. *Island Star* (☎888/677–7238 ⊕www. islandstarexcursions.com) is a 57-foot Columbia offering customized trips out of Mā'alaea. *Cinderella* (☎808/244–0009 ⊕www. maui.net/~sailmaui) is a swift and elegant 50-foot Columbia.

BOATS AND CHARTERS

America II. This onetime America's Cup contender offers an exciting, intimate alternative to crowded catamarans. For fast action, try a morning trade-wind sail. Plan to bring a change of clothes, because you will get wet. Snack and beverages are provided. No one under five years old is permitted. ⊠*Lahaina Harbor Slip 6* ☎*808/667–2195* ⊕*www. sailingonmaui.com.*

Paragon. If you want to snorkel and sail, this is your boat. Many snorkel cruises claim to sail but actually motor most of the way; Paragon is an exception. Both Paragon vessels (one catamaran in Lahaina, the other in Mā'alaea) are ship-shape, and crews are competent and friendly. Their mooring in Molokini Crater is particularly good, and they often stay after the masses have left. The Lāna'i trip includes a picnic lunch on the beach, snorkeling, and an afternoon blue-water swim. Extras on their trips to Lāna'i include mai tais and sodas, hot and cold *pūpū* (Hawaiian tapas), and champagne. A similar spread comes with the sunset sail, which departs from Lahaina Harbor every Monday, Wednesday, and Friday. ⊠*Lahaina and Mā'alaea harbors* ☎*808/244–2087 or 800/441–2087* ⊕*www.sailmaui.com.*

Scotch Mist Charters. Follow the wind aboard this 50-foot Santa Cruz sailing yacht. Three-hour snorkeling, sunset, or whale-watching trips focus on the sail, and usually carry fewer than 25 passengers. Two-hour sunset sails start at $59.95 and include soft drinks, wine, beer, champagne, and chocolate. ⊠*Lahaina Harbor, Slip 2* ☎*808/661–0386* ⊕*www.scotchmistsailingcharters.com.*

Trilogy Excursions. With more than 35 years of sailing tradition and a deep commitment to Hawaiiana and the local ecosystem, Trilogy's reputation is among the best. It is one of only two companies that sail (rather than motor) to Molokini. A two-hour sail starts at $59. Alcohol is not provided on any cruise, but you can bring your choice of libation. Their sunset sail leaves in front of Kā'anapali Beach Hotel. Boarding the catamaran right off the shore can be tricky. Timing is everything and getting wet is inevitable, but after that it's smooth sailing. Book online for a 10% discount. ⊠ *Mā'alaea Harbor, Slip 99, Lahaina Harbor, or by the Kā'anapali Beach Hotel* ☎ *808/661–4743 or 888/225–6284* ⊕ *www.sailtrilogy.com.*

SCUBA DIVING

4

Maui, just as scenic underwater as it is on dry land, has been rated one of the top 10 dive spots in North America. A big advantage here is that divers see more large animals than they would in areas such as the Caribbean. It's common on any dive to see huge sea turtles, eagle rays, and small reef sharks, not to mention many varieties of angelfish, parrotfish, eels, and octopuses. Most of the species are unique to this area, which is unlike other popular dive destinations. For example, of Maui's 450 species of reef fish, 25% are endemic to the island. In addition, the terrain itself is different from other dive spots. Here you'll find ancient and intricate lava flows full of nooks where marine life hide and breed. Although the water tends to be a bit rougher—not to mention colder—here, divers are given a great thrill during humpback-whale season, when you can actually hear whales singing underwater.

Some of the finest diving spots in all of Hawai'i lie along the Valley Isle's western and southwestern shores. Dives are best in the morning, when visibility can hold a steady 100 feet. If you're a certified diver, you can rent gear at any Maui dive shop simply by showing your PADI or NAUI card. Unless you're familiar with the area, however, it's probably best to hook up with a dive shop for an underwater tour. Tours include tanks and weights and start around $130. Wet suits and BCs (buoyancy compensators) are rented separately, for an additional $15 to $30. Shops also offer introductory dives ($100 to $160) for those who aren't certified. ■ TIP→Before signing on with any of these outfitters, it's a good idea to ask a few pointed questions about your guide's experience, the weather outlook, and the condition of the equipment.

Before you head out on your dive, be sure to check conditions. If you have access to the Internet, check the Glenn James weather site, ⊕ *www. hawaiiweathertoday.com*, for a breakdown on the weather, wind, and visibility conditions.

BEST SPOTS

Honolua Bay (⊠ *Between mile markers 32 and 33 on Rte. 30, look for narrow dirt road to left*) has beach entry. This West Maui marine preserve is alive with many varieties of coral and tame tropical fish, including large *ulua* (jack crevalle), *kāhala*, barracuda, and manta rays. With

Snorkelers can see adorable green sea turtles around Maui.

depths of 20 to 50 feet, this is a popular summer dive spot, good for all levels. ■TIP→**High surf often prohibits winter dives.**

Only 3 mi offshore from Wailea on the South Shore, **Molokini Crater** is world renowned for its deep, crystal clear, fish-filled waters. A crescent-shaped islet formed by the eroding top of a volcano, the crater is a marine preserve ranging 10 to 80 feet in depth. The numerous tame fish and brilliant coral dwelling within the crater make it a popular introductory dive site. On calm days, the back side of Molokini (called Back Wall) can be a dramatic sight for advanced divers—giving them visibility of up to 150 feet. The enormous drop-off into the ʻAlalākeiki Channel (to 350 feet) offers awesome seascapes, black coral, and chance sightings of larger pelagic fish and sharks.

On the South Shore, a popular dive spot is **Mākena Landing,** also called Five Graves or Five Caves. About 0.2 mi down Mākena Road, you'll feast on underwater delights—caves, ledges, coral heads, and an outer reef home to a large green-sea-turtle colony (called Turtle Town). ⚠**Entry is rocky lava, so be careful where you step.** This area is for the more experienced diver. Rookies can enter farther down Mākena Road at Mākena Landing, and dive to the right.

South of Mākena Landing, the best diving by far is at ʻĀhihi Bay and La Pérouse Bay, both South Maui marine preserves. ⚠**Unfortunately, ʻĀhihi Bay is part of the newly restricted ʻĀhihi-Kīnaʻu Natural Area Reserve and is closed to all foot traffic until July 31, 2010.** If you're visiting after this date, you can look forward to exploring an area the locals call Fishbowl, which is a small cove right beside the road, next to a hexagonal house. Here you'll find excellent underwater scenery, with many types of fish and coral. ⚠️**Be careful of the rocky bottom entry (wear reef shoes if you have them).** Because no commercial dive boats are allowed in this area, it can only be reached off-shore. It can get crowded, especially in high season. If you want to steer clear of the crowds, look for a second entry ½ mi farther down the road—a gravel parking lot at the surf spot called Dumps. Entry into the bay here is trickier, as the coastline is all lava. **La Pérouse Bay,** formed from the last lava flow 20 years ago, brings you the best variety of fish—more than any other site. The lava rock provides a protective habitat, and all four types of Hawai'i's angelfish can be found here. To dive the spot called Pinnacles, enter anywhere along the shore, just past the private entrance to the beach. Again, wear your reef shoes, as entry is sharp. To the right, you'll be in the marine reserve; to the left, you're outside. Look for the white, sandy bottom with massive coral heads. Pinnacles is for experienced divers only. ⚠️**Although La Pérouse Bay remains open to the public, there are now strict limits to its land access, so check with a guide regarding any trail closures.**

EQUIPMENT, LESSONS AND TOURS

★ **Ed Robinson's Diving Adventures.** Ed wrote the book, literally, on Molokini. Because he knows so much, he includes a "Biology 101" talk with every dive. An expert marine photographer, he offers diving instruction and boat charters to South Maui, the back side of Molokini, and Lāna'i. Weekly night dives are available, and there's a 10% discount if you book three or more days. Check out the Web site for good info and links on scuba sites, weather, and sea conditions. Dives start at $135. ✉️*Box 616, Kīhei* ☎️*808/879–3584 or 800/635–1273* ⊕*www.mauiscuba.com.*

Lahaina Divers. With more than 25 years of diving experience, this West Maui shop offers tours of Maui, Molokini, and Lāna'i. Big charter boats (which can be crowded, with up to 24 divers per boat) leave daily for Molokini Crater, Back Wall, Lāna'i, Turtle Reef, and more. A Continental breakfast and deli lunch are included. Rates range from $109 to $209. For less-experienced divers, they offer a "Discover Scuba" lesson daily. ✉️*143 Dickenson St., Lahaina* ☎️*808/667–7496 or 800/998–3483* ⊕*www.lahainadivers.com.*

Maui Dive Shop. With six locations island-wide, Maui Dive Shop offers scuba charters, diving instruction, and equipment rental. Excursions, offering awe-inspiring beach and boat dives, go to Molokini Back Wall (most advanced dive), Shipwreck Beach on Lāna'i, and more. Night dives and customized trips are available, as are full SSI and PADI certificate programs. ✉️*1455 S. Kīhei Rd., Kīhei* ☎️*808/879–3388 or 800/542–3483* ⊕*www.mauidiveshop.com.*

Mike Severns Diving. This company takes small groups of up to 12 certified divers to both popular and off-the-beaten-path dive sites. Boat trips leave from Kīhei Boat Ramp, and go wherever conditions are best: the Marine Life Conservation District, Molokini's Back Wall, St. Anthony shipwreck, Mākena, La Pérouse, or the Kanaio Coast. You're free to have a guide during your dive, or go into the depths alone. The cost starts at $145 for a two-tank dive. ✉️*Box 627, Kīhei 96753* ☎️*808/879–6596* ⊕*www.mikesevernsdiving.com.*

DIVING 101

If you've always wanted gills, Hawai'i is a good place to get them. Although the bulky, heavy equipment seems freakish on shore, underwater it allows you to move about freely, almost weightlessly. As you descend into another world, you slowly grow used to the sound of your own breathing and the strangeness of being able to do so 30-plus feet down.

Most resorts offer introductory dive lessons in their pools, which allow you to acclimate to the awkward breathing apparatus before venturing out into the great blue. If you aren't starting from a resort pool, no worries. Most intro dives take off from calm, sandy beaches, such as Ulua or Kā'anapali. If you're bitten by the deep-sea bug and want to continue diving, you should get certified. Only certified divers can rent equipment or go on more-adventurous dives, such as night dives, open-ocean dives, and cave dives.

There are several certification companies, including PADI, NAUI, and SSI. PADI, the largest, is the most comprehensive. A child must be at least 10 to be certified. Once you begin your certification process, stick with the same company. The dives you log will not apply to another company's certification. (Dives with a PADI instructor, for instance, will not count toward SSI certification.) Remember that you will not be able to fly or go to the airy summit of Haleakalā within 24 hours of diving. Open-water certification will take three to four days and cost around $350. From that point on, the sky . . . or rather, the sea's the limit!

Shaka Divers. Shaka provides personalized dives including a great four-hour intro dive ($89), a refresher course ($89), scuba certification ($395), and shore dives ($59) to Ulua, Turtle Town, Bubble Cave, and more. Typical dives last about an hour, with 30 to 100 feet visibility. Dives can be booked on short notice, with afternoon tours available (hard to find on Maui). Shaka also offers night dives and torpedo scooter dives. The twilight two-tank dive is nice for day divers who want to ease into night-diving. A fun bit of trivia: owner Shaka Doug holds the world record for thickest diving logbook and most bubble rings, 34, blown in one breath. ⊠ *24 Hakoi Pl., Kīhei* ☎ *808/250–1234* ⊕ *www. shakadivers.com.*

SNORKELING

No one should leave Maui without ducking underwater to meet a sea turtle, moray eel, or humuhumunukunukuāpua'a—the state fish. ■TIP→Visibility is best in the morning, before the wind picks up.

There are two ways to approach snorkeling—by land or by sea. Daily around 7 AM, a parade of boats heads out to Lāna'i or Molokini Crater, that ancient cone of volcanic cinder off the coast of Wailea. Boat trips offer some advantages—deeper water, seasonal whale-watching, crew assistance, lunch, and gear. But you don't need a boat; much of Maui's best snorkeling is found just steps from the road. Nearly the entire leeward coastline from Kapalua south to 'Āhihi-Kīna'u offers prime opportunities to ogle fish and turtles. If you're patient and sharp-eyed, you may glimpse eels, octopuses, lobsters, eagle rays, and even a rare shark or monk seal.

BEST SPOTS

Snorkel sites here are listed from north to south, starting at the northwest corner of the island.

On the west side of the island, just north of Kapalua, **Honolua Bay** (⊠*Between mile markers 32 and 33 on Rte. 30, dirt road to left*) Marine Life Conservation District has a superb reef for snorkeling. When conditions are calm, it's one of the island's best spots with tons of fish and colorful corals to observe. ■TIP→**Make sure to bring a fish key with you, as you're sure to see many species of triggerfish, filefish, and wrasses.** The coral formations on the right side of the bay are particularly dramatic and feature pink, aqua, and orange varieties. Take care entering the water; there's no beach and the rocks and concrete ramp can be slippery.

The northeast corner of this windward-facing bay periodically gets hammered by big waves in winter, and high-profile surf contests are held here. Avoid the bay then, and after a heavy rain (you'll know because Honolua stream will be running across the access path).

Just minutes south of Honolua, dependable **Kapalua Bay** (⊠*From Rte. 30, turn onto Kapalua Pl., and walk through tunnel*) beckons. As beautiful above the water as it is below, Kapalua is exceptionally calm, even when other spots get testy. Needle and butterfly fish dart just past the sandy beach, which is why it's sometimes crowded. ⚠**Sand can be particularly hot here; watch your toes!**

Fodor'sChoice ★ We think **Black Rock** (⊠*In front of Kāʻanapali Sheraton Maui, Kāʻanapali Pkwy.*), at the northernmost tip of Kāʻanapali Beach on West Maui, is tops for snorkelers of any skill level. The entry couldn't be easier— dump your towel on the sand in front of the Sheraton Maui resort and in you go. Beginners can stick close to shore and still see lots of action. Advanced snorkelers can swim beyond the sand to the tip of Black Rock, or Kekaʻa Point, to see larger fish and eagle rays. One of the underwater residents, a turtle named "Volkswagen" for its hefty size, can be found here. He sits very still; you must look closely. Equipment can be rented on-site. Parking, in a small lot adjoining the hotel, is the only hassle.

Along Honoapiʻilani Highway (Route 30) there are several favorite snorkel sites including the area just out from the cemetery at **Hanakaoʻo Beach Park** (⊠*Near mile marker 23 on Rte. 30*). At depths of 5 and 10 feet, you can see a variety of corals, especially as you head south toward Waihikuli Wayside Park. Farther down the highway, the shallow coral reef at **Olowalu** (⊠*South of Olowalu General Store on Rte. 30, at mile marker 14*) is good for a quick underwater tour, though the best spot is a ways out, at depths of 25 feet or more. Closer to shore, the visibility can be hit or miss, but if you're willing to venture out about 50 yards, you'll have easy access to an expansive coral reef with abundant fish life—no boat required. Swim offshore toward the pole sticking out of the reef. Except for during a south swell, this area is calm and good for families with small children; turtles are plentiful. Boats sometimes stop nearby (they refer to this site as "Coral Gardens") on their return trip from Molokini.

Excellent snorkeling is found down the coastline between Kīhei and Mākena on the South Shore. ■ TIP➔The best spots are along the rocky fringes of Wailea's beaches, Mōkapu, Ulua, Wailea, and Polo, off Wailea Alanui Drive. Find one of the public parking lots sandwiched between Wailea's luxury resorts,

and enjoy these beaches' sandy entries, calm waters with relatively good visibility, and variety of fish species. Of the four beaches, Ulua has the best reef. You can glimpse a box-shaped puffer fish here, and listen to snapping shrimp and parrot fish nibbling on coral.

★ Between Maui and neighboring Kahoʻolawe, 3 mi offshore from Wailea, is the world-famous **Molokini Crater**. Its crescent-shaped rim provides a sanctuary for birds and marine life and draws masses of snorkel and dive tours year-round. Most snorkeling tour operators offer a Molokini trip. The journey to this sunken crater takes more than 90 minutes from Lahaina, an hour from Māʻalaea, and half an hour from the South Shore.

At the very southernmost tip of paved road in South Maui lies **ʻĀhihi-Kīnaʻu** (⊠*Just before end of Mākena Alanui Rd., follow marked trails through trees*) Natural Area Reserve, also referred to as La Pérouse Bay. Despite its barren, lava-scorched landscape, the area recently gained such popularity with adventurers and activity purveyors that it had to be closed to commercial traffic and is temporarily closed to all foot traffic (until July 31, 2010). If you're visiting Maui after this date, be sure to visit. A ranger is stationed at the parking lot to assist visitors. It's difficult terrain and sometimes crowded, but if you make use of the rangers' suggestions (stay on marked paths, wear sturdy shoes to hike in and out), you can experience some of the reserve's outstanding treasures, such as the sheltered cove known as the "Fish Bowl." ■ TIP➔Be sure to bring water: this is a hot and unforgiving wilderness.

EQUIPMENT

Most hotels and vacation rentals offer free use of snorkel gear. Beachside stands fronting the major resort areas rent equipment by the hour or day. ■ TIP➔Don't shy away from asking for instructions; a snug fit makes all the difference in the world. A mask fits if it sticks to your face when you inhale deeply through your nose. Fins should cover your entire foot (unlike diving fins, which strap around your heel). If you're squeamish about using someone else's gear (or need a prescription lens), pick up your own at any discount shop. Costco and Long's Drugs have better prices than ABC stores; dive shops have superior equipment.

Maui Dive Shop. You can rent pro gear (including optical masks, boogie boards, and wet suits) from six locations island-wide. Pump these guys for weather info before heading out—they'll know better than last night's

Continued on page 112

SNORKELING IN HAWAI'I

The waters surrounding the Hawaiian Islands are filled with life—from giant manta rays cruising off the Big Island's Kona Coast to humpback whales giving birth in Maui's Mā'alaea Bay. Dip your head beneath the surface to experience a spectacularly colorful world: pairs of milletseed butterflyfish dart back and forth, red-lipped parrotfish snack on coral algae, and spotted eagle rays flap past like silent spaceships. Sea turtles bask at the surface while tiny wrasses give them the equivalent of a shave and a haircut. The water quality is typically outstanding; many sites afford 30-foot-plus visibility. On snorkel cruises, you can often stare from the boat rail right down to the bottom.

Certainly few destinations are as accommodating to every level of snorkeler as Hawai'i. Beginners can tromp in from sandy beaches while more advanced divers descend to shipwrecks, reefs, craters, and sea arches just offshore. Because of Hawai'i's extreme isolation, the island chain has fewer fish species than Fiji or the Caribbean—but many of the fish that are here exist nowhere else. The Hawaiian waters are home to the highest percentage of endemic fish in the world.

The key to enjoying the underwater world is slowing down. Look carefully. Listen. You might hear the strange crackling sound of shrimp tunneling through coral, or you may hear whales singing to one another during winter. A shy octopus may drift along the ocean's floor beneath you. If you're hooked, pick up a waterproof fishkey from Long's Drugs. You can brag later that you've looked the Hawaiian turkeyfish in the eye.

4

IN FOCUS SNORKELING IN HAWAI'I

Picasso Triggerfish	Milletseed Butterflyfish*	Yellow Tang
Moorish Idol	Hawaiian Whitespotted Toby*	Saddleback Wrasse*
Red-lipped Parrotfish	Hawaiian Turkeyfish*	Zebra Moray Eel
Stocky Hawkfish	Green Sea Turtle (Honu)	Spotted Eagle Ray

*endemic to Hawai'i

POLYNESIA'S FIRST CELESTIAL NAVIGATORS: HONU

Honu is the Hawaiian name for two native sea turtles, the hawksbill and the green sea turtle. Little is known about these dinosaur-age marine reptiles, though snorkelers regularly see them foraging for *limu* (seaweed) and the occasional jellyfish in Hawaiian waters. Most female honu nest in the uninhabited Northwestern Hawaiian Islands, but a few sociable ladies nest on Maui and Big Island beaches. Scientists suspect that they navigate the seas via magnetism—sensing the earth's poles. Amazingly, they will journey up to 800 miles to nest—it's believed that they return to their own birth sites. After about 60 days of incubation, nestlings emerge from the sand at night and find their way back to the sea by the light of the stars.

TIPS ON SAFE SNORKELING

■ Snorkel with a buddy and stay together.

■ Choose a location where lifeguards are present.

■ Ask the lifeguard about conditions, especially currents, before getting in the water.

■ Plan your entry and exit points prior to getting in the water.

■ Swim into the current on entering and then ride the current back to your exit point.

■ Pop your head above the water periodically to ensure you aren't drifting too far out, or too close to rocks.

■ Think of the ocean as someone else's home—don't take anything that doesn't belong to you, or leave any trash behind.

■ Don't touch any ocean creatures; they may reveal hidden stingers.

■ Avoid bumping against coral. Touching it can kill the delicate creatures that reside within the hard shell.

■ Wear a rash guard; it will keep you from being fried by the sun.

■ When in doubt, don't go without a snorkeling professional; try a guided tour.

news forecaster, and they'll give you the real deal on conditions. ✉ *1455 S. Kīhei Rd., Kīhei* ☎ *808/873–3388* ⊕ *www.mauidiveshop.com.*

Snorkel Bob's. If you need gear, Snorkel Bob's will rent you a mask, fins, and a snorkel, and throw in a carrying bag, map, and snorkel tips for as little as $9 per week. Avoid the circle masks and go for the split-level ($26 per week); it's worth the extra cash. ✉ *Nāpili Village Hotel, 5425 Lower Honoapi'ilani Hwy., Nāpili* ☎ *808/669–9603* ✉ *Dickenson Sq., Dickenson St., Lahaina* ☎ *808/662–0104* ✉ *1279 S. Kīhei Rd., No. 310, Kīhei* ☎ *808/875–6188* ✉ *Kamaole Beach Center, 2411 S. Kīhei Rd., Kīhei* ☎ *808/879–7449* ⊕ *www.snorkelbob.com.*

TOURS

The same boats that offer whale-watching, sailing, and diving also offer snorkeling excursions. Trips usually include visits to two locales, lunch, gear, instruction, and possible whale or dolphin sightings. Some captains troll for fish along the way, and, if they're lucky, will occasionally catch big game fish such as a marlin or mahimahi.

Molokini Crater, a crescent about 3 mi offshore from Wailea, is the most popular snorkel cruise destination. You can spend half a day floating above the fish-filled crater for about $80. Some say it's not as good as it's made out to be, and that it's too crowded, but others consider it to be one of the best spots in Hawai'i. Visibility is generally outstanding and fish are incredibly tame. Your second stop will be somewhere along the leeward coast, either "Turtle Town" near Mākena or "Coral Gardens" toward Lahaina. ■ TIP➔ Be aware that on blustery mornings, there's a good chance the waters will be too rough to moor in Molokini and you'll end up snorkeling some place off the shore, which you could have driven to for free. For the safety of everyone on the boat, it's the captain's prerogative to choose the best spot for the day.

If you've tried snorkeling and are tentatively thinking about scuba, you may want to try *snuba,* a cross between the two. With snuba, you dive down 20 feet below the surface, only you're attached to an air hose from the boat. Many of the boats now offer snuba as well as snorkeling; expect to pay between $45 and $65 in addition to the regular cost of a snorkel cruise.

Snorkel cruises vary slightly—some serve mai tais and steaks whereas others offer beer and cold cuts. You might prefer a large ferryboat to a smaller sailboat, or vice versa. Whatever trip you choose, be sure you know where to go to board your vessel; getting lost in the harbor at 6 AM is a lousy start to a good day. ■TIP→Bring sunscreen, an underwater camera (they're double the price on board), a towel, and a cover-up for the windy return trip. Even tropical waters get chilly after hours of swimming, so consider wearing a rash guard. Wet suits can usually be rented for a fee. Hats without straps will blow away, and valuables should be left at home.

★ **Ann Fielding's Snorkel Maui.** For a personal introduction to Maui's undersea universe, this guided tour is the indisputable authority. A marine biologist, Fielding—formerly with the University of Hawai'i, Waikīkī Aquarium, and the Bishop Museum, and the author of several guides to island sea life—is the Carl Sagan of Hawai'i's reef cosmos. She'll not only show you fish, but she'll also introduce you to *individual* fish. This is a good first experience for dry-behind-the-ears types. Snorkel trips cost $95 per adult, and include a snack and equipment. These tours take place along the shoreline, and groups travel to snorkel sites by car, not boat. ☎808/572-8437 ⊕*www.maui.net/~annf.*

Maui Classic Charters. This company offers two top-rate snorkel trips at a good value. Hop aboard the *Four Winds II,* a 55-foot, glass-bottom catamaran, for one of the most dependable snorkel trips around. You'll spend more time than the other charter boats do at Molokini and enjoy turtle-watching on the way home. The trip includes optional snuba ($49 extra), Continental breakfast, and a deluxe barbecue lunch, beer, wine, and soda. For a faster ride, try the *Maui Magic,* Mā'alaea's fastest power cat. This boat takes fewer people (45 max) than some of the larger vessels, offers snuba, and plays Hawaiian music on the ride. This one's good for kids. Trips range from $98 to $109; book online at least seven days in advance for a $10 discount. ⊠*Mā'alaea Harbor, Slips 55 and 80* ☎*808/879-8188 or 800/736-5740* ⊕*www.mauicharters.com.*

Maui–Moloka'i Sea Cruises. If you're a landlubber who'd still like to see the sea, book a passage on the 92-foot *Prince Kuhio,* one of the largest air-conditioned cruise vessels in Maui waters. They offer snuba, snorkeling, and complimentary transportation to the harbor, which relieves you from having to park and search for the boat's slip at 7 AM. The cost is $94 per adult, and includes Continental breakfast, deli buffet lunch, and open bar. It's $51 extra for snuba. ⊠*Mā'alaea Harbor* ☎*808/242-8777 or 800/468-1287* ⊕*www.mvprince.com.*

Paragon. With this company, you get to snorkel and sail—they have some of the fastest vessels in the state. As long as conditions are good, you'll hit prime snorkel spots in Molokini, Lāna'i, and occasionally, Coral Gardens. The Molokini trip offers a simple breakfast of fruits and bagels, deli lunch by the crater, juice, soda and beer. The Lāna'i trip includes a Continental breakfast, a picnic lunch on the beach, snacks, open bar, a snorkel lesson, and plenty of time in the water. The friendly crew takes good care of you, making sure you get the most value and enjoyment from your trip. ⊠ *Mā'alaea Harbor Slip 72, or Lahaina Harbor* ☎ *808/244–2087* ⊕ *www.sailmaui.com.*

Teralani Sailing Charters. Snorkel choices vary between a regular trip that serves a deli lunch or a premier snorkel that's one hour longer with two snorkel sites and a barbecue-style lunch. Freshwater showers are available, and so is an open bar after the second snorkel stop. A friendly crew provides all your gear, flotation device, and a snorkeling crash course if necessary. Although there is no official naturalist aboard this comfortable vessel, crew members don't shy from imparting helpful tidbits about the snorkel sites and its marine life. Boarding is right off Dig Me Beach in front of Leilani's at Whalers Village. Parking is convenient and validated. ⊠ *2435 Kā'anapali Pkwy., Kā'anapali* ☎ *808/661–1230* ⊕ *www.teralani.net.*

♻ ★ **Trilogy Excursions.** The longest-running operation on Maui is the Coon family's Trilogy Excursions. In terms of comprehensive offerings, this company's got it: six beautiful multihulled sailing vessels (though they usually only sail for a brief portion of the trip) at three departure sites. All excursions are manned by energetic crews who will keep you well fed and entertained with stories of the Islands and plenty of corny jokes. A full-day catamaran cruise to Lāna'i includes Continental breakfast and barbecue lunch on board, a guided van tour of the island, a "Snorkeling 101" class, and time to snorkel in the waters of Lāna'i's Hulopo'e Marine Preserve (Trilogy has exclusive commercial access). There is a barbecue dinner on Lāna'i and an optional dolphin safari. The company also offers a Molokini and Honolua Bay snorkel cruise that is top-notch. Many people consider a Trilogy excursion the highlight of their trip. ⊠ *Mā'alaea Harbor, Slip 99, Lahaina Harbor, or by Kā'anapali Beach Hotel* ☎ *808/661–4743 or 888/225–6284* ⊕ *www. sailtrilogy.com.*

SURFING

Maui's diverse coastline has surf for every level of waterman or—woman. Waves on leeward-facing shores (West and South Maui) tend to break in gentle sets all summer long. Surf instructors in Kīhei and Lahaina can rent you boards, give you onshore instruction, and then lead you out through the channel, where it's safe to enter the surf. They'll shout encouragement while you paddle like mad for the thrill of standing on water—some will even give you a helpful shove. These areas are great for beginners; the only danger is whacking a stranger with your board or stubbing your toe against the reef.

The North Shore is another story. Winter waves pound the windward coast, attracting water champions from every corner of the world. Adrenaline addicts are towed in by Jet Ski to a legendary, deep-sea break called "Jaws." Waves here periodically tower upward of 40 feet, dwarfing the helicopters seeking to capture unbelievable photos. The only spot for viewing this phenomenon (which happens just a few times a year) is on private property. So, if you hear the surfers next to you crowing about Jaws "going off," cozy up and get them to take you with them.

Stand-up paddle surfing, where you stand on a longboard and paddle out with a canoe oar, is the new "comeback kid" of surf sports. Paddleboarding requires even more balance and coordination than regular surfing. But these days you can almost always see at least one lone paddler amid the pack—watch for them.

> ### HOW BIG IS BIG?
>
> Before heading out for any water activity, be sure to get a weather and wave report, and make sure the surf report you get is the *full face value* of the wave. "Hawaiian style" cuts the wave size in half. For instance, a Hawaiian might say a wave is 5 feet high, which means 10 feet if you're from New Jersey or Florida. For years, scientists and surfers were using different measurements, as Hawai'i locals measured waves from median sea level to the crest. These days, most surf reports are careful to distinguish between the two—but it can still get confusing.

Whatever your skill, there's a board, a break, and even a surf guru to accommodate you. A two-hour lesson is a good intro to surf culture. Surf camps are becoming increasingly popular, especially with women. One- or two-week camps offer a terrific way to build muscle and self-esteem simultaneously. **Maui Surfer Girls** (⊕ *www.mauisurfergirls.com*) immerses adventurous young ladies in wave-riding wisdom during overnight, one- and two-week camps. Coed camps are sponsored by **Action Sports Maui** (⊕ *www.actionsportsmaui.com*).

BEST SPOTS

Beginners can hang 10 at Kīhei's **Cove Park** (⊠ *S. Kīhei Rd., Kīhei*), on the South Shore, a sometimes crowded but reliable 1- to 2-foot break. Boards can easily be rented across the street, or in neighboring Kalama Park parking lot. The only bummer is having to balance the 9-plus-foot board on your head while crossing busy South Kīhei Road. But hey, that wouldn't stop world-famous longboarder Eddie Aikau, now would it?

Long- or shortboarders can paddle out anywhere along Lahaina's coastline. One option is at **Launiupoko State Wayside** (⊠ *Honoapi'ilani Hwy. near mile marker 18*). The east end of the park has an easy break, good for beginners. **Ukumehame** (⊠ *Honoapi'ilani Hwy. near mile marker 12*), also called "Thousand Peaks," is one of the better beginners' spots. You'll soon see how the spot got its name—the waves here break again and again in wide and consistent rows, giving lots of room for beginning and intermediate surfers.

Other **good surf spots** in West Maui include "Grandma's" at **Papalaua Park**, just after the *pali* (cliff)—where waves are so easy a grandma could ride 'em; **Puamana Beach Park** for a mellow longboard day; and **Lahaina Harbor**, which offers an excellent inside wave for beginners (called "Breakwall"), as well as the more-advanced outside (a great lift if there's a big south swell).

For advanced wave riders, **Ho'okipa Beach Park** (⊠ *2 mi past Pā'ia on Hāna Hwy.*) boasts several well-loved breaks, including "Pavilions," "Lanes," "the Point," and "Middles." Surfers have priority until 11 AM, when windsurfers move in on the action. ■TIP➔**Competition is stiff here, and the attitudes can be "agro." If you don't know what you're doing, consider watching from the shore.**

You can get the wave report each day by checking page 2 of the *Maui News*, logging onto the Glenn James weather site at ⊕ *www.hawaii weathertoday.com*, or calling ☎ *808/871–5054* (for the weather forecast) or ☎ *808/877–3611* (for the surf report).

EQUIPMENT AND LESSONS

Big Kahuna Adventures. Rent surfboards (soft-top longboards) here for $20 for two hours, or $30 for the day. The shop also offers surf lessons, and rents kayaks and snorkel gear. Located across from Cove Park, the company has been around for 12 years. ⊠ *1913-C S. Kīhei Rd., Kīhei* ☎ *808/875–6395* ⊕ *www.bigkahunaadventures.com*.

★ **Goofy Foot.** Surfing "goofy foot" means putting your right foot forward. They might be goofy, but we like the right-footed gurus here. Their safari shop is just plain cool and only steps away from "Breakwall," a great beginner's spot in Lahaina. Two-hour classes with five or fewer students are $65, and six-hour classes with lunch and an ocean-safety course are $300. They promise you'll be standing within a two-hour lesson—or it's free. Owner and "stoke broker" Tim Sherer offers private lessons for $200 and will sometimes ride alongside to record video clips and give more-thorough feedback. ⊠ *505 Front St., Suite 123, Lahaina* ☎ *808/244–9283* ⊕ *www.goofyfootsurfschool.com*.

Hāna Highway Surf. If you're heading out to the North Shore surf, you can pick up boards ranging from beginner's soft-tops to high-performance shortboards here for $20 per day. ⊠ *149 Hāna Hwy., Pā'ia* ☎ *808/579–8999*.

Hi-Tech Surf Sports. Locals hold Hi-Tech in the highest regard. They have some of the best boards, advice, and attitudes around. Rent surfboards for $20 per day; $112 for the week. They rent even their best models—choose from longboards, shortboards, and hybrids. All rentals come with board bags, roof racks, and, oh yeah, wax. ⊠ *425 Koloa St., Kahului* ☎ *808/877–2111* ⊕ *www.htmaui.com.*

★ **Nancy Emerson School of Surfing.** Nancy's motto is "If my dog can surf, so can you." Instructors here will get even the most shaky novice riding with their "Learn to Surf in One Lesson" program. A two-hour group lesson (five students max) is $78. Nancy currently lives in Australia, but private lessons with her equally qualified instructors are $165–$200 for two hours. Semiprivate lessons with two people are $130 per person. Multiple-day sessions start at $350. They provide boards and rash guards. ⊠ *505 Front St., Suite 224B, Lahaina* ☎ *808/244–7873* ⊕ *www.mauisurfclinics.com.*

Royal Hawaiian Surf Academy. Owner Kimo Kinimaka grew up rippin' it with uncle and legendary surfer Titus Kinimaka, so it's no wonder his passion translates to a fun, memorable time at the novice-friendly Lahaina Breakwall. Private lessons are available for $130 and semiprivate for $190 total. Group lessons cost $65 per person. Rash guards and shoes are provided. ⊠ *117 Prison St., Lahaina* ☎ *808/276–7873* ⊕ *www.royalhawaiiansurfacademy.com.*

Second Wind. Surfboard rentals at this centrally located shop are a deal— good boards go for $20 per day or $110 per week. They also rent and sell their own *Elua Makani* boards (which means second wind in Hawaiian). Although they don't offer lessons themselves, they will book you with the best surfing, windsurfing, and kiteboarding lessons on the island. ⊠ *111 Hāna Hwy., Kahului* ☎ *808/877–7467 or 800/936–7787* ⊕ *www.secondwindmaui.com.*

WHALE-WATCHING

From December into May, whale-watching becomes one of the most popular activities on Maui. During the season, all outfitters offer whale-watching in addition to their regular activities, and most do an excellent job. Boats leave the wharves at Lahaina and Mā'alaea in search of humpbacks, allowing you to enjoy the awe-inspiring size of these creatures in closer proximity.

As it's almost impossible *not* to see whales in winter on Maui, you'll want to prioritize: is adventure or comfort your aim? If close encounters with the giants of the deep are your desire, pick a smaller boat that promises sightings. Those who think "green" usually prefer the smaller, quieter vessels that produce the least amount of negative impact to the whales' natural environment. If an impromptu marine-biology lesson sounds fun, go with the Pacific Whale Foundation. Two-hour forays into the whales' world are around $30. For those wanting to sip mai tais as whales cruise calmly by, stick with a sunset cruise on a boat with an open bar and *pūpū* (Hawaiian tapas) ($40 and up). ■ TIP→**Afternoon trips are generally rougher because the wind picks up, but some say this is when the most surface action occurs.**

Every captain aims to please during whale season, getting as close as legally possible (100 yards). Crew members know when a whale is

CLOSE UP

The Humpback's Winter Home

The humpback whales' attraction to Maui is legendary. More than half the Pacific's humpback population winters in Hawai'i, especially in the waters around the Valley Isle, where mothers can be seen just a few hundred feet offshore training their young calves in the fine points of whale etiquette. Watching from shore it's easy to catch sight of whales spouting, or even breaching—when they leap almost entirely out of the sea, slapping back onto the water with a huge splash.

At one time there were thousands of the huge mammals, but a history of overhunting and marine pollution dwindled the world population to about 1,500. In 1966 humpbacks were put on the endangered-species list. Hunting or harassing whales is illegal in the waters of most nations, and in the United States boats and airplanes are restricted from getting too close. The word is still out, however, on the effects military sonar testing has on marine mammals.

Marine biologists believe the humpbacks (much like the humans) keep returning

to Hawai'i because of its warmth. Having fattened themselves in subarctic waters all summer, the whales migrate south in the winter to breed, and a rebounding population of thousands cruise Maui waters. Winter is calving time, and the young whales, born with little blubber, probably couldn't survive in the frigid Alaskan waters. No one has ever seen a whale give birth here, but experts know that calving is their main winter activity, since the 1- and 2-ton youngsters suddenly appear while the whales are in residence.

The first sighting of a humpback whale spout each season is exciting and reassuring for locals on Maui. A collective sigh of relief can be heard, "Ah, they've returned." In the not-so-far distance, flukes and flippers can be seen rising above the ocean's surface. It's hard not to anthropomorphize the tail-waving; it looks like such an amiable, human gesture. Each fluke is uniquely patterned, like a human's fingerprint, and is used to identify the giants as they travel halfway around the globe and back.

about to dive (after several waves of its heart-shaped tail) but rarely can predict breaches (when the whale hurls itself up and almost entirely out of the water). Prime-viewing space (on the upper and lower decks, around the railings) is limited, so boats can feel crowded even when half full. If you don't want to squeeze in beside strangers, opt for a smaller boat with fewer bookings. Don't forget to bring sunscreen, sunglasses, a light long-sleeve cover-up, and a hat you can secure. Winter weather is less predictable and at times can be extreme, especially as the wind picks up. Arrive early to find parking.

BEST SPOTS

From December 15 to May 1 the Pacific Whale Foundation has naturalists stationed in two places—on the rooftop of their headquarters and at the scenic viewpoint at **Papawai Point Lookout** (⊠ *Rte. 30, 3 mi west of Māʻalaea Harbor*). Just like the commuting traffic, whales cruise along the *pali*, or cliff-side, of West Maui's Honoapiʻilani Highway

Humpback whale calves are plentiful in winter; this one is breaching off West Maui.

all day long. ⚠Make sure to park safely before craning your neck out to see them.

The northern end of **Keawakapu Beach** (⊠*S. Kīhei Rd. near Kilohana Dr.*) seems to be a whale magnet. Situate yourself on the sand or at the nearby restaurant, and you're bound to see a mama whale patiently teaching her calf the exact technique of flipper-waving.

BOATS AND CHARTERS

Marine Charters. Three-hour cruises narrated by a naturalist are offered aboard *Pride of Maui,* a 65-foot power catamaran (149 passengers max). There's a main cabin, upper sundeck, and swim platform—and you can listen to the whales sing. Trips start at $41.95 per adult, and include *pūpū* (Hawaiian tapas) and an open bar. ⊠*Māʻalaea Harbor, Slip 70* ☎*877/867–7433 or 808/242–0955* ⊕*www.prideofmaui. com.*

⟳ **Pacific Whale Foundation.** This nonprofit organization pioneered whale-
★ watching back in 1979 and now runs four boats, with 15 trips daily. As the most recognizable name in whale-watching, the crew (with a certified marine biologist on board) offers insights into whale behavior (do they *really* know what those tail flicks mean?) and suggests ways for you to help save marine life worldwide. The best part about these trips is the underwater hydrophone that allows you to actually listen to the whales sing. Trips meet at the Foundation's store, where you can buy whale paraphernalia, snacks, and coffee—a real bonus for 8 AM trips. Passengers are then herded much like migrating whales down to the harbor. These trips are more affordable than others, but you'll be sharing the boat with about 100 people in stadium seating. Once you catch

sight of the wildlife up-close, however, you can't help but be thrilled. ✉ *Mā'alaea and Lahaina harbors* ☎ *800/942–5311 or 808/249–8811* ⊕ *www.pacificwhale.org.*

★ **Trilogy Excursions.** Trilogy whale-watching trips consist of smaller crowds of about 20 to 30 passengers, and include beverages and snacks, an onboard marine naturalist, and hydrophones (microphones that detect underwater sound waves). Trips are $39 plus tax. Book online for a discount. ✉ *Loading at Kā'anapali Beach Hotel* ☎ *808/661–4743 or 888/225–6284* ⊕ *www.sailtrilogy.com.*

WINDSURFING

Something about Maui's wind and water stirs the spirit of innovation. Windsurfing, invented in the 1950s, found its true home at Ho'okipa on Maui's North Shore in 1980. Seemingly overnight, windsurfing pros from around the world flooded the area. Equipment evolved, amazing film footage was captured, and a new sport was born.

If you're new to the action, you can get lessons from the experts islandwide. For a beginner, the best thing about windsurfing is (unlike surfing) you don't have to paddle. Instead, you have to hold on like heck to a flapping sail, as it whisks you into the wind. Needless to say, you're going to need a little coordination and balance to pull this off.

Instructors start you out on a beach at Kanahā, where the big boys go. Lessons range from two-hour introductory classes to five-day advanced "flight school." If you're an old salt, pick up tips and equipment from the companies below.

BEST SPOTS

After **Ho'okipa Bay** (✉ *2 mi past Pā'ia on Hāna Hwy.*) was discovered by windsurfers three decades ago, this windy beach 10 mi east of Kahului gained an international reputation. The spot is blessed with optimal wave-sailing wind and sea conditions, and can offer the ultimate aerial experience.

In summer the windsurfing crowd heads south to **Kalepolepo Beach** (✉ *S. Kīhei Rd. near Ohukai St.*) on the South Shore. Trade winds build in strength and by afternoon a swarm of dragonfly-sails can be seen skimming the whitecaps, with the West Maui Mountains as a backdrop.

A great site for speed, **Kanahā Beach Park** (✉ *Behind Kahului Airport*) is dedicated to beginners in the morning hours, before the waves and wind really get roaring. After 11 AM, the professionals choose from their quiver of sails the size and shape best suited for the day's demands. This beach tends to have smaller waves and forceful winds—sometimes sending sailors flying at 40 knots. ■TIP→If you aren't ready to go pro, this is a great place for a picnic while you watch from the beach.

EQUIPMENT AND LESSONS

Action Sports Maui. The quirky, friendly professionals here will meet you at Kanahā on the North Shore, outfit you with your sail and board, and guide you through your first "jibe" or turn. They promise your learning time will be cut in half. Don't be afraid to ask lots of questions. Lessons are held at 9 AM every morning except Sunday at Kanahā, and start at $69 for a two-hour class. Three- and five-day courses cost $225 and $375. ⊠6 E. Waipuilani Rd., Kīhei ☎808/871–5857 ⊕www. actionsportsmaui.com.

Hi-Tech Surf Sports. Known locally as Maui's finest windsurfing school, Hawaiian Sailboarding Techniques (HST, located in Hi-Tech) brings you quality instruction by skilled sailors. Founded by Alan Cadiz, an accomplished World Cup Pro, the school sets high standards for a safe, quality windsurfing experience. Intro classes start at $79 for 2½ hours, gear included. Hi-Tech itself offers excellent equipment rentals; $50 gets you a board, two sails, a mast, and roof racks for 24 hours. ⊠425 Koloa St., Kahului ☎808/877–2111 ⊕www.hstwindsurfing.com.

Second Wind. Located in Kahului, this company rents boards with two sails for $46 per day. Boards with three sails go for $49 per day. Intro classes start at $79. ⊠11 Hāna Hwy., Kahului ☎808/877–7467 ⊕www.secondwindmaui.com.

5

Golf, Hiking, and Outdoor Activities

WORD OF MOUTH

"Walking through the bamboo forest on the Pipiwai Trail on Maui was a unique experience. The waterfall at the end was a worthy payoff."

—iamq

Updated by
Heidi Pool

You may come to Maui to sprawl out on the sand, but you'll soon realize there's much more here than the beach. For a relatively small island, Maui's interior landscapes vary wildly, from the moonlike surface of Haleakalā Crater to the green rain forest of 'Īao Valley State Park. Whether you're exploring waterfalls on a day hike, riding horseback through ranchlands, soaring on a zipline, taking an exhilarating bicycle ride down Haleakalā, or teeing off on a world-class golf course, there's plenty to keep you busy.

Maui's exceptional climate affords year-round opportunities for exploring and participating in the myriad outdoor activities the island has to offer. There's something for every outdoor enthusiast, regardless of age, interest, or fitness level. This chapter will get your toes out of the sand and into your hiking boots or golf shoes. For easy reference, activities are listed in alphabetical order.

AERIAL TOURS

Helicopter flight-seeing excursions can take you over the West Maui Mountains, Hāna, Haleakalā Crater, even the Big Island lava flow or the island of Moloka'i. This is a beautiful, exciting way to see the island, and the *only* way to see some of its most dramatic areas and waterfalls. Tour prices usually include a DVD of your trip so you can relive the experience at home. Prices run from about $200 for a half-hour rainforest tour to more than $500 for a 90-minute megaexperience that includes a champagne toast on landing. Generally the 45- to 50-minute flights are the best value, and if you're willing to chance it, considerable discounts may be available if you call last minute or book online.

It takes about 90 minutes to travel inside the volcano, then down to the village of Hāna. Some companies stop in secluded areas for refreshments. Helicopter-tour operators throughout the state come under sharp scrutiny for passenger safety and equipment maintenance. Don't be shy; ask about a company's safety record, flight paths, age of equipment, and level of operator experience. Generally, though, if they're still in business they're doing something right.

Air Maui Helicopters. Air Maui prides itself on a perfect safety record, and provides 45- to 65-minute flights covering the waterfalls of the West Maui Mountains, Haleakalā Crater, Hāna, even the spectacular sea cliffs of Moloka'i. Prices range from $256 to $338 with considerable discounts available on the Web site. Charter flights are also available. ⊠ *Kahului Heliport, Hangar 110, Kahului* ☎ *877/238–4942 or 808/877–7005* ⊕ *www.airmaui.com.*

Blue Hawaiian Helicopters. This company has provided aerial adventures in Hawai'i since 1985 and has been integral in some of the filming Hollywood has done on Maui. Its EcoStar helicopters are air-conditioned and have noise-blocking headsets for all passengers. Flights are 30 to 90 minutes and cost $220 to $560. Charter flights are also available. ⊠ *Kahului Heliport, Hangar 105, Kahului* ☎ *808/871–8844 or 800/745–2583* ⊕ *www.bluehawaiian.com.*

Sunshine Helicopters. Sunshine offers tours of Maui and Moloka'i in its *Black Beauty* AStar or WhisperStar aircraft. A pilot-narrated DVD of your actual flight is available for purchase. Prices start at $200 for 30 to 105 minutes. First-class seating is available for an additional fee. ⊠ *Kahului Heliport, Hangar 107, Kahului* ☎ *808/270–3999 or 866/501–7738* ⊕ *www.sunshinehelicopters.com.*

BIKING

Maui County biking is safer and more convenient than in the past, but long distances and mountainous terrain keep it from being a practical mode of travel. Still, painted bike lanes enable cyclists to travel all the way from Mākena to Kapalua, and you'll see hardy souls battling the trade winds under the hot Maui sun.

Several companies offer guided bike tours down Haleakalā. This activity is a great way to enjoy an easy, gravity-induced bike ride, but isn't for those not confident in their ability to handle a bike. The ride is inherently dangerous due to the slope, sharp turns, and the fact that you're riding down an actual road with cars on it. That said, the guided bike companies do take every safety precaution. A few companies offer unguided (or as they like to say "self-guided") tours where they provide you with the bike and transportation to the mountain and then you're free to descend at your own pace. Most companies offer discounts for Internet bookings.

Haleakalā National Park no longer allows commercial downhill bicycle rides within the park's boundaries. As a result, tour amenities and routes vary by company. Be sure to ask about sunrise viewing from the Haleakalā summit, if this is an important feature for you. Some lesser-priced tours begin at the 6,500-foot elevation just *outside* the National Park boundaries, where you will be unable to view the sunrise over the crater. Also keep in mind that weather conditions on Haleakalā vary greatly, so a visible sunrise can never be guaranteed. Sunrise is downright cold at the summit, so be sure to dress in layers and wear closed-toe shoes.

Each company has its own age and weight restrictions, and pregnant women are discouraged from participating, although they are generally welcome to ride in the escort van. You should also reconsider this activity if you have difficulty with high altitudes or are taking medications that may cause drowsiness.

BEST SPOTS

Though it's changing, at present there are few truly good spots to ride on Maui. Street bikers will want to head out to scenic **Thompson Road** (⊠ *Off Rte. 37, Kula Hwy., Keokea*). It's quiet, gently curvy, and flanked by gorgeous views on both sides. Plus, because it's at a higher elevation, the air temperature is cooler and the wind lighter. The coast back down toward Kahului on the Kula Highway is worth the ride up. Mountain bikers have favored the remote **Polipoli Spring State Recreation Area** (⊠ *Off Rte. 377, end of Waipoli Rd.*) for its bumpy trail through an unlikely forest of conifers.

EQUIPMENT AND TOURS

Bike It Maui. This small, family-owned company offers only one guided tour down Haleakalā each day. The price of $139 includes pick-up and drop-off at your hotel, a sunrise van tour of the summit, a guided 28-mi bicycle ride down the mountain, and a full sit-down breakfast at Charley's Restaurant in Pāʻia. Gratuity is also included. Riders must be at least 12 years old and weigh no more than 250 pounds. ☎ *808/878–3364 or 866/776–2453* ⊕ *www.bikeitmaui.com.*

Cruiser Phil's Volcano Riders. Owner Phil Feliciano ("Cruiser Phil") has been in the downhill bicycle industry for 25 years. He offers sunrise and morning tours, which cost $150, and include hotel pick-up and drop-off, Continental breakfast at the company's base in Kahului, a van tour of the summit, and a guided 28-mi ride down the mountain. Riders will make a no-host meal stop in either Kula or Pāʻia. Participants should be at least 15 and under 65 years old; be at least 5 feet tall and weigh no more than 275 pounds; and have ridden a bicycle in the past 12 months. ⊠ *58-A Amala Pl., Kahului* ☎ *808/893–2332 or 877/764–2453* ⊕ *www.cruiserphil.com.*

Haleakalā Bike Company. If you're thinking about an unguided Haleakalā bike trip, consider one of the trips offered by this company. Meet at the Old Haʻikū Cannery and take their van shuttle to the summit. Along the way you'll learn about the history of the island, the volcano, and other Hawaiiana. Unlike the guided trips, food is not included but there are several spots along the way down to stop, rest, and eat. The simple, mostly downhill route takes you right back to the cannery where you started. HBC also offers bike sales, rentals, and services. Tour prices range from $60 to $100. ⊠ *810 Haʻikū Rd., Suite 120, Haʻikū* ☎ *808/575–9575 or 888/922–2453* ⊕ *www.bikemaui.com.*

Island Biker. This is the premier bike shop on Maui when it comes to rentals, sales, and service. They offer 2005 Specialized standard front-shock bikes, road bikes, and full-suspension mountain bikes. Daily or weekly rates range from $50 to $150, and include a helmet, pump, water bottle, flat-repair kit, and spare tube. They can suggest routes appropriate for mountain or road biking, or you can join a biweekly group ride. ⊠ *415 Dairy Rd., Kahului* ☎ *808/877–7744* ⊕ *www.islandbikermaui.com.*

Maui Downhill. If biking down the side of Haleakalā sounds like fun, several companies are ready to book you a tour. Maui Downhill vans pick you up at your resort, shuttle you to the mountain, help you onto a bike, and follow you as you coast down through clouds and gorgeous scenery into the town of Pukalani. Ask about different trips: less expensive ones don't go to the summit itself for sunrise viewing. There is also a combination bike and winery tour that gives you an opportunity to visit Maui's winery (also known as Tedeschi Vineyards). Treks cost $125 to $175, and include a Continental breakfast at the company's base. ⊠ *199 Dairy Rd., Kahului* ☎ *808/871–2155 or 800/535–2453* ⊕ *www.mauidownhill.com.*

WORD OF MOUTH

"With the idea of NOT busting your budget, I'd recommend the Maui Lani Dunes course (right outside of Kahului), Pukalani (on the slopes of Haleakalā) or elleair (in Kīhei). Unfortunately, you won't get any ocean views at Maui Lani (though it's a great course)."   –travelinandgolfin

West Maui Cycles. Servicing the west side of the island, WMC offers an assortment of cycles including cruisers for $15 per day ($60 per week); hybrids for $30 per day ($120 per week); and Cannondale road bikes and front-suspension Giantbikes for $50 per day ($200 per week). Sales and service are available. ⊠ *1087 Limahana Pl., No. 6, Lahaina* ☎ *808/661–9005* ⊕ *www.westmauicycles.com.*

EXTREME SPORTS

Maui Canyon Adventures. If the idea of exploring canyons by hiking, climbing, swimming, and rappelling appeals to you, this company stands ready, willing, and able to accommodate. Their friendly, knowledgeable guides encourage and assist you literally every step of the way. You must be at least 10 years old to participate and have a waist size no larger than 54 inches. Rappelling is a fairly strenuous activity, so be prepared for a workout. The tour price of $150 includes all gear, lunch, bottled water, mosquito repellent, and transportation to and from the site from their pickup point in Kahului. Observers may pay a lesser fee ($100) to do all but the rappelling. You can expect to walk over rugged muddy terrain, so be sure to dress accordingly. ☎ *808/270–1500* ⊕ *www.mauicanyons.com.*

GOLF

Maui's natural beauty and surroundings offer some of the most jaw-dropping vistas imaginable on a golf course. Holes run across small bays, past craggy lava outcrops, and up into cool, forested mountains. Most courses have mesmerizing ocean views, some close enough to feel the salt in the air. And although many of the courses are affiliated with resorts (and therefore a little pricier), the general-public courses are no less impressive. You might even consider a ferry ride to the neighbor island of Lāna'i for a round on either of its two championship courses *(see Chapter 11, Lāna'i).*

Green Fees: Green fees listed here are the highest course rates per round on weekdays and weekends for U.S. residents. (Some courses charge non–U.S. residents higher prices.) Discounts are often available for

BEFORE YOU HIT THE 1ST TEE . . .

Golf is golf, and Hawai'i is part of the United States, but Island golf nevertheless has its own quirks. Here are a few tips to make your golf experience in the Islands more pleasant.

■ Sunscreen. Buy it, apply it (minimum 30 SPF). The subtropical rays of the sun are intense, even in December. Good advice is to apply sunscreen, at a minimum, on the 1st and 10th tees.

■ Stay hydrated. Spending four-plus hours in the sun and heat means you'll perspire away considerable fluids and energy.

■ All resort courses and many daily fee courses provide rental clubs. In many cases, they're the latest lines from top manufacturers. This is true both for men and women, as well as for left-handers, which means you don't have to schlep clubs across the Pacific.

■ Pro-shops at most courses are well stocked with balls, tees, and

other accoutrements, so even if you bring your own bag, it needn't weigh a ton.

■ Come spikeless—very few Hawai'i courses still permit metal spikes. And most of the resort courses require a collared shirt.

■ Maui is notorious for its trade winds. Consider playing early if you want to avoid the wind, and remember that although it will frustrate you at times and make club selection difficult, you may very well see some of your longest drives ever.

■ In theory you can play golf in Hawai'i 365 days a year, but there's a reason the Hawaiian Islands are so green. An umbrella and light jacket can come in handy.

■ Unless you play a muni or certain daily fee courses, plan on taking a cart. Riding carts are mandatory at most courses and are included in the green fee.

resort guests and for those who book tee times on the Web. Rental clubs may or may not be included with green fee. Twilight fees are usually offered; call individual courses for information.

■TIP→Resort courses, in particular, offer more than the usual three sets of tees, sometimes four or five. So bite off as much or little challenge as you like. Tee it up from the tips and you'll end up playing a few 600-yard par 5s and see a few 250-yard forced carries.

WEST MAUI

★ **Kā'anapali Golf Resort.** The Royal Kā'anapali (North) Course (1962) is one of three in Hawai'i designed by Robert Trent Jones Sr., the godfather of modern golf architecture. The greens average a whopping 10,000 square feet, necessary because of the often-severe undulation. The par-4 18th hole (into the prevailing trade breezes, with out-of-bounds on the left, and a lake on the right) is notoriously tough. The Kā'anapali Kai (South) Course (Arthur Jack Snyder, 1976) shares similar seaside-into-the-hills terrain, but is rated a couple of strokes easier, mostly because putts are less treacherous. ⊠2290 Kā'anapali Pkwy., Lahaina ☎808/661–9676 or 866/454–4653 ⊕www.kaanapali-golf.

com ✹ *North Course: 18 holes. 6500 yds. Par 71. Slope 126. Green Fee: $235. South Course: 18 holes. 6400 yds. Par 70. Slope 124. Green Fee: $195* ☞ *Facilities: Driving range, putting green, golf carts, rental clubs, lessons, restaurant, bar.*

Fodor's Choice **Kapalua Resort.** Perhaps Hawai'i's best-known golf resort and the crown
★ jewel of golf on Maui, Kapalua hosts the PGA Tour's first event each
January: the Mercedes-Benz Championship at the Plantation Course
at Kapalua. Ben Crenshaw and Bill Coore (1991) tried to incorporate traditional shot values in a very nontraditional site, taking into
account slope, gravity, and the prevailing trade winds. The par-5 18th,
for instance, plays 663 yards from the back tees (600 yards from the
resort tees). The hole drops 170 feet in elevation, narrowing as it goes
to a partially guarded green, and plays downwind and down-grain.
Despite the longer-than-usual distance, the slope is great enough and
the wind at your back usually brisk enough to reach the green with
two well-struck shots—a truly unbelievable finish to a course that will
challenge, frustrate, and reward the patient golfer.

The Bay Course (Arnold Palmer and Francis Duane, 1975) is the more
traditional of Kapalua's courses, with gentle rolling fairways and generous greens. The most memorable hole is the par-3 fifth, with a tee
shot that must carry a turquoise finger of Onelua Bay. The Kapalua
Golf Academy (☒*1000 Office Rd., Kapalua* ☎*808/665–5455 or
877/527–2582*) offers 23 acres of practice turf and 11 teeing areas, a
special golf fitness gym, and an instructional bay with video analysis.
Each of the courses has a separate clubhouse. The Bay Course: ☒*300
Kapalua Dr., Kapalua* ☎*808/669–8044 or 877/527–2582* ⊕*www.
kapaluamaui.com/golf* ✹ *18 holes. 6600 yds. Par 72. Slope 133. Green
Fee: $215* ☞ *Facilities: Driving range, putting green, rental clubs, pro-
shop, lessons, restaurant, bar.* The Plantation Course: ☒*2000 Plantation Club Dr., Kapalua* ☎*808/669–8044 or 877/527–2582* ⊕*www.
kapaluamaui.com/golf* ✹ *18 holes. 7411 yds. Par 73. Slope 135. Green
Fee: $295* ☞ *Facilities: Driving range, putting green, golf carts, pull
carts, rental clubs, pro-shop, golf academy/lessons, restaurant, bar.*

THE SOUTH SHORE

elleair Maui Golf Club. Formerly known as Silversword (1987), elleair
is an exacting test. Fairways tend to be narrow, especially in landing
areas, and can be quite a challenge when the trade winds come up in the
afternoon. The course is lined with enough coconut trees to make them
a collective hazard, not just a nutty nuisance. ☒*1345 Pi'ilani Hwy.,
Kīhei* ☎*808/874–0777* ⊕*elleairmauigolfclub.com* ✹ *18 holes. 6404
yds. Par 71. Slope 117. Green Fee: $120* ☞ *Facilities: Driving range,
putting green, golf carts, rental clubs, pro-shop, lessons.*

Fodor's Choice **Mākena Resort.** Robert Trent Jones Jr. and Don Knotts (not the actor)
★ built the first course at Mākena in 1981. A decade later Jones was
asked to create 18 totally new holes and blend them with the existing
course to form the North and South courses, which opened in 1994.
Both courses—sculpted from the lava flows on the western flank of
Haleakalā—offer quick greens with lots of breaks, and plenty of scenic

ON THE SIDELINES

Maui has a number of golf tournaments, most of which are of professional caliber and worth watching. Many are also televised nationally. One attention-getter is the **Mercedes-Benz Championship** (☎*808/665–9160 or 888/665–9160*) held in January. This is the first official PGA tour event, held on Kapalua's Plantation Course. A clambake feast at the Ritz-Carlton, Kapalua, tops off the **Kapalua Clambake Pro-Am** (☎*808/665–9198*) in July. The **Kapalua LPGA Classic** held in October (☎*808/665–9160*) features the world's top pro women golfers on Kapalua's Bay Course.

Over in Wailea, in May, self-proclaimed "lunatic" golfers play 100 holes of golf from sunrise to sunset in the annual **Ka Lima O Maui Celebrity 100** (☎*808/875–7450*), a fund-raiser for local charity Ka Lima O Maui. The nationally televised **Wendy's Championship Senior Skins** (☎*808/875–7450*) tournament, held on Wailea's Gold Course in January, pits four of the most respected Senior PGA players against one another.

distractions. On the North Course, the fourth is one of the most picturesque inland par 3s in Hawai'i, with the green guarded on the right by a pond. The sixth is an excellent example of option golf: the fairway is sliced up the middle by a gaping ravine, which must sooner or later be crossed to reach the green. Although trees frame most holes on the North Course, the South Course is more open. This means it plays somewhat easier off the tee, but the greens are trickier. The view from the elevated tee of the par-5 10th is lovely with the lake in the foreground mirroring the ocean in the distance. The par-4 16th is another sight to see, with the Pacific running along the left side. Note: at this writing, the South Course was scheduled to be closed for part of 2009. Call to confirm. ✉ *5415 Mākena Alanui, Mākena* ☎*808/891–4000* ⊕*www.princeresortshawaii.com/maui-golf.php* ⚑ *North Course: 18 holes. 6567 yds. Par 72. Slope 135. Green Fee: $200. South Course: 18 holes. 6630 yds. Par 72. Slope 133. Green Fee: $200* ☞ *Facilities: Driving range, putting green, golf carts, rental clubs, pro-shop, golf academy/lessons, restaurant, bar.*

Fodor'sChoice
★   **Wailea.** Wailea is the only Hawai'i resort to offer three different courses: Gold, Emerald, and Old Blue. Designed by Robert Trent Jones Jr. (Gold and Emerald) and Arthur Jack Snyder (Old Blue), these courses share similar terrain, carved into the leeward slopes of Haleakalā. Although the ocean does not come into play, its beauty is visible on almost every hole. ■TIP➔**Remember, putts break dramatically toward the ocean.**

Jones refers to the Gold Course at Wailea (1993) as the "masculine" course. Host to the Championship Senior Skins Game in January, it's all trees and lava and regarded as the hardest of the three courses. The trick here is to note even subtle changes in elevation. The par-3 eighth, for example, plays from an elevated tee across a lava ravine to a large, well-bunkered green framed by palm trees, the blue sea, and tiny Molokini. The course has been labeled a "thinking player's" course because it demands strategy and careful club selection. The Emerald Course at Wailea (1994) is the "feminine" layout with lots of flowers and bunkering away from greens. Although this may seem to render the bunker benign, the opposite is true. A bunker well in front of a green disguises the distance to the hole. Likewise, the Emerald's extensive flower beds are designed to be dangerous distractions because of their beauty. The Gold and Emerald share a clubhouse, practice facility, and 19th hole. At Wailea's first course, the Old Blue Course (1971), judging elevation change is also key. Fairways and greens tend to be wider and more forgiving than on the Gold or Emerald, and run through colorful flora that includes hibiscus, wiliwili, bougainvillea, and plumeria. Old Blue Course: ⊠*100 Wailea Golf Club Dr., Wailea* ☎*808/875–7450 or 888/328–6284* ⊕*www.waileagolf.com* ⅃*18 holes. 6765 yds. Par 72. Slope 129. Green Fee: $225* ⌒*Facilities: Driving range, putting green, golf carts, rental clubs, pro-shop, golf academy/lessons, restaurant, bar.* Gold and Emerald Courses: ⊠*100 Wailea Golf Club Dr., Wailea* ☎*808/875–7450 or 888/328–6284* ⊕*www.waileagolf.com* ⅃*Gold Course: 18 holes. 6653 yds. Par 72. Slope 132. Green Fee: $225. Emerald Course: 18 holes. 6407 yds. Par 72. Slope 130. Green Fee: $225* ⌒*Facilities: Driving range, putting green, golf carts, rental clubs, pro-shop, golf academy/lessons, restaurant, bar.*

CENTRAL MAUI

Fodor'sChoice ★ **The Dunes at Maui Lani.** This is Robin Nelson (1999) at his minimalist best, a bit of British links in the middle of the Pacific. Holes run through ancient, lightly wooded sand dunes, 5 mi inland from Kahului Harbor. Thanks to the natural humps and slopes of the dunes, Nelson had to move very little dirt and created a natural beauty. During the design phase he visited Ireland, and not so coincidentally the par-3 third looks a lot like the Dell at Lahinch: a white dune on the right sloping down into a deep bunker and partially obscuring the right side of the green—just one of several blind to semiblind shots here. Popular with residents, this course has won several awards including "Best 35 New Courses in America" by *Golf Magazine* and "Five Best Kept Secret Golf Courses in America" by *Golf Digest.* ⊠*1333 Maui Lani Pkwy., Kahului* ☎*808/873–0422* ⊕*www.dunesatmauilani.com* ⅃*18 holes. 6841 yds. Par 72. Slope 136. Green Fee: $99* ⌒*Facilities: Driving range, putting green, golf carts, rental clubs, pro-shop, golf academy/lessons, restaurant, bar.*

Kahili Golf Course. The former Sandalwood Course (Robin Nelson, 1991) was completely redone in 2005 by Nelson himself and is now one of two 18-hole courses—one private (King Kamehameha) and one public (Kahili)—that make up the King Kamehameha Golf Club. Course holes run along the slopes of the West Maui Mountains, overlooking Maui's central plain, and feature panoramic ocean views of both the North and South shores. Consistent winds negate the course's shorter length. ⊠*2500 Honoapiʻilani Hwy., Wailuku* ☎*808/242–4653* ⊕*www.kahiligolf.com* ⅃*18 holes. 6570 yds. Par 72. Slope 124. Green Fee: $125* ⌒*Facilities: Driving range, putting green, golf carts, rental clubs, pro-shop, lessons, restaurant, bar.*

Waiehu Golf Course. Maui's lone municipal course, Waiehu is really two courses in one. The front 9 opened in 1930 and features authentic

SAVING THE BEST FOR LAST

Among golf's great traditions is the 19th hole. No matter how the first 18 go, the 19th is sure to offer comfort and cheer, not to mention a chilled beverage. Here's a look at some of the best.

Kapalua boasts three 19th holes with great fare and views—the **Plantation House** has a commanding view of the Plantation Course's 18th hole, the Pailolo Channel, and the island of Moloka'i beyond; the **Pineapple Grill** overlooks the Bay Course's 18th; and **Merriman's Kapalua** sits ocean side at Kapalua Bay.

At Wailea's Gold and Emerald courses, the **Sea Watch** restaurant overlooks the sea in a garden setting and serves excellent food, with a choice selection of single-malt Scotches and cigars.

The **Kahili Restaurant,** a plantation-style clubhouse at the King Kamehameha Golf Club's Kahili Course, offers commanding views of the ocean on both sides of the island and of 10,000-foot Haleakalā. And though not affiliated with elleair, golfers from this course frequent **Lulu's** and **Henry's** in the heart of Kīhei.

seaside links that run along Kahului Bay. The back 9, which climbs up into the lower reaches of the West Maui Mountains through macadamia orchards, opened in 1963 (Arthur Jack Snyder). ⊠ *200 Halewaiu Rd., Wailuku* ☎ *808/270–7400* ⊕ *www.co.maui.hi.us* ⚑ *18 holes. 6330 yds. Par 72. Slope 120. Green Fee: $50 on weekdays/$55 on weekends and holidays, plus $18.50 per cart* ⚐ *Facilities: Driving range, putting green, golf carts, pull carts, rental clubs, pro-shop, restaurant, bar.*

UPCOUNTRY

Pukalani Golf Course. At 1,110 feet above sea level, Pukalani (Bob E. and Robert L. Baldock, 1970) provides one of the finest vistas in all Hawai'i. Holes run up, down, and across the slopes of Haleakalā. The trade winds tend to come up in the late morning and afternoon. This—combined with frequent elevation change—makes club selection a test. The fairways tend to be wide, but greens are undulating and quick. ⊠ *360 Pukalani St., Pukalani* ☎ *808/572–1314* ⊕ *www.pukalanigolf. com* ⚑ *18 holes. 6962 yds. Par 72. Slope 127. Green Fee: $78* ⚐ *Facilities: Driving range, putting green, golf carts, rental clubs, pro-shop, restaurant, bar.*

LĀNA'I

The Island of Lāna'i features two championship-caliber golf courses—the **Challenge at Mānele** and the **Experience at Kō'ele**—that are rarely crowded due to the exclusivity of the island. Both courses require a ferry ride from Lahaina or Mā'alaea harbors on Maui. Transportation–golf packages are available through **Expeditions Ferry** (☎ *808/661–3756 or 800/695–2624* ⊕ *www.go-lanai.com*). *For reviews of the two courses, see Chapter 11, Lāna'i.*

HANG GLIDING AND PARAGLIDING

Hang Gliding Maui. Armin Engert will take you on an instructional powered hang-gliding trip out of Hāna Airport in East Maui. With more than 7,500 hours in flight and a perfect safety record, Armin flies you 1,000 feet over Maui's most beautiful coast. A 30-minute flight lesson costs $130, and a 60-minute lesson is $220. This is easily one of the coolest things you can do in Hāna. Snapshots of your flight from a wing-mounted camera cost an additional $30, and a 34-minute DVD of the flight is available for $70. Reservations are required. ⊠ *Hāna Airport, Hāna* ☎ *808/572–6557* ⊕ *www.hanggglidingmaui.com.*

Maluhialani. The name means "beautiful serenity" in Hawaiian, which is appropriate for an airborne trip taking off from Kula in Upcountry Maui, and soaring as far as the West Maui Mountains. Dwight Mounts, your pilot, built a grass runway on his scenic Upcountry property that serves as home base for his powered hang-gliding lessons. The cost is $125 for a 20- to 30-minute Mini Intro Flight, and $200 for a 50- to 60-minute Full Intro Flight. ☎ *808/280–3307* ⊕ *www.maluhialani.com.*

Proflyght Paragliding. Proflyght is the only paragliding outfit on Maui to offer solo, tandem, and instruction at Polipoli Spring State Recreation Area. The leeward slope of Haleakalā lends itself perfectly to paragliding with breathtaking scenery and Upcountry air currents that increase and rise throughout the day. Polipoli creates tremendous thermals that allow one to peacefully descend 3,000 feet to the landing zone. Owner–pilot Dexter Clearwater boasts a perfect safety record with tandems and student pilots since taking over the company in 2002. Ask and Dexter will bring along his flying duck Chucky or his paragliding puppy Daisy. Prices start at $75, with full certification available. ⊠ *Polipoli Spring State Recreation Area, Kula* ☎ *808/874–5433* ⊕ *www.paraglidehawaii.com.*

HIKING

Hikes on Maui include treks along coastal seashore, verdant rain forest, and alpine desert. Orchids, hibiscus, ginger, heliconia, and anthuriums grow wild on many trails, and exotic fruits like mountain apple, lilikoi (passion fruit), thimbleberry, and strawberry guava provide refreshing snacks for hikers. Ironically, much of what you see in lower-altitude forests is alien, brought to Hawai'i at one time or another by someone hoping to improve upon nature. Plants like strawberry guava and ginger may be tasty, but they grow over native forest plants and have become serious, problematic weeds.

The best hikes get you out of the imported landscaping and into the truly exotic wilderness. Hawai'i possesses some of the world's rarest plants, insects, and birds. Pocket field guides are available at most

Cinder cones, deposits formed around a volcanic vent, are a striking feature in Haleakalā Crater.

grocery or drug stores and can really illuminate your walk. Before you know it you'll be nudging your companion and pointing out trees that look like something out of a Dr. Seuss book. If you watch the right branches quietly you can spot the same honeycreepers or happy-face spiders scientists have spent their lives studying.

BEST SPOTS

HALEAKALĀ NATIONAL PARK
HALEAKALĀ CRATER

Fodor'sChoice Hiking Haleakalā Crater is undoubtedly the best hiking on the island.
★ There are 30 mi of trails, two camping areas, and three cabins. If you're in shape, you can do a day hike descending from the summit (along Sliding Sands Trail) to the crater floor. If you're in shape and have time, consider spending several days here amid the cinder cones, lava flows, and all that loud silence. Going into the crater is like going to a different planet. In the early 1960s NASA actually brought moon-suited astronauts here to practice what it would be like to "walk on the moon." Today, on one of the many hikes—most moderate to stren-uous—you'll traverse black sand and wild lava formations, follow the trail of blooming 'ahinahina (silverswords), watch for nēnē (Hawaiian geese) as they fly above you, and witness tremendous views of big sky and burned-red cliffs. If you're lucky enough to camp or stay in one of the cabins, you'll fall asleep under a wide screen of shooting stars, while the 'alauahio birds murmur around you like a litter of pups.

The best time to go into the crater is in the summer months, when the conditions are generally more predictable. Be sure to bring layered clothing—and plenty of warm clothes if you're staying overnight. It may be scorching hot during the day, but it gets mighty chilly after dark. Ask a ranger about water availability before starting your hike. Note that overnight visitors must get a permit at park headquarters before entering the crater; day-use visitors do not need a permit. Cabins are $75 per night, and fit 12 people. They book months in advance by lottery, though it's possible to get lucky due to last-minute cancellations. To reserve a cabin, write at least two months in advance to **Haleakalā National Park** (⌂ *Box 369, Attn. Cabins, Makawao 96768* ☎*808/572–4459*), or call between 1 and 3 PM Hawaiian Standard Time; you will need a valid credit card to secure a phone reservation. *For detailed information on hikes in the crater, see Haleakalā National Park in Chapter 2, Exploring Maui.*

'OHE'O GULCH

A branch of Haleakalā National Park, 'Ohe'o Gulch is famous for its pools (the area is sometimes called the "Seven Sacred Pools"). Truth is, there are more than seven pools, and there's nothing sacred about them. The owner of the Hotel Hāna started calling the area "Seven Sacred Pools" to attract the masses to sleepy old Hāna. His plan worked and the name stuck, much to the chagrin of most Mauians. The Pools of 'Ohe'o is another name for them.

The best time to visit the pools is in the morning, before the crowds and tour buses arrive. Start your day with a vigorous hike. 'Ohe'o has some fantastic trails to choose from, including our favorite, the Pipiwai Trail. When you're done, nothing could be better than going to the pools, lounging on the rocks, and cooling off in the freshwater reserves.

You'll find 'Ohe'o Gulch on Route 31, 10 mi past Hāna town. All visitors must pay a $10 national park fee (per car not per person), which is valid for three days and can be used at Haleakalā's summit as well.

Kahakai Trail. This easy 0.25-mi hike (more like a walk) stretches between Kuloa Point and the Kipahulu campground. You'll see rugged shoreline views and can stop to gaze at the surging waves below. ⊠*Trailhead: Kuloa Point* ⊙*15 mins, 0.5 mi round-trip.*

Kuloa Point Trail. An easy 0.5-mi walk, this trail takes you from the Kipahulu Visitor Center down to the Pools of 'Ohe'o at Kuloa Point. On the trail you pass native trees and precontact Hawaiian sites. Don't forget to wear your suit and bring your towel if you plan to take a dip in the pools. Keep in mind: no lifeguards are on duty and you'll want to stick to the pools—don't even think about swimming in the ocean. ⊠*Trailhead: Kipahulu Visitor Center (Hāna Hwy., 10 mi past Hāna town)* ⊙*30 mins, 1 mi round-trip.*

Fodor'sChoice   **Pipiwai Trail.** This moderate 2-mi
★   trek upstream leads to the 400-foot
Waimoku Falls, pounding down
in all its power and glory. Follow
signs from the parking lot up the
road, past the bridge overlook, and
uphill into the forest. Along the way
you can take side trips and swim in
the stream's basalt-lined pools. The
trail bridges a sensational gorge and
passes onto a boardwalk through a
mystifying forest of giant bamboo.
This stomp through muddy and
rocky terrain takes around three

KALAUPAPA TRAIL

You can take an overnight trip to
the island of Moloka'i for a day of
hiking down to Kalaupapa Peninsula and back, by means of a 3-mi,
26-switchback trail. The trail is
nearly vertical, traversing the face
of some of the highest sea cliffs
in the world. *See Kalaupapa Peninsula in Chapter 10, Moloka'i, for
more information.*

hours to fully enjoy. It's best done early in the morning, before the
touring crowds arrive (though it can never truly be called crowded).
✉ *Trailhead: On highway toward 'Ohe'o bridge, near mile marker 42*
⊙ *3 hrs, 4 mi round-trip.*

Campsites. Down at the grassy sea cliffs at the Pools of 'Ohe'o, you can
camp, no permit required, although you can stay only three nights. Toilets, grills, and tables are available, but there's no water and open fires
are prohibited. For more information, call the Kipahulu Visitor Center.
☞ *Visitor Center* ☎ *808/248–7375* ⊕ *www.nps.gov/hale.*

POLIPOLI SPRING STATE RECREATION AREA

A good hiking area—and something totally unexpected on a tropical
island—is the Kula Forest Reserve at Polipoli Spring State Recreation
Area (6,200 feet). During the Great Depression the government began
a program to reforest the mountain, and soon cedar, pine, cypress, and
even redwood took hold. Today, the area feels more like Vermont than
Hawai'i. It's cold and foggy here, and often wet, but don't let that stop
you from going. There's something about the enormity of the trees,
quiet mist, and mysterious caves that will make you feel you've discovered an unspoken secret, and one you'll want to keep to yourself.

To reach the forest, take Route 37 all the way out to the far end of
Kula. Then turn left at Route 377. After about ½ mi, turn right at
Waipoli Road. First you'll encounter switchbacks; after that the road
is just plain bad, but passable. Signs say that four-wheel-drive vehicles
are required, though standard cars have been known to make it. Use
your best judgment. There are great trails here for all levels, along with
a small campground, and a cabin that you can rent from the Division
of State Parks. Hikers should wear brightly colored clothing, as hunters
may be in the area.

Reservations for the park's one **cabin** can be made up to a year in
advance by calling Monday through Friday, from 8 AM to 3:30 PM
Hawaiian Standard Time, or by mailing a request in writing (✉ *Box
1049, Wailuku 96793* ☎ *808/587–0300*). For the campground, you can
wait until you arrive in Wailuku and visit the **Division of State Parks** (✉ *54
S. High St., Room 101, Wailuku 96793* ☎ *808/984–8109*).

Continued on page 142

HAWAI'I'S PLANTS 101

Hawai'i is a bounty of rainbow-colored flowers and plants. The evening air is scented with their fragrance. Just look at the front yard of almost any home, travel any road, or visit any local park and you'll see a spectacular array of colored blossoms and leaves. What most visitors don't know is that the plants they are seeing are not native to Hawai'i; rather, they were introduced during the last two centuries as ornamental plants, or for timber, shade, or fruit.

Hawai'i boasts nearly every climate on the planet, excluding the two most extreme: arctic tundra and arid desert. The Islands have wine-growing regions, cactus-speckled ranchlands, icy mountaintops, and the rainiest forests on earth.

Plants introduced from around the world thrive here. The lush lowland valleys along the windward coasts are predominantly populated by non-native trees including yellow- and red-fruited **guava**, silvery-leafed **kukui**, and orange-flowered **tulip trees**.

The colorful **plumeria flower**, very fragrant and commonly used in lei making, and

the giant multicolored **hibiscus flower** are both used by many women as hair adornments, and are two of the most common plants found around homes and hotels. The umbrella-like **monkeypod tree** from Central America provides shade in many of Hawai'i's parks including Kapiolani Park in Honolulu. Hawai'i's largest tree, found in Lahaina, Maui, is a giant **banyan tree.** Its canopy and massive support roots cover about two-thirds of an acre. The native **o'hia tree**, with its brilliant red brush-like flowers, and the **hapu'u**, a giant tree fern, are common in Hawai'i's forests and are also used ornamentally in gardens and around homes.

Bougainvillea

Guava

Monkeypod

Banyan

Ohia Lehua *

Tulip Tree

Plumeria

Pandanus

Hibiscus

Anthurium

Kukui Tree

Hapu'u

*endemic to Hawai'i

DID YOU KNOW?

Over 2,200 plant species are found in the Hawaiian Islands, but only about 1,000 are native. Of these, 282 are so rare, they are endangered. Hawai'i's endemic plants evolved from ancestral seeds arriving on the islands over thousands of years as baggage on birds, floating on ocean currents, or drifting on winds from continents thousands of miles away. Once here, these plants evolved in isolation creating many new species known nowhere else in the world.

IN THE FOOTSTEPS OF KINGS

A much neglected hike in southwestern Maui is the 5.5-mi (allow 4 to 6 hours) coastal **Hoapili Trail** (⊠ *Follow Mākena Alanui to end of paved road at La Pérouse Bay, walk through parking lot along dirt road, follow signs*) beyond the 'Āhihi-Kīna'u Natural Area Reserve. Named after a bygone Hawaiian king, it follows the shoreline, threading through the remains of ancient Hawaiian villages. The once-thriving community was displaced by one of Maui's last lava flows. Later, King Hoapili was responsible for overseeing the creation of an island-wide highway. This remaining section, a wide path of stacked lava rocks, is a marvel to look at and walk on, though it's not the easiest surface for the ankles. (It's rumored to have once been covered in grass.) You can wander over to the Hanamanioa lighthouse, or quietly ponder the rough life of the ancients.

Wear sturdy shoes and bring extra water. This is brutal territory with little shade and no facilities. Beautiful, yes. Accommodating, no.

Boundary Trail. This 4-mi moderate trail begins just past the Kula Forest Reserve boundary cattle guard on Polipoli Road, and descends into the lower boundary southward, all the way to the ranger's cabin at the junction of the Redwood and Plum trails. Link it with these trails, and you've got a hearty 5-mi day hike. The trail crosses many scenic gulches, with an overhead of tall eucalyptus, pine, cedar, and plum trees. Peep through the trees for wide views of Kula and Central Maui. ⊠ *Trailhead: Polipoli campground* ☉ *3–4 hrs, 5-mi loop.*

Redwood Trail. This easy and colorful hike winds through redwoods and conifers past the short Tie Trail down to the old ranger's cabin. Although the views are limited, groves of trees and flowering bushes abound. At the end of the trail is an old cabin site and three-way junction with the Plum Trail and the Boundary Trail. ⊠ *Trailhead: From parking area at Polipoli campground, walk back up road 0.25 mi and look to your left* ☉ *1–2 hrs, 3.4 mi round-trip.*

Upper Waiakoa Trail. This scenic albeit rugged trail starts at the Polipoli Access Road (look for trailheads) and proceeds up Haleakalā through mixed pine and past caves and thick shrubs. It crosses the land of Kaonoulu to the land of Waiakoa, where it reaches its highest point—7,800 feet. Here you'll find yourself in barren, raw terrain with fantastic views. At this point, you can either turn around, or continue on to the 3-mi Waiakoa Loop. Other than a cave shelter, there's no water or other facilities on either of these trails, so come prepared. ⊠ *Trailhead: Look for signs on Polipoli Access Rd.* ☉ *5–6 hrs, 14 mi round-trip.*

'ĪAO VALLEY STATE PARK

★ In Hawaiian, 'Īao means "supreme cloud." When you enter this mystical valley in the middle of an unexpected rain forest, you'll know why. At 750 feet above sea level, the 10-mi valley clings to the clouds as if it's trying to cover its naked beauty. If you've been spending too many days in the sun, the cool shade and moist air may be just the welcome change you need.

Sunrise on top of Haleakalā can be memorable; start early and wear warm clothing.

One of Maui's great wonders, the valley is the site of a famous battle to unite the Hawaiian Islands. Out of the clouds, the ʻĪao Needle, a tall chunk of volcanic rock, stands as a monument to the long-ago lookout for Maui warriors. Today, there's nothing warlike about it: the valley is a peaceful land of lush, tropical plants, clear pools and a running stream, and easy, enjoyable strolls.

To get to ʻĪao Valley State Park, go through Wailuku and continue to the west end of Route 32. The road dead-ends into the parking lot. The park is open daily 7 AM to 7 PM. Facilities are available. (For park information call ☎808/984–8109.)

ʻĪao Valley Trail. Anyone (including your grandparents) can take this easy, short walk from the parking lot at ʻĪao Valley State Park. On your choice of two paved walkways, you can cross the ʻĪao Stream and explore the junglelike area. Ascend the stairs up to the **ʻĪao Needle** for spectacular views of Central Maui, or pause in the garden of Hawaiian heritage plants and marvel at the local youngsters hurling themselves from the bridge into the chilly pools below. ✉ *Trailhead: ʻĪao Valley parking lot* ⏲ *30 mins, 0.5 mi round-trip.*

ADDITIONAL HIKES

Kapalua Resort. The resort offers access to several hiking trails throughout Kapalua's land holdings that are free and open to resort guests and visitors as a self-guided experience. Trail information and maps are available at the **Kapalua Adventure Center.** Access to most trails is via a complimentary resort shuttle. ✉ *Corner of Office and Village Rds., Kapalua* ☎*808/665–4386 or 877/665–4386* ⊕ *www.kapalua. com/adventures.*

TIPS FOR DAY HIKES

Hiking is a perfect way to see Maui. Just wear sturdy shoes to spare your ankles from a crash course in loose lava rock. At upper elevations, the weather is guaranteed to be extreme—alternately chilly or blazing—so layers are good.

When hiking near streams or waterfalls, be cautious: flash floods can occur at any time. Don't drink stream water or swim in streams if you have open cuts; bacteria and parasites are not the souvenir you want to take home with you.

Here's a checklist for what to take for a great hike.

■ Water (at least 2 quarts per person; drink even if you're not thirsty)

■ Food—fruit and trail mix

■ Rain gear—especially if going into the crater

■ Sturdy hiking shoes

■ Layered clothing

■ Wide-brimmed hat and sunglasses

■ Sunscreen (SPF 30 or higher recommended)

■ Mosquito repellent (a must around waterfalls and pools)

Waihe'e Ridge. This moderately strenuous hike offers a generous reward at the top: breathtaking panoramic views of the windward coast and the ridges that rise inland, as well as Mt. Lanilili, Pu`u Kukui, Eke Crater, and the remote village of Kahakuloa. A picnic table enables you to enjoy a comfortable lunch before making the descent back to your car. It's best to avoid this hike during rainy conditions as the trail can quickly turn into a muddy, slippery affair. ⊠ *Trailhead: From Hwy. 340, turn left across the highway from Mendes Ranch and call box 4. Drive ¾ mi up a partially paved road to a signed trailhead on the left in a pasture* ⊙ *2–3 hrs, 4¾ mi round-trip.*

GOING WITH A GUIDE

Guided hikes can help you see more than you might on your own. If the company is driving you to the site, be sure to ask about drive times; they can be long.

Fodor's Choice
★ **Friends of Haleakalā National Park.** This nonprofit offers day and overnight service trips into the crater and in the Kipahulu region. The purpose of your trip, the service work itself, isn't too much—mostly removing invasive plants and light cabin maintenance. Chances are you'll make good friends and have more fun than on a hike you'd do on your own. Trip leader Farley, or one of his equally knowledgeable cohorts, will take you to places you'd never otherwise see, and teach you about the native flora and birds along the way. Visit the Web site to learn more about the trips before calling to make a reservation. Admission is free. ☎ *808/248–7660* ⊕ *www.fhnp.org.*

Hawai'i Nature Center. In 'Iao Valley, the Hawai'i Nature Center leads easy, interpretive rain-forest walks for children and their families. The daily walks, which cost $29.95 for adults and $19.95 for children,

These horses on the less-developed North Shore seem to be taking in the ocean view.

include a visit to the Nature Center's interactive museum. Participants must be at least five years old and should wear closed-toe shoes suitable for uneven terrain. Advance reservations are suggested. Another option is to just visit the museum, which costs $6 for adults and $4 for kids (children under four are free). ⊠ *875 ʻIao Valley Rd., Wailuku* ☎ *808/244–6500* ⊕ *www.hawaiinaturecenter.org.*

Hike Maui. Started in 1983, Hike Maui is the oldest hiking company in the Islands. Its waterfall and rain forest, mountain ridge, crater, coastline, and combination hikes are led by enthusiastic trained naturalists who weave botany, geology, ethnobotany, culture, and history into the outdoor experience. Prices range from $75 to $154 for excursions of 3 to 10 hours (discounts are available for advance, online bookings). Private and custom tours are also available. Hike Maui supplies day packs, rain gear, water shoes, mosquito repellent, first-aid supplies, bottled water, lunch and/or snacks for the longer trips, and transportation to and from the site. ☎ *808/879–5270 or 866/325–6284* ⊕ *www.hikemaui.com.*

Maui Eco Adventures. For excursions into remote areas, Maui Eco Adventures is your choice. The ecologically minded company leads hikes into private or otherwise inaccessible areas. Hikes explore botanically rich valleys in Kahakuloa and East Maui, as well as Hāna, Haleakalā, and more. They also offer a hike/kayak combination at Kapalua Bay, and a Haleakalā Heli-Hike with Sunshine Helicopters. Guides are botanists, mountaineers, boat captains, and backcountry chefs. Excursions are priced from $80 for a "waterfall experience" to $400 for the Heli-Hike. ⊠ *180 Dickenson St., Suite 102, Lahaina* ☎ *808/661–7720 or 877/661–7720* ⊕ *www.ecomaui.com.*

COWBOY FUN: RODEOS & POLO

Cowboys aren't always working, and you can watch them having fun at rodeos and polo matches.

With working cattle ranches throughout the Islands, many youngsters learn to ride a horse before they can drive a car. Mauians love their rodeos and put on several for students at high schools.

Paniolos (Hawaiian cowboys) get in on the action, too, at three major annual events: the **Oskie Rice Memorial Rodeo**, usually staged the weekend after Labor Day; the **Cancer Benefit Rodeo** in April; and Maui's biggest event, drawing competitors from all the Islands as well as the U.S. mainland, the **4th of July Rodeo**, which comes with a full parade in Makawao town and festivities that last for days.

Polo is popular with the Upcountry *paniolos* (Hawaiian cowboys). From April through June, Haleakalā Ranch hosts "indoor" or arena contests on a field flanked by side boards. The field is on Route 377, 1 mi from Route 37. During the "outdoor" polo season, September to mid-November, matches are held at Olinda Field, 1 mi above Makawao on Olinda Road. There's a $5 admission for most games, which start at 1 PM on Sunday. The **Manduke Baldwin Memorial Tournament** (☎ 808/877–7744 ⊕ www.mauipolo club.com) occurs on Memorial Day and is a popular two-day event. The Maui Polo Club draws challengers from Argentina, England, South Africa, New Zealand, and Australia. For information, call or visit the Web site.

Maui Hiking Safaris. Hikes with Maui Hiking Safaris are limited to groups of eight or less. Excursions include hikes to waterfalls, Haleakalā, rain forests, and more. You can choose two half-day hikes to customize your own full-day tour. Hikes range from $60 to $140. ✉ 273 Leolani Pl., Pukalani ☎ 808/573–0168 or 888/445–3963 ⊕ www.mauihikingsafaris.com.

★ **Sierra Club.** A great avenue into the island's untrammeled wilderness is Maui's chapter of the Sierra Club. Rather than venturing out on your own, join one of the club's hikes into pristine forests and Valley Isle watersheds, or along ancient coastal paths. Several hikes a month are led by informative leaders who carry first-aid kits and make arrangements to access private land. Some outings include volunteer service, but most are just for fun. Bring your own food and water, sturdy shoes, and a suggested donation of $5—a true bargain. ✉ Box 791180, Pāʻia 96779 ☎ 808/573–4147 ⊕ www.hi.sierraclub.org/maui.

HORSEBACK RIDING

Several companies on Maui offer horseback riding that's far more appealing than the typical hour-long trudge over a dull trail with 50 other horses.

GOING WITH A GUIDE

FodorsChoice **Maui Stables.** Hawaiian-owned and run, this company provides a trip
★ back in time, to an era when life moved more slowly and reverently—though galloping is allowed, if you're able to handle your horse! Educational tours begin at the stable in remote Kipahulu (near Hāna), and

pass through several historic Hawaiian sites. Before heading up into the forest, your guides intone the words to a traditional *oli,* or chant, asking for permission to enter. By the time you reach the mountain pasture overlooking Waimoku Falls, you'll feel lucky to have been a part of the tradition. Both morning and afternoon rides are available at $150 per rider. ✉*Between mile markers 40 and 41 on Hwy. 37, Hāna* ☎*808/248–7799* ⊕*www.mauistables.com.*

Fodor'sChoice
★
Mendes Ranch. Family-owned and run, Mendes operates out of the beautiful ranchland of Kahakuloa on the windward slopes of the West Maui Mountains. Two-hour morning and afternoon trail rides ($110) are available with an optional barbecue lunch ($20). Cowboys will take you cantering up rolling pastures into the lush rain forest to view some of Maui's biggest waterfalls. Mendes caters to weddings and parties and offers private trail rides on request. Should you need accommodations they have a home and bunk for rent right on the property. ✉*3530 Kahekili Hwy., Wailuku* ☎*808/244–7320 or 800/871–5222* ⊕*www.mendesranch.com.*

Pi'iholo Ranch. The local wranglers here will lead you on a rousing ride through family ranchlands—up hillside pastures, beneath a eucalyptus canopy, and past many native trees. Morning and afternoon "country" rides last two hours and cost $120. Their well-kept horses navigate the challenging terrain easily, but hold on when axis deer pass by! Private rides and lessons are available. ✉*End of Waiahiwi Rd., Makawao* ☎*808/357–5544* ⊕*www.piiholo.com.*

Pony Express Tours. Pony Express Tours offers trips on horseback into Haleakalā Crater. The half-day ride goes down to the crater floor for a picnic lunch, and is a great way to see the top of the dormant volcano. The company also offers 1½- and 2-hour rides on the slopes of the Haleakalā Ranch. Prices range from $95 to $182. ☎*808/667–2200* ⊕*www.ponyexpresstours.com.*

TENNIS

Most courts charge by the hour but will let players continue after their initial hour for free, provided no one is waiting. In addition to the facilities listed below, many hotels and condos have courts open to nonguests for a fee.

BEST SPOTS

Kapalua Tennis Garden. This complex, home to the Kapalua Tennis Club, serves the Kapalua Resort with 10 courts, 4 lighted for night play, and a pro-shop. You'll pay $14 an hour if you're a guest, $16 if you're not. ✉*100 Kapalua Dr., Kapalua* ☎*808/665–9112* ⊕*www. kapalua.com.*

ON THE SIDELINES

At the **Kapalua Jr. Vet/Sr. Tennis Championships** in May, players compete in singles and doubles events. Over Labor Day weekend, the **Kapalua Open Tennis Tournament** calls Hawai'i's hitters to Kapalua's Tennis Garden. Both events are put on by the **Kapalua Tennis Club** (☎*808/665–9112*). **The Wailea Open Tennis Championship** is held at the Wailea Tennis Club in May (☎*808/879–1958*).

Lahaina Civic Center. The best free courts are the five at the Lahaina Civic Center, near Wahikuli State Park. They all have overhead lighting for night play, and are available on a first-come, first-served basis. ✉*1840 Honoapi'ilani Hwy., Lahaina* ☎*808/661–4685.*

Mākena Tennis Club. Mākena features six Plexipave courts, two of which are lighted for night play. Private lessons, rentals, ball machines, racquet stringing, and weekly clinics are available. ✉*5415 Mākena Alanui Dr., Mākena* ☎*808/891–4050.*

Wailea Tennis Club. The club has 11 Plexipave courts (its famed grass courts are, sadly, a thing of the past), lessons, rentals, and ball machines. Daily clinics are offered to help you improve ground strokes, serve, volley, or doubles strategy. Rates are $15 per player, with three lighted courts available for night play. ✉*131 Wailea Ike Pl., Kīhei* ☎*808/879–1958 or 800/332–1614* ⊕*www.waileatennis.com.*

ZIPLINE TOURS

Ziplining lets you satisfy your inner Tarzan by soaring high above deep gulches and canyons. A harness keeps you supported on each ride. There are weight restrictions, and you should wear closed-toe athletic-type shoes and expect to get dirty. ■**TIP➜ Although zipline tours are completely safe, you may want to reconsider this activity if you are uncomfortable with heights or have serious back or joint problems.**

Kapalua Adventures Mountain Outpost. Opened in 2008, the zipline at Kapalua Adventures Mountain Outpost has almost 2 mi of parallel lines, enabling two riders to zip side by side. Prices range from $60 to $299. You must be at least 10 years old and weigh between 60 and 250 pounds. The Mountain Outpost also has a high-ropes challenge course, and a 35-foot pole from which you can leap to catch a trapeze. ✉*2000 Village Rd., Kapalua* ☎*808/665–4386 or 877/665–4386* ⊕*www.kapalua.com/adventures.*

Pi'iholo Ranch Zipline. The Pi'iholo Ranch complex, opened in 2008, has six ziplines—five parallel lines and one quadruple—plus a 12-person climbing tower. Ziplines range from 500 to 3,200 feet, and prices are $140 for four lines and $190 for five lines. You must be at least 10 years old and weigh between 60 and 275 pounds. Nonparticipants can watch the action from the shady "tree-house" observation deck. ✉*Pi'iholo Rd., Makawao* ☎*808/572–1717* ⊕*www.piiholo.com.*

Skyline Eco Adventures. Skyline Eco Adventures operates in two locations on Maui: the original course on the slope of Haleakalā, and the newer venue at 1,000 feet above Kā'anapali. Good-natured guides give expert instruction and have you "zipping" confidently in no time. You must be at least 10 years old, weigh between 80 and 260 pounds, and be able to hike a moderate distance over uneven terrain in order to participate. For the Haleakalā tour ($89), dress in layers, as it can get chilly at the 4,000-plus foot elevation, especially in the morning. The Kā'anapali tour ($150) includes breakfast or lunch. Advance reservations are suggested, especially in summer, and discounts are available for online bookings. ☎*808/878–8400* ⊕*www.zipline.com.*

Shops and Spas

WORD OF MOUTH

"The [Westin Maui] Spa was as they say, heavenly! Arrive early for your appointment to enjoy the facilities! I could have died and gone to heaven in my white bathrobe waiting for my facial in the 'quiet room.' The facilities were excellent!"

—saxbe

Updated by
Eliza Escaño-
Vasquez

We hope you've saved room in your suitcase. With the help of our shopping guide, you'll find the top shops for everything "Maui grown," from *lilikoi* (passion fruit) jams and fresh pineapples to koa wood bowls and swimwear. Even fashionistas can get their fill of bohemian-resort chic style in Pā'ia, luxury brands in Wailea and *paniolo* (cowboy) threads in Upcountry's quiet Makawao town. If you're seeking authentic Hawaiian artisanal goods, check out handcrafted Mele Ukulele, Randy Jay Braun photography, and Robert Wyland's marine-life paintings.

But before packing up your plunder, conjure up some Zen by soaking in Maui's natural resources. Rejuvenate in a yoga class, then enter one of the island's world-class spas to unwind. Among the best are the Waihua Spa at the Ritz-Carlton in Kapalua, the Grand Wailea Resort's Spa Grande, and the Four Seasons Resort's spa in Wailea. Most treatments are infused with ingredients indigenous to the Valley Isle, like *kukui* nut, coconut, ginger, and eucalyptus. Plus, you're sure to find a spa product or two to bring home. Lavender salt bath, anyone?

SHOPS

Whether you're searching for a dashboard hula dancer or an original Curtis Wilson Cost painting, you can find it on Front Street in Lahaina or at the Shops at Wailea. Art sales are huge in the resort areas, where artists regularly show up to promote their work. Alongside the flashy galleries are standards like Quicksilver and ABC store, where you can stock up on swim trunks, sunscreen, and flip-flops.

Don't miss the great boutiques lining the streets of small towns like Pā'ia and Makawao. You can purchase boutique fashions and art while strolling through these charming, quieter communities. Notably, several local designers—Tamara Catz, Letarte, and Maui Girl—all produce top-quality island fashions. In the neighboring galleries, local artisans turn out gorgeous work in a range of prices. Special souvenirs include rare hardwood bowls and boxes, prints of sea life, Hawaiian quilts, and blown glass.

Specialty food products—pineapples, coconuts, or Maui onions—and "Made in Maui" jams and jellies make great, less-expensive souvenirs. Cook Kwee's Maui Cookies have gained a following, as have Maui Potato Chips. Coffee sellers now offer Maui-grown-and-roasted beans alongside the better-known Kona varieties. Remember that fresh fruit must be inspected by the U.S. Department of Agriculture before it can leave the state, so it's safest to buy a box that has already passed inspection.

Business hours for individual shops on the island are usually 9 to 5, seven days a week. Shops on Front Street and in shopping centers tend to stay open later (until 9 or 10 on weekends).

WEST MAUI

From weekend craft fairs under the town's historical banyan tree, to golf apparel at Kapalua, or the art galleries on Front Street, there are plenty of shopping options to peruse on the island's West Shore. Souvenir tchotchkes can be found in local swap meets and Hawaiian confectionery items are available in most grocery stores.

SHOPPING CENTERS

Lahaina Cannery Mall. In a building reminiscent of an old pineapple cannery are 50 shops and an active stage. The mall hosts fabulous free events year-round (like the Keiki Hula Festival and annual ice-sculpting competition). Recommended stops include Na Hoku, purveyor of striking Hawaiian heirloom jewelry and pearls; and Kite Fantasy, one of the best kite shops on Maui. An events schedule is on the Web site. ⊠*1221 Honoapi'ilani Hwy., Lahaina* ☎*808/661–5304* ⊕*www.lahainacannerymall.com.*

Lahaina Center. Island department store Hilo Hattie Fashion Center anchors the complex and puts on a free hula show at 2:30 PM every Wednesday. In addition to the Hard Rock Cafe, Warren & Annabelle's Magic Show, and a four-screen cinema, you can find a replica of an ancient Hawaiian village complete with three full-size thatch huts built with 10,000 feet of Big Island 'ōhi'a wood, 20 tons of *pili* grass, and more than 4 mi of hand-woven coconut *senit* (twine). There's all that *and* validated parking. ⊠*900 Front St., Lahaina* ☎*808/667–9216* ⊕*www.lahainacenter.com.*

Lahaina Gateway. This plaza, newly opened in 2008, includes restaurants; Barnes & Noble; Lahaina Farms, a gourmet grocery store; Sunglass Hut; Office Max; and a host of other stores featuring sporting goods and trendy apparel. ⊠*305 Keawe St., Lahaina* ☎*808/877–7073* ⊕*www.lahainagateway.com.*

Whalers Village. Chic Whalers Village has a whaling museum and more than 50 restaurants and shops. Upscale haunts include Louis Vuitton, Coach, and Tiffany & Co. The complex also offers some interesting diversions: Hawaiian artisans display their crafts daily; hula dancers perform on an outdoor stage weeknights from 6:30 to 7:30; sunset jazz is featured every first Sunday of the month; and Taiko drums and island rhythms beat on Saturday. ⊠*2435 Kā'anapali Pkwy., Kā'anapali* ☎*808/661–4567* ⊕*www.whalersvillage.com.*

BEST MADE-ON-MAUI GIFTS

- *Koa* jewelry boxes from **Maui Hands.**

- Fish-shaped sushi platters and bamboo chopsticks from the **Maui Crafts Guild.**

- Black pearl pendant from **Maui Divers.**

- Handmade Hawaiian quilt from **Hāna Coast Gallery.**

- Jellyfish paperweight from **Hot Island Glass.**

- Fresh plumeria lei, made by you!

6

BOOKSTORES

FodorśChoice **Old Lahaina Book Emporium.** Down a narrow alley you will find this book-
★ store stacked from floor to ceiling with new and antique finds. Spend
a few moments (or hours) browsing the maze of shelves filled with
mystery, sci-fi, nature guides, art, military history, and more. Collectors
can scoop up rare Hawaiian memorabilia: playing cards, coasters, rare
editions, and out-of-print books chronicling Hawai'i's colorful past. ✉
834 Front St., in alley next door, Lahaina ☎*808/661–1399* ⊕*www.
oldlahainabookemporium.com.*

CLOTHING

Hilo Hattie Fashion Center. Hawai'i's largest manufacturer of aloha shirts
and mu'umu'u also carries brightly colored blouses, skirts, and children's
clothing. ✉*Lahaina Center, 900 Front St., Lahaina* ☎*808/667–7911*
⊕*www.hilohattie.com.*

Honolua Surf Company. If you're not in the mood for a matching aloha
shirt and mu'umu'u ensemble, check out this surf shop—popular with
young men and women for surf trunks, casual clothing, and accessories.
✉*845 Front St., Lahaina* ☎*808/661–8848* ⊕*www.honoluasurf.com.*

Maggie Coulombe. Maggie Coulombe's cutting-edge fashions have the
style of SoHo and the heat of the Islands. The svelte, body-clinging
designs are unique and definitely worth a look. ✉*505 Front St., Lahaina* ☎*808/662–0696* ⊕*www.maggiecoulombe.com.*

Mahina. Work the latest styles without breaking the bank. A friendly
staff, easy-breezy jersey dresses, and resort-perfect rompers await the
smart shopper at this shop. ✉*335 Keawe St., Lahaina* ☎*808/661–0383*
✉*1913-B S. Kīhei Rd., Kīhei* ☎*808/879–3453* ✉*23 Baldwin Ave.,
Pā'ia* ☎*808/579–9131* ⊕*www.mahinamaui.com.*

FOOD

Lahaina Square Shopping Center Foodland. This Foodland serves West
Maui and is open daily from 6 AM to midnight. ✉*878 Front St., Lahaina* ☎*808/661–0975.*

Safeway. Safeway has three stores on the island open 24 hours daily. ✉*Lahaina Cannery Mall, 1221 Honoapi'ilani Hwy., Lahaina* ☎*808/667–4392.*

GALLERIES

Lahaina Galleries. Works of both national and international artists are
displayed at the gallery's two locations in West Maui. ✉*828 Front
St., Lahaina* ☎*808/661–6284* ✉ *The Shops at Wailea, 3750 Wailea
Alanui Dr., Wailea* ☎*808/874–8583* ⊕*www.lahainagalleries.com.*

Lahaina Printsellers Ltd. Hawai'i's largest selection of original antique maps
and prints pertaining to Hawai'i and the Pacific is available here. You
can also buy museum-quality reproductions and original oil paintings
from the Pacific Artists Guild. There's a second, smaller shop is at 505
Front Street. ✉*Whalers Village, 2435 Kā'anapali Pkwy., Kā'anapali*
☎*808/667–7617* ⊕*www.printsellers.com.*

Martin Lawrence Galleries. Martin Lawrence displays the works of noted
mainland artists, including Andy Warhol and Keith Haring, in a bright
and friendly gallery. ✉*Lahaina Market Pl., Front St. at Lahainaluna Rd.,
Lahaina* ☎*808/661–1788* ⊕*www.martinlawrence.com.*

Village Gallery. This gallery, with two locations on the island, showcases the works of such popular local artists as Betty Hay Freeland, Margaret Bedell, George Allan, Joyce Clark, Pamela Andelin, Stephen Burr, and Macario Pascual. ⊠*120 Dickenson St., Lahaina* ☎*808/661–4402* ⊠*Ritz-Carlton, 1 Ritz-Carlton Dr., Kapalua* ☎*808/669–1800* ⊕*www.villagegalleriesmaui.com.*

Wyland Galleries. Robert Wyland is a globally celebrated artist known for his ubiquitous gigantic murals of whales, dolphins, and other marine life. Enjoy his artwork—along with some from other fine artists—at his namesake gallery in Lahaina. ⊠*711 Front St., Lahaina* ☎*808/667–2285* ⊕*www.wyland.com.*

JEWELRY

Jessica's Gems. Jessica's has a good selection of Hawaiian heirloom jewelry, including custom designs by Maui designer David Welty. Both stores specialize in black pearls. ⊠ *Whalers Village, 2435 Kā'anapali Pkwy., Kā'anapali* ☎*808/661–4223* ⊠*858 Front St., Lahaina* ☎*808/661–9200* ⊕*www.jessicasgems.com.*

Lahaina Scrimshaw. Here you can buy brooches, rings, pendants, cuff links, tie tacks, and collector's items adorned with intricately carved sailors' art. ⊠*845A Front St., Lahaina* ☎*808/661–8820* ⊠*Whalers Village, 2435 Kā'anapali Pkwy., Kā'anapali* ☎*808/661–4034* ⊕*www.lahainascrimshaw.net.*

Maui Divers. This company has been crafting gold and coral into jewelry for more than 40 years. ⊠*640 Front St., Lahaina* ☎*808/661–0988* ⊕*www.mauidivers.com.*

CENTRAL MAUI

While locals come here in droves for their monthly Costco run or to catch the latest flick at Queen Ka'ahumanu Center, Central Maui can be an ideal shopping destination for visiting families who are passing time on their way to or from the airport. Most of the stores here can be found on the mainland; however, there are some specialty shops worth a peek for Hawaiiana or water-sports goods.

SHOPPING CENTERS

Maui Mall. The anchor stores here are Longs Drugs and Star Market, and there's a decent Chinese restaurant, Dragon Dragon. The Tasaka Guri Guri Shop is an oddity—it's been around for nearly a hundred years, selling an ice-cream–like confection called "guri guri." The mall also has a whimsically designed 12-screen megaplex. ⊠*70 E. Ka'ahumanu Ave., Kahului* ☎*808/872–4320* ⊕*www.mauimall.com.*

Maui Marketplace. On the busy stretch of Dairy Road, just outside Kahului Airport, this behemoth marketplace couldn't be more conveniently located. The 20-acre complex houses several outlet stores and big retailers, such as Pier One Imports, Sports Authority, and Borders Books & Music. Sample local food at the Kau Kau Corner food court. ⊠ *270 Dairy Rd., Kahului* ☎*808/873–0400.*

Queen Ka'ahumanu Center. This is Maui's largest mall with 75 stores, a movie theater, an active stage, and a food court. The mall's interesting rooftop, composed of a series of manta ray–like umbrella shades, is easily spotted. Stop at Camellia Seeds for what the locals call "crack seed," a snack made from dried fruits, nuts, and lots of sugar. Other stops here include mall standards such as Macy's, Pacific Sunwear, and American Eagle Outfitters. ⊠*275 W. Ka'ahumanu Ave., Kahului* ☎*808/877–3369* ⊕*www. queenkaahumanucenter.com.*

ARTS AND CRAFTS

Mele Ukulele. For those looking for a professional quality, authentically Maui 'ukulele, skip the souvenir shops. Mele's crafted beauties are made of koa or mahogany, and strung by hand by the store's owner, Michael Rock. ⊠*1750 Ka'ahumanu Ave., Wailuku* ☎*808/244–3938* ⊕*www.meleukulele.com.*

CLOTHING

Bohemia. Find vintage Hawaiiana, top-quality designer resale, *and* new pieces by upscale designers like Letarte, Chanel, Roberto Cavalli, and Juicy Couture, all at affordable prices. ⊠*105 N. Market St., Wailuku* ☎*808/244–9995.*

Hi-Tech. Stop here immediately after deplaning to stock up on surf trunks, windsurfing gear, bikinis, and sundresses. ⊠*425 Koloa St., Kahului* ☎*808/877–2111* ⊕*www.htmaui.com.*

FOOD

Maui Coffee Roasters. This café and roasting house near Kahului Airport is the best stop for Kona and Island coffees. The salespeople give good advice and will ship items. You even get a free cup of joe in a signature to-go cup when you buy a pound of coffee. ⊠*444 Hāna Hwy., Unit B, Kahului* ☎*808/877–2877* ⊕*www.mauicoffeeroasters.com.*

Safeway. Safeway has three stores on the island open 24 hours daily. ⊠*170 E. Kamehameha Ave., Kahului* ☎*808/877–3377.*

FLEA MARKETS

Lahaina Civic Center Craft Fair. An eclectic mix of vendors and artists set up shop at the Lahaina Civic Center property. You'll find the whole gamut of souvenir shopping, from towels to aloha prints. ⊠ *1840 Honoapi'ilani Hwy., Lahaina* ⬛*$1 suggested donation* ⊙ *Most Sun. 9 AM–4 PM.*

Maui Swap Meet. This Saturday flea market in Central Maui is the biggest bargain on the island, with crafts, souvenirs, fruit, shells, and lots more. ⊠ *310 Ka'ahuman Ave., Kahului* ☎*808/877–3100* ⬛*50¢* ⊙*Sat. 7 AM–1 PM.*

▪TIP➔Check out ⊕www.maui markets.com for information.

Continued on page 158

ALL ABOUT LEIS

Leis brighten every occasion in Hawai'i, from birthdays to bar mitzvahs to baptisms. Creative artisans weave nature's bounty—flowers, ferns, vines, and seeds—into gorgeous creations that convey an array of heartfelt messages: "Welcome," "Congratulations," "Good luck," "Farewell," "Thank you," "I love you." When it's difficult to find the right words, a lei expresses exactly the right sentiments.

WHERE TO BUY THE BEST LEIS

These florists carry a nice variety of leis: **A Special Touch** (Emerald Plaza, 142 Kupuohi St., Ste. F-1, Lahaina, 808/661—3455); **Kahului Florist** (Maui Mall, 70 E. Ka'ahumanu Ave., Kahului, 808/877–3951 or 800/711—8881); **Nāpili Florist** (5059 Nāpilihau St., Lahaina, 808/669-4861); and **Kīhei-Wailea Flowers by Cora** (1280 S. Kīhei Rd., Ste. 126, Kīhei, 808/879-7249 or 800/339—0419). **Costco**, **Kmart**, **Wal-Mart**, and **Safeway** sell basic leis, such as orchid and plumeria.

LEI ETIQUETTE

■ To wear a closed lei, drape it over your shoulders, half in front and half in back. Open leis are worn around the neck, with the ends draped over the front in equal lengths.

■ Pīkake, ginger, and other sweet, delicate blossoms are "feminine" leis. Men opt for cigar, crown flower, and ti leaf, which are sturdier and don't emit as much fragrance.

■ Leis are always presented with a kiss, a custom that supposedly dates back to World War II when a hula dancer fancied an officer at a U.S.O. show. Taking a dare from members of her troupe, she took off her lei, placed it around his neck, and kissed him on the cheek.

■ You shouldn't wear a lei before you give it to someone else. Hawaiians believe the lei absorbs your *mana* (spirit); if you give your lei away, you'll be giving away part of your essence.

ORCHID

Growing wild on every continent except Antarctica, orchids—which range in color from yellow to green to purple—comprise the largest family of plants in the world. There are more than 20,000 species of orchids, but only three are native to Hawai'i—and they are very rare. The pretty lavender vanda you see hanging by the dozens at local lei stands has probably been imported from Thailand.

MAILE

Maile, an endemic twining vine with a heady aroma, is sacred to Laka, goddess of the hula. In ancient times, dancers wore maile and decorated hula altars with it to honor Laka. Today, "open" maile leis usually are given to men. Instead of ribbon, interwoven lengths of maile are used at dedications of new businesses. The maile is untied, never snipped, for doing so would symbolically "cut" the company's success.

'ILIMA

Designated by Hawai'i's Territorial Legislature in 1923 as the official flower of the island of O'ahu, the golden 'ilima is so delicate it lasts for just a day. Five to seven hundred blossoms are needed to make one garland. Queen Emma, wife of King Kamehameha IV, preferred 'ilima over all other leis, which may have led to the incorrect belief that they were reserved only for royalty.

PLUMERIA

This ubiquitous flower is named after Charles Plumier, the noted French botanist who discovered it in Central America in the late 1600s. Plumeria ranks among the most popular leis in Hawai'i because it's fragrant, hardy, plentiful, inexpensive, and requires very little care. Although yellow is the most common color, you'll also find plumeria leis in shades of pink, red, orange, and "rainbow" blends.

PĪKAKE

Favored for its fragile beauty and sweet scent, pīkake was introduced from India. In lieu of pearls, many brides in Hawai'i adorn themselves with long, multiple strands of white pīkake. Princess Kaiulani enjoyed showing guests her beloved pīkake and peacocks at Āinahau, her Waikīkī home. Interestingly, pīkake is the Hawaiian word for both the bird and the blossom.

KUKUI

The kukui (candlenut) is Hawai'i's state tree. Early Hawaiians strung kukui nuts (which are quite oily) together and burned them for light; mixed burned nuts with oil to make an indelible dye; and mashed roasted nuts to consume as a laxative. Kukui nut leis may not have been made until after Western contact, when the Hawaiians saw black beads from Europe and wanted to imitate them.

THE SOUTH SHORE

Browse ornate beaded accessories while listening to island rhythms at Kīhei Kalama Village Marketplace, or splurge on high-end labels at the Shops at Wailea. Otherwise, stumble upon a strip mall—or seven—to fulfill your gifting needs.

SHOPPING CENTERS

Azeka Place Shopping Center. Azeka II, on the *mauka* (toward the mountains) side of South Kīhei Road, has the Coffee Store (the place for iced mochas), Who Cut the Cheese (the place for aged Gouda), and the Nail Shop (the place for shaping, waxing, and tweezing). Azeka I, the older half on the *makai* (toward the ocean) side of the street, has a decent Vietnamese restaurant and Kīhei's post office. ✉ *1280 S. Kīhei Rd., Kīhei* ☎ *808/879–5000.*

Kīhei Kalama Village Marketplace. This is a fun place to investigate. Shaded outdoor stalls sell everything from printed and hand-painted T-shirts and sundresses to jewelry, pottery, wood carvings, fruit, and gaudily painted coconut husks—some, but not all, made by local craftspeople. ✉ *1941 S. Kīhei Rd., Kīhei* ☎ *808/879–6610.*

Rainbow Mall. This mall is one-stop shopping for condo guests—it offers video rentals, Hawaiian gifts, plate lunches, and a liquor store. ✉ *2439 S. Kīhei Rd., Kīhei* ☎ *808/879–1145* ⊕ *www.rainbowmallmaui.com.*

The Shops at Wailea. Stylish, upscale, and close to most of the resorts, this mall brings high fashion to Wailea. Luxury boutiques such as Gucci, Fendi, Cos Bar, and Tiffany & Co. have shops, as do less-expensive chains like Gap, Guess, and Tommy Bahama's. Several good restaurants face the ocean, and regular Wednesday-night events include live entertainment, art exhibits, and fashion shows. ✉ *3750 Wailea Alanui Dr., Wailea* ☎ *808/891–6770* ⊕ *www.shopsatwailea.com.*

CLOTHING

Cruise. This upscale resort boutique has sundresses, swimwear, sandals, bright beach towels, and a few nice pieces of resort wear. ✉ *In Grand Wailea, 3850 Wailea Alanui Dr., Wailea* ☎ *808/875–1234.*

The Enchantress. Painted silk Sue Wong gowns and glittering tiaras command attention in the window of the Enchantress—the only boutique on the island where you can buy a fantasy wedding gown off the rack. Indulge the little girl within by flaunting a feather-fringed handbag, or hand-painted cowboy boots. It's true—Paris shops here. ✉ *The Shops at Wailea, 3750 Wailea Alanui Dr., Wailea* ☎ *808/891–6360* ⊕ *www.mauienchantress.com.*

Hilo Hattie Fashion Center. Hawai'i's largest manufacturer of aloha shirts and mu'umu'u also carries brightly colored blouses, skirts, and children's clothing. ✉ *297 Pi'ikea Ave., Kīhei* ☎ *808/875–4545* ⊕ *www.hilohattie.com.*

SIMPLE SOUVENIRS

Take Home Maui. The folks at this colorful grocery and deli in West Maui will supply, pack, and deliver produce to the airport or your hotel. ✉ *121 Dickenson St., Lahaina* ☎ *808/661–8067 or 800/545–6284.*

Honolua Surf Company. If you're in the mood for colorful print tees and sundresses, check out this surf shop. It's popular with young men and women for surf trunks, casual clothing, and accessories. ⊠*2411 S. Kīhei Rd., Kīhei* ☎*808/874–0999* ⊕*www.honoluasurf.com.*

Sisters & Company. Opened by four sisters, this little shop has a lot to offer—current brand-name clothing such as True Religion and Da-nang, locally made jewelry, beach sandals, and gifts. Sister No. 3, Rhonda, runs a tiny, ultrahip hair salon in back while Caroline, Sister No. 2, offers mani-pedis. ⊠*The Shops at Wailea, 3750 Wailea Alanui Dr., Wailea* ☎*808/874–0003* ⊕*www.sistersandco.com.*

Tommy Bahama's. It's hard to find a man on Maui who *isn't* wearing a TB–logo aloha shirt. For better or worse, here's where you can get yours. Make sure to grab a Barbados Brownie on the way out at the restaurant attached to the shop. ⊠*The Shops at Wailea, 3750 Wailea Alanui Dr., Wailea* ☎*808/879–7828* ⊕*www.tommybahamas.com.*

FOOD

Foodland. In Kīhei town center, this is the most convenient supermarket for those staying in Wailea. It's open round-the-clock. ⊠*1881 S. Kīhei Rd., Kīhei* ☎*808/879–9350.*

Safeway. Safeway has three stores on the island open 24 hours daily. ⊠*277 Pi'ikea Ave., Kīhei* ☎*808/891–9120.*

6

UPCOUNTRY, THE NORTH SHORE, AND HĀNA

Discover Upcountry Maui's treasures like Ali'i Kula Lavender products (only available on Maui) and gourmet cheeses from Surfing Goat Dairy. Traipse around Makawao for fashion-forward tropical pieces and Hawaiian cowboy, or *paniolo,* gear. Shopping in the North Shore's Pā'ia is as diverse as the town's history and eclectic as its residents. Owned by local artists, Maui Crafts Guild provides alternatives to the run-of-the-mill souvenirs, while fashion havens Nuage Bleu or Biasa Rose Boutique will make the brand-savvy set feel right at home. Hāna's shopping scene consists mainly of flower and fruit stands, but you won't want to miss the fine art collection of Hāna Coast Gallery.

ARTS AND CRAFTS

Hāna Cultural Center. The center sells distinctive island quilts and other Hawaiian crafts. ⊠*4974 Uakea Rd., Hāna* ☎*808/248–8622.*

Hot Island Glass. With furnaces glowing bright orange and loads of mesmerizing sculptures on display, this is an exciting place to visit. The working studio, set back from Makawao's main street in a little courtyard, is owned by a family of glassblowers. ⊠*3620 Baldwin Ave., Makawao* ☎*808/572–4527* ⊕*www.hotislandglass.com.*

CLOTHING

Biasa Rose. This boutique offers hip island styles for the whole family. Charming gifts—pillows, napkins, photo albums—are on display along with comfy cotton Splendid and James Perse tees, airy tunics, and vintage aloha shirts. There's a consignment area in the back where you can score designer pieces on a dime. ⊠*104 Hāna Hwy., Pā'ia* ☎*808/579–8602.*

Collections. This eclectic boutique is brimming with pretty jewelry, humorous gift cards, housewares, leather goods, yoga wear, and Asian print silks. ✉3677 *Baldwin Ave., Makawao* ☎808/572–0781.

Moonbow Tropics. If you're looking for an aloha shirt that won't look out of place on the mainland, make a stop at this little store, which sells the best-quality shirts on the island. ✉36 *Baldwin Ave., Pā'ia* ☎808/579–8592.

Nuage Bleu. Los Angeles meets Maui at trendy Nuage Bleu, where you'll find summery Trina Turk dresses, Paige denim, and hip children's clothing. The entrance emanates a scent reminiscent of fresh bouquets, thanks to a display of Tocca candles and fragrance sticks covered in lavender-scented oil. ✉76 *Hāna Hwy., Pā'ia* ☎808/579–9792 ⊕*www.nuagebleu.com.*

MAUI'S BEST OMIYAGE

Omiyage is the Japanese term for food souvenirs.

■ Lavender salt seasoning from **Ali'i Kula Lavender**, a brand sold only on Maui.

■ Horseradish or apple-banana curry goat cheese from local producer **Surfing Goat Dairy**.

■ Aloha Taro pancake mix from any grocery store.

■ Maui Gold Pineapple from **Take Home Maui**.

■ Maui Peaberry beans from **Maui Coffee Company**, sold in many grocery stores.

■ Nicky Beans from **Maui Coffee Roasters**.

Pink By Nature. Stay ahead of the style curve with coveted lines like Ella Moss, Tart, and Paige Denim. Owner Desiree Martinez's penchant for refined nautical details and easy wearability keeps this rustic store stocked with select pieces from Free People and T-Bag, or showstoppers from local designers Fighting Eel and Tamara Catz. Trendsetting moms can gush about adorable vintage onesies and baby tanks by Annie K. for the wee fashionista-in-training. ✉3663 *Baldwin Ave., Makawao* ☎808/572–9576.

Fodor's Choice ★ **Tamara Catz.** This Maui designer already has a worldwide following, and her sarongs and superstylish beachwear have been featured in many fashion magazines. If you're looking for a sequined bikini or a delicately embroidered sundress, this is the place to check out. And for the blushing beach bride, Catz has recently launched a bridal line that is superhaute. ✉83 *Hāna Hwy., Pā'ia* ☎808/579–9184 ⊕*www.tamaracatz.com.*

FOOD

Mana Foods. Stock up on local fish and grass-fed beef for your barbecue here. You can find the best selection of organic produce on the island, as well as a great bakery and deli at this typically crowded health-food store. ✉49 *Baldwin Ave., Pā'ia* ☎808/579–8078 ⊕*www.manafoodsmaui.com.*

GALLERIES

★ **Hāna Coast Gallery.** One of the best places to shop on the island, this 3,000-square-foot gallery has fine art and jewelry on consignment from local artists. ✉*Hotel Hāna-Maui, Hāna Hwy., Hāna* ☎808/248–8636 or 800/637–0188.

FodorśChoice
★
Maui Crafts Guild. This is one of the more interesting galleries on Maui. Set in a two-story wooden building alongside the highway, the Guild is crammed with treasures. Resident artists craft everything in the store—from *raku* (Japanese lead-glazed) pottery to original sculpture. The prices are surprisingly low. ✉ *43 Hāna Hwy., Pā'ia* 🕾 *808/579–9697* ⊕ *www.mauicraftsguild.com.*

★ **Maui Hands.** This gallery shows work by hundreds of local artists, including *paniolo*- (Hawaiian cowboy) theme lithographs. ✉ *3620 Baldwin Ave., Makawao* 🕾 *808/572–5194* ⊕ *www.mauihands.com.*

Randy Jay Braun Gallery. A local favorite, Randy Jay Braun's black-and-white hula photographs, sepia *paniolo* (Hawaiian cowboy) images, and vivid landscapes are instant classics. His gallery features a slew of his own work, along with satin lei, fused-glass collectibles, and ceramics. ✉ *1152 Makawao Ave., Makawao* 🕾 *808/573–1176* ⊕ *wwwrandy jaybraun.com.*

JEWELRY

Maui Master Jewelers. The exterior of this shop is as rustic as all the old buildings of Makawao, so there's no way to prepare yourself for the elegance of the handcrafted jewelry displayed within. ✉ *3655 Baldwin Ave., Makawao* 🕾 *808/573–5400.*

SWIMWEAR

Hāna Hwy. Surf. You can grab trunks and bikinis, and a board, if needed, at this surf shack on the North Shore. ✉ *149 Hāna Hwy., Pā'ia* 🕾 *808/579–8999* ⊕ *www.hanahwysurf.com.*

FodorśChoice
★
Maui Girl. This is *the* place for swimwear, cover-ups, beach hats, and sandals. Maui Girl designs its own suits and imports teenier versions from Brazil as well. Tops and bottoms can be purchased separately, greatly increasing your chances of finding a suit that actually fits. ✉ *12 Baldwin Ave., Pā'ia* 🕾 *808/579–9266* ⊕ *www.maui-girl.com.*

SPAS

Traditional Swedish massage and European facials anchor most spa menus, though you'll also find shiatsu, ayurveda, aromatherapy, and other body treatments drawn from cultures across the globe. *Lomilomi,* traditional Hawaiian massage involving powerful strokes down the length of the body, is a regional specialty passed down through generations. Many treatments incorporate local plants and flowers. *Awapuhi,* or Hawaiian ginger, and *noni,* a pungent-smelling fruit, are regularly used for their therapeutic benefits. *Limu,* or seaweed, and even coffee are employed in rousing salt scrubs and soaks. And this is just the beginning.

Heavenly Spa at the Westin Kā'anapali Ocean Resort Villas. Find tranquillity at this stellar and fairly new (opened in May 2008) spa near Kā'anapali's Airport Beach. The decor is modern and Asian-inspired, and treatments incorporate Hawaiian elements. Try the *Lilikoi* Fruit Melody, which infuses the fruit in a gentle body exfoliation, luxurious body wrap, and an uplifting oil massage. Couples can opt for tandem *lomilomi* massages (traditional Hawaiian massage involving powerful strokes down the length of the body), all in the privacy of a beautiful tropical suite. Although access to the gym next door is reserved for resort guests only, other amenities such as the steam room and nail salon more than suffice. A little basket hangs on each doorknob, in which guests are asked to place all worries before entering the treatment room. ⊠ *Westin Kā'anapali Ocean Resort Villas, 6 Kai Ala Dr., Kā'anapali* ☎*808/662–2642* ⊕*www.westin. com* ☞*$125 50-min massage, $245 spa package. Steam room, couples suites, relaxation lounges, hot tub, nail salon. Services: aromatherapy, body wraps, facials, hydrotherapy, massage, nail services.*

> **BUDGET-FRIENDLY SPAS**
>
> Try **Spa Luna** (⊠ *810 Ha'ikū Rd., Ha'ikū* ☎ *808/575–2440* ⊕ *www. spaluna.com*), a day spa, which is also an aesthetician's school. In the former Ha'ikū Cannery, it offers services ranging from massage to microdermabrasion. You can opt for professional services, but the student clinics are the real story here. The students' services are offered at a fraction of the regular cost ($30 for a 50-minute massage).

★ **Heavenly Spa by Westin at the Westin Maui.** An exquisite 80-minute Lavender Body Butter treatment is the star of this spa's menu, thanks to a partnership with a local lavender farm. Other options include cabana massage (for couples, too) and water lily sunburn relief with green tea. The facility is flawless, and it's worth getting a treatment just to sip lavender lemonade in the posh ocean-view waiting room. The open-air yoga studio and the gym offer energizing workouts. Bridal parties can request a private area within the salon. ⊠ *Westin Kā'anapali, 2365 Kā'anapali Pkwy., Kā'anapali* ☎*808/661–2588* ⊕*www.westinmaui.com* ☞*$130 50-min massage, $285 day spa packages. Hair salon, hot tub, sauna, steam room. Gym with: cardiovascular machines, free weights, weight-training equipment. Services: aromatherapy, body wraps, facials, hydrotherapy, massage, Vichy shower. Classes and programs: aquaerobics, yoga.*

Fodor'sChoice **Honua Spa at Hotel Hāna-Maui.** A bamboo gate opens into an outdoor
★ sanctuary with a lava-rock basking pool and hot tub; at first glimpse this spa seems to have been organically grown, not built. The decor here can hardly be called decor—it's an abundant, living garden. Taro varieties, orchids, and ferns still wet from Hāna's frequent downpours nourish the spirit as you rest with a cup of jasmine tea, or take an invigorating dip in the plunge pool. Signature aromatherapy treatments utilize *Honua*, the spa's own sumptuous blend of sandalwood, coconut, ginger, and vanilla orchid essences. The Hāna Wellness package is a blissful eight hours of treatments, which can be shared between the family, or enjoyed alone. ⊠ *Hotel Hāna-Maui, 5031 Hāna Hwy., Hāna* ☎*808/270–5290* ⊕*www.hotelhanamaui.com* ☞*$140 60-min massage, $265 spa packages. Hair salon, outdoor hot tub, steam room. Gym with: cardiovascular machines, free weights, weight-training equipment. Services: aromatherapy, body wraps, facials, hydrotherapy, massage. Classes and programs: meditation, Pilates, yoga.*

Fodor'sChoice **The Spa at Four Seasons Resort Maui.** The Four Seasons' hawklike attention
★ to detail is reflected here. Thoughtful gestures like fresh flowers beneath the massage table (to give you something to stare at), organic herbal tea in the

Honua Spa at Hotel Hāna-Maui

"relaxation room," and your choice of music begin to ease your mind and muscles before your treatment even begins. The spa is genuinely stylish and serene, and the therapists are among the best. Warm up for your treatment with a hot ginger blast before hopping into the steam room. You will feel cleansed and nurtured from the inside out. Thanks to an exclusive partnership, the spa offers treatments created by celebrity skin-care specialist Kate Somerville. The "Ultimate Kate" is 80 minutes of superhydrating, collagen-increasing magic, incorporating light therapy and powerful, tingling products that literally wipe wrinkles away. And if you don't mind shelling out for the ultimate indulgence, reserve one of the seaside open-air *hale hau* (traditional thatch-roof houses). You can have not just one, but two or more

SPA TIPS
■ Arrive early for your treatment so you can enjoy the amenities.
■ Bring a comfortable change of clothing and remove your jewelry.
■ Most spas are clothing-optional. If a swimsuit is required, you will be notified.
■ If you're pregnant, or have allergies, say so before you book a treatment.
■ Your therapist should be able to explain the ingredients of products being used in your treatment. If anything stings or burns, say so.
■ Gratuities of 15%–20% are suggested.

therapists realign your body and spirit with a meditative *lomilomi* (traditional Hawaiian massage involving powerful strokes down the length of the body) as you listen to the soothing waves of Wailea Beach. ⊠*3900 Wailea Alanui Dr., Wailea* ☎*808/874–8000 or 800/334–6284* ⊕*www. fourseasons.com/maui* ☞*$150 50-min massage, $450 3-treatment packages. Hair salon, steam room, seaside cabanas. Gym with: cardiovascular machines, free weights, weight-training equipment. Services: aromatherapy, body wraps, facials, hydrotherapy, massage. Classes and programs: aquaerobics, meditation, personal training, Pilates, Spinning, tai chi, yoga.*

Fodor'sChoice **Spa Grande, Grand Wailea Resort.** Built to satisfy an indulgent Japanese bil-
★ lionaire, this 50,000-square-foot spa makes others seem like well-appointed closets. Slathered in honey and wrapped up in the steam room (if you go for the Ali'i honey steam wrap), you'll feel like royalty. All treatments include a loofah scrub and a trip to the *termé,* a hydrotherapy circuit including a Roman Jacuzzi, furo bath, plunge pool, powerful waterfall and Swiss jet showers, and five therapeutic baths. (Soak for 10 minutes in the moor mud to relieve sunburn or jellyfish stings.) To fully enjoy the baths, plan to arrive an hour before your treatment. Free with treatments, the termé is also available separately for $55 for two hours. At times—especially during the holidays—this wonderland can be crowded. ⊠*3850 Wailea Alanui Dr., Wailea* ☎*808/875–1234 or 800/888–6100* ⊕*www. grandwailea.com* ☞*$150 50-min massage, $255 half-day spa packages. Hair salon, hot tub, sauna, steam room. Gym with: cardiovascular machines, free weights, racquetball, weight-training equipment. Services: aromatherapy, body wraps, facials, hydrotherapy, massage, Vichy shower. Classes and programs: aquaerobics, cycling, Pilates, qigong (activities focusing on the body's qi, or energy), yoga.*

Fodor'sChoice ★

Spa Grande, Grand Wailea Resort

The Spa at the Four Seasons Resort Maui

Spa Grande, Grand Wailea Resort

Spa Kea Lani, Fairmont Kea Lani. This small spa is a little cramped, but nicely appointed: fluffy robes and Italian mints greet you upon arrival. We recommend the excellent *lomilomi* massage—a series of long, soothing strokes combined with gentle stretching—or the *ili ili* hot stone therapy. Both treatments employ indigenous healing oils: rich *kukui* nut, kava, and *noni* (a pungent-smelling fruit), and tropical fragrances. Poolside massages by the divinely serene adult pool can be reserved on the spot. Not in a lounging mood? Check out the state-of-the-art 1,750-square-foot fitness center. ⊠ *4100 Wailea Alanui Dr., Wailea* ☎ *808/875–4100 or 800/441–1414* ⊕ *www.kealani.com* ☞ *$145 50-min massage, $340 spa packages. Hair salon, steam room. Gym with: cardiovascular machines, free weights, weight-training equipment. Services: aromatherapy, body wraps, facials, hydrotherapy, massage. Classes and programs: aquaerobics, body sculpting, personal training, yoga.*

Spa Moana, Hyatt Regency Maui. Spa Moana's oceanfront salon has a million-dollar view. It's a perfect place to beautify before your wedding or special anniversary, and it's a convenient beach stroll from its adjacent parking lot. An older facility, it's spacious and well-appointed, offering traditional Swedish and Thai massage, Reiki, and shiatsu, in addition to numerous innovative treatments such as the hydrating vitamin C facial for sun lovers, invigorating Ka'anapali coffee salt scrub, and the immune-boosting Ali'i Royal Experience, a papaya-pineapple–grapeseed scrub and propolis lotion rub combined with a facial and *kukui* nut oil scalp massage. For body treatments, the oceanfront rooms are a tad too warm—request one in back. ⊠ *200 Nohea Kai Dr., Lahaina* ☎ *808/661–1234 or 800/233–1234* ⊕ *www.maui.hyatt.com* ☞ *$140 50-min massage, $266 spa packages. Hair salon, hot tub, sauna, steam room. Gym with: cardiovascular machines, free weights, weight-training equipment. Services: aromatherapy, body wraps, facials, massage, Vichy shower. Classes and programs: aquaerobics, Pilates, tai chi, yoga.*

★ **Waihua Spa, Ritz-Carlton, Kapalua.** This gorgeous 17,500-square-foot spa reopened as part of the hotel's recent renovation. Enter this blissful maze where floor-to-ceiling riverbed stones lead to serene treatment rooms, couples' *hales* (cabanas), and a wet grotto with a Jacuzzi, dry sauna, and steam rooms. With cucumber water in hand, hang out in the co-ed waiting area, where sliding glass doors open to a whirlpool overlooking a taro patch garden. Get any rough skin exfoliated with a pineapple papaya scrub; then wash it off in a private outdoor shower garden before indulging in a traditional *lomilomi* massage (traditional Hawaiian massage involving powerful strokes down the length of the body). The spa's caviar of beauty treatments uses advanced oxygen technology to tighten mature skin. Attention fitness junkies: personal TVs are attached to the state-of-the-art cardiovascular machines in the oceanview fitness center. ⊠ *1 Ritz-Carlton Dr., Kapalua* ☎ *808/669–6200 or 800/262–8440* ⊕ *www.ritzcarlton.com* ☞ *$150 50-min massage, $375 half-day spa packages. Hair salon, hot tubs (outdoor and indoor), sauna, steam room. Gym with: cardiovascular machines, free weights, weight-training equipment. Services: aromatherapy, body wraps, facials, massage. Classes and programs: aquaerobics, cycling, nutrition, Pilates, yoga.*

Entertainment
and Nightlife

WORD OF MOUTH

"Drums of the Pacific at the Hyatt has the best fire knife dancer on Maui. This lū'au also has a better variety of dances from many countries. [Old Lahaina Lū'au] does not have a fire knife dancer."
—dusty56438

Updated by
Eliza Escaño-
Vasquez

Looking for wild island nightlife? We can't promise you'll always find it here—and sometimes you'll just have to be the party. This island has little of Waikīkī's after-hours decadence, and the club scene can be quirky, depending on the season and the day of the week. But sometimes Maui will surprise you with a big-name concert, world-class DJ, outdoor festival, or special event. And if the event promises to draw a big crowd, chances are it's at the Maui Arts & Cultural Center in Wailuku, or the MACC, as it is known.

Lahaina and Kīhei are your best bets for action. Lahaina tries to uphold its reputation as a party town, and succeeds every Halloween when thousands of masqueraders converge for a Mardi Gras–style party on Front Street. Kīhei is a bit more local and can be something of a rough-and-rowdy crowd in parts. On the right night, both towns stir with activity, and if you don't like one scene, there's always next door.

Outside Lahaina and Kīhei, you might be able to hit an "on" night in Pā'ia (North Shore) or Makawao (Upcountry), especially on weekend nights. Your best bet? Pick up the free *MauiTime Weekly,* or Thursday's edition of the *Maui News,* where you'll find a listing of all your after-dark options, island-wide.

ENTERTAINMENT

Before 10 PM, there's a lot to offer by way of lū'au shows, dinner cruises, and tiki-lighted cocktail hours. Aside from that, you should at least be able to find some down-home DJ-spinning or the strum of acoustic guitars at your nearest watering hole or restaurant.

DINNER CRUISES AND SHOWS

There's no better place to see the sun set on the Pacific than from one of Maui's many boat tours. You can find a tour to fit your mood, as you can choose anything from a quiet, sit-down dinner to a festive, beer-swigging booze cruise. Note, however, that many cocktail cruises have recently put a cap on the number of free drinks offered with open bars, instead including a limited number of drinks per ticket.

Tours leave from Mā'alaea or Lahaina harbors. Be sure to arrive at least 15 minutes early (count in the time it will take to park). The dinner cruises typically feature music and are generally packed—which is great if you're feeling social, but you might have to fight for a good seat. You can usually get a much better meal at one of the local restaurants, and opt instead for a different type of tour. Most nondinner cruises offer *pūpū* (appetizers) and sometimes a chocolate-and-champagne toast.

CLOSE UP — Slack-Key Guitars and 'Ukuleles

You may not think about Hawai'i's music until you step off a plane on the Islands, and then there's no escaping it. It's a unique blend of the strings and percussion favored by the early settlers and the chants and rituals of the ancient Hawaiians. Hawaiian music today includes Island-devised variations on acoustic guitar—slack key and steel guitar—along with the 'ukulele (a small, four-string guitar about the size of a violin), and vocals that have evolved from ritual chants to more-melodic compositions.

This is one of the few folk music traditions in the United States that is fully embraced by the younger generation, with no prodding from their parents or grandparents. Many of the radio stations on Maui play plenty of Hawaiian music, and concerts performed by

Island favorites are filled with fans of all ages.

One don't-miss opportunity to hear Hawaiian music on Maui is the outstanding Masters of the Slack-Key Guitar Concert series, weekly concerts held at the Nāpili Kai Beach Resort. You can catch Grammy-winning slack-key legends in an intimate setting. The mellow *ki ho'alu* (slack key) music will show you to a bit of Hawaii's *paniolo* (cowboy) history and knee-slapping banter among the musicians as they tune their guitars. Call ☎ 888/669–3858 for reservations, or check at ⊕ www.slackkey.com.

Check ads and listings in local papers, and the Maui Arts & Cultural Center, for information on concerts, which take place in indoor and outdoor theaters, hotel ballrooms, and cozy nightclubs.

Winds are consistent in summer, but variable in winter—sometimes making for a rocky ride. If you're worried about seasickness, you might consider a catamaran, which is much more stable than a monohull. Keep in mind, the boat crews are experienced in dealing with such matters. The best advice? Take Dramamine before the trip, and if you feel sick, sit in the shade (but not inside the cabin), place a cold rag or ice on the back of your neck, and *breathe* as you look at the horizon. In the worst-case scenario, aim downwind—and shoot for distance.

America II Sunset Sail. The star of this two-hour cruise is the craft itself—a 1987 America's Cup 12-meter class contender that will take you on a wild ride. This trip is all about the sail, so you can count out any cocktails or fancy food. But if it's adventure you're looking for, you will go fast, you will get wet—and you will have fun. Private charters are available. ⊠ *Slip 6, Lahaina Harbor, Lahaina* ☎ *808/667–2195* ⊕ *www.sailingonmaui.com* 🖃 *$40* ⊙ *Daily 4–6* PM.

Hula Girl Dinner Cruise. This custom-charter catamaran is one of the best-equipped boats on the island, complete with a VIP lounge for 12 people. The company offers a different approach to a dinner cruise: everything is cooked to order by an onboard chef. The trips are on the pricier side, mainly because the initial cost doesn't include the meal. But if you're willing to splurge for a comfy set-up and upscale service, then it can be worth it. Three-hour dinner sails run from April 1 to December 15 and also include a hula show. Two-hour whale-watching trips fill the calendar gap. ✉ *Check-in in front of Leilani's restaurant at Whalers Village, Kāʻanapali* ☎ *808/665–0344 or 808/667–5980* ⊕ *www.sailingmaui.com* 🖥 *$68.62 adult, $54.13 child 2–12* ☼ *Daily, call for seasonal check-in times.*

Kaulana Cocktail Cruise. This two-hour sunset cruise prides itself on its live music and festive atmosphere. Accommodating up to 100 people, the cruise generally attracts a younger, more-boisterous crowd. *Pūpū*, such as meatballs, crab and shrimp platters, and teriyaki pineapple chicken are served, and there is a full bar (two drinks included). Freshly baked chocolate-chip cookies are passed around toward the end of the trip. ✉ *Lahaina Harbor, Slip 3* ☎ *800/244–7400* ⊕ *www.tombarefoot.com/maui/kaulana_sunset.html* 🖥 *$49* ☼ *Mon., Wed., and Fri. 4:30–7:30 PM.*

Maui Princess Dinner Cruise. This 118-foot yacht is set up with a dance floor, open-air deck, snack bar, and cocktail lounge. Dinner is prepared fresh daily and not catered by an outside company. Unlike other sunset cruises, there's no need to rush to get a good seat—the upper-deck tables are already reserved for each party. Guests have a choice of roasted chicken with sesame sauce, a 12-ounce prime rib with au jus and horseradish, or a vegetarian Mediterranean couscous pocket with tomato, mushroom, and herb sauce, all with table-side service. ✉ *Lahaina Harbor, Slip 3* ☎ *877/500–6284 or 808/667–6165* ⊕ *www.mauiprincess.com* 🖥 *$96.44 adult, $66.63 child 7–12* ☼ *5 PM–8 PM.*

Pacific Whale Foundation Dinner or Cocktail Cruise. All aboard a sleek double-deck power catamaran for a dinner of grilled steak and chicken, mahimahi, vegetable tofu stir-fry, and orange-glazed pound cake. This cruise holds up to 100 people, so it can be crowded. Note that if the water is choppy and the wind is blowing, it won't be a comfortable experience with napkins and utensils flying around. You might just opt for a relaxing "booze cruise," with hot and cold appetizers, live entertainment, and bar (three drinks included). ✉ *Ocean Discovery Store, 612 Front St., Lahaina* ☎ *808/249–8811* ⊕ *www.pacificwhale.org* 🖥 *$84.95 dinner cruise; $49.95 cocktail cruise* ☼ *Daily, call for seasonal check-in times.*

Paragon Champagne Sunset Sail. This 47-foot catamaran brings you a performance sail within a personal setting. Limited to groups of 24 (with private charters available), you can spread out on deck and enjoy the gentle trade winds. It's free for children three and under. An easygoing, attentive crew will serve you hot and cold *pūpū*, such as grilled chicken skewers, spring rolls, and a fruit platter, along with beer, wine, mai tais, and champagne at sunset. This is one of the best trips around. ✉ *Loading Dock, Lahaina Harbor* ☎ *808/244–2087* ⊕ *www.sailmaui.*

Hula, music, and traditional foods are all part of the popular Old Lahaina Lū'au.

com ✉$47.60 adult, $33.15 child 4–12, free for children 3 and under ⊙ Mon., Wed., Fri. evenings only; call for check-in times.

Pride Charters. A 65-foot catamaran built specifically for Maui's waters, the *Pride of Maui* has a spacious cabin, dance floor, and large upper deck for unobstructed viewing. Evening cruises include premium, top-shelf cocktails and an impressive spread of baby back ribs, grilled chicken, roasted veggies, artichoke dip, and penne pasta salad. Desserts include tropical cake and assorted tarts. ⊠ *Mā'alaea Harbor, Mā'alaea* ☎877/867–7433 ⊕*www.prideofmaui.com* ✉$69.95 ⊙*Tues., Thurs., and Sat. 5–7:30* PM.

Scotch Mist Charters. Sailing is at its best on this two-hour champagne cruise. The 25-passenger, 50-foot *Scotch Mist II* will give you an intimate and exhilarating ride, with complimentary champagne, chocolate, fresh pineapple, juice, beer, and wine. Private charters are available. ⊠ *Lahaina Harbor, Slip 2, Lahaina* ☎808/661–0386 ⊕*www.scotchmistsailingcharters.com* ✉$59.95 ⊙*Daily; call for seasonal check-in times.*

Spirit of Lahaina Dinner Cruise. This double-deck, 65-foot catamaran offers a family-style dinner cruise, featuring appetizers, warm taro rolls, freshly grilled steak, *huli-huli* chicken (barbecued with flavors like brown sugar cane, ginger, and soy), shrimp skewered on sugarcane, and fabulous desserts. The trip also features contemporary Hawaiian music, hula, and a comedy magic show that will definitely cure you of any motion sickness. ⊠ *Lahaina Harbor, Slip 4, Lahaina* ☎808/662–4477 ⊕*www. spiritoflahaina.com* ✉$99 adult, $59 child ⊙*Daily 5–7:15* PM.

Teralani Sailing Charters. Teralani catamarans are modern, spotless, and laid out comfortably for dining. Check-in for this trip is at 3 PM and the boat heads back shortly after sunset, which means plenty of light to enjoy the food and view. During whale watching season the best seats are the corner booths at the front of the boat. The buffet is a few notches up from other dinner cruise spreads, featuring vegetable crudite, chipotle citrus rotisserie chicken, and grilled ono fish with roasted red pepper sauce. The trip departs from the shore of *Kā'anapali's Dig Me Beach in front of Leilani's at Whalers Village.* ✉ ⊕ *2435 Kā'anapali Pkwy., Kā'anapali* ☎*808/661–1230* ⊕*www.teralani.net* ✉*$79 adult, $69 teen 13–19, $59 child 3–12.*

> ## STARGAZING
>
> For nightlife of a different sort, children and astronomy buffs can try **Tour of the Stars,** a one-hour stargazing program on the roof or patio of the Hyatt Regency Maui. **Romance of the Stars,** with champagne and chocolate-covered strawberries, is held on Friday and Saturday at 11 PM. Check-in at the hotel lobby 15 minutes prior to starting time. ✉*Lahaina Tower, Hyatt Regency Maui Resort & Spa, 200 Nohea Kai Dr., Kā'anapali* ☎*808/661–1234 Ext. 4727* ⊕ *www.maui.hyatt.com* ✉*$20–$25 adult, $15 child 12 and under* ☉ *Tues.–Sat. 8, 9, and 10; Fri. and Sat. romantic program 11 PM.*

LŪ'AU

A trip to Hawai'i isn't complete without a good lū'au. With the beat of drums and the sway of hula, lū'au give you a snippet of Hawaiian culture left over from a long-standing tradition. Early Hawaiians celebrated many occasions with lū'au—weddings, births, battles, and more. The feasts originally brought people together as an offering to the gods, and to practice *ho'okipa,* the act of welcoming guests. The word *lū'au* itself refers to the taro root, a staple of the Hawaiian diet, which, when pounded, makes a gray, pudding-like substance called *poi.* You'll find poi at all the best feasts, along with platters of salty fish, fresh fruit, and *kālua* (baked underground) pork. *For more information about Hawaiian food and lū'au, see the Authentic Taste of Hawai'i feature in Chapter 8, Where to Eat.*

Lū'au are still held by locals today to mark milestones or as informal, family-style gatherings. For tourists, they are a major attraction and, for that reason, have become big business. Keep in mind—some are watered-down tourist traps just trying to make a buck, others offer a night you'll never forget. As the saying goes, you get what you pay for. ■ TIP➡Many of the best lū'au book weeks, sometimes months, in advance, so reserve early. Plan your lū'au night early on in your trip to help you get into the Hawaiian spirit.

★ **The Feast at Lele.** "Lele" is an older, more traditional name for Lahaina. This feast redefines the lū'au by crossing it with island-style fine dining in an intimate beach setting. Each course of this succulent sit-down meal expresses the spirit of specific island cultures—Hawaiian, Samoan, Tongan, Tahitian—and don't forget dessert. Dramatic Polynesian entertainment accompanies the dinner, along with excellent wine and liquor selections. Tables are arranged to fit the size of your group. This is the most expensive lū'au on the island for a reason: Lele is top-notch. ✉ *505 Front St., Lahaina* ☎ *808/667–5353* ⊕ *www.feastatlele.com* ⚓ *Reservations essential* 💲 *$110 adult, $80 child 2–12* ⊙ *Nightly at sunset; 5:30* PM *in winter, 6* PM *in summer.*

★ **Ho'omana'o at Old Lahaina Lū'au.** Save yourself the hangover and get into the Island culture instead with this morning event. Start off with a lovely hula show accompanied by a scrumptious breakfast buffet of *kālua* (baked underground) pork hash with *lomilomi* (rubbed with herbs and onions) salmon, French toast with mango orange marmalade, *haupia* (coconut pudding) oatmeal, tropical fruits, and Kona coffee. (Sorry, no all-you-can-drink mimosas.) Then proceed to three *kūlana*, or villages, to explore the lives of indigenous Hawaiians through interactive presentations. You'll get to pass around fascinating artifacts, play with traditional weaponry, apply tattoos, and learn the hula with instruments. It's ideal for the whole family, but note that it's three hours long and younger children could get fussy halfway through. ✉ *1251 Front St., Lahaina* ☎ *808/667–1998* ⊕ *www.oldlahainaluau.com/hoomanao* 💲 *$69 adult, $49 child 12 and under* ⊙ *Wed. and Fri. 9-noon.*

Hyatt Regency Maui Drums of the Pacific Lū'au. Located by the *Kā'anapali* beach, this lū'au excels in every category—breathtaking location, well-made food, smooth-flowing buffet lines, and a wonderfully authentic program that covers the Hawaiian, Samoan, Tahitian, Fijian, Tongan, and Maori cultures. The cast offers an exhilarating show as you feast on delicious Hawaiian delicacies like *kālua* (baked underground) pork, *huli-huli* chicken (barbecued with flavors like brown sugar cane, ginger, and soy), 'Ulupalakua beef, Polynesian rice, *lomilomi* (rubbed with onions and herbs) salmon, Pacific 'ahi *poke* (pickled raw tuna, tossed with herbs and seasonings), *poi* (taro root paste), and desserts. An open bar features beer, wine and the usual tropical concoctions. ✉ *200 Nohea Kai Dr., Kā'anapali* ☎ *808/667–4727* ⊕ *www.maui.hyatt.com* 💲 *$96 adult ($119 for premium seating), $61 teen 13–20 ($86 for premium seating), $49 child 6–12 ($75 for premium seating), free for children 5 and under ($30 for premium seating)* ⊙ *Nightly, 5–8* PM.

Fodor's Choice ★ **Old Lahaina Lū'au.** Many consider this the best lū'au on Maui; it's certainly the most traditional. Located right on the water, at the northern end of town, the Old Lahaina Lū'au is small, personal, and as authentic as it gets. Sitting either at a table or on a *lauhala* mat, you'll dine on all-you-can-eat Hawaiian cuisine: pork *laulau* (wrapped with taro sprouts in *tī* leaves), 'ahi *poke* (pickled raw tuna, tossed with herbs and seasonings), *lomilomi* salmon (rubbed with onions and herbs), Maui-style mahimahi, *haupia* (coconut pudding), and more. At sunset the show begins a historical journey that relays key periods in Hawai'i's history, from the arrival of the Polynesians to the influence of the missionaries and, later, tourism. The tanned, talented performers will charm you with their music, chanting, and variety of hula styles (modern and *kahiko*, the ancient way of communicating with the gods). But if it's fire dancers you want to see, you won't find them here, as they aren't considered traditional. Although it's performed nightly, this lū'au sells out regularly. Make your reservations when planning your trip to Maui. You can cancel up until 10 AM the day of the scheduled show. ✉ *1251*

Front St., makai (toward the ocean) of Lahaina Cannery Mall, Lahaina ☎*808/667–1998* ⊕*www.oldlahainaluau.com* ⚑*Reservations essential* ⌨*$92 adult, $62 child 2–12* ⊙*Nightly at 5:15* PM *in winter, 5:45* PM *in summer.*

Wailea Beach Marriott Honua'ula Lū'au. This lū'au offers an open bar, a tasty buffet, and a sunset backdrop that can't be beat. The stage is placed right next to the water, and the show features an *imu* (underground oven) ceremony to start, and Polynesian dancers performing a blend of modern acrobatics (including an impressive fire-knife dance) and traditional hula. ✉*3700 Wailea Alanui Dr., Wailea* ☎*808/879–1922* ⊕*www.marriotthawaii.com* ⚑*Reservations essential* ⌨*$94 adult ($104 for premium seating), $49 child 6–12 ($78 for premium seating)* ⊙*Mon. and Thurs.–Sat. 5–8* PM.

Westin Maui Resort and Spa Wailele Polynesian Lū'au. Held at the hotel's oceanfront Aloha Pavilion, this event offers a picturesque setting where dinner is served family-style during the performance. This option can be too pricey for some, but it might be ideal if you prefer tableside service over buffet lines. Traditional dishes such as ahi *poke* (chopped, pickled raw tuna), fire-roasted teriyaki beef, and Molokai sweet potato with coconut are accompanied by a delicious dessert spread. The show features authentic songs and dances from Hawai'i, Tahiti, New Zealand, and Samoa, and while the costumes may not be as elaborate as elsewhere, the pulse-raising five-member fire knife dance is a thrilling highlight. ✉*2365 Kā'anapali Pkwy., Kā'anapali* ☎*808/669–2992* ⊕*www.westinmaui.com* ⌨*$105 adult ($120 for premier seating), $75 child 5–12 ($90 for premier seating)* ⊙*Tues. 5:30* PM.

ARTS CENTER

★ **Maui Arts & Cultural Center.** The hub of all highbrow arts and quality performances has an events calendar that features everything from rock to reggae to Hawaiian slack-key guitar, international dance and circus troupes, political and literary lectures, art films, cult classics—you name it. Each Wednesday (and occasionally Friday) evening, the MACC hosts movie selections from the Maui Film Festival. The complex includes the 1,200-seat Castle Theater, a 4,000-seat amphitheater for large outdoor concerts, the 350-seat McCoy Theater for plays and recitals, and a courtyard café offering preshow dining and drinks. For information on current events, check the Events Box Office (☎*808/242–7469* ⊕*www. mauiarts.org*) or *Maui News.* ✉*1 Cameron Way, above harbor on Kahului Beach Rd., Kahului* ☎*808/242–2787.*

FILM

In the heat of the afternoon, a theater may feel like paradise. There are megaplexes showing first-run movies in Kukui Mall (Kīhei), Lahaina Center, and Maui Mall and Ka'ahumanu Shopping Center (Kahului).

★ **Maui Film Festival.** In this ongoing celebration, the Maui Arts & Cultural Center features art-house films every Wednesday (and sometimes Friday) evening at 5 and 7:30 PM, accompanied by live music, dining, and poetry in the Candlelight Café & Cinema. In summer, an international weeklong festival attracts big-name celebrities to Maui for cinema under

Continued on page 180

MORE THAN A FOLK DANCE

Hula has been called "the heartbeat of the Hawaiian people" and also "the world's best-known, most misunderstood dance." Both are true. Hula isn't just dance. It is storytelling. No words, no hula.

Chanter Edith McKinzie calls it "an extension of a piece of poetry." In its adornments, implements, and customs, hula integrates every important Hawaiian cultural practice: poetry, history, genealogy, craft, plant cultivation, martial arts, religion, protocol. So when 19th century Christian missionaries sought to eradicate a practice they considered depraved, they threatened more than just a folk dance.

With public performance outlawed and private hula practice discouraged, hula went underground for a generation, to rural villages. The fragile verbal link by which culture was transmitted from teacher to student hung by a thread. Even increasing literacy did not help because hula's practitioners were a secretive and protected circle.

As if that weren't bad enough, vaudeville, Broadway, and Hollywood got hold of the hula, giving it the glitz treatment in an unbroken line from "Oh, How She Could Wicky Wacky Woo" to "Rock-A-Hula Baby." Hula became shorthand for paradise: fragrant flowers, lazy hours. Ironically, this development assured that hundreds of Hawaiians could make a living performing and teaching hula. Many danced 'auana (modern form) in performance; but taught kahiko (traditional), quietly, at home or in hula schools.

Today, 30 years after the cultural revival known as the Hawaiian Renaissance, language immersion programs have assured a new generation of proficient—and even eloquent—chanters, songwriters, and translators. Visitors can see more, and more authentic, traditional hula than at any other time in the last 200 years.

Like the culture of which it is the beating heart, hula has survived.

Lei *po'o*. Head lei. In kahiko, greenery only. In 'auana, flowers.

Face emotes appropriate expression. Dancer should not be a smiling automaton.

Shoulders remain relaxed and still, never hunched, even with arms raised. No bouncing.

Eyes always follow leading hand.

Lei. Hula is rarely performed without a shoulder lei.

Arms and hands remain loose, relaxed, below shoulder level— except as required by interpretive movements.

Traditional hula skirt is loose fabric, smocked and gath- ered at the waist.

Hip is canted over weight-bearing foot.

Knees are always slightly bent, accentuating hip sway.

Kupe'e. Ankle bracelet of flowers, shells, or— traditionally—noise- making dog teeth.

In kahiko, feet are flat. In 'auana, they may be more arched, but not tiptoes or bouncing.

BASIC MOTIONS

Speak or Sing

Moon or Sun

Grass Shack or House

Mountains or Heights

Love or Caress

At backyard parties, hula is performed in bare feet and street clothes, but in performance, adornments play a key role, as do rhythm-keeping implements.

In hula kahiko (traditional style), the usual dress is multiple layers of stiff fabric (often with a pellom lining, which most closely resembles *kapa*, the paperlike bark cloth of the Hawaiians). These wrap tightly around the bosom but flare below the waist to form a skirt. In pre-contact times, dancers wore only kapa skirts. Monarchy-period hula is performed in voluminous Mother Hubbard mu'umu'u or high-necked muslin blouses and gathered skirts. Men wear loincloths or, for monarchy period, white or gingham shirts and black pants—sometimes with red sashes.

In hula 'auana (modern), dress for women can range from grass skirts and strapless tops to contemporary tea-length dresses. Men generally wear aloha shirts, but sometimes grass skirts over pants or even everyday gear. (One group at a recent competition wore wetsuits to do a surfing song!)

SURPRISING HULA FACTS

- Grass skirts are not traditional; workers from Kiribati (the Gilbert Islands) brought this custom to Hawai'i.
- In olden-day Hawai'i, *mele* (songs) for hula were composed for every occasion—name songs for babies, dirges for funerals, welcome songs for visitors, celebrations of favorite pursuits.
- Hula *ma'i* is a traditional hula form in praise of a noble's genitals; the power of the *ali'i* (royalty) to procreate gave *mana* (spiritual power) to the entire culture.
- Hula students in old Hawai'i adhered to high standards: scrupulous cleanliness, no sex, daily cleansing rituals, certain food prohibitions, and no contact with the dead. They were fined if they broke the rules.

WHERE TO WATCH

- Kā'anapali Beach Hotel: Employees break into song at any excuse, teach daily hula lessons, and staff a free nightly hour-long hula show and torchlighting ceremony. ☎ 808/661-0011.
- Feast at Lele: Nightly beachside lū'au includes show that strives for authenticity. ☎866/244-5353.
- Whalers Village: Three weekly free evening hula shows (usually Monday, Wednesday, and Saturday, but check schedule). ☎808/661-4567.
- Hula festivals: Festival of Hula, January, Lahaina Cannery Mall; Na Mele O Maui/Emma Farden Sharpe Hula Festival, December, Kā'anapali Resort (call to check month).

The 'ukulele, a smaller four-string guitar, is part of Hawaiian music's unique sound.

the stars. ☎*808/579–9244 recorded program information* ⊕*www.mauifilmfestival.com.*

THEATER

For live theater, check local papers for events and showtimes.

Maui Academy of Performing Arts. For more than 30 years, this nonprofit performing-arts group has offered fine productions, as well as dance and drama classes for children and teens. Recent shows have included *Peter Pan,* the *Complete Works of William Shakespeare,* and the *Wizard of Oz.* Call ahead for performance venue. ✉*81 N. Church St., Wailuku* ☎*808/244–8760* ⊕*www.mauiacademy.org* 💲*$10–$35.*

Maui OnStage. Located at the Historic 'Iao Theater, this nonprofit theater group stages four to six shows per season. Each October, they hold an "Evening of Stars" Masquerade Ball, which can be a hoot of the costumed kind. ✉*'Iao Theater, 68 N. Market St., Wailuku* ☎*808/242–6969* ⊕*www.mauionstage.com* 💲*$15–$20.*

⊙ ★ **"'Ulalena" at Maui Theatre.** One of Maui's hottest tickets, "'Ulalena" is a 75-minute musical extravaganza that is well received by audiences and Hawaiian-culture experts alike. Cirque du Soleil–inspired, the ensemble cast (20 singer-dancers and a five-musician orchestra) mixes native rhythms and stories with acrobatic performance. High-tech stage wizardry gives an inspiring introduction to island culture. It has auditorium seating, and beer and wine are for sale at the concession stand. There are dinner-theater packages in conjunction with top Lahaina restaurants. ✉*878 Front St., Lahaina* ☎*808/661–9913 or 877/688–4800* ⊕*www.mauitheatre.com* ⌨*Reservations essential* 💲*$59.50–$129.50 for a dinner package* ⊙*Mon.–Sat. 6:30* PM.

Warren & Annabelle's. This is one show not to miss—it's serious comedy with amazing sleight of hand. Magician Warren Gibson entices guests into his swank nightclub with red carpets and a gleaming mahogany bar, and plies them with à la carte appetizers (coconut shrimp, crab cakes), desserts (rum cake, crème brûlée), and "smoking cocktails." Then, he performs

table-side magic while his ghostly assistant, Annabelle, tickles the ivories. This is a nightclub, so no one under 21 is allowed. ✉ *Lahaina Center, 900 Front St., Lahaina* ☏ *808/667–6244* ⊕ *www.hawaiimagic. com* ✍ *Reservations essential* 🖃 *$56 or $94.50, including food and drinks* 🕐 *Mon.–Sat. 5 and 7:30* PM.

NIGHTLIFE

Your best bet when it comes to bars on Maui? If you walk by and it sounds like it's happening, go in. If you want to scope out your options in advance, be sure to check the free *MauiTime Weekly,* found at most stores and restaurants, to find out who's playing where. *Maui News* also publishes an entertainment schedule in its Thursday edition of the "Maui Scene." With an open mind (and a little luck), you can usually find a good scene for fun.

WEST MAUI

BARS AND RESTAURANTS

Cheeseburger in Paradise. This Front Street joint is known for—what else?—big beefy cheeseburgers (not to mention a great spinach-nut burger). This is a casual place to start your evening, as they usually have live music and big, fruity cocktails for happy hour. There's no dance floor, but the second-floor balcony gives you a bird's-eye view of Lahaina's Front Street action. ✉ *811 Front St., Lahaina* ☏ *808/661–4855.*

Cool Cat Café. One could easily miss this casual 1950's-style diner while strolling through Lahaina. Tucked in the second floor of the Wharf Cinema Center, its semi-outdoor area plays host to rockin' local music nightly. The entertainment lineup covers jazz, contemporary Hawaiian, and traditional island rhythms. It doesn't hurt that the kitchen dishes out specialty burgers, fish that's fresh from the harbor, and delicious homemade sauces from the owner's family recipes. ✉ *658 Front St., Lahaina* ☏ *808/667–0908* ⊕ *www.coolcatcafe.com*

Hard Rock Cafe. You've seen one Hard Rock Cafe, you've seen them all. However, Maui's Hard Rock brings you Reggae Monday, featuring beloved local reggae star Marty Dread ($5 cover, 10 PM). ✉ *Lahaina Center, 900 Front St., Lahaina* ☏ *808/667–7400.*

7

Mai Tai Lounge. You have to pass through a lot of "bling" to get to this swanky joint. Perched atop a jewelry store, the oceanfront lounge has a DJ who spins hip-hop, Hawaiian, and reggae music on Friday and Saturday evenings. You might want to ask the bartender to ease up on the ice. ⊠ *839 Front St., Lahaina* ☎ *808/661–5288* ⏱ *11–11.*

Sansei Seafood Restaurant and Sushi Bar. Sansei has stayed a favorite among locals and visitors alike for years. The atmosphere is always spirited. If you're more prone to doing the entertaining yourself,

MAI TAI

Don't let your sweet tooth fool you. Maui's favorite drink—the mai tai—can be as lethal as it is sweet. The Original Trader Vic's recipe calls for 2 ounces of aged dark rum, mixed with almond syrup, orange curaçao, the juice of one lime, and (wouldn't you know it) rock-candy syrup. Mama's Fish House on the North Shore (⇨ *see Chapter 8, Where to Eat*) makes the best-tasting mai tai in town.

why not indulge in some mai tai–induced karaoke and get half-off fresh sushi at the same time? Karaoke nights are Thursday and Friday, and live music is scheduled on Saturday. ⊠ *600 Office Rd., Kapalua* ☎ *808/669–6286* ⊕ *www.sanseihawaii.com* ⏱ *5:30 PM–1 AM.*

CLUB

The Cellar 744. This late-night subterranean spot, formerly known as Paradice Bluz, re-opened in late 2008 without any major renovation but with cushy new lounge seating having replaced its pool tables. Tuesday features hip-hop and reggae but if you're jonesing for some bass-heavy funky house, Friday will give you the necessary fix. ⊠ *744 Front St., Lahaina* ☎ *808/661–3744* ⊕ *www.thecellar744maui.com.*

Moose McGillycuddy's. The Moose offers no-cover live or DJ music on most nights, drawing a young, mostly single crowd who come for the burgers, beer, and dance-floor beats. There's live music on Sunday. ⊠ *844 Front St., Lahaina* ☎ *808/667–7758.*

THE SOUTH SHORE

BARS AND RESTAURANTS

Ambrosia Blues and Jazz Club. For or a chill night out, Ambrosia is a South Maui favorite. It's a cozy hangout for blues, jazz, and folk music, as well as the occasional absinthe drink. The crowd is more sophisticated—less rowdy, but a lot of fun. ⊠ *1913 S. Kīhei Rd., Kīhei* ☎ *808/891–1011* ⊕ *www.ambrosiamaui.com* ⏱ *5 PM–2 AM.*

Kahale's Beach Club. A friendly, casual dive bar, Kahale's offers live music (usually Hawaiian), drinks, and burgers every day from 10 AM until 2 in the morning. If the place is empty, try the Tiki Bar or Lulu's next door. ⊠ *36 Keala Pl., Kīhei* ☎ *808/875–7711.*

Life's a Beach. This place brings in a young, rambunctious bunch looking to par-tay (read: meat market). But hey, if you dig lingerie contests and half-price Jägermeister shots, who are we to judge? Friday and Saturday is live music, Sunday is karaoke. ⊠ *1913 S. Kīhei Rd., Kīhei* ☎ *808/891–8010.*

Lulu's. Lulu's could be your favorite bar in any beach town. It's a second-story, open-air tiki and sports bar, with a pool table, small stage, and dance floor to boot. The most popular night is Salsa Thursday, with dancing and lessons until 11. Wednesday is karaoke night, Friday is classic rock night, and Saturday features guest hip-hop DJs. ⊠ *1945 S. Kīhei Rd., Kīhei* ☎ *808/879–9944.*

> **WHAT'S A LAVA FLOW?**
>
> Can't decide between a piña colada or strawberry daiquiri? Go with a Lava Flow—a mix of light rum, coconut and pineapple juice, and a banana, with a swirl of strawberry puree. Add a wedge of fresh pineapple and a paper umbrella, and mmm . . . good. Try one at Lulu's in Kīhei.

★ **Mulligan's on the Blue.** Frothy pints of Guinness and late-night fish-and-chips—who could ask for more? Saturday and Sunday nights feature foot-stomping Irish jams that will have you dancing a jig, and singing something about "a whiskey for me-Johnny." Other nights bring in various local bands. ⊠ *Blue Golf Course, 100 Kaukahi St., Wailea* ☎ *808/874–1131.*

Sansei Seafood Restaurant and Sushi Bar. Sansei's sister location in Kihei offers the same fun atmosphere and is just as popular among locals and visitors. While the core menu is the same, the ambience is brighter and more casual than Sansei Kapalua's resort-style polish. The place always draws a good crowd on karaoke nights (from Thursday to Saturday) when sushi is half off. ⊠ *1881 S. Kīhei Rd., Kīhei* ☎ *808/879–0004* ⊕ *www.sanseihawaii.com* ☉ *5:30 PM–1 AM.*

South Shore Tiki Lounge. Good eats are paired with cool tunes in this breezy, tropical tavern. Local acts and DJs are featured most evenings; if you're craving some old-school hip-hop, Thursday is your night. ⊠ *1913-J S. Kīhei Rd., Kīhei* ☎ *808/874–6444.*

UPCOUNTRY AND THE NORTH SHORE

BARS AND RESTAURANTS

Casanova Italian Restaurant and Deli. Casanova can bring in some big acts, which in the past have included Kool and the Gang, Los Lobos, and Taj Majal. Most Friday and Saturday nights, though, it attracts a hip, local scene with live bands and eclectic DJs spinning house, funk, and world music. Don't miss the costume theme nights. Wednesday is for Wild Wahines (code for ladies get in free), which can be on the smarmy side. There's a $5 to $25 cover. ⊠ *1188 Makawao Ave., Makawao* ☎ *808/572–0220.*

Charley's. The closest thing to country Maui has to offer, Charley's is a down-home, dive bar in the heart of Pā'ia. It also hosts disco, house, industry, and lounge nights. ⊠ *142 Hāna Hwy., Pā'ia* ☎ *808/579–9453.*

Stopwatch Sportsbar & Grill. This friendly dive bar books favorite local bands on Friday and charges only $3. ⊠ *1127 Makawao Ave., Makawao* ☎ *808/572–1380.*

CLUBS

Jacques. Who could resist a place once voted by locals as the "best place to see suspiciously beautiful people from around the world"? On Friday nights, the crowd spills onto the cozy streets of Pā'ia, as funky DJs spin Latino, world lounge, salsa, and live jazz. ✉ *120 Hāna Hwy., Pā'ia* ☎ *808/579–8844.*

Where to Eat

WORD OF MOUTH

"We still love the informal atmosphere of the Hula Grill bar. You and your husband would have fun and have what we value most— dinner on the beach with the sand under your feet and the sound of the waves."

—chicgeek

WHERE TO EAT PLANNER

Eating Out Strategy

Where should we eat? With dozens of eateries competing for your attention, it may seem like a daunting question. But our expert writers and editors have done most of the legwork—the dozens of selections here represent the best eating experiences Maui has to offer. Search "Best Bets" for top recommendations by price, cuisine, and experience. Or find a restaurant quickly; reviews are ordered alphabetically within their geographic area.

With Kids

Hawai'i is kid-friendly in many ways. The vibe is casual, and even the fancy joints have a *keiki*, or kids' menu, and perhaps a box of crayons hidden somewhere. Some of the hotel restaurants feature cute-as-a-button "knee-high buffets" for the little ones. Take advantage of local treats and experiences such as shave ice and lū'aus.

Smoking

No butts about it: smoking is prohibited in all Hawai'i restaurants and bars.

Reservations

Maui is one of the top tourist islands in the world, and in peak months, it's best to make reservations in advance, at your earliest convenience. If you're dying to go to Mama's Fish House or the Old Lahaina Lū'au, make reservations before leaving home. Everywhere else you may be able to squeeze into, at least at the bar, at the last minute.

What to Wear

Maui's last jacket-required dining room closed years ago. Wear evening resort attire, meaning covered shoes and collared shirts for men (you can get away with dress shorts) and a nice outfit for women at the better restaurants. Refrain from tank tops at family establishments as it's still considered too casual. Bring a sweater or cover-up in winter months—many restaurants are breezy and open-air.

Hours and Prices

Many restaurants on Maui are packed from 5 PM to 7 PM— the early-bird special hours and the best time for viewing sunsets. By 8:30 many dining rooms have quieted down, and by 9:30 most are closed. If the place has a rowdy bar (or is a karaoke hangout), you may be able to get food until 10 or even midnight.

Unless a resort is noted for its culinary department, you may find hotel restaurants somewhat overpriced and underwhelming. We've listed the best of the bunch. To dine well on the cheap, go for coupons advertised in the *Maui News*. Even upscale restaurants go half-price during the slow months (September through November). As for tips, 18% to 20% is standard for quality service.

WHAT IT COSTS AT DINNER				
¢	$	$$	$$$	$$$$
Under $10	$10–$17	$18–$26	$27–$35	Over $35

Restaurant prices are for a main course at dinner.

BEST BETS FOR MAUI DINING

Where can I find the best food the island has to offer? Fodor's writers and editors have selected their favorite restaurants by price, cuisine, and experience in the lists below. In the first column, the Fodor's Choice properties represent the "best of the best" across price categories. You can also search by area for excellent eats—just peruse our complete reviews on the following pages.

★ FODOR'S CHOICE

Cafe O'Lei, $$
Capische, $$$
Gerard's, $$$$
Mama's Fish House, $$$$
A Saigon Café, $$
Waterfront Restaurant, $$$$

By Price

¢
Alexander's Fish & Chips
Maui Bake Shop

$
Cafe Mambo
Cilantro
Jacques
Joy's Place
WokStar International Noodle Café

$$
Cafe O'Lei
Matteo's
A Saigon Café
Sansei
Stella Blues

$$$
Cascades
Pineapple Grill
Roy's Kahana Bar & Grill

$$$$
Ferraro's
Gerard's
Humuhumunu-kunukuāpua'a
Lahaina Grill
Mama's Fish House

By Cuisine

MODERN HAWAIIAN
Hāli'imaile General Store, $$$
Hula Grill, $$$
Mala Ocean Tavern, $$
Roy's Kahana Bar & Grill, $$$

PLATE LUNCH
Aloha Mixed Plate, $
Cafe O'Lei, $$
Four Sisters Kitchen, $
Honokowai Oka-zuya, $

SUSHI
Cascades, $$$
Genki Sushi, $
Sansei, $$

By Experience

MOST KID-FRIENDLY
Alexander's Fish & Chips, ¢
Flatbread Company, $$
Genki Sushi, $
Matteo's, $$
Seascape Mā'alaea, $$
Stella Blues, $$

MOST ROMANTIC
Cafe Mambo, $
Chez Paul, $$$$
Son'z at Swan Court, $$$

BEST VIEW
Capische, $$$
The Gazebo Restaurant, ¢
Mala Ocean Tavern, $$
Sea House Restaurant, $$$

8

By Carla Tracy   In the mid-1990s, Maui and the rest of Hawai'i erupted as a gastronomic force. Bold colors and bold flavors were coaxed from the island's freshest ingredients and Hawai'i Regional Cuisine (modern Hawaiian fare) was born.

Menus began to feature dishes such as 'ahi caught in deep water off of Keanae, grilled with peppercorn in Hanakua mushroom-basil sauce; crunchy tempura 'ahi roll with pea shoot slaw, wasabi tobiko crème fraîche, and pickled cucumber; and succulent Kona lobster with ginger carrot risotto, tarragon, and coral butter. Even desserts got a makeover, bending all culinary conventions to create such specialties as the Polynesian Black Pearl (as seen on the Rachel Ray Show), which looks as if it were an oversize chocolate replica of the real thing; and macadamia-nut tacos packed with tropical fruits and liliko'i (passion fruit) custard.

This sustainable style of cooking is no flash in the pan and its popularity continues throughout the Islands. The premise is to raise awareness of the state's indigenous cuisine, and to encourage farmers to grow more produce and fishers to know they have a source for their days of work on the water. Maui can now boast award-winning Surfing Goat Dairy cheeses, a host of lavender food products from Ali'i Kula Lavender, island grass-fed beef from Maui Cattle Co., and juicy vine-ripened tomatoes from Olowalu Nui Farms. The list goes on and on.

Some of Hawai'i Regional Cuisine's original 12 chefs still live on the island and remain successful restaurateurs. They include Beverly Gannon of Hāli'imaile General Store and Joe's, Peter Merriman of Hula Grill and Merriman's Kapalua, and Mark Ellman of Mala restaurants, Maui Tacos, and Penne Pasta fame. They have been around so long that they've spawned a whole other culinary generation called the Hawaii Island Chefs. Leading many top kitchens here, some of these HIC wunderkinds are huge successes and have their own farms. Countless chefs in small mom-and-pop shops also either grow their own, or buy locally to support the vast agricultural resources in this remote tropical state, reducing the carbon footprint and offering up fresh tastes of island cuisine. When mango trees are loaded with juicy fruit, hey, there's no reason to ship in hard-as-a-rock, under-ripe peaches from 6,000 mi away in Georgia.

If you want to get off the beaten path and hunt down ethnic and local-style restaurants, you can eat well at thrifty prices. Check out historic downtown Wailuku on First Friday (the first Friday of every month) with its market-style atmosphere. Restaurants take their foods out onto the sidewalks, and entertainment is on every corner. Head Upcountry to Makawao for a taste of *paniolo* (cowboy) country, or for fun restaurants and bars try the small town of Pā'ia on the booming North Shore. Do be a little forgiving about the ambience in some of these places, especially Lower Main Street in Wailuku, as they may be stuck in a time warp with no renovations in sight. But that's part of the real deal, the eccentricity that makes Maui *nō ka 'oi* (the best).

WEST MAUI

West Maui encompasses the area from tiny Olowalu, with its famous mom-and-pop store and the state's oldest French restaurant, all the way north to the ritzy Kapalua Resort. In between lies Lahaina, the historic former capital of Hawai'i, with its myriad touristy restaurants on Front Street as well as a host of new establishments opening up in the ever-burgeoning shopping district; and the resort area of Kā'anapali, which is undergoing some changes with several new establishments scheduled to open in the coming year or two. And, don't forget about the restaurants in the nooks and crannies of Kahana, Honokowai, and Nāpili. Throughout the West Side, you'll find a rainbow of cuisines in just about every price category and level of service.

LAHAINA

$ ✕**Aloha Mixed Plate.** Set right on the ocean in Lahaina, this walk-up
HAWAIIAN open-air bar and restaurant with seating under the kiawe shade trees is a great casual place for *'ono grinds*—"good food." Chinese roast duck, Hawaiian *laulau* (taro-leaf-wrapped bundles of meats and fish) plate, and Korean *kalbi* ribs (marinated and cooked on a grill) are indicative of the mixed-plate culture that is part of Hawai'i. We recommend the Ali'i Plate with Hawaiian laulau, *lomilomi* salmon, poi, rice, and coconut *haupia* (a light, pudding-like sweet) for dessert. The plates go well with drinks such as the Lava Flow, Peachy Passion, and Hawaiian Punch. This place is well regarded by locals and is a good pit stop for lunch. ✉ *1286 Front St., Lahaina* ☎ *808/661–3322* ▭ *AE, D, DC, MC, V.*

¢ ✕**Amigo's.** You don't have to travel south of the border to enjoy the
MEXICAN savory style of Mexican fare—just head to the Wharf Cinema Center in Lahaina to the latest Amigo's in the Maui franchise. Owner Jesus Ortega calls his tiny hot-as-a-tamale eateries "the three amigos" because there are three on Maui; the others are in Kīhei and Kahului. Popular items include chile verde, chimichangas, and taco salads. Eat on the sunny lānai or catch some shade under one of the umbrellas, or at one of the few seats tucked inside. In a rush or having a party? There's takeout and a catering menu. ✉ *Wharf Cinema Center, 658 Front St., Unit 145, Lahaina* ☎ *808/661–0210* ▭ *AE, MC, V.*

$$$$ ✕**Chez Paul.** Legendary since 1975, this intimate affair in tiny Olowalu
FRENCH (between Mā'alaea and Lahaina) is the oldest French restaurant in the state of Hawai'i. Owner-chef Patrick Callarec, who hails from Provence, honed his skills at many Ritz-Carltons. Let the Edith Piaf music and sensual artwork transport you to France as you dine on whole duck à l'orange; seared papio Provençale in the niçoise style with shrimp; or rack of lamb *paniolo*-style with fruit marinade. For dessert, try the pineapple tart tatin with tapioca pudding and caramel sauce. Chef Patrick is a lively firebrand, so do chat him up. The restaurant's offbeat exterior belies the elegant interior, which is complete with linen-draped tables and a wine cellar. ✉ *Honoapi'ilani Hwy., 4 mi south of Lahaina, Olowalu* ☎ *808/661–3843* ⚏ *Reservations essential* ▭ *AE, D, MC, V* ☾ *No lunch.*

8

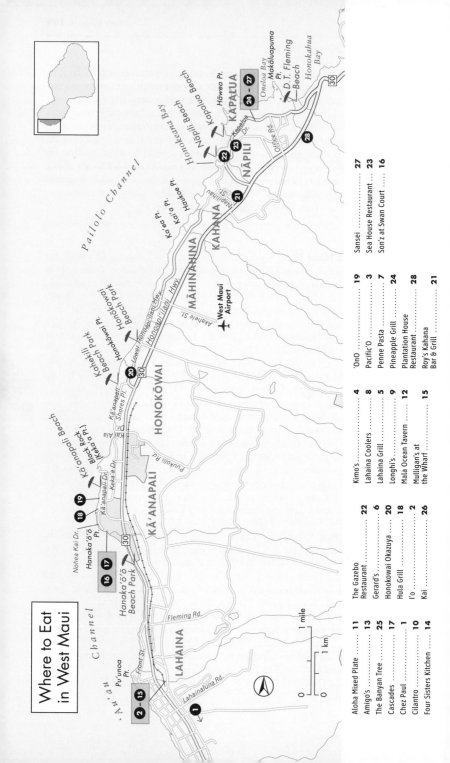

Where to Eat in West Maui

$ ✕**Cilantro.** The flavors of Old Mexico are given new life here, where
MEXICAN   the tortillas are hand-pressed and no fewer than nine chilies are used
to create the salsas. Owner Paris Nabavi, a former high-end food and
beverage pro, spent three years visiting authentic eateries in 40 Mexican cities. Let him take you south of the border with spinach, mushroom, and poblano enchiladas (a first-place winner in Taste of Lahaina);
or scallops and prawns chile relleno with ancho tomato sauce, crema
fresca, and roasted corn. The rotisserie chicken tacos with jicama slaw
are also mouthwatering—and healthful. Look for Nabavi's collection
of tortilla presses worn from duty, now hand-painted and displayed
up on the wall. ⊠*Old Lahaina Center, 170 Papalaua Ave., Lahaina*
☎*808/667–5444* ▤*AE, MC, V.*

$ ✕**Four Sisters Kitchen.** Maybe your friend craves local grinds (food) such
ECLECTIC   as mango barbecued pork ribs or chicken long rice, but you want something more touristy, such as New York steak with mashed potatoes.
Both of you can get your fill at this neat-as-a-pin spot with tablecloths,
friendly service, and extremely reasonable prices. The owners' Filipino heritage shines through with grandma's favorite of *tortang talong*
(charbroiled eggplant with the skin peeled off, dipped in egg batter and
panfried). It's served with white rice and fried plantains. New house
favorites are the chicken papaya and the oxtail soup. This is the real
Maui deal, and you won't find better Filipino specialties anywhere. ⊠*In
Lahaina Center, 900 Front St., Lahaina* ☎*808/667–5809* ▤*MC, V.*

$$$$ ✕**Gerard's.** French-born owner and top Lahaina chef Gerard Reversade
Fodor's Choice   honors the French tradition yet adds an island twist in such exqui-
★   site appetizers as shrimp sautéed in hazelnut oil, and 'ahi and smoked
FRENCH   salmon carpaccio with lemon Chantilly. The rack of lamb Persillade
offers a mint and lemon jus crust and is served with potatoes au gratin
and stuffed tomatoes. You will be in heaven with the pineapple tart
tatin à la mode. Located in the Plantation Inn, Gerard's resembles a
country estate with balustrades and gingerbread latticework. Antique
furnishings and wallpaper along with a wide veranda for dining make
this perfect for special occasions. A first-class wine list and celebrity-
spotting round out the experience. ⊠*Plantation Inn, 174 Lahainaluna
Rd., Lahaina* ☎*808/661–8939* ▤*AE, D, DC, MC, V* ☽*No lunch.*

$ ✕**Honokowai Okazuya.** Don't expect to sit down at this miniature res-
HAWAIIAN   taurant sandwiched between a dive shop and a salon—this is strictly
a takeout joint. It has a good reputation with the locals, so it's always
packed. Sink your teeth into mahimahi with lemon capers, ono with a
sun-dried tomato sauce, or spicy kung pao chicken. Or try chicken *katsu*
(Japanese-style breaded and fried chicken), pork, and peas piled with the
requisite two scoops of rice and macaroni-potato salad. You'll also find
lighter fare such as vegetarian plates, sandwiches, and Chinese food. The
spicy eggplant is delicious, and the fresh *chow fun* noodles (flat, wide
Chinese rice noodles) sell out quickly. ⊠*3600-D Lower Honoapi'ilani
Hwy., Lahaina* ☎*808/665–0512* ▤*No credit cards* ☽*Closed Sun.*

$$$ ✕**I'o.** From its opening, this oceanfront restaurant established itself
PACIFIC RIM   with its theatrical interior designed by the artist Dado and its contem-
porary Pacific Rim menu. Now its claim to fame is the produce from
the owner's 8-acre, Upcountry organic farm, and the fresh catch caught

8

by local fishermen using the trolling method. Menu favorites include a crispy 'ahi roll with root vegetables; the Road to Hāna grilled fish with jasmine rice and fresh fruit; and the rainbow catch with goat cheese fondue and truffle oil. Desserts to savor are the Hawaiian vintage chocolate mousse and the chocolate pâté with Kula strawberries. The monthly I'o Wine Club affairs can be quite entertaining. ⊠*505 Front St., Lahaina* ☎*808/661–8422* ⊟*AE, D, DC, MC, V* ⊘*No lunch.*

$$
SEAFOOD
✕**Kimo's.** On a warm Lahaina day, it's a treat to relax at an umbrella-shaded table on this restaurant's lānai as you sip a mai tai and watch the tour boats glide in and out of nearby Lahaina Harbor. The deck area hangs directly over the water so you might even spot some of Maui's tropical fish swimming below. A good portion of the menu is devoted to fresh fish, with five or six varieties and preparations to choose from each night—a highlight is the panko-crusted catch with beurre blanc. Try the signature dessert, Hula Pie: vanilla–macadamia nut ice cream topped with chocolate fudge and whipped cream in an Oreo-cookie crust. Or pop in mid-afternoon to enjoy happy hour. ⊠*845 Front St., Lahaina* ☎*808/661–4811* ⊟*AE, DC, MC, V.*

$
AMERICAN
✕**Lahaina Coolers.** Breezy, small, and popular with locals, this café and bar with a replica of a record-winning 955-pound blue marlin hanging on the wall serves such tantalizing fare as Evil Jungle Pasta (pasta with grilled chicken in spicy Thai peanut sauce) and Pork Chops with Chinese Five-Spice Marinade. The restaurant likes to buy its fish from nearby Lahaina Harbor fishermen, who are often spotted eating huevos rancheros with *kālua* pork (baked underground in an *imu*) or *loco moco* (a hamburger patty and over-easy egg on top of rice, slathered in brown gravy) for breakfast on the sunny lānai. The café is a couple of blocks down from busy Front Street, so expect a nice mix of locals and tourists. ⊠*180 Dickenson St., Lahaina* ☎*808/661–7082* ⊟*AE, MC, V.*

$$$$
AMERICAN
✕**Lahaina Grill.** A culinary force since 1990, Lahaina Grill lost the "David Paul's" part of its name late in 2007, but under the latest owner Jurg Munch, executive chef at the Mandarin Oriental in Hong Kong for years, the celebrated updated American food and the service remain consistent. Beautifully designed with stamped-tin ceilings, splashy artwork, and overhead fans, it is part of an elegant historic building and boasts a sommelier who rules over an extensive wine cellar and pastry chefs who do magic in the in-house bakery. Try the seared 'ahi with foie gras or the crispy-fried blue corn–crusted chile relleno filled with Hawaiian Big Island prawns, scallops, and Monterey Jack cheese. Save room for the scrumptious triple-berry pie. Smaller portions are available at the bar. ⊠*127 Lahainaluna Rd., Lahaina* ☎*808/667–5117* ⊟ *AE, DC, MC, V* ⊘*No lunch.*

$$$$
ITALIAN
✕**Longhi's.** A Lahaina landmark, Longhi's has been drawing in throngs of visitors since 1976. Its authentic Italian pastas, sandwiches, seafood, beef, and chicken dishes were created by owner Bob Longhi, "the man who loves to eat." The in-house bakery turns out breakfast pastries, desserts, and pizza bread, the latter complimentary with your meal. Definitely for two, the signature lobster Longhi includes two lobsters over linguine and pomodoro sauce with mussels, clams, and prawns. Another must try is the fillet Longhi, served with red and yellow bell peppers. There are two

spacious, open-air levels from which to choose; and there's a second Maui restaurant on the South Shore, at the Shops at Wailea. ⊠ *888 Front St., Lahaina* ☎808/667–2288 ⊟*AE, D, DC, MC, V.*

$$ ✕**Mala Ocean Tavern.** On the water's edge, above the tide-tossed rocks,
MODERN stands this cheery yellow-walled, open-air restaurant owned by noted
HAWAIIAN Hawai'i Regional Cuisine chef Mark Ellman and his wife, Judy. The menu, composed of mostly organic and locally sourced ingredients, includes flavorful flat breads and a Kobe burger with Maytag blue cheese. Don't miss the calamari, battered and fried with lemon slices and served with a spicy *mojo verde* (jalapeño cilantro pesto). This is a good place to try *moi*, the fish of Hawaiian royalty, wok-fried with ginger and spicy black-bean sauce. Fans of the Caramel Miranda dessert at Avalon (Ellman's former restaurant) can find it here. In the evening, the bar is a coveted hangout, and weekend brunch is lively. In addition, a much bigger Mala Ocean Tavern opened in Wailea in mid-2008 as a co-venture between Ellman and a number of celeb partners, including Clint Eastwood and Alice Cooper. ⊠ *1307 Front St., Lahaina* ☎808/667–9394 ⊟*AE, MC, V.*

$ ✕**Mulligan's at the Wharf.** Lahaina's only authentic Irish pub offers the
IRISH freshest and finest pint of Guinness on the island. Stomp your feet to Irish music as you dine on fish-and-chips, bangers and mash, and corned beef and cabbage, or try Pancho Mulligan's Mexican specialties and island selections. Satellite sports such as soccer, rugby, football, baseball, and hockey are on the TVs, especially for weekend college and pro sports. Owner Kevin O'Kennedy often jumps onstage to contribute his signature tin whistle to the nightly live music—traditional and contemporary. It's fun for the whole family until 10 PM, when it morphs into a happening late-night spot for those 21 and over until 2 AM. ⊠ *Wharf Cinema Center, 658 Front St., Unit 145-C, Lahaina* ☎808/661–8881 ⊟*AE, MC, V.*

$$$ ✕**Pacific'O.** You can sit outdoors at umbrella-shaded tables near the
SEAFOOD water's edge, or find a spot in the breezy, marble-floor interior of this seafood haven. All the produce comes from the owner's Upcountry organic farm, just as it does at its sister restaurant I'o. The exciting menu features the appropriately named bling bling, which is grilled petit filet mignon topped with Gorgonzola cheese and ginger butter; and poached lobster with potato du jour and tempura asparagus. Another fun dish is fresh 'ahi-and-ono tempura, in which the two kinds of fish are wrapped around *tobiko* (flying-fish roe), then wrapped in nori, and wok-fried. For dessert, try the banana pineapple *lumpia* served hot with homemade banana ice cream. ⊠ *505 Front St., Lahaina* ☎808/667–4341 ⊟*AE, D, DC, MC, V.*

$ ✕**Penne Pasta.** A couple of blocks off the beaten path in Lahaina, little
ITALIAN Penne Pasta packs a powerhouse of a menu, as might be expected from a place owned by chef Mark Ellman of the Mala Ocean Tavern. Heaping plates of reasonably priced, flavorful pasta and low-key service make this restaurant the perfect alternative to an expensive night in the resort areas. House favorites are cheesy baked penne in tomato cream sauce and linguine in clam sauce with lemon butter. The osso buco (Wednesday's special) is a lamb shank with fettuccine, lamb ragout, and

salad. The salade niçoise overflows with olives, peppers, garlic 'ahi, and potatoes. Couples should split a salad and entrée, as portions are large. ✉ *180 Dickenson St., Lahaina* ☎ *808/661–6633* ▤ *AE, D, DC, MC, V* ◷ *No lunch weekends.*

KĀ'ANAPALI

$$$

PACIFIC RIM

✕ **Cascades.** Above the Hyatt's wonderland of swimming pools and beneath a canopy of *hau* trees, you can enjoy a sampler of island treats—pot stickers, teriyaki beef skewers, and *poke.* Toast your good fortune with a kitschy tropical cocktail or *junmai ginjo,* a high-grade sake made from polished sushi rice. While there is something for the whole family, the real reason to dine here is the sushi. Savor lobster mango summer rolls with Thai basil and peanut chili sauce, and fun specialties such as the pizza roll. All are garnished with freshly grated wasabi root, a rare treat on Maui. For hot food, try the New York steak, sautéed lobster, and prawns. Note: you can order sushi and light fare until 10 PM. ✉ *Hyatt Regency Maui, Kā'anapali Beach Resort, 200 Nohea Kai Dr., Kā'anapali* ☎ *808/661–1234* ▤ *AE, D, DC, MC, V* ◷ *No lunch.*

$$$

MODERN HAWAIIAN

✕ **Hula Grill.** Genial chef-restaurateur Peter Merriman, the pied piper of Hawai'i Regional Cuisine, has teamed with TS Restaurant Group in this bustling, family-oriented restaurant. They have re-created a 1930s Hawaiian beach house, and every table has an ocean view. You can also dine on the beach, toes in the sand, at the Barefoot Bar where Hawaiian entertainment is presented every evening. Lunch items include such tasty dishes as shrimp, spinach, and Asian pear salad and Bahn Mi, a Vietnamese steak sandwich using local Maui Cattle Co. beef. Two types of fresh fish are offered nightly, often with lobster risotto or mango-jasmine rice and fresh local vegetables. Children of all ages scream for the ice-cream sandwich made with baked brownies and drizzled with raspberry sauce. ✉ *Whalers Village, 2435 Kā'anapali Pkwy., Kā'anapali* ☎ *808/667–6636* ▤ *AE, DC, MC, V.*

$$$

HAWAIIAN

✕ **'OnO.** Casual and fun, this restaurant has all outdoor seating under umbrellas next to the Westin Maui's magnificent pool; streams also meander by the tables. It features a host of island fare such as golden calamari strips; Haiku salad with lime, tomato, and Chinese black-bean salsa; and furikake seared 'ahi on sesame focaccia with wasabi cream and daikon relish. This is a good place to bring the kids, who can munch away on the beef tenderloin kebabs while you sample the Hokkaido scallops and asparagus doused in a not-too-spicy kimchi cream. Tourists keep coming back for the popular dinner of macadamia-nut chicken with jasmine rice and grilled vegetables in katsu butter. Changing varieties of fresh fish are offered nightly. ✉ *Westin Maui Resort & Spa, 2365 Kā'anapali Pkwy., Kā'anapali* ☎ *808/667–2525* ▤ *AE, DC, MC, V.*

$$$

CONTINENTAL

✕ **Son'z at Swan Court.** Robin Leach once named this the most romantic restaurant in the world in *Lifestyles of the Rich and Famous,* and it's perfect for couples celebrating special occasions. Descend the grand staircase into an amber-lighted dining room with soaring ceilings and a massive artificial lagoon with swans, waterfalls, and tropical gardens. Choose your evening's libation from one of 3,000 bottles of wine,

Continued on page 199

LŪʻAU: A TASTE OF HAWAIʻI

The best place to sample Hawaiian food is at a backyard lūʻau. Aunties and uncles are cooking, the pig is from a cousin's farm, and the fish is from a brother's boat.

But invitations to those occasions are rare. So your choice is most likely between a commercial lūʻau and a restaurant that serves Hawaiian food.

Most commercial lūʻau will offer you some of the authentic diet; they're also about umbrella drinks, laughs, spectacle, and fun. Expect to spend a leisurely evening and no small amount of cash.

For greater authenticity, folksy experiences, and rock-bottom prices, visit a Hawaiian restaurant (most are in simple, anonymous storefronts in residential neighborhoods). Locals will be happy to help you negotiate the menu.

In either case, much of what is known today as Hawaiian food would be as foreign to a 16th-century Hawaiian as risotto or chow mien. The pre-contact diet was simple and healthy–mainly raw and steamed seafood and vegetables. Early Hawaiians used earth ovens and heated stones to cook seafood, taro, sweet potatoes, and breadfruit and seasoned their food with sea salt and ground kukui nuts. Seaweed, fern shoots, sweet potato vines, coconut, banana, sugarcane, and select greens and roots rounded out the diet.

Successive waves of immigrants added their favorites to the ti leaf–lined table. So it is that foods as disparate as salt salmon and chicken long rice are now Hawaiian—even though there is no salmon in Hawaiian waters and long rice (cellophane noodles) is Chinese.

AT THE LŪ'AU: KĀLUA PORK

The heart of any lū'au is the *imu*, the earth oven in which a whole pig is roasted. The preparation of an imu is a bonding affair for most families, who tackle it only once a year or so, for a baby's first birthday or at Thanksgiving, when many Islanders prefer to imu their turkeys. Commercial lū'au operations have it down to a science, however.

THE ART OF THE STONE

The key to a proper imu is the *pohaku*, the stones. Imu cook by means of long, slow, moist heat released by special stones that can withstand a hot fire without exploding. Many Hawaiian families treasure their imu stones, keeping them in a pile in the backyard and passing them on through generations.

PIT COOKING

The imu makers first dig a pit about the size of a re-frigerator, then lay down *kiawe* (mesquite) wood and stones, and build a white-hot fire that is allowed to burn itself out. The ashes are raked away, and the hot stones covered with banana and ti leaves. Well-wrapped in ti or banana leaves and a net of chicken wire, the pig is lowered onto the leaf-covered stones. *Laulau* (leaf-wrapped bundles of meats, fish, and taro leaves) may also be placed inside. Leaves—ti, banana, even ginger—cover the pig followed by wet burlap sacks (to create steam). The whole is topped with a canvas tarp and left to steam overnight.

OPENING THE IMU

This is the moment everyone waits for: The imu is unwrapped like a giant present and the imu keep-ers gingerly wrestle out the steaming pig. When it's unwrapped, the meat falls moist and smoky-flavored from the bone, looking and tasting just like Southern-style pulled pork, but without the barbecue sauce.

WHICH LŪ'AU?

The Feast at Lele. Top-notch value and price, great wine list.

Old Lahaina Lū'au. Intimate and the most traditional; a perennial sell-out.

Wailea Beach Marriott Honua'ula Lū'au. Imu ceremony and buffet.

MEA 'AI 'ONO.
GOOD THINGS TO EAT.

LAULAU
Steamed meats, fish, and taro leaf in ti-leaf bundles: fork-tender, a medley of flavors; the taro resembles spinach.

LOMI LOMI SALMON
Salt salmon in a piquant salad or relish with onions, tomatoes.

POI (DON'T CALL IT LIBRARY PASTE.)
Poi, a paste made of pounded taro root, is an acquired taste, but give it a try.

Consider: The Hawaiian Adam is descended from *kalo* (taro). Young taro plants are called "keiki"–children. Poi is the first food after mother's milk for many Islanders. 'Ai, the word for food, is synonymous with poi in many contexts.

Not only that, we like it. "There is no meat that doesn't taste good with poi," the old Hawaiians said.

But you have to know how to eat it: with something rich or powerfully flavored. "It is salt that makes the poi go in," is another adage. When you're served poi, try it with a mouthful of smoky kālua pork or salty lomi lomi salmon. Its slightly sour blandness cleanses the palate. And if you don't like it, smile and say something polite. (And slide that bowl over to a local.)

Laulau

Lomi Lomi Salmon

Poi

IN FOCUS LŪ'AU: A TASTE OF HAWAI'I

8

E HELE MAI 'AI! COME AND EAT!

Hawaiian restaurants tend to be inconveniently located in well-worn storefronts with little or no parking, outfitted with battered tables and clattering Melmac dishes, open odd (and usually limited) hours and days, and often so crowded you have to wait. But they personify aloha, invariably run by local families who welcome tourists who take the trouble to find them.

Many are cash-only operations and combination plates are a standard feature: one or two entrées, a side such as chicken long rice, choice of poi or steamed rice and—if the place is really old-style—a tiny portion of coarse Hawaiian salt and some raw onions for relish.

Most serve some foods that aren't, strictly speaking, Hawaiian, but are beloved of

kama'āina, such as salt meat with watercress (preserved meat in a tasty broth), or *akubone* (skipjack tuna fried in a tangy vinegar sauce).

Our two favorites: **Aloha Mixed Plate** and **A.K.'s Café**.

MENU GUIDE

Much of the Hawaiian language encountered during a stay in the Islands will appear on restaurant menus and lists of lū'au fare. Here's a quick primer.

'ahi: *yellowfin tuna.*

aku: *skipjack, bonito tuna.*

'ama'ama: *mullet; it's hard to get but tasty.*

bento: *a box lunch.*

chicken lū'au: *a stew made from chicken, taro leaves, and coconut milk.*

haupia: *a light, pudding-like sweet made from coconut.*

imu: *the underground ovens in which pigs are roasted for lū'au.*

kālua: *to bake underground.*

kaukau: *food. The word comes from Chinese but is used in the Islands.*

kimchee: *Korean dish of pickled cabbage made with garlic and hot peppers.*

Kona coffee: *coffee grown in the Kona district of the Big Island.*

laulau: *literally, a bundle. Laulau are morsels of pork, chicken, butterfish, or other ingredients wrapped with young taro leaves and then bundled in ti leaves for steaming.*

liliko'i: *passion fruit, a tart, seedy yellow fruit that makes delicious desserts, juice, and jellies.*

lomi lomi: *to rub or massage; also a massage. Lomi lomi salmon is fish that has been rubbed with onions and herbs; commonly served with minced onions and tomatoes.*

lū'au: *a Hawaiian feast; also the leaf of the taro plant used in preparing such a feast.*

lū'au leaves: *cooked taro tops with a taste similar to spinach.*

mahimahi: *mild-flavored dolphinfish, not the marine mammal.*

mai tai: *potent rum drink with orange and lime juice, from the Tahitian word for "good."*

malasada: *a Portuguese deep-fried doughnut without a hole, dipped in sugar.*

manapua: *dough wrapped around diced pork or other fillings.*

manō: *shark.*

niu: *coconut.*

'ōkolehao: *a liqueur distilled from the ti root.*

onaga: *pink or red snapper.*

ono: *a long, slender mackerel-like fish; also called wahoo.*

'ono: *delicious; also hungry.*

'opihi: *a tiny shellfish, or mollusk, found on rocks; also called limpets.*

pāpio: *a young ulua or jack fish.*

pohā: *Cape gooseberry. Tasting a bit like honey, the pohā berry is often used in jams and desserts.*

poi: *a paste made from pounded taro root, a staple of the Hawaiian diet.*

poke: *chopped, pickled raw tuna or other fish, tossed with herbs and seasonings.*

pūpū: *Hawaiian hors d'oeuvre.*

saimin: *long thin noodles and vegetables in broth, often garnished with small pieces of fish cake, scrambled egg, luncheon meat, and green onion.*

sashimi: *raw fish thinly sliced and usually eaten with soy sauce.*

ti leaves: *a member of the agave family. The fragrant leaves are used to wrap food while cooking and removed before eating.*

uku: *deep-sea snapper.*

ulua: *a member of the jack family that also includes pompano and amberjack. Also called crevalle, jack fish, and jack crevalle.*

the largest cellar in the state. Must-haves on chef Geno Samiento's contemporary, Mediterranean-influenced menu include tiger shrimp penne à la vodka; goat-cheese ravioli of fresh Kula corn, edamame, and Hamakua mushrooms; and *opakapaka* (blue snapper) served with artichokes, sweet-potato hash browns, and tomato puree. ✉ *Hyatt Regency Maui, Kāʻanapali Beach Resort, 200 Nohea Kai Dr., Kāʻanapali* ☎ *808/661–1234* ☐ *AE, D, DC, MC, V* ☾ *No lunch*

NORTH OF KĀʻANAPALI

$$$$
PACIFIC RIM

✗ **The Banyan Tree.** The signature restaurant of the Ritz-Carlton, Kapalua is better than ever after the resort's late 2007 makeover. Drink in views of the Pailolo Channel and Molokaʻi from the outdoor bar and lounge with covered terrace. The *dukka* (Middle Eastern spices) delivered with your bread is a tip that this elegant dining hall offers plenty of worldly influences. Chef Ryan Urig excels with pine-nut-crusted ʻahi with cucumber noodles and Thai-basil pesto; crispy ehu with creamy Surfing Goat Dairy cheese polenta with beets and watercress; and Kona lobster with ginger-carrot risotto, tarragon, and coral butter. The open-beam restaurant's subdued atmosphere is sometimes charged with the sounds of live world music by Ranga Pae. ✉ *Ritz-Carlton, Kapalua, 1 Ritz-Carlton Dr., Kapalua* ☎ *808/669–6200* ☐ *AE, D, DC, MC, V.*

¢
DINER

✗ **The Gazebo Restaurant.** Even locals will stand in line up to half an hour to have diner fare at a table overlooking the beach at this slightly hard-to-find restaurant, an open-air gazebo (albeit an old and funky one) overlooking magnificent Nāpili Bay. Sunsets are phenomenal, and turtle and spinner dolphin sightings are common. The food is standard diner fare, but it's thoughtfully prepared. Breakfast choices include pancakes with macadamia-nuts, pineapple, and bananas; and the

> ### WORD OF MOUTH
>
> "With gorgeous views and whale sightings while standing in line during whale season, [Gazebo] is worth the wait. The macadamia pancakes are so light and fluffy and the fried rice is very good. It would be worth getting half-orders if you are with only 2 people because the portions are huge." —historygirl

Kahuna omelet with Portuguese sausage, mushrooms, onions, bacon, avocado, and pepper-jack cheese. At lunch, there are satisfying bacon and avocado burgers and Southwestern salads. The friendly resort staff puts out coffee for those waiting in line. ✉ *Nāpili Shores Resort, 5315 Lower Honoapiʻilani Hwy., Nāpili* ☎ *808/669–5621* ☐ *No credit cards* ☾ *No dinner.*

$$$
JAPANESE

✗ **Kai.** This popular sushi restaurant in the Ritz-Carlton, Kapalua takes design inspiration from the arrival of the ancient Hawaiians over the sea. Hand-carved ceiling beams resemble outrigger canoes, and the back wall of the bar glows like lava. This is a great place to meet friends and raise your chopsticks to a rainbow roll or fresh ʻahi sashimi before heading to the neighboring Alaloa Lounge. The menu also includes hot Japanese entrées such as baked crab dynamite, but your best bet is to let Tokyo native, chef Tadashi Yoshino, design the meal. His top sellers include tuna tataki salad in ponzu sauce and the Yamato Roll with fresh hamachi (yellowtail) and spicy tuna. The kitchen is open until 9 PM. ✉*Ritz-Carlton, Kapalua, 1 Ritz-Carlton Dr., Kapalua* ☎*808/669–6200* ⊟*AE, D, DC, MC, V.*

$$$
MODERN
HAWAIIAN
✕**Pineapple Grill.** With a menu built almost entirely around local ingredients, Pineapple Grill attracts those foodies who appreciate exceptional Pacific Island cuisine such as stuffed Kamuela vine-ripened tomatoes, 'ahi and salmon tartare, Moloka'i sweet potatoes, and Maui Gold pineapple upside-down cake for dessert. A Maui Seafood Watch participant, the restaurant only serves seafood that has been harvested sustainably. So go on—order the Kona lobster. The restaurant also features *Wine Spectator*'s annual top 100 wines by the glass. At night, you can witness spectacular sunsets overlooking the golf greens and the Pacific; the outdoor tables facing the West Maui Mountains can be even nicer than those with an ocean view. There's live entertainment and 50% off the bar menu every Wednesday night. ✉*200 Kapalua Dr., Kapalua* ☎*808/669–9600* ⊟*AE, D, DC, MC, V.*

$$$
MODERN
HAWAIIAN
✕**Plantation House Restaurant.** It's hard to decide which is better here, the food or the view. Perched high above Kapalua's coastline, this estate-like restaurant at the Plantation Course has the misty Maui Mountains behind, and views of Moloka'i and the Pailolo Channel in front. The menu is on par with the surroundings and features Mediterranean flavors blended with local ingredients. Longtime Chef Alex Stanislaw began doing the sustainability thing even before it became widespread. He uses neighboring Kapalua Farms' vegetables and prepares two or three fresh Hawaiian fish seven different ways nightly. A favorite is the Venice: panko-crusted and sautéed fish on risotto with Kula sugar peas, O'ahu asparagus, and Pacific shrimp. Breakfast here is luxurious; try the Bloody Mary with pickled asparagus and one of the famous Benedicts. ✉*Plantation Course Clubhouse, 2000 Plantation Club Dr., past Kapalua* ☎*808/669–6299* ⊟*AE, MC, V.*

$$$
MODERN
HAWAIIAN
✕**Roy's Kahana Bar & Grill.** Founder Roy Yamaguchi is a James Beard Award–winning chef who now has almost 40 restaurants to his name from Japan to Florida. This is one of his first, and regulars keep returning for his Hawaiian-fusion specialties and private-label wines and beers. Favorites include Kona kampachi tataki with sizzling yuzu soy and sesame snap peas; crisp Sonoma duck breast with Makawao mushroom risotto cake; and pepper-seared scallops and seared white shrimp with saffron rice. Locals know to order the incomparable chocolate soufflé immediately after being seated. Both branches, in Kahana and Kīhei, are in supermarket parking lots—it's not the view that excites; it's the fantastic food and the welcoming and professional service. ✉*Kahana Gateway Shopping Center, 4405 Honoapi'ilani Hwy., Kahana* ☎*808/669–6999* ⊟*AE, D, DC, MC, V..*

$$
PACIFIC RIM
✕**Sansei Seafood Restaurant & Sushi Bar.** One of the best-loved restaurants in Hawai'i with locations on four of the Islands, Sansei is Japanese with a contemporary Hawaiian twist. Inspired dishes include a *panko* (Japanese bread crumb)-crusted 'ahi sashimi roll, rock shrimp in creamy garlic aioli, spicy fried calamari with *kochujang* (Korean hot pepper paste), and the signature mango-and-crab-salad roll. Those who love French cuisine will appreciate the decadent foie gras nigiri sushi. Desserts

such as deep-fried tempura ice cream are worth the calories. The Kapalua location uses colors such as pumpkin, butterscotch, and sage that all add a tasty touch. Both this and the Kīhei locations are popular karaoke hangouts, serving early-bird and late-night sushi at half price. ⊠*600 Office Rd., Kapalua* 🕾*808/669–6286* ▭*AE, D, MC, V* ⊗*No lunch.*

$$$

HAWAIIAN

✕**Sea House Restaurant.** Built in the 1960s at Nāpili Kai Beach Resort, this restaurant came before laws that forbid buildings to be so close to the beach—and what a beach it is. Nāpili Bay is drop-dead gorgeous. Wear your beach wrap during the day or come for a casual meal after a day of water sports. The breakfast, lunch, and dinner menus are varied; best bets include the Molokaʻi sweet-potato egg frittata with chicken sausage and spinach, the berry pancakes, and the Reuben sandwich. For dinner, go for the popular Taste of Lahaina sampler of *huli huli* (a sugar, soy, and ginger sauce for barbecue) lamb chops, macadamia nut shrimp, and sushi. ⊠*5900 Lower Honoapiʻilani Hwy., Nāpili* 🕾*808/669–1500* ▭*AE, D, DC, MC, V.*

> ### SUSHI FOR ALL
>
> On Maui, there's a sushi restaurant for everyone—even those who don't like sushi! Sansei has the most diverse menu: everything from lobster ravioli to sea urchin. People love designer rolls such as the "69" (unagi eel slathered in sweet sauce paired with crab) or the "caterpillar" (avocado and tuna wrapped around rice, complete with radish-sprout antennae).

THE SOUTH SHORE

8

South Maui's dining scene begins at Māʻalaea Harbor, with the landmark Waterfront Restaurant. From here, the food trail blossoms as you head south, with literally hundreds of restaurants scattered throughout the towns of Kīhei and Wailea, all the way south toward Makena. The food and drink epicenter is arguably the Kīhei Triangle (the area around Foodland on South Kīhei Road), where you'll find WokStar International Noodle Café among others. In Wailea, restaurants tend to be high-end, although there are spots of budget-minded eateries here and there. At the "end of the restaurant road" in Makena, things are in flux due to proposed developments.

Besides restaurants listed below, you'll find branches of Roy's, Sansei, Mala Ocean Tavern, and Longhi's in this area. *For reviews of these establishments, see the West Maui section.*

KĪHEI AND NORTH (MĀʻALAEA)

KĪHEI

¢

☽

SEAFOOD

✕**Alexander's Fish & Chips.** Across from the beach in sunny Kīhei, Alexander's has been an affordable Maui favorite since 1990. Famous for its tempura batter, this mostly takeout spot uses sauces from secret family recipes. Select from daily fish such as ʻahi, ono, and mahimahi, and have it charbroiled, grilled Cajun style, or fried with tempura. Pile on sides such as Southern coleslaw, french fries, or *hapa* rice: a blend of brown

Where to Eat on the South Shore

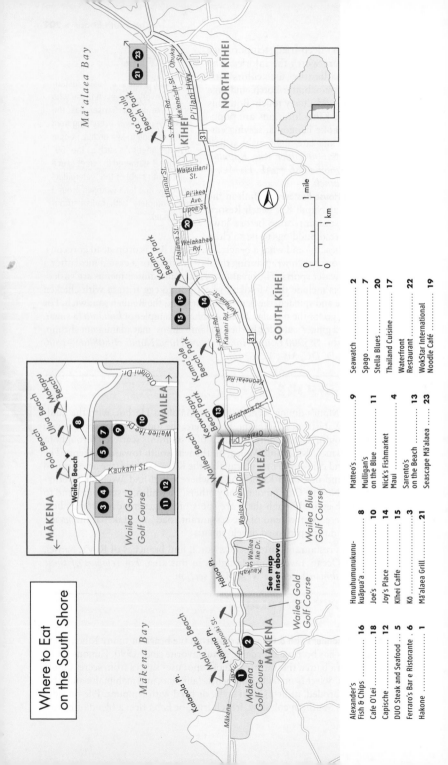

Alexander's
Fish & Chips 16
Cafe O'Lei 18
Capische 12
DUO Steak and Seafood ... 5
Ferraro's Bar e Ristorante .. 6
Hakone 1

Humuhumunukunu-
kuāpua'a 8
Joe's 10
Joy's Place 14
Kihei Caffe 15
Kō 3
Mā'alaea Grill 21

Matteo's 9
Mulligan's
on the Blue 11
Nick's Fishmarket
Maui 4
Sarento's
on the Beach 13
Seascape Mā'alaea 23

Seawatch 2
Spago 7
Stella Blues 20
Thailand Cuisine 17
Waterfront
Restaurant 22
WokStar International
Noodle Café 19

and white. You've got to try the lovely Cajun fish tacos with mango salsa. There are also kiawe-smoked barbecue ribs and kids' meals. You can carry your meal to the beach, or dine at one of the outdoor tables. ⊠*1913 S. Kīhei Rd., Kīhei* ☎808/874–0788 ▭*MC, V.*

$$ ✕**Cafe O'Lei.** This is where locals go on their day off. Chef-owners
Fodor'sChoice Michael and Dana Pastula are known to dish up fabulously fresh tastes
★ at affordable prices. Huge portions at lunch and dinner include Manoa
AMERICAN lettuce wraps filled with chicken, mushrooms, and water chestnuts; crab cakes; and quinoa salads packed with local eggplant and creamy goat cheese. Order sushi from the bar in back or baked clams and giant tiger prawns from the brick oven. Other popular items are fresh fish, macadamia-nut chicken breast, and Asian short ribs. Gauze curtains separate tables nicely set with white linens and bright tableware, and the spacious octagonal bar is great for sharing pūpū and sipping cocktails. The Pastulas also have Café O'Lei restaurants in Kahului and Wailuku. ⊠*2439 S. Kīhei Rd., Kīhei* ☎808/891–1368 ▭*AE, MC, V.*

$ ✕**Joy's Place.** You may see Joy in the back of this small spot, whipping up
VEGETARIAN one of the fantastic, vitamin-packed soups that reflect her healthful culinary wizardry. Try a sandwich or collard-green wrap filled with veggies and a creamy spread, or a nut burger with nondairy cheese. Joy's is also known for free-range turkey, avocado, and cheese sandwiches, and they poach fresh, locally caught tuna for fresh tuna salad. Almost everything is made from scratch, including organic cookies and vegan brownies. If you have a hint of a cold, a spicy potion called Cold Buster is available to ward it off. Other healthful refreshers include the CranMint Cooler and the Spiced Iced Tea. Children will find a fun menu; and adults may sign up for occasional vegetarian cooking classes. ⊠*In Island Surf Bldg., 1993 S. Kīhei Rd., Suite 17, Kīhei* ☎808/879–9258 ▭*MC, V.*

¢ ✕**Kīhei Caffe.** People-watching is fun over a cup of coffee at this casual
AMERICAN breakfast and lunch joint right across from the beach in Kīhei. Hearty, affordable portions will prepare you for surfing across the street at Kalama Park. The bowl-shaped egg scramble is tasty and almost enough for two, or try signature dishes such as the Hawaiian favorite *loco moco* (a hamburger patty and over-easy egg on top of rice, slathered in brown gravy), pork fried rice, and chorizo and eggs. *Opakapaka* (blue snapper) with *liliko'i* (passion fruit) beurre blanc is popular lunch fare. The resident rooster, one of many that live under the building, may come a-beggin' for some of your muffin. This place closes at 3. ⊠*1945 S. Kīhei Rd., Kīhei* ☎808/879–2230 ▭*MC, V* ☺*No dinner.*

$$$$ ✕**Sarento's on the Beach.** This upscale Italian restaurant's setting right on
ITALIAN spectacular Keawakapu Beach, with views of Molokini and Kaho'olawe, is irresistible. Chef Geno Sarmiento heads the kitchen which turns out such gems as wild tiger shrimp served over house-made ravioli of ricotta cheese, Yukon Gold potato puree, and white truffle oil; seafood *fra diavolo* (in a tomato sauce spiced with chilies); and swordfish saltimbocca, a strangely successful entrée with a prosciutto, Bel Paese cheese, radicchio, and porcini sauce. Meat lovers should try the fall-off-the-bone tender osso buco with spicy gremolata. The wine list includes some great finds. The owner's wife is a personal trainer, so there's also a "Trainer's Menu" of healthful picks. ⊠*2980 S. Kīhei Rd., Kīhei* ☎808/875–7555 ▭*AE, D, DC, MC, V* ☺*No lunch.*

8

$$ × **Stella Blues.** Centrally located in Azeka Mauka marketplace, this free-
☺   standing restaurant is affordable and spacious. It wins die-hard fans for
AMERICAN   unpretentious service and cuisine, and its open-beam, warmly lighted
dining room is unexpectedly classy. The menu is a major hit, especially
with families, and the bar is great for surfer-dude watching. Plus, there
is a private party room complete with pool tables and other games.
Comfort food of every sort is served at breakfast, lunch, and dinner,
including grilled New York steak (dry-aged and all-natural from Maui
Cattle Co.); Sunshine Daydream seafood stew in a white saffron tomato
broth; and yellow coconut curry for vegetarians. The ample Bananas
Foster Our Way features vanilla ice cream topped with caramelized
bananas, macadamia nuts, and whipped cream. ⊠*1279 S. Kīhei Rd.,
Kīhei* ☎*808/874–3779* ⊟*AE, D, DC, MC, V.*

$ × **Thailand Cuisine.** Fragrant tea and coconut-ginger chicken soup begin
THAI   a satisfying meal at this excellent Thai restaurant, set unassumingly in
the middle of a casual shopping mall. The care and expense that goes
into the decor—reflected in the glittering Buddhist shrines, fancy nap-
kin folds, and matching blue china—also applies to the cuisine. Take
an exotic journey with pad thai noodles; beef salad with scallions,
tomatoes, cucumber, and mint; or yellow curry with potatoes, carrots
and your choice of protein. Can't decide? Try the family dinners for
two or four. The fried bananas with ice cream are wonderful. If you
are in Central Maui, there is a second location in Kahului's Maui Mall.
⊠*In Kukui Mall, 1819 S. Kīhei Rd., Kīhei* ☎*808/875–0839* ⊟*AE,
D, DC, MC, V.*

$ ×**WokStar International Noodle Café.** This fun, easy-on-the-budget eatery,
PACIFIC RIM   across the street from the humpback whale sculpture in Kīhei, has a
walk-up counter and picnic tables. The name may imply that it's part of
some global conglomerate, but this is the first and only one of its kind.
You'll find everything from Thai red curry with seasonal vegetables to
Japanese miso ramen soup and Balinese stir-fries. The young owners try
to stay open until midnight seven nights a week for those hungry after
"pub crawling" through the many nearby bars and lounges. ⊠*Kīhei
Kalama Village, 1913D S. Kihei Rd., Kīhei* ☎*808/495–0066* ⊟*AE,
MC, V.*

MĀ'ALAEA

$$ × **Mā'alaea Grill.** Large French doors are kept open so that you can
AMERICAN   view Mā'alaea Harbor and feel the ocean breezes in this casual sea-
side restaurant. The teak and bamboo furniture, intimate lounge area,
and exhibition kitchen lend sophistication to this otherwise happily
relaxed establishment. Enjoy the light but satisfying blackened mahimahi with tropical fruit salsa, kiawe-wood-grilled New York steak with
house-made onion rings, or shrimp prepared a variety of ways: coconut
fried, sautéed Provençale, or garlic grilled with pesto. Live jazz music
is performed Wednesday through Sunday. This may be one of the only
restaurants on Maui in which you can enjoy ocean views until 9 PM, as
the harbor and Kīhei beyond are backlighted. ⊠*In the Harbor Shops,
300 Mā'alaea Rd., Mā'alaea* ☎*808/243–2206* ⊟*AE, MC, V.*

$$
$$ ✕**Seascape Māʻalaea.** A good choice for a seafood lunch, the Maui
☺ Ocean Center's signature restaurant offers harbor views from its open-
SEAFOOD air perch above the parking lot. On the back wall, giant windows look
into the famous aquarium's Edge of the Reef exhibit. Two popular
dishes are the Local Boy club, a triple-decker sandwich with layers of
lobster and shrimp salads in dill aioli; and the Molokini, grilled sashimi
grade ʻahi with shiitake mushrooms and sun-dried tomato buerre blanc.
Dining here is a heart-healthful, ocean-friendly experience featuring
sustainable seafood and trans-fat-free items. Kids love their own menu.
Aquarium admission is not required; ask directions at the front gate.
✉ *192 Māʻalaea Rd., Māʻalaea* ☎ *808/270–7000* ▭ *AE, D, DC, MC,
V* ☉ *No dinner.*

$$$$ ✕**Waterfront Restaurant.** The Smith
Fodor'sChoice family lures you in hook, line,
★ and fresh catch at this award-
SEAFOOD winning harborside establishment
with an outstanding menu, great
wine list, and exceptional service.
Choose from six types of fresh fish
prepared in nine different ways,
including baked in buttered parchment paper; captured in ribbons of
angel-hair potato; and topped with
tomato salsa, smoked chili pepper,
and avocado. The varied menu also
lists outstanding game meats along
with rack of lamb and veal scalop-

> **WORD OF MOUTH**
>
> "The Waterfront Restaurant had to
> be my favorite as far as the food
> went. I had ʻahi just about every-
> where, and this was the best. The
> decor is not island style but more
> classy supper club; we sat outside
> so we couldn't enjoy that aspect
> as much. Finding the place at night
> was a little challenge, but that
> won't stop me. I shall return!"
> —TMWeddle

pine. Do try the Caesar salad, tossed in an entertaining show table-side.
Enter Māʻalaea at the Maui Ocean Center and then follow the blue
WATERFRONT RESTAURANT signs to the third condominium. Come early
if you want to dine at sunset on the lānai. ✉ *50 Hauʻoli St., Māʻalaea*
☎ *808/244–9028* ▭ *AE, D, DC, MC, V* ☉ *No lunch.*

WAILEA AND SOUTH SHORE (MĀKENA)

MĀKENA

$$$ ✕**Hakone.** The Japanese food served at this popular restaurant in the
JAPANESE Maui Prince Hotel has a great reputation with locals. Saturday, the all-
you-can-eat Japanese Buffet ($48) draws them in like moths to a flame.
Indulge in seaweed salads, kabocha pumpkin and cranberries, miso
butterfish, shrimp tempura, and kalbi beef. The regular menu offers
numerous dishes of raw, cooked, hot, cold, sweet, and savory items.
Impeccably fresh sushi, traditional cooked dishes, and an impressive
sake list round out the menu. You may even get a degree in sake to take
home with you if you try one of the samplers. The ambience takes you
into the heart of Tokyo with its shoji screens, austere look, and servers
dressed in kimonos. ✉ *Maui Prince, 5400 Mākena Alanui Rd., Mākena*
☎ *808/874–1111* ▭ *AE, MC, V* ☉ *No lunch.*

8

CLOSE UP

The Plate Lunch Tradition

To experience island history first-hand, take a seat at one of Hawai'i's ubiquitous "plate lunch" eateries, and order a segmented Styrofoam plate piled with two scoops of rice, macaroni salad, and maybe a pickled vegetable condiment. On the sugar plantations, immigrant workers from many different countries ate together in the fields, sharing food from their kaukau kits, the utilitarian version of the Japanese *bento* (Japanese divided box filled with savory items) lunchbox. From this stir fry of people came the vibrant language of pidgin and its equivalent in food: the plate lunch.

At beaches and public parks, you will probably see locals eating plate lunches from nearby restaurants. Favorite combos include deep-fried chicken *katsu* (rolled in Japanese panko flour and spices), marinated beef teriyaki, and miso butterfish. *Saimin*, a noodle soup with Japanese fish stock and Chinese red-tinted barbecue pork, is a distinctly local medley. Koreans have contributed spicy barbecue *kal-bi* ribs, often served with chili-laden *kimchi* (pickled cabbage). Portuguese bean soup and tangy Filipino adobo stew are also favorites. The most popular Hawaiian contribution to the plate lunch is the *laulau*, a mix of meat and fish and young taro leaves, wrapped in more taro leaves and steamed.

WAILEA

$$$
Fodor'sChoice
★
ITALIAN

✕**Capische.** Hidden up at the quiet Diamond Hawaii Resort & Spa, this Italian restaurant is one local patrons would like kept secret. A circular stone atrium with soaring ceilings gives way to a small piano lounge and balcony, where you can find some of the best sunset views on the island. Below is a lovely garden seating area. It's as romantic as it gets. Capische favorites include cioppino with saffron tomato basil broth; braised lamb shank osso buco style with lemon risotto; and truffle grilled 'ahi with sautéed butternut squash, Kula corn sauce, and wilted frisée. Intimate and well conceived, this restaurant, with its seductive flavors and ambience, ensures a lovely night out. Il Teatre downstairs is owner-chef Brian Etheredge's fine-dining concept, where he designs and cooks your menu in front of you. ⊠*Diamond Hawaii Resort & Spa, 555 Kaukahi St., Wailea* ☎*808/879–2224* ▤*AE, D, DC, MC, V* ⊘*No lunch.*

$$$$
STEAK

✕**DUO Steak and Seafood.** At the Four Seasons Resort Maui's newest restaurant in tony Wailea, slicing into a well-marbled porterhouse steak is just one of the pleasures. All of the beef on the menu is prime and perfectly aged. Dip the meaty morsels into fun sauces including green peppercorn, béarnaise, and merlot, and sip a frothy martini in a colorful designer glass. Or try the fish specialties, from oysters Rockefeller to the seafood tower served in a silver-coated octopus sculpture. Sides range from creamed spinach to macaroni and cheese. Don't forget to check out the foyer bar with its chic contemporary decor and crowd of beautiful people, and take a peek into the state-of-the-art open kitchen. By day, this fine-dining restaurant is transformed by screens into the main breakfast room. ⊠ *Four Seasons Resort Maui, 3900 Wailea Ala Nui Drive, Wailea* ☎*808/874–8000* ▤*AE, DC, MC, V* ⊘*No lunch.*

$$$$ ╳ **Ferraro's Bar e Ristorante.** Overlooking the ocean from a bluff above
ITALIAN Wailea Beach, this outdoor Italian restaurant at the Four Seasons Resort
Maui is beautiful both day and night, with unparalleled service. For
lunch, indulge in a lobster sandwich, salad niçoise, or a bento. At dinner
you might begin your feast with the arugula and endive salad and move
on to the lobster risotto and veal Milanese while enjoying live classical
music under the stars. Try the wine list's excellent Italian choices, and
if chef Michael Cantin is offering one of his periodic tasting menus—
such as white Alba truffles in fall—go for it. Occasionally you can
catch celebrities gossiping at the bar. ⊠*Four Seasons Resort Maui at
Wailea, 3900 Wailea Alanui Dr., Wailea* ☎*808/874–8000* ▭*AE, D,
DC, MC, V.*

$$$$ ╳ **Humuhumunukunukuāpua'a.** You don't have to wrestle with the restau-
MODERN rant's formidable name (it's Hawai'i's state fish); simply tell the valet
HAWAIIAN or concierge that you're headed to Humuhumu. Romantic, exotic, and
good for a special occasion, this oceanfront thatch-roof restaurant at the
Grand Wailea has delectable sunsets. From your table, you can watch
the fish swim by in the surrounding lagoon and there is a large tank
of colorful sea critters at the bar. As for the food, chef Michael Lofaro
will impress with such dishes as Malaysian-style rack of lamb finished
with mustard, mild *sambal* (an Asian condiment), and brioche crust;
and blue-crab-stuffed *hamachi* (yellowtail) with garlic-sautéed baby
spinach. The cocktails are over the top, especially the tropical ones.
⊠*Grand Wailea Resort Hotel & Spa, 3850 Wailea Alanui Dr., Wailea*
☎*808/875–1234* ▭*AE, D, DC, MC, V.*

$$$$ ╳ **Joe's.** Owners Joe and Beverly Gannon, who run the immensely popu-
AMERICAN lar Hāli'imaile General Store in Upcountry Maui, have brought their
flair for food to this comfortable treetop-level restaurant at the Wailea
Tennis Club. Views include the sparkling Pacific on one side and vistas
of Haleakalā on the other. This place is named after Joe, who's been
in show biz for decades, instead of his celebrity chef wife. So his gold
records and other memorabilia hang on the walls. Friendly service and
the best burger on the island draw residents as well as visitors. Top
menu items include Joe's favorite meat loaf, grilled thick-cut pork chop,
seafood potpie, and Joe's pastry chef daughter Cheech's chocolate bread
pudding. ⊠*131 Wailea Ike Pl., Wailea* ☎*808/875–7767* ▭*AE, MC,
V* ☺*No lunch*.

$$$ ╳ **Kō.** Translated from Hawaiian, this restaurant's name means "cane,"
PACIFIC RIM as in sugarcane. The menu borrows treasured family recipes and cui-
sines from the sugar plantation camp days of old and adds a modern,
gourmet twist. Kō opened in 2008 in the Fairmont Kea Lani Maui's
open-air Caffe Ciao location (though Caffe Ciao's gourmet deli remains
a popular pit stop next door). Its plantation-inspired cuisine covers
all the bases from Japanese lobster tempura to Filipino steamed fresh
Manila clams with chorizo. Kō is bigger than a concept, says Executive
Chef Tylun Pang: it's about the people in Hawai'i. Represented cultures
include Chinese, Korean, Puerto Rican, Portuguese, and Hawaiian. For
dessert, you've gotta try the gourmet shave ice or the hot *malassadas*
(a kind of fried doughnut). ⊠*Fairmont Kea Lani, 4100 Wailea Alanui
Dr., Wailea* ☎*808/875–4100* ▭*AE, D, DC, MC, V.*

8

$$
☺
ITALIAN
✕**Matteo's.** Chef Matteo Mitsura—a bona-fide Italian—may be heard singing as he pounds dough in the kitchen of this miraculous pizzeria. The former chef of Ferraro's at the Four Seasons, this man can cook! And he does so at reasonable prices. (Trust us, discovering handsomely size Margherita and Portofino pizzas for $17 in Wailea is truly a miracle.) The Cowboy is a wild one with barbecue sauce, chicken, and fontina cheese. Handmade pappardelle pasta is loaded with luxurious braised lamb, wild mushrooms, and fresh-shaved Parmesan. Located on the Wailea Blue golf course, this casual, open-air restaurant benefits from gentle trade winds in the afternoon and a sky full of stars at night. A voluptuous wine list and desserts such as tiramisu top it off. ⊠ *100 Wailea Ike Dr., Wailea* ☎ *808/874–1234* ▤ *AE, D, MC, V.*

> **BEST BETS FOR BREAKFAST**
>
> **Colleen's** (North Shore). Eavesdrop on surfers here, while munching on a scone or breakfast burrito.
>
> **Gazebo Restaurant** (West Maui). It's worth the wait if you're a sucker for macadamia-nut pancakes and a Pacific view.
>
> **Plantation House** (West Maui). Which is better, the crab-cake Benedict or the view of Moloka'i?
>
> **Kīhei Caffe** (South Shore). Hearty portions prepare you for surfing.
>
> **Seawatch** (South Shore). Continue the debate at the Plantation House's sister restaurant—are the Benedicts better with this view?

$$
IRISH
✕**Mulligan's on the Blue.** When you have a hankering for Irish fare such as bangers and mash, shepherd's pie, and corned beef and cabbage, head to this popular pub and restaurant on the Wailea Blue golf course. A nearly all-Irish staff greets you, and before you know it, you'll be sipping a heady pint of Guinness with a four-leaf clover drawn on top. The Wailea Nights dinner show with different kinds of live music is outstanding—and a terrific deal to boot. This is *the* St. Paddy's Day and Cinco de Mayo headquarters of Maui, never mind the latter is a Mexican holiday. Breakfast is a good value for the area, and the view of the golf course and ocean is one of the best. ⊠ *100 Kaukahi St., Wailea* ☎ *808/874–1131* ▤ *AE, D, DC, MC, V.*

$$$$
SEAFOOD
✕**Nick's Fishmarket Maui.** This romantic spot serves fresh seafood using the simplest preparations. Savor the grilled 'ahi mignon served medium rare with polenta fries and sauce au poivre; or the seared diver scallops with herb gnocchi, local mushrooms, asparagus tips, and Parmesan nage. Everyone seems to love the Greek Maui Wowie salad made with local onions, tomatoes, avocado, feta cheese, and bay shrimp. The service is formal—even theatrical—but it befits the beautiful food presentations and extensive wine list. If you are a repeat diner, the staff will probably remember what drink is your favorite. ⊠ *Fairmont Kea Lani, 4100 Wailea Alanui Dr., Wailea* ☎ *808/879–7224* ▤ *AE, D, DC, MC, V* ☉ *No lunch.*

$$$
AMERICAN
✕**Seawatch.** The Plantation House's South Shore sister restaurant has equally outstanding views and an equally delicious menu. Breakfast is especially nice here—the outdoor seating is cool in the morning and overlooks the parade of boats heading out to Molokini. The crab-cake

Benedicts are a well-loved standard. For dinner, try longtime chef Todd Carlos' Thai beef in a martini glass with fresh coconut milk and lemongrass; or his Huikau Eke of island catch, Alaskan scallops and tiger prawns in parchment paper—opened table-side to release the aromatics. Regarding the "brownie all the way" dessert, one regular says it "serves a deep need." Weddings and other large functions may be booked here. ⊠ *100 Golf Club Dr., Wailea* ☎ *808/875–8080* ⊟ *AE, D, DC, MC, V.*

$$$$ ✕ **Spago.** Celebrity chef and own-
PACIFIC RIM er Wolfgang Puck wisely brought his fame to this gorgeous, popular-with-celebs restaurant set lobby level and oceanfront at the Four Seasons Resort Maui. Giant sea-anemone prints, modern-art-inspired lamps, and views of the shoreline give you something to look at while waiting. The cutting-edge menu delivers with appetizers such as spicy 'ahi *poke* in sesame miso cones and entrées such as Thai seafood in red coconut curry; pan-roasted organic free-range chicken breast; and lamb chops with spicy Hunan eggplant, sweet peas, and chili mint vinaigrette. Chef Cameron Lewark's tasting menu, paired with wines, is a treat. ⊠ *Four Seasons Resort Maui at Wailea, 3900 Wailea Alanui Dr., Wailea* ☎ *808/879–2999* ⊟ *AE, D, DC, MC, V* ⊗ *No lunch.*

SHAVE ICE

Nothing goes down quite so nice as shave ice on a hot day. This favorite island treat has been likened to a snow cone, but that description doesn't do a good shave ice justice. Yes, it is ice served up in a cone-shaped cup and drenched with sweet syrup, but the similarities end there. The ice should be well shaved, feathery, and light—the texture of snowflakes, not frozen slush. Alongside the standard cherry and grape are all sorts of exotic island flavorings. But the true beauty of a shave ice is what's underneath. Devotees have theirs with adzuki beans; just about everyone wants vanilla ice cream for the base.

CENTRAL MAUI

Central Maui is where the locals live and you'll find just about every ethnic cuisine represented on the Islands here. Savory saimin noodle shops and small joints dishing up hamburger patties set atop two scoops of rice with rich brown gravy are particularly plentiful. Be sure to check out Wailuku. Drive up Lower Main Street and take a chance on dozens of mom-and-pop eateries. It's truly an adventure in dining. If you walk along historic Market Street, you can peruse antiques shops between bites.

Kahului offers more variety as it's in the main traffic corridor and near the big-box stores; you'll even find potatoes instead of rice on a few menus. The most important thing to know about dining in Central Maui? It's all about deals.

8

KAHULUI

¢ VIETNAMESE **Ba Le.** Tucked into a mall's food court, this eatery is the best and cheapest Vietnamese fast food on the island. *Pho,* the famous soups, come laden with seafood or rare beef, fresh basil, bean sprouts, and lime. Tasty sandwiches are served on crisp French rolls—lemongrass chicken is a favorite. The word is out, so the place gets busy at lunchtime, though the wait is never long. Make sure to try one of the flavored tapiocas for dessert and take home some freshly baked croissants. Also check out Ba Le's latest incarnation in Wailuku. ✉ *Kau Kau Corner food court, Maui Marketplace, 270 Dairy Rd., Kahului* ☎ *808/877–2400* ▭ *AE, D, DC, MC, V.*

$$ CHINESE **Dragon Dragon.** Whether you're a party of 10 or 2, this is the place to share Cantonese West Lake beef soup, honey walnut prawns, and lamb-back ribs with garlic sauce. Tasteful, simple decor that focuses on feng shui and sharp angles complements the solid Chinese menu. Dim sum is served at lunch only. Can't decide what to order? Try the set meals for two, four, or six people. The restaurant shares parking with the Maui Megaplex and makes a great pre- or postmovie stop. ✉ *In Maui Mall, 70 E. Ka'ahumanu Ave., Kahului* ☎ *808/893–1628* ▭ *AE, D, MC, V.*

$ JAPANESE **Genki Sushi.** At this automated sushi bar, it's fun to watch items go around in circles on dual conveyor belts. There are 220 locations in Japan, 35 in Singapore, and 2 on Maui (this is the first; it's sister restaurant opened at Lahaina Gateway in 2008). Watch fresh spicy 'ahi tuna and other sushi treats parade past you, then grab what you like, pop items in your mouth, and grab for more. Sit in large booths or on stools in cool, air-conditioned comfort. Children love the show, and there's a kid-friendly menu. In addition, you can choose plenty of cooked items such as shrimp tempura. Ordering to go is easy with a walk-up counter. Prices are very reasonable. ✉ *In the Maui Mall, 70 E. Ka'ahumanu Ave., Kahului* ☎ *808/873–7776* ▭ *AE, D, MC, V.*

$ AMERICAN **Koho Grill and Bar.** Over 20 years in the same location is a major feat for any restaurant and that's exactly what Koho Grill and Bar has going for it. Open all day every day, except Christmas, Koho is a family-oriented restaurant known for value, consistency, and friendly service. At breakfast, try the Road to Hāna eggs served in a hot skillet, a steaming bowl of saimin, or one of the classic eggs Benedict. Lunch has lots of options, from local plate lunches to fresh Island Catch Salad. Substitutions are never a problem and the lunch and "pūpū" menu are available all day. Located only six minutes from the Kahului airport, the restaurant is convenient and offers enough variety to please most. ✉ *275 Ka'ahumanu Ave., Kahului* ☎ *808/877–5588* ▭ *AE, MC, V.*

$$ ITALIAN **Marco's Grill & Deli.** Outside Kahului Airport at the busy intersection of Hāna Highway and Dairy Road, this convenient restaurant (look for the green awning) serves the best Italian food in Central Maui. Owner Marco Defanis was a butcher in his former life and makes all his meatballs and sausages from scratch. Homemade pastas appear on the extensive menu and the vodka rigatoni is a must try. The Reuben sandwich is unforgettably good, the Greek Salad crunchy and fresh, and the tiramisu all cakey and creamy at the same time. Even the coffee,

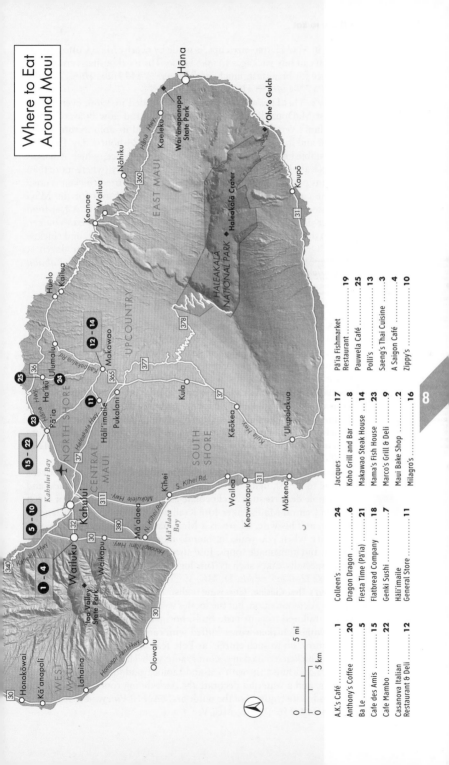

Where to Eat Around Maui

served in Mad Hatter–size cups, is made by nearby Maui Coffee Roasters; you can buy packages to take home. The local business crowd fills the place for breakfast, lunch, and dinner. ✉ *444 Hāna Hwy., Kahului* ☎ *808/877–4446* ⊟ *AE, D, DC, MC, V.*

$ ✕ **Zippy's.** This Hawaiian favorite was founded in 1966, even before
HAWAIIAN the first McDonald's opened in the Islands, and now boasts 27 outlets. Maui's version is the latest to emerge and its architecture, cushy booths, and local art make it quite posh for a 24-hour-a-day, Denny's-type establishment. It's famous for its chili and rice, which it barges over to Kahului Harbor from its main O'ahu facility (where more than 110 tons per month are made in giant vats). The fried chicken is crisp and the curry stew is *ono* (delicious). But watch out for the MSG (monosodium glutamate): many of the entrées contain it. A fast-food counter does a brisk business of Zip Pacs (mini bento boxes you can take to the beach) as well as pūpū platters of fried noodles and chicken katsu. Order the famous Napples (apple turnovers) by the dozen at the Napoleans' Bakery counter up front. ✉ *15 Ho'okele St., Kahului* ☎ *808/856–7599* ⊟ *AE, D, MC, V.*

WAILUKU

$ ✕ **A.K.'s Café.** Nearly hidden between auto-body shops and karaoke bars
HAWAIIAN is this wonderful, bright café serving good island fare. Affordable, tasty entrées such as grilled tenderloin with wild mushrooms or garlic-crusted ono with ginger-cucumber relish come with a choice of two sides. The flavorful dishes are healthful, too—chef Elaine Rothermal previously instructed island nutritionists on how to prepare health-conscious versions of local favorites. (She's trying to get away from that somewhat, as most people like the bad stuff at least sometimes.) Try the Hawaiian french-fried sweet potatoes or the poi, the Hawaiian classic made from taro root. Solo musicians entertain on weekends. ✉ *1237 Lower Main, Wailuku* ☎ *808/244–8774* ⊟ *D, MC, V* ☉ *Closed Sun.*

¢ ✕ **Maui Bake Shop.** Wonderful French breads baked in old brick ovens
AMERICAN (dating to 1935), light lunch fare such as quiche and sandwiches, and irresistible desserts such as chocolate éclairs make this a popular lunch spot in Central Maui. Baker José Krall was trained in his homeland of France, and his wife, Claire, is a Maui native whose friendly face you often see when you walk in. Standouts include the focaccia, Caesar salads, and homemade soups. José also creates impressive wedding and other specialty cakes such as Yule logs. ✉ *2092 Vineyard St., Wailuku* ☎ *808/242–0064* ⊟ *AE, D, MC, V* ☉ *Closed Sun. No dinner.*

$$ ✕ **Saeng's Thai Cuisine.** Choosing a dish from the six-page menu here
THAI requires determination, but the food is worth the effort, and most dishes can be tailored to your taste buds: hot, medium, or mild. Begin with angel wings (chicken wings stuffed with carrots and bean-thread noodles); move on to such entrées as Poh Teak (spicy seafood soup), Evil Prince Chicken (cooked in coconut sauce with Thai herbs), or red-curry shrimp; and finish up with tea and tapioca pudding. Asian artifacts, flowers, and a waterfall decorate the dark dining room, and tables on a veranda satisfy lovers of the outdoors. ✉ *2119 Vineyard St., Wailuku* ☎ *808/244–1567* ⊟ *AE, MC, V.*

$$ ✕ **A Saigon Café.** The only storefront sign announcing this delightful
Fodor'sChoice Vietnamese hideaway is one reading OPEN. Once you find it (below the
★ historic bridge in Wailuku), treat yourself to the Vietnamese *pho* (soup)
VIETNAMESE in rich beef broth, rice in a clay pot, or *banh hoi chao tom,* more com-
monly known as "shrimp pops burritos" (ground marinated shrimp,
steamed and grilled on a stick of sugarcane). Wok-fried or steamed
whole *opakapaka* (blue snapper) is always available, and vegetarian
fare is well represented—try the green-papaya salad or tofu with lem-
ongrass. The simple white interior serves as a backdrop for Vietnamese
carvings, and booths make for some privacy. Owner Jennifer Nguyen
really makes the place, so ask to talk story with her if she's in. ✉ *1792
Main St., Wailuku* ☎ *808/243–9560* ▭ *D, MC, V.*

UPCOUNTRY

Take the drive up the slopes of magnificent Mount Haleakalā and you
will find a plethora of restaurants catering to both locals and visitors.
Hāliʻimaile General Store is a landmark in the middle of a pineapple
field; the small town of Pukalani dishes up everything from pizza to
sushi; and little Makawao will let you saddle up to everything from a
steak house to an Italian restaurant to a Mexican cantina. Upcountry
also encompasses cool Kula with the famous Kula Lodge and a few
mom-and-pop's. Many visitors opt to check out the farm tours between
bites at eateries.

$$$ ✕ **Casanova Italian Restaurant & Deli.** An authentic Italian dinner house and
ITALIAN nightclub, this place is smack in the middle of *paniolo* (cowboy) country,
and it has remained an Upcountry institution for decades. The pizzas,
baked in a brick wood-burning oven imported from Italy, are the best
around, especially the *tartufo,* or truffle oil pizza. All entrées come with
either creamy risotto, steamy polenta, or garlicky mashed potatoes. The
daytime deli serves outstanding sandwiches and espresso. After dining
hours, local and visiting entertainers heat up the dance floor. ✉ *1188
Makawao Ave., Makawao* ☎ *808/572–0220* ▭ *D, DC, MC, V.*

$$$ ✕ **Hāliʻimaile General Store.** What do you do with a lofty wooden building
MODERN surrounded by sugarcane and pineapple fields that was a tiny town's
HAWAIIAN camp store in the 1920s? If you're Beverly and Joe Gannon, you invent
a now legendary restaurant known for Hawaiʻi Regional Cuisine. This
landmark celebrated 20 successful years in 2008, and it continues to
wow with bamboo steamer fish with dumplings; Kurobuta pork shank;
and Asian bouillabaisse with green tea noodles. For lunch, dig into the
Kobe beef burger with fontina cheese; or the Brie-and-grape quesadilla
with sweet-pea guacamole. The back room houses a rotating art exhibit,
courtesy of some of the island's top artists. The restaurant even has its
own cookbook, but Beverly will never reveal the recipe for her famous
"crab" dip. ✉ *900 Hāliʻimaile Rd., take left exit halfway up Haleakalā
Hwy., Hāliʻimaile* ☎ *808/572–2666* ▭ *MC, V.*

$$$ ✕ **Makawao Steak House.** A restored 1927 house on the slopes of
STEAKHOUSE Haleakalā is the setting for this Hawaiian cowboy restaurant, which
serves consistently good prime rib, rack of lamb, and fresh fish. The
New York pepper steak is a signature, as is the Mud Pie dessert with

Kona coffee ice cream and Oreo cookie crust. Three fireplaces, friendly service, and an intimate lounge create a cozy, welcoming atmosphere. The salad bar, albeit small, is always a big hit. In addition, ladies will love the tearoom in the back, perfect for all kinds of girly get-togethers with its frilly ambience and antique china. ⊠*3612 Baldwin Ave., Makawao* ☎*808/572-8711* ▭*D, DC, MC, V* ⊗*No lunch.*

$$
MEXICAN
✕**Polli's.** The sign at the front reads, "Come In and Eat or We'll Both Starve" and the interior is plastered with colorful sombreros and other cantina knickknacks. Menu items include such Mexican standards as enchiladas, chimichangas, and fajitas; and you can request any item on the menu with seasoned tofu or vegetarian taco mix—and the meatless dishes are just as good as the real thing. A special treat are the *buñuelos*—light pastries topped with cinnamon, maple syrup, and ice cream. Call ahead and ask for the nightly promotion. The bar is always packed with the same regulars, just as it has been for decades. ⊠*1202 Makawao Ave., Makawao* ☎*808/572–7808* ▭*AE, D, DC, MC, V.*

THE NORTH SHORE

The North Shore sets the dramatic stage for Maui's most famous restaurant, Mama's Fish House in Kū'au. Visitors to Maui all want to dine there and residents wish they could afford it more often. The area also encompasses the great food town of Pā'ia, which boasts one fun restaurant after another. People-watching from any number of these spots should be high on your agenda. The North Shore is a feast for the senses as well as for the eyes. Don't miss it for a minute. And, make sure to bring your bathing suit for a dip in the ocean at one of the nearby beaches.

HAʻIKŪ

$
AMERICAN
✕**Colleen's.** On the main road in jungly yet up-and-coming Ha'ikū, this is the neighborhood hangout for windsurfers, yoga teachers, and just plain beautiful people. Many regulars stop in for takeout on their way home from commutes in the touristy areas. At breakfast, pastries tend to be jam-packed with berries and nuts, rather than being flaky and full of butter. Sandwiches are especially good, served on giant slices of homemade bread. For dinner you can't go wrong with the 'ahi niçoise salad, pepper-crusted mahimahi, or red-ale-and-mango-glazed ribs with sour cream and herb mashed potatoes. ⊠*In Ha'ikū Cannery, 810 Kokomo Rd., Ha'ikū* ☎*808/575–9211* ▭*AE, DC, MC, V.*

¢
AMERICAN
✕**Pauwela Café.** Ultracasual and ultrafriendly, this slightly hard-to-find spot (a few miles off Hāna Highway in the historic Pauwela Cannery) is worth the ride. Order a *kālua* (baked underground) turkey sandwich and a piece of homemade coffee cake and hang out for a while. The large breakfast burritos, Belgian waffles, and, if you're here on the weekend, eggs Benedict are also good. This is where you'll find the hippies and trust-fund babies of Maui's North Shore. ⊠*375 W. Kuiaha Rd., off Hāna Hwy. past Ha'ikū Rd., Ha'ikū* ☎*808/575–9242* ▭*AE, MC, V* ⊗*No dinner.*

KŪ'AU

$$$$
Fodor'sChoice
★
SEAFOOD

✕**Mama's Fish House.** For over 35 years Mama's has been *the* Maui destination for special occasions. A stone path leads you through the cool coconut grove to what would be, in an ideal world, a good friend's house. The Hawaiian nautical theme is hospitable and fun— the menu even names which boat reeled in your fish. Despite its high

prices—even for Maui—the restaurant is always full; dinner reservations start at 4:30 PM. Chef Perry Bateman outdoes himself with lobster guacamole; Kula corn and crab chowder; and Big Island hearts of palm salad. The daily catch steamed in traditional lū'au leaves is outstanding—and worth the cash. Follow up with the Polynesian Pearl—a gorgeous affair of chocolate mousse and passion-fruit cream. Look for the old fishing boat perched above the entrance to Mama's, about 1½ mi east of Pā'ia on Hāna Highway. ⌂*799 Poho Pl., Kū'au* ☎*808/579–8488* ⌕*Reservations essential* ⊟*AE, D, DC, MC, V.*

PĀ'IA

¢
AMERICAN

✕**Anthony's Coffee.** Here's a great place to eavesdrop on the local windsurfing crowd. The coffee is excellent—they roast their own beans. For breakfast, try eggs done Benedict style with toppings such as veggies, *kālua* (baked underground) pork, fresh catch, or lox. The catch-of-the-day breakfast includes two eggs, toast, potatoes, and fruit. Picnic lunches, such as turkey or ham sandwiches with chips, are available, and there's an ice-cream counter. Bonus: free Wi-Fi. ⌂*90 Hāna Hwy., Pā'ia* ☎*808/579–8340* ⊟*AE, DC, MC, V* ☾*No dinner.*

$
FRENCH

✕**Cafe des Amis.** Papier-mâché wrestlers pop out from the walls at this small creperie that has been newly expanded with a breezy and shaded outdoor courtyard. French crepes with Gruyère, and Indian wraps with lentil curry are among the choices, all served with wild greens and sour cream or homemade chutney on the side. The giant curry bowls are mild but tasty, and also come with a delicious side of chutney. For dessert there are crepes filled with chocolate, Nutella, cane sugar, or banana. It may take some time for your order to arrive, but the people-watching in eccentric Pā'ia makes it worth the wait—so do the smoothies. ⌂*42 Baldwin Ave., Pā'ia* ☎*808/579–6323* ⊟*AE, D, MC, V.*

$
MEDITERRANEAN

✕**Cafe Mambo.** Pā'ia is arguably Maui's most interesting food town, and this Mediterranean-inspired place is right in the thick of it. The husband-and-wife owners, from England and Spain respectively, tiled the walk-up counter with Moroccan clay pieces, and teak- and coconut-wood tables are set in the middle of benches with Middle Eastern pillows. The seafood tapas platter sizzles with shrimp, calamari, and mussels cooked in garlic butter, white wine, and herbs. Fajita platters and paella are all the rage in Pā'ia, and we recommend them here. On Saturday, come watch a classic movie on the big screen before ordering

8

hot and crunchy popcorn, or lime cheesecake. ⊠ *30 Baldwin Ave., Pāʻia* ☎ *808/579–8021* ⊟ *AE, D, MC, V.*

¢ ✕**Fiesta Time.** Surfers say nothing tastes better after a day in the waves

MEXICAN than Fiesta Time's fish tacos with Spanish rice and black beans topped with melted cheese and fresh salsa. If you're out for a day of sunbathing or driving around the island, stop in here and fill your belly with burritos, enchiladas, and chiles rellenos. The pickled vegetables available in take-home tubs are especially tasty. Decorated with fanciful Mexican murals, the restaurant has limited seating and is mainly take-out, but it's as authentic as it gets on Maui. ⊠ *149 Hāna Hwy., Pāʻia* ☎ *808/579–8269* ⊟ *AE, MC, V.*

$$ ✕**Flatbread Company.** Sit inside this popular pizzeria and watch the chef

☺ stir the giant cauldron of organic fresh tomatoes over kiawe wood. Every

PIZZA item on the menu screams that it's fresh, sustainable, and oh-so-good for you. Wood-fired pizzas are baked in a clay oven, and meats include nitrate-free pepperoni and free-range pork. Partake in the "Mopsy's Pork Pie" with *kālua* (baked underground) pork, barbecue sauce, and pineapple goat cheese; or the "Pele's Pesto" with Roma tomatoes, goat cheese, and olives. Portions are large and service is prompt and friendly, despite the near-constant crowds. It can get hot inside with all of those clay ovens, so dress accordingly or opt to sit in the breezy courtyard. ⊠ *375 Hāna Hwy., Pāʻia* ☎ *808/579–8989* ⊟ *MC, V.*

$ ✕**Jacques North Shore.** An amiable French chef, Jacques Pauvert won the

ECLECTIC hearts of the windsurfing crowd when he opened this hip, ramshackle bar and restaurant. It's a youthful hangout with fairly sophisticated fare for the price, and makes a great dating spot for twentysomethings on a budget. French-Caribbean dishes like Jacques' Crispy Little Poulet (chicken) reveal the owner's expertise. The tropical outdoor area can be a little chilly at times; coveted spots at the sushi bar inside are snatched up quickly. On Friday nights, a DJ moves in and the dining room becomes a packed dance floor. ⊠ *120 Hāna Hwy., Pāʻia* ☎ *808/579–8844* ⊟ *AE, D, MC, V.*

$$ ✕**Milagro's.** Delicious fish tacos are found at this corner restaurant, along

LATIN-AMERICAN with a selection of fine tequilas and Latin-fusion recipes that ignite the taste buds. Try the lava-rock grilled ʻahi burrito with house-made beans and rice; and the seafood enchiladas with ʻahi, ono, and mild green Anaheim chili sauce. The location at the junction of Baldwin Avenue and Hāna Highway makes people-watching from under the awning shade fun, but the constant stream of traffic makes it a bit noisy. Mostly tourists dine here as it's such a convenient location. Lunch and happy hour (3 to 5) are the best values; prices jump at dinnertime. ⊠ *3 Baldwin Ave., Pāʻia* ☎ *808/579–8755* ⊟ *AE, D, DC, MC, V.*

$ ✕**Pāʻia Fishmarket Restaurant.** The line leading up to the counter of this

SEAFOOD tiny corner fish market should attest to the popularity of the tasty fish sandwiches—though the great location right in the middle of Pāʻia doesn't hurt. Bench seating is somewhat grimy, but you will find a good fish sandwich. Don't bother with the other items—go for your choice of fillet on a soft bun with a dollop of slaw and some grated cheese. As we say in Hawaiʻi, *ʻono* (delicious)! ⊠ *2A Baldwin Ave., Pāʻia* ☎ *808/579–8030* ⊟ *AE, DC, MC, V.*

Where to Stay

WORD OF MOUTH

"Kā'anapali would be my choice, for the things to do and the shopping in Lahaina (one of my favorite towns in the U.S.). It is so central to everything on Maui and taking a day trip to get away from the noise/hustle is just a beach or waterfall away."

—eamc

WHERE TO STAY PLANNER

Lodging Strategy

With resorts, condos, and bed-and-breakfasts around the island, there's no shortage of lodging options. Our team of expert writers and editors has compiled their top recommendations, organized by geographical area.

Hotels and Resorts

Maui's resorts are clustered along the island's leeward (West and South) shores, so they offer near-perfect weather year-round. Kā'anapali, in West Maui, has the most action. Kapalua, farther north, is more private and serene. Among the South Shore resort communities, posh Wailea has excellent beaches and golf courses.

Condos and Rentals

If you compromise on luxury, you will find convenient condos in West Maui in Nāpili, Honokōwai, or Kahana, and on the South Shore in Kīhei. Many are oceanfront and offer the amenities of a hotel without the cost, through central air-conditioning is rare. Besides the condos listed here, Maui has condos rented through central agents.

B&Bs and Inns

As of this writing, Maui County is in the midst of a controversy over the licensing of B&Bs and what are technically called TVRs (transient vacation rentals). Part of the problem stems from the fact that glorious inns are lumped together—for the county's legal purposes—with what may be nothing more than a bed set up in someone's garage. To avoid disappointment (some places may have to close), our best advice is to ask whether the property is licensed by the county. You might even ask for the permit number, which should be posted on the property's Web site.

Reservations

The farther ahead you book, the more likely you are to get exactly the room you want. This is especially true at the big resort hotels for December 20 through April, and again during July and August, Maui's busiest times. At these times, booking a year in advance is not uncommon. Even at other times, booking less than four to six months ahead may mean settling for a second, third, or fourth choice.

Prices

Assume that hotels have private bath, phone, and TV and that prices do not include meals unless we state otherwise. We always list facilities but not whether you'll be charged an extra fee to use them; ask when you book. Most resorts charge parking and facility fees—a "resort fee." Always ask about packages and discounts. In Hawai'i room prices can rise dramatically if a room has an ocean view. To save money, ask for a garden or mountain view.

WHAT IT COSTS IN HOTELS				
¢	$	$$	$$$	$$$$
Under $100	$100–$180	$181–$260	$261–$340	Over $340

Hotel prices are for two people in a double room in high season. Condo price categories reflect studio and one-bedroom rates. Prices exclude 11.41% tax.

BEST BETS FOR MAUI LODGING

Fodor's writers and editors have selected their favorite hotels, resorts, condos, vacation rentals, and B&Bs by price and experience. Fodor's Choice properties represent the "best of the best" across price categories. You can also search by area for excellent places to stay—check out our complete reviews on the following pages.

★ FODOR'S CHOICE

Four Seasons Resort Maui at Wailea, $$$$

Hale Ho'okipa Inn, $–$$

Hotel Hāna-Maui, $$$$

The Old Wailuku Inn at Ulupono, $

Ritz-Carlton, Kapalua, $$$$

By Price

¢

Pu'ukoa Maui Rentals

$

Banyan Tree House

Hale Ho'okipa Inn

Luana Kai

The Old Wailuku Inn at Ulupono

$$

Hāna Kai-Maui Resort Condominiums

Plantation Inn

$$$

Kā'anapali Beach Hotel

Kama'ole Sands

Maui Eldorado

Nāpili Kai Beach Resort

$$$$

Four Seasons Resort Maui at Wailea

Hotel Hāna-Maui

Mākena Surf

Polo Beach Club

Ritz-Carlton, Kapalua

Wailea Beach Villas

By Experience

BEST BEACH

Kā'anapali Ali'i, $$$$

Mana Kai Maui, $$–$$$

Nāpili Kai Beach Resort, $$$–$$$$

Polo Beach Club, $$$$

BEST HOTEL BAR

Four Seasons Resort Maui at Wailea, $$$$

Kā'anapali Beach Hotel, $$$–$$$$

Ritz-Carlton, Kapalua, $$$$

Sheraton Maui Resort, $$$$

BEST B&BS & INNS

Hale Ho'okipa Inn, $–$$

The Old Wailuku Inn at Ulupono, $

BEST SPA

Four Seasons Resort Maui at Wailea, $$$$

Hotel Hāna-Maui, $$$$

Wailea Beach Marriott Resort & Spa, $$$$

The Westin Maui Resort & Spa, $$$$

MOST KID-FRIENDLY

Banyan Tree House, $–$$

Fairmont Kea Lani Maui, $$$$

Kama'ole Sands, $$$

Mana Kai Maui, $$–$$$

Nāpili Kai Beach Resort, $$$–$$$$

MOST ROMANTIC

Four Seasons Resort Maui at Wailea, $$$$

Hale Ho'okipa Inn, $–$$

Hotel Hāna-Maui, $$$$

The Old Wailuku Inn at Ulupono, $

Ritz-Carlton, Kapalua, $$$$

The Westin Maui Resort & Spa, $$$$

9

Updated
by Bonnie
Friedman

Maui's accommodations run the gamut from a rural B&B listed on the State and National Historic Registers to one particularly over-the-top, superopulent megaresort. But hey, each to his or her own taste, right? In between the extremes, there's something for every vacation style and budget.

If the latest and greatest is your style, be prepared to spend a small fortune. Newly renovated properties like the Ritz-Carlton Kapalua and the Four Seasons Resort Maui at Wailea and the newest condo complexes such as the Wailea Beach Villas may set you back at least $600 a night, though the weaker economy has brought more deals. Ask for these wherever you stay and consider the alternatives.

Although there aren't many of them, small bed-and-breakfasts are charming. They tend to be in residential or rural neighborhoods around the island, sometimes beyond the resort areas of West Maui and the South Shore. The B&Bs offer both a personalized experience and a window onto authentic local life. The prices tend to be the lowest available on Maui, often less than $200 per night.

Apartment and condo rentals are perfect for modest budgets, for two or more couples traveling together, and for families. Not only are the nightly rates lower than hotel rooms, but "eating in" (all have kitchens of some description) is substantially less expensive than dining out. There are literally hundreds of these units, ranging in size from studios to luxurious four-bedrooms with multiple baths, all over the island. The vast majority are along the sunny coasts—from Mākena to Kīhei on the South Shore and Lahaina up to Kapalua on West Maui. Prices are dependent on the size of the unit and its proximity to the beach, as well as on the amenities and services offered. For about $250 a night, you can get a perfectly lovely one-bedroom apartment without many frills or flourishes, close to but probably not on the beach. Many rentals have minimum stays (usually three to five nights), and don't forget to ask if a discount is offered on stays of a week or more.

Most of Maui's resorts—several are megaresorts—have opulent gardens, fantasy swimming pools, championship golf courses, and full-service fitness centers and spas. Expect to spend at least $350 a night at the resort hotels; they are all located in the Wailea and Mākena resort area on the South Shore and Kā'anapali and Kapalua on West Maui. At all hotels, ask about discounts and deals (free nights with longer stays, for example), which have proliferated.

WEST MAUI

Along the coast, West Maui is a long string of small communities, beginning with Lahaina at the south end and meandering north into Kā'anapali, Honokōwai, Kahana, Nāpili, and Kapalua. Here's the breakdown on what's where: Lahaina, a former whaling town, is the business district with all the action: shops, shows, restaurants, historic buildings, churches, and rowdy side streets. Kāʻanapali, the island's original resort area, is all glitz: fancy resorts set on Kāʻanapali Beach. Honokōwai, Kahana, and Nāpili are quiet little nooks characterized by comfortable condos built in the late 1960s. All face the same direction and get the same consistently hot, humid weather. Kapalua, at the northern tip, faces windward and has a cooler climate and slightly more rain. It has become synonymous with the utmost in luxury in accommodations from hotels to condos to residences.

LAHAINA

Lahaina doesn't have a huge range of accommodations, but it does make a great headquarters for active families, or those not looking to spend a bundle on resorts. One major advantage is the proximity of restaurants, shops, and activities—everything is within walking distance. It's a business district, however, and won't provide the same peace and quiet as resorts or secluded vacation rentals. Still, Lahaina has a nostalgic charm, especially early in the morning before the streets have filled with visitors and vendors.

$-$$ **Best Western Pioneer Inn.** Fans of author Tom Robbins will recognize
HOTEL the Pioneer Inn as one of the settings in his novel *Still Life with Woodpecker*. Built in 1901 when Lahaina was the bawdy heart of the Pacific's whaling industry, the small, right-in-town hotel has been substantially remodeled, updated, and rebranded as a Best Western. Rooms are clean and basic but the price is certainly right. The grounds are well tended and there's a gazebo and private room designed specifically for weddings. The restaurant is open from 7 AM to 10 PM daily and is a popular hangout (especially at sunset) for folks who work at the harbor as well as hotel guests. **Pros:** Lahaina town shops and restaurants are within easy walking distance; proximity to Lahaina Harbor makes for easy access to oceangoing activities. **Cons:** few in-room amenities; facing Front Street on one side and the busy harbor on the other; can be noisy. ⊠*658 Wharf St., Lahaina* ☎*808/661–3636 or 800/457–5457* ⊕*www.pioneerinnmaui.com* ⚲*31 rooms, 3 suites* ⌂ *In-hotel: restaurant, pool, public Wi-Fi, no-smoking rooms* ⊟*AE, D, DC, MC, V.*

$ **House of Fountains Bed & Breakfast.** Authentic, traditional Hawaiiana
B&B/INN pervades the six guest rooms and common areas of this large home, located in a mountainside neighborhood just outside Lahaina. Handcrafted koa furniture and Hawaiian artworks and artifacts are in every room. There are two studios plus the smaller Ginger/Hibiscus bedroom on the lower level, and three suites on the upper level, all with queen-size bed, private bath, air-conditioning, TV, phone, refrigerator, and toiletries. A stone fireplace (more for show than warmth in Lahaina's tropical climate) is the centerpiece of the upstairs common area, which is filled with displays of Hawaiian works and descriptions of their history. There's a full kitchen and games and books fill the downstairs living room. The Hawaiian touches continue poolside with two thatched *hale* (huts): one where guests can learn Hawaiian crafts such as *lauhala* weaving and one where they can just relax in

WHERE TO STAY IN WEST MAUI

PROPERTY NAME	Worth Noting	Cost $	Pools	Beach	Golf Course	Tennis Courts	Gym	Spa	Children's Programs	Rooms	Restaurants	Other	Location
Hotels & Resorts													
❷ Best Western Pioneer Inn	Convenient location in Lahaina	169–250	1							34	1		Lahaina
❸ Hyatt Regency Maui	130-ft water slide	365–580	1	yes	priv.	6	yes	yes	3–12	806	5		Kā'anapali
❻ Kā'anapali Beach Hotel	Hula & lei-making classes	235–485	1	yes	priv.					432	3		Kā'anapali
⓰ Mauian Hotel	On Nāpili Bay	120–280	1	yes						44		no TVs	Nāpili
⓲ Ritz-Carlton, Kapalua	Environmental education center	505–875	1	yes	priv.	10	yes	yes	5–12	463	6	shops	Kapalua
❾ Royal Lahaina Resort	New tower wing	235–650	3	yes	priv.	11	yes	yes	5–12	333	2		Kā'anapali
❼ Sheraton Maui Resort & Spa	Nightly torch-lighting ritual	360–680	1	yes		3	yes	yes	5–12	540	2		Kā'anapali
❿ The Westin Kā'anapali Ocean Resort Villas		690–1050	3	yes	priv.	2	yes	yes	5–12	1021	2	shops	Kā 'anapali
❺ The Westin Maui Resort	The Heavenly Spa	525–810	5	yes	priv.		yes	yes	5–12	758	2		Kā'anapali
Condos & Vacation Rentals													
⓫ Aston Mahana at Kā'anapali	Spacious rooms	391–715	1	yes		2				215		kitchens	Honokowai
⓬ Aston at Papakea Resort	Cultural classes	315–650	2			4			5–12	364		kitchens	Honokowai
⓳ Kapalua Villas	Gorgeous views	299–829	10	yes	yes	10				564		kitchens	Kapalua
❹ Kā'anapali Ali'i	Great location	405–675	2	yes	yes	6				264		kitchens	Kā'anapali
❶ Lahaina Shores	Oceanfront	225–385	1	yes						145		Kitchens	Lahaina
⓮ Mahina Surf Oceanfront Resort	Free parking and phone	170–320	1							50		kitchens	Mahinahina
⓭ Makani Sands	Small private beach	180–435	1	yes						21		kitchens	Honokowai
❽ Maui Eldorado	On golf course	259–419	3	yes	yes					204		kitchens	Kā'anapali
⓱ Nāpili Kai Beach Resort	Outstanding beach	275–965	4	yes					6–10	163		some kitchens	Nāpili
⓯ Sands of Kahana	Kids' putting green	265–500	2	yes		3				162		kitchens	Kahana

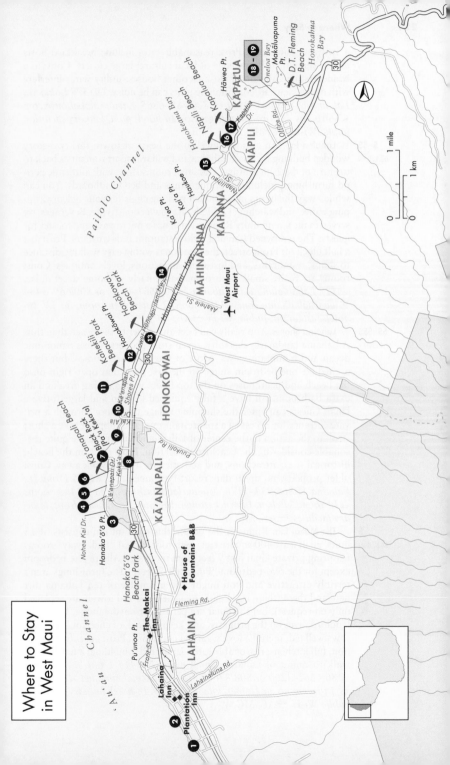

Where to Stay in West Maui

Pailolo Channel

'Au'au Channel

KAPALUA
Makāluapuma Pt.
Oneloa Bay
D. T. Fleming Beach
Hāwea Pt.
Honokahua Bay
18 – 19

Kapalua Beach
Nāpili Beach
Honokeana Bay
NĀPILI
Office Rd.
16 17
15
Hawea Pt.
Kai'a Pt.
Ko'ea Pt.
KAHANA
MĀHINAHINA
Nāpilihau St.
Kahekili Hwy.
West Maui Airport
Kahele St.

Honokōwai Beach Park
HONOKŌWAI
Honokōwai Pt.
Lower Honoapi'ilani Hwy.
14
13
12
Puukolii Rd.

Kahekili Beach Park
11
'Ākāhele Shores Pt.
Kai Ala Dr.
10
9
Black Rock (Pu'u Keka'a)
Kā'anapali Dr.
Keka'a Dr.
7
8
KĀ'ANAPALI
Kō'anapali Beach
Nohea Kai Dr.
6
5
4
3
Hanaka'ō'ō Pt.

Hanaka'ō'ō Beach Park
♦ House of Fountains B&B
Fleming Rd.
30

♦ The Makai Inn
LAHAINA
Front St.
Pu'unoa Pt.
Lahainaluna Rd.
♦ Lahaina Inn
♦ Plantation Inn
2
1

N

1 mile
1 km
0
0

a swinging hammock. **Pros:** reasonable rates include breakfast; hosts like to share their knowledge of local culture; large closets. **Cons:** in a residential neighborhood close to other houses; utility wires interfere with ocean view; air-conditioning units can be noisy. ⊠ *1579 Lokia St., Lahaina* ☎ *808/667–2121 or 800/789–6865* ⊕ *www.alohahouse.com* ➥ *6 rooms* ⌂ *In-room: refrigerator. In-hotel: pool, laundry facilities, public Wi-Fi AE, MC, V.*

$–$$
B&B/INN

⊡ **Lahaina Inn.** An antique jewel in the heart of town, this two-story wooden building is classic Lahaina and will transport romantics back to the turn of the 20th century. The small rooms shine with authentic period furnishings, including antique lamps and bed headboards. You can while away the hours in a wooden rocking chair on your balcony, sipping coffee and watching Old Lahaina town come to life. Beverages are served in the Community Room, which has a microwave and toaster for guests. The renowned Lahaina Grill restaurant is downstairs. **Pros:** just a half block off Front Street, the location is within easy walking distance to shops, restaurants, and historical attractions; lovely antiques. **Cons:** rooms are really small, bathrooms particularly so; some street noise. ⊠ *127 Lahainaluna Rd., Lahaina* ☎ *808/661–0577 or 800/669–3444* ⊕ *www.lahainainn.com* ➥ *10 rooms, 2 suites* ⌂ *In-room: no TV. In-hotel: restaurant, public Wi-Fi* ▤ *AE, MC, V.*

$$–$$$
RENTAL

⊡ **Lahaina Shores.** You really can't get any closer to the beach than this. A Lahaina landmark, this lofty, seven-story property offers panoramic ocean and mountain views. Most of the units are studios, but there are deluxe one-bedroom suites on the first floor that open right onto the beach and penthouses on the top floors with a dining area and an extra bathroom. All have a fully equipped kitchen and large, private lānai. Guests can enter the shopping village next door through a private entrance for access to a spa, restaurants, and shops or take a short stroll to the action in the center of Lahaina town. Prices are quite reasonable considering the beachfront location. **Pros:** right on the beach; historical sites, attractions, and activities are a short walk away. **Cons:** older property, no up-to-date resort-type amenities. ⊠ *475 Front St., Lahaina* ☎ *866/934–9176* ⊕ *www.lahainashores.com* ➥ *145 rooms* ⌂ *In-room: kitchen, Internet (some). In-hotel: pool, beachfront, laundry facilities* ▤ *AE, MC, V.*

$
B&B/INN

⊡ **The Makai Inn.** Right on the ocean, this pleasant inn consists of 18 units, all at least 400 square feet, with four special "Hideaway" rooms featuring private lānai just 9 feet from the water. All are one-bedroom except for the two-bedroom "Pineapple Sweet." The furnishings aren't terribly attractive and you might find a smudge of red Lahaina dirt here and there (there is no daily maid service, and towels are replaced only on request), but the lānai are perfect for daydreaming. Suzie, the landlord, lives on the property, and keeps a flock of cheerful Java sparrows well fed; there's a lovely garden courtyard. **Pros:** oceanfront location; full kitchens; reasonable rates. **Cons:** older building; a few blocks' walk to center of Lahaina; small units. ⊠ *1415 Front St., Lahaina* ☎ *808/662–3200 or 808/870–9004* ⊕ *www.makaiinn.net* ➥ *18 units* ⌂ *In-room: no a/c (some), kitchen, no TV. In-hotel: laundry facilities, public Wi-Fi* ▤ *AE, MC, V.*

$$–$$$
B&B/INN
🖼 **Plantation Inn.** Charm and some added amenities set this inn, tucked into a corner of a busy street in the heart of Lahaina, apart. Filled with Victorian and Asian furnishings, it's reminiscent of a southern plantation home. Secluded lānai draped with hanging plants face a central courtyard, pool, and a garden pavilion perfect for morning coffee. Each guest room or suite is decorated differently, with hardwood floors, French doors, and slightly dowdy antiques. (We think No. 10 is nicest.) Suites have kitchenettes and whirlpool baths. A generous breakfast is included in the room rate, and one of Hawai'i's best French restaurants, Gerard's, is on-site. Breakfast, coupled with free parking in downtown Lahaina, makes this a truly great value, even if it's 10 minutes from the beach. **Pros:** guests have full privileges at the sister Kā'anapali Beach Hotel, 3 mi north; walk to shops, sights, and restaurants. **Cons:** Lahaina town can be noisy; Wi-Fi connection is hit-or-miss (try the lānai). ⊠ *174 Lahainaluna Rd., Lahaina* ☎ *808/667–9225 or 800/433–6815* ⊕ *www.theplantationinn.com* 🛏 *15 rooms, 4 suites* ⚉ *In-room: safe, kitchen (some), refrigerator, Wi-Fi. In-hotel: restaurant, pool* ⊟ *AE, D, DC, MC, V.*

KĀ'ANAPALI

With its long stretch of beach lined with over-the-top resorts, shopping, and restaurants, Kā'anapali is a playground. Expect top-class service here, and everything you could want is just a few steps from your room—including the calm waters of sun-kissed Kā'anapali Beach. Wandering along the beach path between resorts is a recreational activity unto itself. Weather is dependably warm, and for that reason as well as all the others, Kā'anapali is a popular—at times downright crowded—destination.

$$$$
RESORT
🖼 **Hyatt Regency Maui Resort & Spa.** Fantasy landscaping with splashing waterfalls, swim-through grottoes, a lagoonlike swimming pool, and a 130-foot waterslide wow guests of all ages at this active Kā'anapali resort. Stroll through the lobby past museum-quality art, brilliant parrots, and South African penguins (as we said, this is not reality). The Hyatt is not necessarily Hawaiian, but it is photogenic. The grounds are the big deal, but rooms are elegantly decorated with plantation-style wood furniture; each has a private sitting area and lānai. At the southern end of Kā'anapali Beach, this resort is in the midst of the action. Also on the premises is Spa Moana, an oceanfront, full-service facility. **Pros:** nightly lū'au show on-site; recent upgrades of linens; refurbished restaurant. **Cons:** it can be difficult to find a space in self-parking; the hotel staff's service can be uneven. ⊠ *200 Nohea Kai Dr., Kā'anapali* ☎ *808/661–1234 or 800/233–1234* ⊕ *www.maui.hyatt.com* 🛏 *806 rooms* ⚉ *In-room: safe, refrigerator, Internet. In-hotel: 5 restaurants, bars, golf courses, tennis courts, pool, gym, spa, beachfront, water sports, children's programs (ages 3–12)* ⊟ *AE, D, DC, MC, V.*

$$$$
RENTAL
🖼 **Kā'anapali Ali'i.** Four 11-story buildings are laid out so well that the feeling of seclusion you enjoy may make you forget you're in a condo complex. Instead of tiny units, you'll be installed in an ample (1,500–1,900 square feet) one- or two-bedroom apartment. All units

9

VACATION RENTAL COMPANIES

There are many real-estate companies that specialize in short-term vacation rentals. They may represent an entire resort property, most of the units at one property, or even individually owned units. The companies listed here have a long history of excellent service to Maui visitors.

AA Oceanfront Condominium Rentals. As the name suggests, the specialty is "oceanfront." With rental units in more than 25 condominium complexes on the South Shore from the northernmost reaches of Kīheiall the way to Wailea, there's something for everyone at prices that range from $130 to $435 a night. ⊠ 1279 S. Kīhei Rd., Kīhei ☎ 808/879-7288 or 800/488-6004 ⊕ www.aaocean front.com.

Aston Hotels & Resorts. Formerly ResortQuest Hawai'i, the company manages hotels and condos throughout the islands, including nine properties on Maui. Most are on or near the beach, concentrated in the resort areas of Kā'anapali, Kīhei, and Wailea. Studios to three-bedroom units range in price from $120 to $695 per night. The company offers some interesting value-added programs like "Kids Stay, Play and Eat Free." ⊠ 2511 S. Kīhei Rd., Kīhei ☎ 808/879-5445 or 800/822-4409 ⊕ www.astonhotels. com.

Bello Maui Vacations. The Bellos are Maui real-estate experts and have a full range of vacation rentals in 20 South Shore condominium complexes. They also have gorgeous houses for rent. Condos start at right around $100 per night (most are $200 or less); a seven-bedroom oceanfront estate rents for $1,500 per night. ⊠ 115 E. Lipoa, No. 101, Kīhei ☎ 808/879-3328 or 800/541-3060 ⊕ www.bellomauivacations.com.

Chase 'n Rainbows. Family-owned and -operated, this is the largest property management company on West Maui, with the largest selection of rentals from studios to three-bedrooms. Rentals are everywhere from Lahaina town up to Kahana. Prices range from about $100 to $525 per night. The company has been in business since 1980, and it's good. ⊠ 118 Kupuohi St., Lahaina ☎ 808/667-7088 or 800/367-6092 ⊕ www.chasenrain bows.com.

Destination Resorts Hawai'i. If it's the South Shore luxury of Wailea and Mākena you seek, look no further. This company has a full complement of many dozens of condominiums and villas ranging in size from studios to four bedrooms, and in price from $240 a night for a studio at Wailea 'Ekahi, an older property, to more than $3,500 for the new Wailea Beach Villas. The company offers excellent personalized service and is known for particularly fine housekeeping services. ⊠ 3750 Wailea Alanui Dr., Wailea ☎ 808/879-1595 or 866/384-1365 ⊕ www.drhmaui.com.

Mā'alaea Bay Realty and Rentals. Mā'alaea, a little strip of condominiums within the isthmus that links Central and West Maui, is often overlooked, but it shouldn't be. This company has 140 one-, two-, and three-bedroom units from $100 to $235 per night. The wind is usually strong here, but there's a nice beach, a harbor, and some good shopping and decent restaurants. ⊠ 280 Hau'oli St., Mā'alaea ☎ 808/244-5627 or 800/367-6084 ⊕ www.maalaeabay.com.

have great amenities: a chaise in an alcove, a sunken living room, a whirlpool, and a separate dining room, though some of the furnishings are dated. It's the best of both worlds: homelike condo living with hotel amenities—daily maid service, an activities desk, small store with video rentals, and 24-hour front-desk service. **Pros:** large, comfortable units on the beach; good location in heart of the action in Kā'anapali Resort. **Cons:** elevators are notoriously slow; crowded parking; no onsite restaurant. ⊠ *50 Nohea Kai Dr., Kā'anapali* ☎ *808/667–1400 or 800/642–6284* ⊕ *www.kaanapalialii.com* ⤶ *264 units* ⚝ *In-room: safe, kitchen, DVD. In-hotel: golf course, tennis courts, pools, beachfront, laundry facilities* ▭ *AE, D, DC, MC, V.*

$$$–$$$$
HOTEL
🏨 **Kā'anapali Beach Hotel.** Older but still attractive, this small hotel is full of aloha. Locals say that it's one of the few resorts on the island where visitors can get a true Hawaiian experience. The entire staff takes part in the hotel's ongoing Po'okela program to learn about the history, traditions, and values of Hawaiian culture, and shares its knowledge and stories with guests. Also, you can take complimentary classes in authentic hula dancing, lei making, *lauhala* weaving, 'ukulele playing, and other Hawaiian activities. The spacious rooms are decorated with Hawaiian motifs, wicker, and rattan; each has a lānai and faces either the beach beyond the courtyard or the lush mountains. The departure ceremony makes you want to come back. **Pros:** exceptional Hawaiian culture program; friendly staff. **Cons:** a bit run-down; fewer amenities than other places along this beach. ⊠ *2525 Kā'anapali Pkwy., Kā'anapali* ☎ *808/661–0011 or 800/262–8450* ⊕ *www.kbhmaui.com* ⤶ *432 rooms* ⚝ *In-room: safe, refrigerator, Internet. In-hotel: 3 restaurants, bar, pool, beachfront* ▭ *AE, D, DC, MC, V.*

$$$–$$$$
RENTAL
🏨 **Maui Eldorado.** The Kā'anapali golf course's fairways wrap around this fine condo complex that offers several perks, most notably air-conditioning in the units and access to a fully outfitted beach cabana on a semiprivate beach. The complex itself isn't exactly on the beach—it's a quick golf-cart trip away. While guests at other resorts get scolded for dragging lounge chairs onto neighboring resort beaches, here you can relax in luxury. Not only will you have beach chairs at your disposal, but a full kitchen and lounge area at the cabana, too. The privately owned units are tastefully decorated with modern appliances and have spacious bathrooms. These condos are a good value for pricey Kā'anapali. **Pros:** privileges at five resort golf courses; daily maid service. **Cons:** not right on beach; some distance from attractions of the Kā'anapali Resort; some units are privately owned so condition of units may vary. ⊠ *2661 Keka'a Dr., Kā'anapali* ☎ *808/661–0021* ⊕ *www. mauieldorado.com* ⤶ *204 units* ⚝ *In-room: kitchen, Internet. In-hotel: golf course, pools, laundry facilities, concierge* ▭ *AE, D, DC, MC, V.*

$$$–$$$$
RESORT
🏨 **Royal Lahaina Resort.** Built in 1962 as the first hotel in the Kā'anapali Resort, this grand property has hosted millionaires and Hollywood stars. In the 21st century, major upgrades have taken place including renovation of the 333 rooms in the 12-story Lahaina Kai Tower, which now feature dark teak furnishings set against light-color walls, plush beds with 300-count Egyptian cotton linens, sound systems with an iPod and MP3 docking station, and 32-inch, high-definition flat-

9

screen TVs. The resort's quaint low-rise cottages were scheduled to be replaced with individually owned luxury villas but those plans are on hold. So, you can still stay in one of the 27 plantation-style cottages that have been updated with new bedding, furnishings, and amenities. Another option at the Royal Lahaina Resort is the Kā'anapali Ocean Inn where you can stay for less money and a little less comfort

> **WORD OF MOUTH**
>
> "The Sheraton Maui is at Black Rock, which is great for snorkeling right at the beach (that also means, however, that that part of Kā'anapali Beach is pretty busy, because everyone comes there to snorkel and because it's the widest part of the beach)."   –sf7307

(it's a three-story building with no elevator), but enjoy the services and amenities of the resort. To experience the spirit of the hotel's early days, head to the poolside Don the Beachcomber bar, billed as "the Home of the Original Mai Tai," where the retro-Tiki style of Hawai'i's early days as a vacation paradise lives on. **Pros:** on-site lū'au nightly; variety of accommodation types; tennis ranch with 11 courts and pro shop. **Cons:** older property still in need of updating. ⊠*2780 Keka'a Dr., Kā'anapali* ☎*808/661–3611 or 800/447–6925* ⊕*www.hawaiian hotels.com* ➴*333 rooms* ⌂*In-room: safe, refrigerator, Internet, Wi-Fi. In-hotel: 2 restaurants, tennis courts, pools, beachfront* ▭*AE, D, DC, MC, V.*

$$$$ RESORT   ⌘ **Sheraton Maui Resort & Spa.** Set among dense gardens on Kā'anapali's best stretch of beach, the Sheraton offers a quieter, more low-key atmosphere than its neighboring resorts. The open-air lobby has a crisp, cool look with understated furnishings and decor, and sweeping views of the pool area and beach. The majority of the spacious rooms come with ocean views; only one of the six buildings has rooms with mountain or garden views. All rooms have plenty of amenities, including a 32-inch flat-screen TV with video games and on-command movies; all suites also have Bose stereo systems. The huge swimming pool looks like a natural lagoon, with rock waterways and wooden bridges; and the Spa at Black Rock has been renovated and expanded. Best of all, the hotel sits next to and on top of the 80-foot-high Pu'u Keka'a (Black Rock), from which divers leap in a nightly torch-lighting and cliff-diving ritual. **Pros:** luxury resort with terrific beach location; great snorkeling right off the beach. **Cons:** extensive property can mean a long walk from your room to the lobby, restaurants, and beach; staff not overly helpful. ⊠*2605 Kā'anapali Pkwy., Kā'anapali* ☎*808/661–0031 or 888/488–35358* ⊕*www.sheraton-maui.com* ➴*508 rooms, 32 suites* ⌂*In-room: safe, refrigerator, Internet. In-hotel: 2 restaurants, bar, tennis courts, pool, gym, spa, beachfront, children's programs (ages 5–12), laundry facilities, public Wi-Fi* ▭*AE, D, DC, MC, V.*

$$$$ RESORT   ⌘ **The Westin Kā'anapali Ocean Resort Villas.** Farther up the beach from its sister property, the Westin Maui, these newly built villas are available for vacation ownership and hotel accommodations. Large studio, one-, and two-bedroom units are designed to provide the comforts of home (fully equipped kitchens, washer and dryer, LCD flat-screen TV, DVD player, and Internet access) and then some (Westin Heavenly beds,

Westin Heavenly Bath with dual showerheads, and separate whirlpool tub). Resort amenities abound: the Heavenly Spa by Westin opened in 2008 and incorporates Hawaiian elements in massage and treatments. There is also a fitness center, tennis courts, general store, and fine-dining restaurant on the property. Even though the villas are oceanfront, you may never see the beach because of the acres of water features—a meandering lagoon, cascading waterfalls, a huge heated pool with a 90-foot waterslide, a revitalizing pool, whirlpool spas, and a separate children's pool complete with a pirate ship. **Pros:** just about anything you could ever want inside and out. **Cons:** large complex could be overwhelming; not right in the Kā'anapali Resort. ⊠6 Kai Ala Dr., Lahaina ☎808/667–8112 ⊕www.westinkaanapali.com ➲500 studios, 521 1-bedroom units ⌂In-room: kitchen, DVD, Internet. In-hotel: 2 restaurants, tennis courts, pools, gym, spa, beachfront, children's programs (ages 5–12) ☰AE, D, DC, MC, V.

$$$$
RESORT
The Westin Maui Resort & Spa. The cascading waterfall in the lobby of this hotel gives way to an "aquatic playground" with five heated swimming pools, abundant waterfalls (15 at last count), lagoons complete with pink flamingos, and a premier beach. The water features combined with a spa and fitness center and privileges at two 18-hole golf courses make this an active resort—great for families. Relaxation is by no means forgotten, though. The 15,000-square-foot Heavenly Spa has 16 treatment rooms and a yoga studio. Elegant dark-wood furnishings in the rooms accentuate the crisp linens of the chain's "Heavenly Beds." Rooms in the Beach Tower are newer and slightly larger than those in the Ocean Tower. **Pros:** complimentary shuttle to Westin Kā'anapali Ocean Resort Villas and to Lahaina, where parking can be difficult; activity programs for all ages; one pool just for adults. **Cons:** you could end up with fantasy overload; can seem a bit stuffy at times. ⊠2365 Kā'anapali Pkwy., Kā'anapali ☎808/667–2525 or 888/488–3535 ⊕www.starwood.com/hawaii ➲758 rooms ⌂In-room: Internet. In-hotel: 2 restaurants, bar, pools, gym, spa, beachfront, children's programs (ages 5–12), public Wi-Fi ☰AE, D, DC, MC, V.

NORTH OF KĀ'ANAPALI (UPPER WEST SIDE)

The Upper West Side is how locals refer to the neighborhoods north of Kā'anapali: Honokōwai, Mahinahina, Kahana, Nāpili, and finally, Kapalua. They seamlessly blend into one another along Lower Honoapi'ilani Highway. Each has a few shops and restaurants and a secluded bay or two to call its own. Many visitors have found a second home here, at one of the condominiums nestled between beach-access roads and groves of mango trees. You won't get the stellar service of a resort, but you'll be among the locals here, in a relatively quiet part of the island. Be prepared for a long commute, though, if you're planning to do much exploring elsewhere on the island. Kapalua is the town farthest north, but well worth all the driving to stay at the elegant Ritz-Carlton, which is surrounded by misty greenery and overlooks beautiful D.T. Fleming Beach.

9

$$$–$$$$
RENTAL
☾

▦ **Aston Mahana at Kā'anapali.** Though the address claims Kā'anapali, this 12-story condominium complex is really in quiet, neighboring Honokōwai. All of the studio, one-, and two-bedroom units in this building are oceanfront, with views of the ocean and nearby islands, and the spacious rooms and living areas can accommodate families easily. Built in 1974, the property has been regularly updated since, but the decor in individually owned units may vary. An elegant pool faces a sandy beach, which is good for snorkeling because of the shallow reef. **Pros:** the private lānai and floor-to-ceiling windows are great for watching Maui's spectacular sunsets; daily maid service. **Cons:** high-rise with an elevator; furnishings in some units may be worn; no shops or restaurants on property. ⊠ *110 Kā'anapali Shores Pl., Honokōwai* ☏ *808/661–8751 or 866/774–2924* ⊕ *www.astonhotels.com* ⤵ *215 units* ♨ *In-room: safe, kitchen, Internet, Wi-Fi (some). In-hotel: tennis courts, pool, beachfront, public Wi-Fi* ▤ *AE, D, DC, MC, V.*

$$$–$$$$
RENTAL
☾

▦ **Aston at Papakea Resort.** Although this oceanfront condominium with studios and one- and two-bedroom units has no beach, there are several close by. And with classes on swimming, snorkeling, pineapple cutting, and more, you'll have plenty to keep you busy. Papakea has built-in privacy because its units are spread out among 11 low-rise buildings on about 13 acres of land; bamboo-lined walkways between buildings and fish-stocked ponds add to the serenity. Fully equipped kitchens and laundry facilities make longer stays easy here. **Pros:** units have large rooms, lovely garden landscaping. **Cons:** no beach in front of property, pool can get crowded, no on-site shops or restaurants. ⊠ *3543 Lower Honoapi'ilani Hwy., Honokōwai* ☏ *808/669–4848 or 866/774–2924* ⊕ *www.astonhotels.com* ⤵ *364 units* ♨ *In-room: kitchen, Wi-Fi. In-hotel: tennis courts, pools, children's programs (ages 5–12)* ▤ *AE, MC, V.*

$$ $$$
RENTAL

▦ **Makani Sands.** Centrally located in Honokōwai, on the lower road between two roads that access West Maui's main highway, this slightly older complex offers an economical way to see West Maui. Rooms have wide lānai, which hang over a small sandy beach below. The corner rooms (ending in 01) are best, with wraparound views. A small freshwater pool is available for cooling off. The back bedrooms may be noisy at night, as they're close to the road. **Pros:** beachfront; reasonable rates. **Cons:** older buildings; few amenities; road noise. ⊠ *3765 Lower Honoapi'ilani Hwy., Honokōwai* ☏ *808/669–8223 or 800/227–8223* ⊕ *www.makanisands.com* ⤵ *21 units* ♨ *In-room: kitchen, DVD, Internet, Wi-Fi (some). In-hotel: pool, beachfront, laundry facilities* ▤ *MC, V.*

$–$$
RENTAL

▦ **Mahina Surf Oceanfront Resort.** Mahina Surf stands out from the many condo complexes lining the ocean-side stretch of Honoapi'ilani Highway by being both well managed and affordable. You won't be charged fees for parking, check-out, or local phone use, and discount car rentals are available. The individually owned units are typically overdecorated (lots of rattan furniture, silk flowers, and decorative items), but each one has a well-equipped kitchen and an excellent ocean view.

The quiet complex is a short amble away from Honokōwai's grocery shopping, beaches, and restaurants. **Pros:** oceanfront barbecues; no "hidden" fees. **Cons:** set among a row of relatively nondescript condo complexes; oceanfront but with rocky shoreline rather than a beach. ⊠*4057 Lower Honoapi'ilani Hwy., Mahinahina* ☎*808/669–6068 or 800/367–6068* ⊕*www.mahinasurf.com* ⟟*50 units* ⟐*In-room: safe, kitchen, Internet. In-hotel: pool, laundry facilities* ☰*MC, V.*

KAHANA

$$$
RENTAL
☷**Sands of Kahana.** Meandering gardens, spacious rooms, and an on-site restaurant distinguish this large condominium complex. Primarily a time-share property, a few units are available as vacation rentals and are managed by Sullivan Properties. The upper floors benefit from their height—matchless ocean views stretch away from private lānai. The oceanfront penthouse, which accommodates up to eight, is a bargain at $495 during peak season. One-, two-, and three-bedroom units are also available in the rental pool. Kids can enjoy their own swimming pool area near a putting green and ponds filled with giant koi. **Pros:** spacious units at reasonable prices; restaurant on the premises. **Cons:** you may be approached about buying a unit; street-facing units may get a bit noisy. ⊠*4299 Lower Honoapi'ilani Hwy., Kahana* ☎*808/669–0400* ⊕*www.sands-of-kahana.com* ⟟*162 units* ⟐*In-room: no a/c (some), kitchen, Internet. In-hotel: restaurant, tennis courts, pools, beachfront* ☰*AE, D, MC, V.*

NĀPILI

$–$$
HOTEL
☷**Mauian Hotel.** If you're looking for a quiet place to stay, this nostalgic hotel way out in Nāpili may be for you. The rooms have neither TVs nor phones—such noisy devices are relegated to the 'Ohana Room, where a Continental breakfast is served daily. The simple two-story buildings date from 1959 but have been renovated with new flooring and new island-style furnishings. Rooms include well-equipped kitchens. Best of all, the 2-acre property opens out onto lovely Nāpili Bay. **Pros:** reasonable rates; friendly staff. **Cons:** older building; few amenities. ⊠*5441 Lower Honoapi'ilani Hwy., Nāpili* ☎*808/669–6205 or 800/367–5034 9* ⊕*www.mauian.com* ⟟*44 rooms* ⟐*In-room: no a/c, no phone, kitchen (some), no TV. In-hotel: pool, beachfront, laundry facilities, public Wi-Fi* ☰*AE, D, MC, V.*

$$$–$$$$
RENTAL
☺
☷**Nāpili Kai Beach Resort.** On 10 beautiful beachfront acres—the beach here is one of the best on West Maui for swimming and snorkeling—the Nāpili Kai draws a loyal following. Hawaiian-style rooms have plantation-theme furnishings with shoji doors opening onto a private lānai. The rooms closest to the beach have no air-conditioning, but ceiling fans usually suffice. "Hotel" rooms have only mini-refrigerators and coffeemakers, whereas studios and suites have fully equipped kitchenettes. This is a family-friendly place, with children's programs and free classes in hula and lei making. A 5th Night Free package is offered seasonally. **Pros:** free kids' hula performance every week; fantastic swimming and sunning beach; old Hawaiian feel. **Cons:** older property; some might call it "un-hip." ⊠*5900 Lower Honoapi'ilani Hwy., Nāpili* ☎*808/669–6271 or 800/367–5030* ⊕*www.napilikai.com* ⟟*163 units* ⟐*In-room: no a/c (some), kitchen (some), Internet.*

9

Ritz-Carlton, Kapalua

In-hotel: pools, beachfront, children's programs (ages 6–10), laundry service ⊟*AE, D, MC, V.*

KAPALUA

$$$–$$$$ ⛰ **Kapalua Villas.** Set among the 23,000 sprawling acres of the Kapalua Resort, these condominiums are named for their locations: the Golf Villas line the fairways of Kapalua's championship golf courses; the Ridge Villas are perched along a cliff overlooking the ocean; and the Bay Villas are at the water's edge. There are one-, two-, and three-bedroom units. All are fully furnished with kitchens and washers and dryers, and include free Wi-Fi and a lānai. Throughout these three complexes, certain accommodations are continually being upgraded to "Gold Villas." Not only do Gold Villas have newly refurbished kitchens, baths, and decor, they also include such amenities as daily maid service, nightly turn down service, robes and slippers, and daily newspaper delivery, as well as extras such as a free shuttle to shopping, dining, and activities within the resort, and resort-wide charging privileges. Gold Villas typically run $70 to $120 more per night. **Pros:** large, well-appointed condos; amazing views. **Cons:** you may hear noise from neighboring condos; some units do not have direct beach access; Kapalua can be windy. ⊠*500 Office Road, Lahaina* ☎*808/665–5400 or 800/527–2582* ⊕*www. kapalua.com* ⇄*564 rooms* ⏦*In-room: safe, kitchen, Wi-Fi. In-hotel: golf courses, tennis courts, pools* ⊟*AE, D, MC, V.*

$$$$
RESORT
Fodor's Choice
★
⛰ **Ritz-Carlton, Kapalua.** After a multimillion-dollar going-over, this elegant hillside property reopened in early 2008 with upgraded accommodations, spa, restaurants, and pool, along with a new education center and an enhanced Hawaiian sense of place. The result is one of Maui's most notable resorts. Refurbished guest rooms and 107 newly created one- and two-bedroom condominium residential suites (some of which are available for rent) are decorated in themes incorporating the rich colors of the ocean, mountains, and rain forests that surround the resort. The expanded spa facility includes a fitness center, yoga studio, 15 treatment rooms, private outdoor shower gardens, and Hawaiian design elements. Set amid the lush grounds of the resort, the renovated multilevel pool and hot tubs are open 24 hours. There is a new Environmental Education Center, as well as a full-time cultural advisor who instructs employees and guests in Hawaiian traditions. Although not set directly on the sand, the Ritz does front D.T. Fleming Beach, recognized as one of America's best. **Pros:** luxury and service you'd expect from a Ritz; newly renovated; many cultural and recreational programs. **Cons:** extremely expensive; can be windy on the grounds and at the pool; the hotel is not on the beach and is far from major attractions such as Lahaina and Haleakalā. ⊠*1 Ritz-Carlton Dr., Kapalua* ☎*808/669–6200 or 800/262–8440* ⊕*www.ritzcarlton.com/en/prop erties/kapaluamaui* ⇄*463 rooms* ⏦*In-room: safe, Wi-Fi. In-hotel: 6 restaurants, bar, tennis courts, pool, gym, spa, children's programs (ages 5–12), laundry service* ⊟*AE, D, DC, MC, V.*

9

THE SOUTH SHORE

The South Shore is composed of two main communities: resort-filled Wailea and down-to-earth Kīhei. In general, the farther south you go, the fancier the accommodations get. ■TIP➔**North Kīhei tends to have great prices, but it has windy beaches scattered with seaweed. (This isn't a problem if you don't mind driving 5 to 10 minutes to save a few bucks.)** As you travel down South Kīhei Road, you can find condos both fronting and across the street from inviting beach parks, and close to shops and restaurants. Once you hit Wailea, the opulence quotient takes a giant leap—this is the land of perfectly groomed resorts. Wailea and West Maui's Kāʻanapali continuously compete over which is more exclusive and which has better weather—in our opinion it's a draw.

KĪHEI

If you're a beach lover, you won't find many disadvantages to staying in Kīhei. A string of welcoming beaches stretches from tip to tip. Snorkeling, boogie boarding, and barbecuing find their ultimate expression here. Affordable condos line South Kīhei Road; however, some find the busy traffic and the strip-mall shopping distinctly un-Maui and prefer quieter hideaways.

$$–$$$
RENTAL

Hale Hui Kai. Bargain hunters who stumble across this small three-story condo complex of two-bedroom units will think they've died and gone to heaven. The beachfront units are older, but many of them have been renovated. Some have marble countertops in the kitchens and all have outstanding views. But never mind the interior; you'll want to spend all of your time outdoors—in the shady lava-rock lobby that overlooks a small pool perfect for kids, or on gorgeous Keawakapu Beach just steps away. Light sleepers should avoid the rooms just above the neighboring restaurant, Sarento's, but do stop in there for dinner. **Pros:** far enough from the noise and tumult of "central" Kīhei, close enough to all the conveniences. **Cons:** "older" can sometimes mean a bit shabby; nondescript '70s architecture. ✉2994 S. Kīhei Rd., Kīhei ☎808/879–1219 or 800/809–6284 ⊕www.halehuikaimaui.com ➪40 units ♿In-room: no a/c (some), safe, kitchen, DVD. In-hotel: pool, beachfront, laundry facilities ⊟ MC, V.

$$$
RENTAL
☺

Kamaʻole Sands. At this south Kīhei property, a good choice for active families, there are tennis courts for a friendly game, and the ideal family beach (Kamaʻole III) is just across the street. Ten four-story buildings wrap around 15 acres of grassy slopes with swimming pools, a small waterfall, and barbecues. Condos with one to three bedrooms are equipped with modern conveniences, but there's a relaxed, almost retro feel to the place. All units have two bathrooms, kitchens, laundry facilities, and private lānai. The property has a 24-hour front desk and an activities desk. **Pros:** in the seemingly endless strip of Kīhei condos, this stands out for its pleasant grounds and well-cared-for units. **Cons:** the complex of buildings may seem a bit too "city-like"; all buildings look the same, so remember a landmark to help you find your unit. ✉2695 S. Kīhei Rd., Kīhei ☎808/270–1200 or 800/367–5004 ⊕ www.castleresorts.com ➪204 units managed by Castle Resorts ♿In-room:

CONDO COMFORTS

When you stay in a condo, you'll want to find the best places for food shopping, takeout, and other comforts. Here's a rundown of the best spots around Maui.

WEST MAUI

Foodland. This large grocery store should have everything you need, including video rentals and a Starbucks. ✉ *Old Lahaina Center, 845 Waine'e St., Lahaina* ☎ *808/661–0975.*

Gaby's Pizzeria and Deli. The friendly folks here will toss a pie for takeout. ✉ *505 Front St., Lahaina* ☎ *808/661–8112.*

The Maui Fish Market. It's worth stopping by this little fish market for an oyster or a cup of fresh-fish chowder. You can also get live lobsters and fillets marinated for your barbecue. ✉ *4405 Lower Honoapi'ilani Hwy., Honokōwai* ☎ *808/665–9895.*

SOUTH SHORE

Eskimo Candy. Stop here for fresh fish or fish-and-chips. ✉ *2665 Wai Wai Pl., Kīhei* ☎ *808/879–5686.*

Safeway. Find every variety of grocery at this giant superstore. ✉ *277 Pi'ikea Ave., Kīhei* ☎ *808/891–9120.*

Who Cut the Cheese. This shop has great party foods. ✉ *Azeka Marketplace, 1279 S. Kīhei Rd., Suite 309, Kīhei* ☎ *808/874–3930.*

CENTRAL MAUI

Safeway. This supermarket has a deli, prepared-foods section, and bakery that are all fantastic. There's a great wine selection, tons of produce, and a flower shop where you can treat yourself to a fresh lei. ✉ *170 E. Ka'ahumanu Ave., Kahului* ☎ *808/877–3377.*

UPCOUNTRY

Pukalani Terrace Center. Stop by for pizza, a bank, post office, hardware store, and Starbucks. There's also a **Foodland** (☎ *808/572–0674*), which has fresh sushi and a good seafood section in addition to the usual grocery store fare. ✉ *55 Pukalani St., Pukalani.*

NORTH SHORE

Ha'ikū Cannery. This marketplace is home to **Ha'ikū Grocery** (☎ *808/575–9291*), a somewhat limited grocery store where you can find the basics: veggies, meats, wine, snacks, and ice cream. Also part of the cannery are a few restaurants, a laundromat, and a yoga studio. The post office is across the street. ✉ *810 Ha'ikū Rd., Ha'ikū.*

kitchen, DVD (some), Internet (some), Wi-Fi (some). In-hotel: tennis courts, pool ☐AE, D, DC, MC, V.

$
RENTAL
Luana Kai. If you don't need everything to be totally modern, consider setting up house at this North Kīhei condominium-by-the-sea. Units are older and some have slightly dated furnishings, but each one comes with everything you need to make yourself at home: a fully equipped kitchen with dishwasher, laundry facilities, TV, DVD, and stereo equipment. There are three different room plans suited for couples, families, or friends traveling together. The pool area and its new deck is a social place, with five gas grills, a full outdoor kitchen, hot tub, men's and women's sauna rooms, and a shuffleboard court. The property adjoins a grassy county park with tennis courts, and the beach is

WHERE TO STAY ON THE SOUTH SHORE

Hotels & Resorts

	PROPERTY NAME	Worth Noting	Cost $	Pools	Beach	Golf Course	Tennis Courts	Gym	Spa	Children's Programs	Rooms	Restaurants	Other	Location
3	Fairmont Kea Lani	Villas available	485–4000	3	yes	priv.		yes	yes	5–13	450	4	shops	Wailea
4	Four Seasons Resort	Luxurious	495–12,800	3	yes	priv.	2	yes	yes	5–12	380	3	poolside cabanas	Wailea
5	Grand Wailea Resort	Spa Grande	700–15,000	3	yes	priv.		yes	yes	5–12	780	5	shops	Wailea
13	Mana Kai Maui	Fabulous beach	190–438	1	yes						158	1		Kihei
15	Maui Coast Hotel	Beach across the street	265–345	1			2				265	1		Kihei
11	Maui Prince	Beautiful beach	425–1500	2	yes	yes	6	yes		5–12	310	4	Sunday Brunch	Makena
6	Wailea Beach Marriott Resort & Spa	Package deals avail.	350–600	3	yes	priv.		yes	yes		546	2	Large rooms	Wailea

Condos & Vacation Rentals

	PROPERTY NAME	Worth Noting	Cost $	Pools	Beach	Golf Course	Tennis Courts	Gym	Spa	Children's Programs	Rooms	Restaurants	Other	Location
12	Hale Hui Kai	Oceanfront lounge	225–385	1	yes						40		kitchens	Kihei
14	Kama'ole Sands	Beach across the street	305–555	1			4				204		kitchens	Kihei
16	Luana Kai	Poolside BBQs	109–299	1			4				113		no A/C	Kihei
1	Mākena Surf	Secluded gated community	625–1800	2	yes	priv.	4				107		kitchens	Wailea
17	Maui Sunseeker Resort	Beach across the street	109–295	1	yes						17		kitchens	Kihei
2	Polo Beach Club	Location, location, location	445–800	1	yes	priv.					71		kitchens	Wailea
7	Wailea Beach Villas	Ultimate luxury	1,000–3,000	2	yes	priv.			yes		98		kitchens	Wailea
9	Wailea 'Ekahi	Studios available	275–1,400	4	yes	priv.					300		kitchens	Wailea
8	Wailea 'Elua	Gated community	275–1,400	2	yes	priv.					150		kitchens	Wailea
10	Wailea 'Ekolu	Hillside view	275–1,400	2	no	priv.					160		kitchens	Wailea

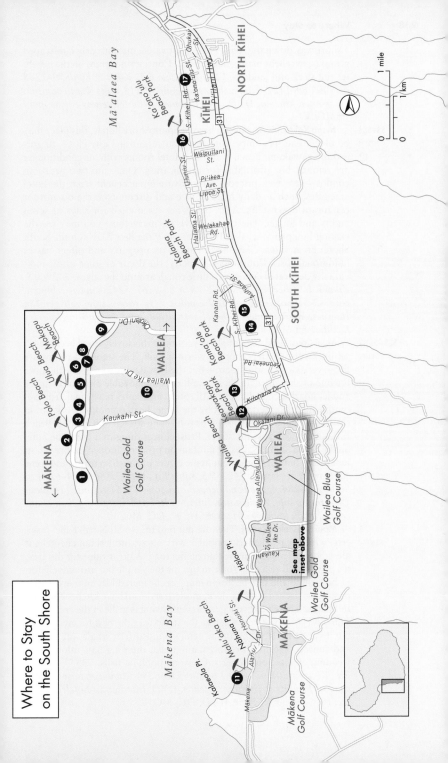

Where to Stay on the South Shore

Māʻalaea Bay

NORTH KĪHEI

Kaʻonoʻulu
Beach Park

17

16

Waipuilani
St.

Piʻikea
Ave.
Lipoa St.

Welakahao
Rd.

KĪHEI

Pi'ilani Hwy

31

S. Kihei Rd.
Ka'ono'ulu St.
Ohukai St.

Uluniu St.

Halama St.

Kalama Park Beach Park

Kamaʻole Beach Park

Kanani Rd.

Auhana St.

S. Kihei Rd.

15

14

31

Keonekai Rd.

SOUTH KĪHEI

Kilohana Dr.

13

12

Okalani Dr.

Wailea Beach

Keawakapu Beach Park

MĀKENA

Polo Beach
ʻUlua Beach
Mokapu Beach

9

8
6 7

5

4

3

2

1

Kaukahi St.

Okolani Dr.

Wailea ʻIke Dr.

10

WAILEA

Wailea Gold
Golf Course

See map
inset above

WAILEA

Wailea Alanui Dr.

Wailea
ʻIke Dr.
Kaukahi St.

Wailea Blue
Golf Course

Wailea Gold
Golf Course

MĀKENA

Mākena Bay

Kalaeola Pt.

Maluʻaka Beach

Maluʻaka Pt.

Nāhuna Pt.

Honoiki St.

Mākena
Alanui Dr.

Hāloa Pt.

11

Mākena
Golf Course

N

0   1 mile

0   1 km

a short way down the road. **Pros:** great value; meticulously landscaped grounds; excellent management team. **Cons:** it's not right on the beach; it's not sleek and modern. ⊠ *940 S. Kīhei Rd., Kīhei* ☎ *808/879–1268 or 800/669–1127* ⊕ *www.luanakai.com* ➫ *113 units* ☖ *In-room: no a/c (some), kitchen, DVD, Wi-Fi (some). In-hotel: tennis courts, pool* ▤ *MC, V.*

$$–$$$ **Mana Kai Maui.** An unsung hero of South Shore hotels, this place may
HOTEL   be older than its competitors, but you cannot get any closer to gor-
ⓒ   geous Keawakapu Beach than this. Hotel rooms with air-conditioning
are remarkably affordable for the location. One- and two-bedroom
condos—very well priced—with private lānai benefit from the hotel
amenities, such as daily maid service and discounts at the oceanfront
restaurant downstairs. Also, prices are discounted for stays of seven
nights and longer. The ocean views are marvelous; you may see the
visiting humpback whales. **Pros:** arguably the best beach on the South
Shore; great value; Maui Yoga Path is on property and offers classes
(additional cost). **Cons:** older property; the decor of some of the individually decorated condos is a little rough around the edges. ⊠ *2960 S.
Kīhei Rd., Kīhei* ☎ *808/879–2778 or 800/367–5242* ⊕ *www.crhmaui.
com* ➫ *51 hotel rooms, 107 condos* ☖ *In-room: safe, refrigerator,
Internet, Wi-Fi (some). In-hotel: restaurant, pool, beachfront, laundry
facilities* ▤ *MC, V.*

$$$–$$$$ **Maui Coast Hotel.** You might never notice this lovely hotel because it's
HOTEL   set back off the street, but it's worth a look. The standard rooms are
fine—very clean and modern—but the best deal is to pay a little more
for one of the suites. In these you'll get an enjoyable amount of space
and jet nozzles in the bathtub. All rooms and suites have lānai. You can
sample nightly entertainment by the large, heated pool or work out in
the fitness center until 10 PM. The 6-mi-long stretch of Kamaʻole Beach
I, II, and III is across the street. **Pros:** closest thing to a boutique hotel
on the South Shore; Spices Restaurant on property is open for breakfast,
lunch, and dinner. **Cons:** right in the center of Kīhei, so traffic and some
street noise are issues. ⊠ *2259 S. Kīhei Rd., Kīhei* ☎ *808/874–6284 or
800/895–6284* ⊕ *www.mauicoasthotel.com* ➫ *151 rooms, 114 suites*
☖ *In-room: safe, refrigerator, Internet. In-hotel: restaurant, bar, tennis
courts, pool, laundry service* ▤ *AE, D, DC, MC, V.*

$ **Maui Sunseeker Resort.** The care put into this small North Kīhei prop-
RENTAL   erty, which is particularly popular with a gay and lesbian clientele, is
already noticeable from the sign on the road. A great value for the area,
it's private and relaxed. You can opt for the simple but attractively fur-
nished studio and one-bedroom units, or the incredible, more-expensive
penthouse decked out in a sleek, modern style; all have kitchenettes and
full baths. There's a lovely gazebo with two gas grills in the courtyard.
The 4-mi stretch of beach across the street isn't the best for swimming,
but it's great for strolling and watching windsurfers, whales (in winter),
and sunsets. **Pros:** impeccably maintained; there's a hair salon and a
wedding officiate on property. **Cons:** no pool; no frills. ⊠ *551 S. Kīhei
Rd., Kīhei* ☎ *808/879–1261 or 800/532–6284* ⊕ *www.mauisunseeker.
com* ➫ *17 units* ☖ *In-room: kitchen, DVD, Internet. In-hotel: laundry
facilities, public Wi-Fi* ▤ *AE, D, DC, MC, V.*

WAILEA AND MĀKENA

Warm, serene, and luxurious, Wailea is less action packed than West Maui resorts. The properties here tend to focus on ambience—thoughtful details and big scenery. Nightlife is pretty much nil, save for a few swank bars and a boisterous Irish pub. However, you'll have your choice of sandy beaches with good snorkeling. Farther south, Mākena is a little less developed, a little more wild; more stars can be seen here at night. Expect everything—even bottled water—to double in price when you cross the line from Kīhei to Wailea.

WAILEA

$$$$
RESORT
☾

Fairmont Kea Lani Maui. Gleaming white spires and tiled archways are the hallmark of this stunning resort that's particularly good for families. Spacious suites have microwaves, stereos, and marble bathrooms. The villas are the real lure, though. Each is two-story and has a private plunge pool, two (or three) large bedrooms, a laundry room, and a fully equipped kitchen—barbecue and margarita blender included. Best of all, maid service does the dishes. A fantastic haven for families, the villas are side by side, creating a sort of miniature neighborhood. Request one on the end, with an upstairs sundeck. The resort also boasts a fantastic new restaurant, Kō, and offers a small, almost private beach. **Pros:** for families, this is the best of the South Shore luxury resorts; excellent restaurant; on-site deli good for picnic fare. **Cons:** some feel the architecture and design scream anything *but* Hawai'i; great villas but price puts them out of range for many. ⊠*4100 Wailea Alanui Dr., Wailea* ☎*808/875–4100 or 800/659–4100* ⊕*www.Fairmont.com/kealani* ⟲*413 suites, 37 villas* ♿*In-room: kitchen (some), refrigerator, DVD, Internet. In-hotel: 4 restaurants, bar, pools, gym, spa, beachfront, water sports, children's programs (ages 5–13), laundry facilities* ⊟*AE, D, DC, MC, V.*

$$$$
RESORT
Fodor'sChoice
★

Four Seasons Resort Maui at Wailea. Impeccably stylish, subdued, and relaxing describe most Four Seasons properties; this one fronting award-winning Wailea beach is no exception. Thoughtful luxuries—like Evian spritzers poolside and twice-daily housekeeping—earned this Maui favorite its reputation. The property has an understated elegance, with beautiful floral arrangements, courtyards, and private cabanas. Most rooms have an ocean view (avoid those over the parking lot in the North Tower), and terry robes and a mini-refrigerator (stocked with your favorites on request) are among the amenities. Choose among three restaurants, including Wolfgang Puck's Spago and DUO. The spa is small but expertly staffed and impeccably appointed, or you can opt for poolside spa mini-treatments. Families: request Suite 301, with its round tub and private lawn. **Pros:** the most low-key elegance on Maui; known for exceptional service. **Cons:** extremely expensive; a bit too pretentious for some. ⊠*3900 Wailea Alanui Dr., Wailea* ☎*808/874–8000 or 800/332–3442* ⊕*www.fourseasons.com/maui* ⟲*305 rooms, 75 suites* ♿*In-room: safe, refrigerator, DVD, Internet. In-hotel: 3 restaurants, bars, tennis courts, pools, gym, spa, beachfront, children's programs (ages 5–12)* ⊟*AE, D, DC, MC, V.*

9

Four Seasons Resort Maui at Wailea

$$$$
RESORT

🏨 **Grand Wailea Resort Hotel & Spa.** Following a renovation of all rooms in 2008, "Grand" is no exaggeration for this opulent, sunny, 40-acre resort with elaborate water features such as a "canyon riverpool" with slides, caves, a Tarzan swing, and a water elevator. Tropical garden paths meander past artwork by Léger, Warhol, Picasso, Botero, and noted Hawaiian artists—sculptures even hide in waterfalls. Spacious ocean-view rooms are outfitted with stuffed chaises, comfortable desks, and oversize marble bathrooms. Spa Grande, also upgraded in 2008, is the island's most comprehensive spa facility, offering everything from mineral baths to massage. For kids, Camp Grande has a full-size soda fountain, game room, and movie theater. Definitely not the place to go for a quiet retreat or for attentive service, the resort is astounding or way over the top, depending on your point of view. **Pros:** you can meet every vacation need without ever leaving the property; many shops. **Cons:** at these prices, service should be extraordinary, and it isn't; sometimes too much is too much. ✉3850 Wailea Alanui Dr., Wailea ☎808/875–1234 or 800/888–6100 ⊕www.grandwailea.com ⇨728 rooms, 52 suites ⚒In-room: safe, Internet. In-hotel: 5 restaurants, bars, pools, gym, spa, beachfront, children's programs (ages 5–12) ▭AE, D, MC, V.

$$$$
RENTAL

🏨 **Mākena Surf.** For travelers who've done all there is to do on Maui and just want simple but luxurious relaxation, this is the spot. The security-gate entrance gives way to manicured landscaping dotted with palm trees. The secluded complex is designed to belie its size—from the road it's hard to tell that the units are actually three-story buildings. "B" building is oceanfront; "A," "C," and "G" are the best value, just a bit farther from the shore. Water aerobics and tennis clinics are regularly offered. Privacy envelops the grounds—which makes the place a favorite with visiting celebrities. **Pros:** away from it all, yet still close enough to "civilization"; laundry facilities in every unit. **Cons:** too secluded and "locked-up" for some; Hawaiian legend has it that spirits may have been disturbed here. ✉3750 Wailea Alanui Dr., Wailea ☎808/879–1595 or 800/367–5246 ⊕www.drhmaui.com ⇨107 units ⚒In-room: safe, kitchen, DVD, Wi-Fi. In-hotel: tennis courts, pools, beachfront ▭AE, MC, V.

$$$$
RESORT

🏨 **Maui Prince.** This isn't the most luxurious resort on the South Shore—it could actually use a face-lift—but it has many pluses that more than make up for the somewhat dated decor. The location is superb. Just south of Mākena, the hotel is on a secluded piece of land surrounded by a magnificent golf course and abutting a beautiful, near-private beach. The pool area is simple (two round pools), but surrounded by beautiful gardens that are quiet and understated compared to the other big resorts. The attention given to service is apparent from the minute you walk into the open-air lobby—the staff is excellent. Rooms on five levels all have ocean views (in varying degrees) and surround the courtyard, which has a Japanese garden with a bubbling stream. **Pros:** the restaurant serves, arguably, the best Sunday brunch on Maui; for quiet and a great beach, the location is ideal. **Cons:** the rooms and common areas are in dire need of face-lifts; the property is far from attractions. ✉5400 Mākena Alanui Rd., Mākena ☎808/874–1111 or 800/321–6284 ⊕www.princeresortshawaii.com or www.mauiprince.com ⇨291 rooms, 19 suites ⚒In-room: safe, Internet, Wi-Fi. In-hotel:

9

4 restaurants, golf course, tennis courts, pools, gym, beachfront, children's programs (ages 5–12) ▤*AE, DC, MC, V.*

$$$$
RENTAL **Polo Beach Club.** Lording over a hidden section of Polo Beach, this wonderful old eight-story property somehow manages to stay under the radar. From your giant corner window, you can look down at the Fairmont Kea Lani villas and know you've scored the same great locale at a fraction of the price (and daily housekeeping service is included). Individually owned one- and two-bedroom apartments are well cared for and feature top-of-the-line amenities, such as stainless-steel kitchens, marble floors, and valuable artwork. An underground parking garage keeps vehicles out of the blazing Maui sun. **Pros:** you can pick fresh herbs for dinner out of the garden; beach fronting the building is a beautiful, very private crescent of sand. **Cons:** some may feel isolated. ⊠*3750 Wailea Alanui Dr., Wailea* ☎*808/879–1595 or 800/367–5246* ⊕*www.drhmaui.com* ⟿*71 units* ☍*In-room: kitchen, DVD, Wi-Fi. In-hotel: pool, beachfront, laundry facilities* ▤*AE, MC, V.*

$$$$
RESORT **Wailea Beach Marriott Resort & Spa.** The Marriott was built before current construction laws, so rooms sit much closer to the crashing surf than at most resorts. If you like to be lulled to sleep by the sound of the ocean, this is the place. Wailea Beach is a few steps away, as are the Shops at Wailea. In 2007, the hotel completed a $60 million renovation with redesigned guest rooms, the new 10,000-square-foot Mandara Spa, a gorgeous, adults-only "Serenity" pool, and Maui celebrity chef Mark Ellman's Mala Wailea. All rooms have private lānai and have been restyled with a contemporary residential feel; the new mattresses, quilts, and bed linens make for a great night's sleep. You have golf privileges at three nearby courses, as well as tennis privileges at the Wailea Tennis Club. **Pros:** spa is one of the best in Hawai'i; Mala restaurant is outstanding; near good shopping. **Cons:** it's not quite "beachfront" but has a rocky shore, so you must walk left or right to sit on the sand; building exteriors are showing their age. ⊠*3700 Wailea Alanui Dr., Wailea* ☎*808/879–1922 or 800/292–45326* ⊕*www.waileamarriott. com* ⟿*499 rooms, 47 suites* ☍*In-room: safe, Internet. In-hotel: 2 restaurants, pools, gym, spa, beachfront, laundry service* ▤*AE, D, DC, MC, V.*

$$$$
RENTAL **Wailea Beach Villas.** The most luxurious vacation rentals on Maui include units that are bigger than many houses—about 3,000 square feet. The furnishings and accessories are gorgeous; some kitchens are fit for the likes of Wolfgang Puck, some units have plunge pools, some have outdoor showers. Combined with stunning grounds and all the

services of the finest resort hotel—the concierge will arrange anything from in-room spa treatments to a personal trainer or a chef—you've got the vacation accommodation of a lifetime. **Pros:** steps away from the luxurious Shops at Wailea; near several excellent restaurants. **Cons:** lots of walking and up and down steps required; certainly not in everyone's budget. ✉*3750 Wailea Alanui, Wailea* ☎*808/879–1595 or 800/367–5246* ⊕*www.drhmaui.com* ⤶*98 units* ⚷*In-room: safe, DVD, kitchen, Wi-Fi. In-hotel: pools, beachfront, gym, laundry facilities, parking, concierge* ▤*AE, MC, V.*

> **LĀNAI**
>
> Islanders love their porches, balconies, and verandas, all wrapped up in the single Hawaiian word lānai. When booking your lodging, ask about the lānai and be sure to specify the view (understanding that top views command top dollars). Also, check that the lānai is not merely a step-out or Juliet balcony, with just enough room to lean against a railing. You want a lānai that is big enough for patio seating.

$$$–$$$$
RENTAL

🏠 **Wailea 'Ekahi, 'Elua, and 'Ekolu.** The Wailea Resort started out with three upscale condominium complexes named, appropriately, 'Ekahi, 'Elua, and 'Ekolu (One, Two, and Three). The individually owned units, managed by Destination Resorts Hawai'i, represent some of the best values in this high-class neighborhood; there's a wide range of prices. All benefit from daily housekeeping, air-conditioning, high-speed Internet, free long distance, lush landscaping, and preferential play at the neighboring world-class golf courses and tennis courts. You're likely to find custom appliances and sleek furnishings befitting the million-dollar locale. ■TIP→**The concierges here will stock your fridge with groceries—even hard-to-find dietary items—for a nominal fee.** 'Ekolu, farthest from the water, is the most affordable and benefits from a hillside view; 'Ekahi is a large V-shaped property focusing on Keawakapu Beach; 'Elua has 24-hour security and overlooks Ulua Beach. **Pros:** probably the best value in this high-rent district; close to good shopping and dining. **Cons:** the oldest complexes in the neighborhood; it can be tricky to find your way around the buildings. ✉*3750 Wailea Alanui Dr., Wailea* ☎*808/879–1595 or 800/367–5246* ⊕*www.drhmaui.com* ⤶*594 units* ⚷*In-room: kitchen, DVD, Wi-Fi. In-hotel: pools, beachfront, laundry facilities* ▤*AE, MC, V.*

9

CENTRAL MAUI

Kahului and Wailuku, the commercial, residential, and government centers that make up Central Maui, are not known for their lavish accommodations, but there are options that meet some travelers' needs perfectly.

¢
HOSTEL

🏠 **Banana Bungalow Maui Hostel.** A typical lively and cosmopolitan hostel, the yellow Banana Bungalow offers the cheapest accommodations on the island. Private rooms have one queen or two single beds; bathrooms are down the hall. Dorm rooms are available for $29 per night. Free daily tours to waterfalls, beaches, and Haleakalā Crater make this a stellar deal. The property's amenities include free high-speed Internet access in the common room, kitchen privileges, a Jacuzzi, and banana and mango trees ripe for the picking. Though it's tucked in a slightly rough-around-the-edges corner of Wailuku, the old building does have mountain views. **Pros:** on an expensive island, this is as inexpensive as it gets; you can walk to Takamiya Market for some of the island's best bento boxes (lunches). **Cons:** you get what you pay for; no luxury or serenity here. ⊠*310 N. Market St., Wailuku* ☎*808/244–5090 or 800/846–7835* ⊕*www.mauihostel.com* ⟿*28 rooms* ♿*In-room: no a/c. In-hotel: laundry facilities, public Internet, public Wi-Fi* ⊟*MC, V.*

$ 🖵**The Old Wailuku Inn at Ulupono.** Built in 1924 and listed on the State
B&B/INN   and National Registers of Historic Places, this home may be the ultimate
Fodor'sChoice   Hawaiian B&B. Each room is decorated with the theme of a Hawaiian
★   flower, and the flower motif appears in the heirloom Hawaiian quilt on each bed. Other features include 10-foot ceilings and floors of native hardwoods; some rooms have delightful whirlpool tubs. The first-floor rooms have private gardens. A newer addition has three gorgeous rooms, each with a standing spa shower and bed coverings designed by Hawai'i's premier fabric designer, Sig Zane. A hearty and delicious breakfast is included. **Pros:** the charm of old Hawai'i; knowledgeable innkeepers; walking distance to Maui's best ethnic restaurants. **Cons:** closest beach is a 20-minute drive away; you may hear some traffic at certain times. ⊠*2199 Kaho'okele St., Wailuku* ☎*808/244–5897 or 800/305–4899* ⊕*www.mauiinn.com* ⟿*10 rooms* ♿*In-room: VCR, Internet* ⊟*AE, D, DC, MC, V.*

UPCOUNTRY

Upcountry accommodations (those in Kula, Makawao, and Hāli'imaile) are generally on country properties—with the exception of Kula Lodge—and are privately owned vacation rentals. At high elevation, these lodgings offer splendid views of the island, temperate weather, and a "getting away from it all" feeling—which is actually the case, as most shops and restaurants are a fair drive away, and beaches even farther. You'll definitely need a car here.

$-$$ 🖵**The Banyan Tree House.** If a taste of rural Hawai'i life in plantation
B&B/INN   days is what you crave, you'll find it here. The setting is pastoral—the
♺   2-acre property is lush with tropical foliage, has an expansive lawn, and is fringed with huge monkeypod and banyan trees. The cottages (bedrooms, really, with updated baths and kitchenettes) are simple and functional. The gem, though, is the 1927 plantation house with its sprawling living and dining rooms, a kitchen any cook will adore, and a lānai that will take you back in time. The configuration of the property allows for lots of combinations; you can rent one, two, or all three bedrooms in the house or even add the adjoining one-bedroom cottage. And you can rent the entire property for a family reunion or a retreat and have access to a large yoga and meditation space complete with audio and video capabilities. **Pros:** one cottage and the pool are outfitted for travelers with disabilities; you can walk to Makawao town for dining and shopping. **Cons:** the furniture in the cottages is pretty basic; few amenities. ⊠*3265 Baldwin Ave., Makawao* ☎*808/572–9021* ⊕*www.*

The Old Wailuku Inn at Ulupono

Hale Ho'okipa Inn

FAMILY REUNION HEADQUARTERS

Maui is a great place for a family gathering. Here are a few suggestions for good places to get away together.

The configuration of the seven-room property at the **Banyan Tree House** (✉ *3265 Baldwin Ave., Makawao* ☎ *808/572–9021* ⊕ *www.banyan treehouse.com*) with a main house and little cottages around it, makes this perfect for a family reunion in Upcountry Maui. The pool, the expansive lawn, and the old-fashioned swing on one of the huge trees will keep the kids busy for hours. Groceries are just minutes away in Makawao town.

Kama'ole Sands (✉ *2695 S. Kīhei Rd., Kīhei* ☎ *808/270–1200 or 800/ 367–5004* ⊕ *www.castleresorts. com*) is an easy spot for launching

family activities. Two-bedroom units have everything a family needs: kitchens, laundry facilities, and pool access. The complex is across the street from Kama'ole III beach park to boot—a great place for family barbecues, Frisbee championships, or kite-flying contests.

On the other end of the spectrum there are the villas at the **Fairmont Kea Lani Maui** (✉ *4100 Wailea Alanui Dr., Wailea* ☎ *808/875–4100 or 800/659–4100* ⊕ *www.kealani. com*). Twice as luxurious (and about six times more costly), a two-story villa is a posh hangout zone for the family. In-laws and cousins can book suites, and activities focus around the villa with its fully equipped kitchen, plunge pool, and grill.

banyantreehouse.com ⏎*7 rooms* ⟡*In-room: kitchen (some), Wi-Fi. In-hotel: pool, laundry facilities* ☐*AE, D, MC, V.*

$ $$
B&B/INN
Fodor'sChoice
★

🖼 **Hale Ho'okipa Inn.** A handsome 1924 Craftsman-style house in the heart of Makawao town, this inn on both the Hawai'i and the National Historic Registers provides a great base for excursions to Haleakalā or to Hāna. Owner Cherie Attix has furnished it with antiques and fine art, and she allows guests to peruse her voluminous library of Hawai'i-related books. She's also a fountain of local knowledge. The house is divided into three single rooms, each prettier than the next, and the South Wing, which sleeps four and includes the kitchen. Two rooms have wonderful claw-foot tubs. The lush, serene grounds have a koi pond and the biggest Norfolk pine tree you've ever seen. **Pros:** genteel rural setting, price includes full island-style breakfast including organic fruit from the garden. **Cons:** a 20-minute drive to the nearest beach; this is not the sun, sand, and surf surroundings of travel posters. ✉*32 Pakani Pl., Makawao* ☎*808/572–6698* ⊕*www.maui-bed-and-breakfast. com* ⏎*3 rooms, 1 suite* ⟡*In-room: Wi-Fi. In-hotel: no kids under 9* ☐*MC, V.*

$–$$
HOTEL

🖼 **Kula Lodge.** Don't expect a local look despite being out in the country: the lodge inexplicably resembles a chalet in the Swiss Alps, and two units even have gas fireplaces. Charming and cozy in spite of the nontropical ambience, it's a good spot for a short romantic stay. Units are in two wooden cabins; four have lofts in addition to the ample bed space downstairs. On 3 acres, the lodge has striking, expansive views of Haleakalā and two coasts, enhanced by the surrounding tropical gardens. The property has an art gallery and a protea store that will

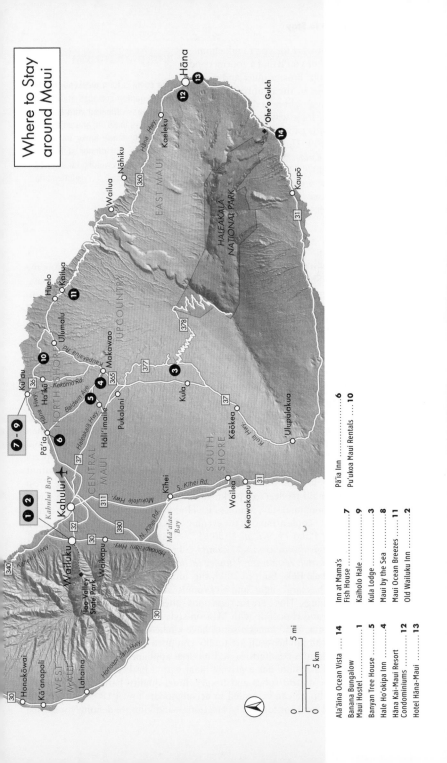

Where to Stay around Maui

Alaʻāina Ocean Vista **14**
Banana Bungalow **1**
Maui Hostel
Banyan Tree House **5**
Hale Hoʻokipa Inn **4**
Hāna Kai-Maui Resort
Condominiums **12**
Hotel Hāna-Maui **13**

Inn at Mama's **7**
Fish House
Kaiholo Hale **9**
Kula Lodge **3**
Maui by the Sea **8**
Maui Ocean Breezes **11**
Old Wailuku Inn **2**

Pāʻia Inn **6**
Puʻukoa Maui Rentals **10**

pack flowers for you to take home; next door you'll find a gourmet and gift shop. **Pros:** a quiet and peaceful place in the country; excellent shopping right next door. **Cons:** it's a long, long way to the beach; in winter, it can get downright cold. ⊠*15200 Haleakalā Hwy., Rte. 377, Kula* ☎*808/878–1535 or 800/233–1535* ⊕*www.kulalodge. com* ⇱*5 units* ⚿*In-room: no a/c, no phone, no TV. In-hotel: restaurant* ▤*AE, MC, V.*

WORD OF MOUTH

"We spent a long weekend in one of the garden cottages at The Inn at Mama's—affiliated with Mama's Fish House in Kū'au, and enjoyed it immensely. Kinda funky, but clean and quiet—and dinner at Mama's Fish House was waiting for us just a few steps away!"   –auntiemaria

THE NORTH SHORE

You won't find any large resorts or condominium complexes along the North Shore, yet there are a variety of accommodations along the coastline from the surf town of Pā'ia, through tiny Kū'au, and along the rainforested Hāna Highway through Ha'ikū. Some are oceanfront but not necessarily beachfront (with sand); instead, look for tropical gardens overflowing with ginger, bananas, papayas, and nightly bug symphonies. Some have heart-stopping views or the type of solitude that seeps in, easing your tension before you know it. You may encounter brief, powerful downpours, but that's what makes this part of Maui green and lush. You'll need a car to enjoy staying on the North Shore.

$ $$
B&B/INN 🖭**The Inn at Mama's Fish House.** Nestled in gardens adjacent to one of Maui's most popular dining spots, Mama's Fish House ($$$$), these well-maintained one- and two-bedroom cottages have a retro-Hawaiian style with rattan furnishings and local artwork. Each has a kitchen and a private garden patio. There is a small beach in front of the property known as Kū'au Cove. It's best to make reservations for the restaurant when you book your accommodations or you may not get a table. **Pros:** daily maid service; free parking; next to Ho'okipa Beach. **Cons:** three-night minimum stay; Mama's Fish House is very popular, so there can be a lot of people around in the evenings (it's more mellow during the day). ⊠*799 Poho Pl., Kū'au* ☎*808/579–9764 or 800/860–4852* ⊕*www. mamasfishhouse.com* ⇱*12 units* ⚿*In-room: safe, kitchen, DVD, Wi-Fi. In-hotel: restaurant, laundry facilities* ▤*AE, D, DC, MC, V.*

$$–$$$
B&B/INN 🖭**Kaiholo Hale.** Built in 2005, this immaculately maintained vacation house has large, light, and airy rooms with comfortable contemporary furnishings. There are four spacious suites decorated in muted colors of cream and chocolate with Mission-style teak furniture. The Hibiscus, Gardenia, and Plumeria suites have kitchenettes and the Orchid Suite has a full kitchen—all are totally equipped and beautifully appointed with granite countertops and modern appliances such as glass cooktops. Each suite has a private lānai with a barbecue. Special touches include cotton robes and luxury, hotel-quality bath amenities. The entire house can be rented to accommodate up to 18 guests, making it a perfect spot for family vacations—and kids are definitely welcome

here. **Pros:** big rooms; beautiful furnishings; lots of kitchen equipment and beach gear. **Cons:** no views; it's a 100-yard walk to the beach. ⊠*25 Kaiholo Pl., Pā'ia* ☎*808/870–3481* ⊕*www.northshoremauivacations. com* ➷*5 rooms* ⌂*In-room: DVD, kitchen. In-hotel: public Wi-Fi* ▤*MC, V.*

$$
RENTAL ⊡**Maui by the Sea.** Just past Pā'ia on the other side of a stucco wall from Hāna Highway, this cute, small but clean one-bedroom apartment decorated with tropical prints and Hawaiian quilts is bright and

airy. You can park your car in the garage below and climb the stairs to this second-floor unit, which has a broad lānai with a gas grill and a dining table. The lānai captures gentle cooling breezes, and it has a fantastic ocean view. You're just steps away from the ocean here, although there is no sand beach, just a rocky access; Tavares Bay is a mere 200 yards away for windsurfing or swimming. **Pros:** free interisland, mainland, and Canada phone calls; host is lifelong Maui resident and will share island stories with you. **Cons:** road noise from Hāna Highway; another house is right next door; no resort amenities. ⊠*523 Hāna Hwy., Pā'ia* ☎*808/579–9865* ⊕*www.mauibythesea.com* ➷*1 unit* ⌂*In-room: kitchen, DVD, Internet. In-hotel: laundry facilities* ▤*AE, D, MC, V*

$
RENTAL ⊡**Maui Ocean Breezes.** The warm ocean breeze rolls through these pretty rentals and shoos the mosquitoes away, making this a perfect spot if you want quiet, gorgeous scenery. The decor is both whimsical and calming—expect colorfully painted walls and sheer curtains. The saltwater pool is fed by a waterfall. Fully equipped kitchens and Wi-Fi make these studios an ideal home away from home. Allergy-prone travelers can relax here—no chemicals or pesticides are used on the property. Although it seems far from civilization, you are only 5 minutes from Ha'ikū and 10 from Pā'ia. **Pros:** good for people sensitive to harsh chemicals; one of few licensed rentals in area. **Cons:** 15 minutes from closest beach; rather remote location; the owner prefers stays of seven nights or longer, though will negotiate depending on availability. ⊠*240 N. Holokai Rd., Ha'ikū* ☎*808/572–2775* ⊕*www.mauivacationhide away.com* ➷*3 units* ⌂*In-room: no a/c, kitchen, Wi-Fi. In-hotel: pool, laundry facilities* ▤*MC, V.*

$$
B&B/INN ⊡**Pā'ia Inn Hotel.** Built in 1927 as a boarding house when Pā'ia was a bustling plantation town, this building was completely renovated and reopened as an inn in 2008. Set right in the heart of Pā'ia on busy Hāna Highway, it is amazingly quiet inside the lobby and guest rooms. The rooms are air-conditioned and each has a phone, flat-screen television, iPod clock/radio, and fully stocked minibar. All have private bathrooms with travertine tile and salon-quality amenities. Guests enter through a pleasant courtyard to the lobby; the guest rooms are up a set of stairs

on the second floor. Also on the second floor is a lounge where complimentary coffee and tea, along with muffins and scones, are served daily. For guests desiring room service, a coffeehouse across the street will deliver. Access to secluded and sandy Pāʻia Bay is along a pathway between two private residences behind the inn. **Pros:** friendly and knowledgeable staff; no minimum-night stay required; guests receive a complimentary membership at Upcountry Fitness in Haʻikū. **Cons:** no elevator; guest rooms are extraordinarily small and have no closets. ✉ *93 Hāna Hwy., Pāʻia* 🕾 *808/579–6000* ⊕ *www.paiainn.com* ↩ *5 rooms* ⚓ *In-hotel: laundry facilities, Wi-Fi* ☰ AE, MC, V.

¢   🏠 **Puʻukoa Maui Rentals.** Off a peaceful cul-de-sac in a residential area,
RENTAL these two well-maintained and immaculately clean homes offer studio and one-bedroom accommodations. Studios have an efficiency-style kitchen with a small refrigerator, hot plate, microwave, toaster oven, and coffeemaker. One-bedroom apartments have fully equipped kitchens, a separate bedroom, and a large living area. All units have private bathrooms and a lānai or patio, some with ocean views. The large yard with tropical flowers and fruit trees is great for a sunset barbecue or just relaxing. **Pros:** very clean; reasonable rates; good spot for a group. **Cons:** 10-minute drive to the beach; set in quiet residential area. ✉ *Puʻukoa Pl., Haʻikū* 🕾 *808/573–2884* ⊕ *www.puukoa.com* ↩ *7 rooms* ⚓ *In-room: no a/c, kitchen, DVD, Wi-Fi. In-hotel: laundry facilities* ☰ AE, MC, V.

HĀNA

Why stay in Hāna when it's so far from everything? In a world where everything moves at high speed, Hāna still travels on horseback, ambling along slowly enough to smell the flowers. But old-fashioned and remote do not mean tame—this is a wild coast, known for heart-stopping scenery and downpours. Leave city expectations behind: the single grocery may run out of milk, and the only videos to rent may be several years old. The dining options are slim. ■ TIP➔**If you're staying for several days, or at a vacation rental, stock up on groceries before you head out to Hāna.** Even with these inconveniences, Hāna is a place you won't want to miss.

$ 🏠 **Alaʻāina Ocean Vista.** This B&B is on the grounds of an old banana
B&B/INN plantation past ʻOheʻo Gulch (about a 40-minute drive from Hāna). Banana trees still populate the property alongside mango, papaya, and avocado trees. There's also a Balinese garden, complete with a lotus-shaped pond. The single room has a private lānai with an outdoor kitchenette, outdoor shower (there's a regular shower in the room as well), and astonishing views of the coastline. Sam and Mercury, a

SHOPPING IN HĀNA

Hasegawa General Store. Hāna's one-stop shopping option is charming, filled-to-the-rafters Hasegawa's. Buy fishing tackle, hot dogs, ice cream, and eggs here. You can rent videos and buy the newspaper, which isn't always delivered on time. Check out the bulletin board for local events. ✉ *5165 Hāna Hwy. Haʻikū 96713* 🕾 *808/248–8231.*

Hotel Hāna-Maui

mother-daughter team, live in the main house on-site and are available to give tips and advice about exploring the area. This is a simple, back-to-nature kind of spot. **Pros:** quiet and secluded; no pesticides or chemicals used on property. **Cons:** travel time from Kahului Airport is quite long; remote location with no restaurants nearby. ⊠ *Off Hwy. 31, 10 mi past Hāna* ⊅ *SR 184-A, Hāna96713* ☎ *808/248–7824 or 877/216–1733* ⊕ *www.hanabandb.com* ↩ *1 room* ⚲ *In-room: no a/c, kitchen* ⊟ *No credit cards.*

$$–$$$
RENTAL

⌘ **Hāna Kai-Maui Resort Condominiums.** Perfectly situated on Hāna Bay, this resort complex has a long history (it opened in 1970) and excellent reputation for visitor hospitality. All you have to do is take your morning coffee out onto the lānai of any of these lovely units to know why Hāna is often referred to as "heavenly." The units are tastefully and comfortably furnished with tropical-pattern fabrics and light-color wood, and have well-equipped kitchens with all the appliances, table settings, and tools you need to prepare meals. They even have 100% Egyptian cotton sheets on the beds and all-natural soaps and shampoos. **Pros:** it's a stone's throw to Hāna Bay, where you can take a swim or have a Roselani mac-nut ice-cream cone at Tutu's; one-night rentals are accepted. **Cons:** early to bed and early to rise—no nightlife or excitement here. ⊠ *1533 Uakea Rd., Hāna* ☎ *808/248–8426 or 800/346–2772* ⊕ *www.hanakaimaui.com* ↩ *17 units* ⚲ *In-room: kitchen, no TV, Wi-Fi* ⊟ *MC, V.*

$$$$
HOTEL
Fodor'sChoice
★

⌘ **Hotel Hāna-Maui.** Small, secluded, and quietly luxurious, with unobstructed views of the Pacific, this tranquil property is a departure from the usual resort destinations on Maui. Here, horses nibble wild grass on the sea cliff nearby. Spacious rooms (680 to 830 square feet) have bleached-wood floors, authentic kapa-print fabric furnishings, and sumptuously stocked minibars at no extra cost. Spa suites and a heated *watsu* (massage performed in warm water) pool complement a state-of-the-art spa-and-fitness center. The Sea Ranch Cottages with individual hot tubs are the best value. A shuttle takes you to beautiful Hāmoa Beach. **Pros:** if you want to get away from it all, there's no better or more beautiful place; spa is incredibly relaxing. **Cons:** everything moves slowly; if you can't live without your Blackberry, this is not the place for you; it's oceanfront but does not have a sandy beach (red- and black-sand beaches are nearby). ⊠ *5031 Hāna Hwy.* ⊅ *Box 9, Hāna 96713* ☎ *808/248–8211 or 800/321–4262* ⊕ *www.hotelhanamaui.com* ↩ *69 rooms, 47 cottages, 1 house* ⚲ *In-room: refrigerator, no TV, Internet. In-hotel: 2 restaurants, bar, tennis courts, pools, gym, spa, public Wi-Fi* ⊟ *AE, D, DC, MC, V.*

Moloka'i

WORD OF MOUTH

"My wife and I did the day trip from Lahaina to Moloka'i, and things are soooo different there. People are few and far between, and the pace very slow. I never could get over all those beautiful tropical beaches with only a few people. Be prepared to create most of your own nightlife."

—kanunu

WELCOME TO MOLOKA'I

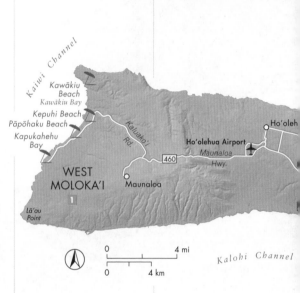

TOP REASONS TO GO

★ **Kalaupapa Peninsula:** Hike or take a mule ride down the world's tallest sea cliffs to a fascinating, historic community that once housed patients suffering from leprosy.

★ **Hike to a waterfall in Hālawa:** A fascinating guided hike through private property takes you past ancient ruins, restored taro patches, and a sparkling cascade.

★ **Deep-sea fishing:** Sport fish are plentiful in these waters, as are gorgeous views of several islands. Fishing is one of the island's great adventures.

★ **Get close to nature:** Deep valleys, sheer cliffs, and the untamed ocean are the main attractions on Moloka'i.

★ **Pāpōhaku Beach:** This 3-mi stretch of golden sand is one of the most sensational beaches in all of Hawai'i. Sunsets and barbecues are perfect here.

1 **West Moloka'i.** The most arid part of the island, known as the west end, has two inhabited areas: the coastal stretch includes a few condos and luxury homes, and the largest beaches on the island. Nearby is the hilltop hamlet of Maunaloa.

2 **Central Moloka'i.** The island's only true town, Kaunakakai, with its mile-long wharf, is here. Nearly all the island's eateries and stores are in or close to Kaunakakai. Highway 470 crosses the center of the island, rising to the top of the sea cliffs and the Kalaupapa overlook. At the base of the cliffs is Kalaupapa National Historic Park, a top attraction.

PACIFIC OCEAN

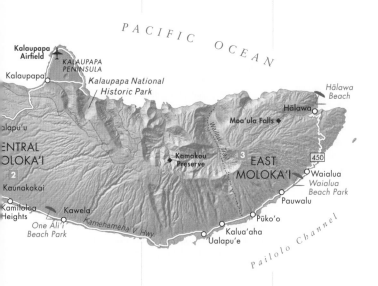

3 East Moloka'i. The scenic drive around this undeveloped area, also called the east end, passes through the green pastures of Pu'u O Hoku Ranch and climaxes with a descent into Hālawa Valley. As you continue east, the road becomes increasingly narrow and the island ever more lush.

GETTING ORIENTED

Shaped like a long bone, Moloka'i is only about 10 mi wide on average, and four times that long. The north shore thrusts up from the sea to form the tallest sea-cliffs on Earth, while the south shore slides almost flat into the water, then fans out to form the largest shallow-water reef system in the United States. Surprisingly, the highest point on Moloka'i rises only to about 4,000 feet.

MOLOKA'I PLANNER

What You Won't Find on Moloka'i

Moloka'i is a great place to be outdoors. And that's a good thing, because with only about 8,000 residents Moloka'i has very little of what you would call "indoors." There are no tall buildings, no traffic lights, no streetlights, no stores bearing the names of national chains, and nothing at all like a resort. Among the Hawaiian Islands, Moloka'i has distinguished itself as the one least interested in attracting tourists. At night the whole island grows dark, creating a velvety blackness and a wonderful, rare thing called silence.

Will It Rain?

Moloka'i's weather mimics that of the other islands: mid- to low 80s year-round, slightly rainier in winter. Because the island's accommodations are clustered at low elevation or along the leeward coast, warm weather is a dependable constant for visitors (only 15 to 20 inches of rain fall each year on the coastal plain). As you travel up the mountainside, the weather changes with bursts of forest-building downpours.

Timing Is Everything

If you're keen to explore Moloka'i's beaches, coral beds, or fishponds, summer is your best bet for nonstop calm seas and sunny skies. For a taste of Hawaiian culture, plan your visit around a festival. In January, islanders and visitors compete in ancient Hawaiian games at the Ka Moloka'i Makahiki Festival. The Moloka'i Ka Hula Piko, an annual daylong event in May, draws premiere hula troupes, musicians, and storytellers. Long-distance canoe races from Moloka'i to O'ahu are in late September and early October. Although never crowded, the island is busier during these events—book accommodations and transportation six months in advance.

Dining and Lodging on Moloka'i

Moloka'i appeals most to travelers who appreciate genuine Hawaiian ambience rather than swanky digs. Most hotel and condominium properties range from adequate to funky. Visitors who want to lollygag on the beach should choose one of the condos or home rentals in West Moloka'i. Locals tend to choose Hotel Moloka'i, located seaside just 2 mi from Kaunakakai. Travelers who want to immerse themselves in the spirit of the island should seek out a condo or cottage, the closer to East Moloka'i the better.

Dining on Moloka'i is more a matter of eating. There are no fancy restaurants, just pleasant low-key places to eat out. Try the Hotel Moloka'i dining room for a selection of fresh, local-style food. Other options include plate lunch, pizza, coffee-shop-style sandwiches, and make-it-yourself health food fixings.

Cell Phones and Internet

There are many locations on the island where cell phone reception is difficult, if not impossible, to obtain. Your best bet for finding service is in Kaunakakai. There is in-room, high-speed Internet access at the Hotel Moloka'i.

Updated by
Joana Varawa

Moloka'i is generally thought of as the last bit of "real" Hawai'i. Tourism has been held at bay by the island's unique history and the deep pride of the island's predominantly native Hawaiian population, despite the fact that the longest white-sand beach in Hawai'i can be found along its western shore.

With sandy beaches to the west, sheer sea cliffs to the north, and a rainy, lush eastern coast, Moloka'i offers a bit of everything, including a peek at what the islands were like 50 years ago. No one is in much of a hurry, and a favorite expression is "Slow down, you're on Moloka'i.

Only 38 mi long and 10 mi wide at its widest point, Moloka'i is the fifth-largest island in the Hawaiian archipelago. Eight thousand residents call Moloka'i home, nearly 60% of whom are Hawaiian.

GEOLOGY

Roughly 1½ million years ago two large volcanoes—Kamakou in the east and Maunaloa in the west—broke the surface of the Pacific Ocean and created the island of Moloka'i. Shortly thereafter a third and much smaller caldera, Kauhako, popped up to form the Makanalua Peninsula on the north side. After hundreds of thousands of years of rain, surf, and wind, an enormous landslide on the north end sent much of the mountain into the sea, leaving behind the sheer sea cliffs that make Moloka'i's north shore so spectacularly beautiful.

HISTORY

Moloka'i is named in chants as the child of the moon goddess Hina. For centuries, the island was occupied by natives who took advantage of the excellent reef fishing and ideal conditions for growing taro. When leprosy broke out in the Hawaiian Islands in the 1840s, the Makanalua Peninsula, surrounded on three sides by the Pacific and accessible only by a steep, switchback trail, was selected as the place to exile people suffering from the disease. The first patients were thrown into the sea to swim ashore as best they could, and left with no facilities, shelter, or supplies. In 1873 a missionary named Father Damien, who is expected to soon be canonized, arrived and began to serve the peninsula's suffering inhabitants. Though leprosy, now known as Hansen's disease, is no longer contagious and can be remitted, the buildings and infrastructure created by those who were exiled here still exist, and some longtime residents have chosen to stay in their homes. Visitors are welcome but must book a tour operated by Damien Tours of Kalaupapa. No one is allowed to wander unescorted, and no one may take photographs without the written permission of the resident.

THE BIRTHPLACE OF HULA

Tradition has it that centuries ago La'ila 'i came to Moloka'i and lived on Pu'u Nana at Ka'ana. She brought the art of hula and taught it to the people, who kept it secret for her descendents, making sure the sacred dances were performed only at Ka'ana. Five generations later Laka was born into the family and learned hula from an older sister. She chose to share the art and traveled throughout the Islands teaching the dance, though she did so without her family's consent. The yearly Ka Hula Piko Festival, held on Moloka'i in May, celebrates the birth of hula at Ka'ana.

EXPLORING MOLOKA'I

The first thing to do on Moloka'i is to drive everywhere. It's a feat you can accomplish comfortably in two days. Depending on where you stay, spend one day exploring the west end and the other day exploring the east end. Basically you have one 40-mi west–east highway (two lanes, no stoplights) with three side trips: the little west-end town of Maunaloa; the Highway 470 drive (just a few miles) to the top of the north shore and the overlook of Kalaupapa Peninsula; and the short stretch of shops in Kaunakakai town. After you learn the general lay of the land, you can return to the places that interest you most. ■ TIP→ Directions on the island are often given as mauka (toward the mountains) and makai (toward the ocean).

WEST MOLOKA'I

The remote beaches and rolling pastures on Moloka'i's west end are presided over by Maunaloa, a dormant volcano, and a sleepy little former plantation town of the same name. Pāpōhaku, the Hawaiian Islands' second-longest white sand beach, is here, as is the 53,000-acre Moloka'i Ranch, which is currently shuttered due to a land dispute.

TOP ATTRACTIONS

★ **Maunaloa.** This quiet, small town was built in 1923 to house the workers on the island's pineapple plantation. Although the fields of golden fruit are long gone, some of the old dwellings have been restored, anchoring the west end of Moloka'i. You'll find a kite shop, a gallery with local and imported art and jewelry, and an eclectic general store on the short main street. This is the last place to buy supplies before heading out to explore the beaches of the west end. ⊠ *Western end of Maunaloa Hwy., Rte. 460.*

Fodor'sChoice **Pāpōhaku Beach.** The most splendid stretch of golden-white sand on
★ Moloka'i, Pāpōhaku is also the island's largest beach—it stretches 3 mi along the western shore. Even on busier days you're likely to see only a handful of other people. If the waves are high, swimming is dangerous. ⊠ *Kaluako'i Rd., 2 mi beyond the deserted Kaluako'i Hotel and Golf Club* .

WORTH NOTING

Kaluako'i Hotel and Golf Club. This late-1960s resort passed through several owners, and is now closed and forlorn. The last owner, Moloka'i Ranch, has given up resort operations and is no longer maintaining the property. The abandoned golf course and landscaping is dying, and the buildings are boarded up. Some very nice condos are still operating nearby, however, and the white sand beach along the coast (Kepuhi Beach) is still worth a visit. ⊠ *Kaluako'i Rd., Maunaloa.*

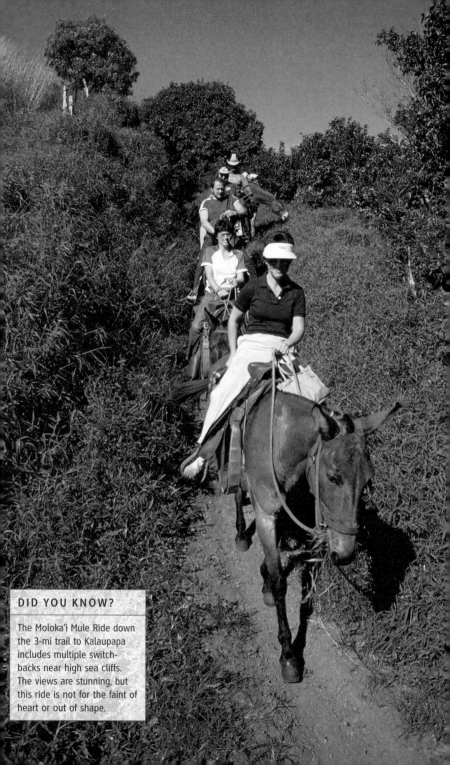

DID YOU KNOW?

The Moloka'i Mule Ride down the 3-mi trail to Kalaupapa includes multiple switch-backs near high sea cliffs. The views are stunning, but this ride is not for the faint of heart or out of shape.

CENTRAL MOLOKA'I

Most residents live centrally, near the island's one and only true town, Kaunakakai. It's just about the only place on the island to get food and supplies. It *is* Moloka'i. Go into the shops along and around Ala Mālama Street. Buy stuff. Talk with people. Take your time and you'll really enjoy being a visitor. Also in this area, on the north side, is Coffees of Hawai'i, a 500-acre coffee plantation, and the Kalaupapa National Historic Park, one of the island's most notable sights.

TOP ATTRACTIONS

Coffees of Hawai'i. Visit the headquarters of a 500-acre Moloka'i coffee plantation, where you can enjoy a mule-pulled wagon tour then stay for lunch. The espresso bar serves freshly made sandwiches, *liliko'i* (passion fruit) cheesecake, and java in artful ways. Their "moca mamma" is a special Moloka'i treat. This is the place to pick up additions to your picnic lunch if you're headed to Kalaupapa. The gift shop offers a wide range of Moloka'i handicrafts, memorabilia, and, of course, coffee. Call in advance to ask about various tours (fee) of the plantation. *630 Farrington Hwy., off Rte. 470, Kualapu'u* 🕾*877/322–3276 or 808/567–9490* ⊕*www.coffeesofhawaii.com* ⊙*Café and gift shop weekdays 7–5, Sat. 8–4, Sun. 8–2.*

Kalaupapa. *See photo feature, Kalaupapa Peninsula: A Tale of Tragedy and Triumph.*

★ **Kaunakakai.** Central Moloka'i's main town looks like a fading 1940s movie set. Along the one-block main drag is a cultural grab bag of restaurants and shops. Many people are friendly and willing to supply directions. The preferred dress is shorts and a tank top, and no one wears anything fancier than a cotton skirt or aloha shirt. ⊠*Rte. 460, about 3 blocks north of Kaunakakai Wharf.*

NEED A BREAK? Stop for some of Dave's Hawaiian Ice Cream at the **Kamo'i Snack-n-Go** (⊠*28 Kamo'i St., Kaunakakai* 🕾*808/553–3742*). Sit on one of the benches in front for a Moloka'i rest stop. Snacks, crack seed, cold drinks, and water are also available.

Fodor'sChoice **Moloka'i Mule Ride.** Mount a friendly, well-trained mule and wind along a
★ 3-mi, 26-switchback trail to reach the town of Kalaupapa, which was once home to patients with leprosy who were exiled to this remote spot. The path was built in 1886 as a supply route for the settlement below. Once in Kalaupapa, you will take a guided tour of the town. A light picnic lunch is provided. The trail is very steep, down some of the highest sea cliffs in the world. ■TIP→ Only those in good shape should attempt the ride, as two hours each way on a mule can take its toll. The entire event takes seven hours.

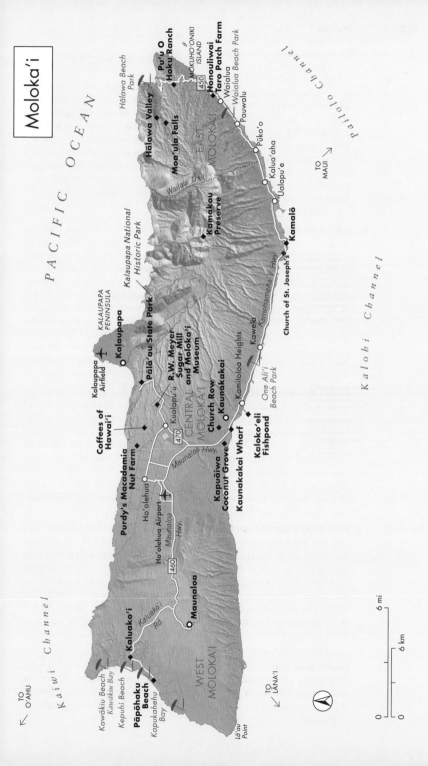

Moloka'i

PACIFIC OCEAN

Kaiwi Channel

TO O'AHU

Kawākiu Beach
Kawākiu Bay
Kepuhi Beach

Kapukahehu Bay

Lā'au Point

TO LĀNA'I

Pāpōhaku Beach

Kaluako'i

Kaluako'i Rd.

Maunaloa

WEST MOLOKA'I

Ho'olehua Airport

Maunaloa Hwy.

460

Ho'olehua

Purdy's Macadamia Nut Farm

Coffees of Hawai'i

Kualapu'u

470

Maunaloa Hwy.

Pāla'au State Park

R.W. Meyer Sugar Mill and Moloka'i Museum

KALAUPAPA PENINSULA

Kalaupapa Airfield

Kalaupapa

Kalaupapa National Historic Park

Kalaupapa Trail

CENTRAL MOLOKA'I

Church Row

Kaunakakai

Kamiloloa Heights

Kapuāiwa Coconut Grove

Kaunakakai Wharf

Kaloko'eli Fishpond

One Ali'i Beach Park

Kawela

Church of St. Joseph's

Kamehameha V. Hwy.

Kamalō

Ualapu'e

Kalua'aha

Pūko'o

Pauwalu

Waialua

Waialua Beach Park

Honouliwai Taro Patch Farm

450

Pu'u O Hoku Ranch

MOKUHO'ONIKI ISLAND

Hālawa Beach Park

Hālawa Valley

Moa'ula Falls

Wailau Trail

Kamakou Preserve

EAST MOLOKA'I

TO MAUI

Pailolo Channel

Kalohi Channel

6 mi

6 km

0

Make reservations ahead of time, as spots are limited. The same outfit can arrange for you to hike down or fly in, or some combination of a hike in and fly out. No one is allowed in the park or on the trail without booking a tour. *See Kalaupapa Peninsula: A Tale of Tragedy and Triumph photo feature, below, for more information.* ⊠ *100 Kala'e Hwy., Rte. 470, Kualapu'u* ☎ *808/567–6088 or 800/567–7550* ⊕ *www.muleride. com* ☒ *$165* ⊙ *Mon.–Sat. 8–3.*

WORD OF MOUTH

"I've done both the mule ride and flown in. The mule ride isn't as dangerous as it may appear as the animals are smart, well trained and very experienced. The plane ride made me more nervous as the runway isn't very long. However, the plane would be quicker and you won't get a saddle sore!" –offlady

★ **Pālā'au State Park.** One of the island's few formal recreation areas, this cool retreat covers 233 acres at a 1,000-foot elevation. A short path through an ironwood forest leads to **Kalaupapa Lookout,** a magnificent overlook with views of the town of Kalaupapa and the 1,664-foot-high sea cliffs protecting it. Informative plaques have facts about leprosy, Father Damien, and the colony. The park is also the site of **Kauleonānāhoa** (the phallus of Nānāhoa)—women in old Hawai'i would come to the rock to enhance their fertility, and it is said some still do. It is a sacred site, so be respectful and don't deface the boulders. The park is well maintained, with trails, camping facilities, restrooms, and picnic tables. ⊠ *Take Rte. 460 west from Kaunakakai and then head mauka (toward the mountains) on Rte. 470, which ends at park* ☎ *No phone* ☒ *Free* ⊙ *Daily dawn–dusk.*

Purdy's Macadamia Nut Farm. Moloka'i's only working macadamia-nut farm is open for educational tours hosted by the knowledgeable and entertaining owner. A family business on Hawaiian homestead land in Ho'olehua, the farm takes up 1½ acres with a flourishing grove of some 50 trees more than 70 years old. Taste a delicious nut right out of its shell or home roasted, and dip it into macadamia-blossom honey; then buy some at the shop on the way out. Look for Purdy's sign behind Moloka'i High School. ⊠ *Lihipali Ave., Ho'olehua* ☎ *808/567–6601* ⊕ *www.molokai-aloha.com/macnuts* ☒ *Free* ⊙ *Weekdays 9:30–3:30, Sat. 10–2, Sun. and holidays by appointment.*

R. W. Meyer Sugar Mill and Moloka'i Museum. Built in 1877, this three-room mill has been reconstructed as a testament to Moloka'i's agricultural history. Some of the equipment may still be in working order, including a mule-driven cane crusher, redwood evaporating pans, some copper clarifiers, and a steam engine. A small museum with changing exhibits on the island's early history and a gift shop are on-site as well. The facility serves as a campus for Elderhostel educational programs. ⊠ *Rte. 470, 2 mi southwest of Pālā'au State Park, Kala'e* ☎ *808/567–6436* ☒ *$3.50* ⊙ *Mon.–Sat. 10–2.*

WORTH NOTING

Church Row. Standing together along the highway are several houses of worship with primarily native Hawaiian congregations. Notice the unadorned, boxlike style of architecture so similar to missionary homes. ⊠ *Mauka (toward the mountains) side of Rte. 460, 5½ mi southwest of airport.*

Kapuāiwa Coconut Grove. At first glance this looks like a sea of coconut trees. Close-up you can see that the tall, stately palms are planted in long rows leading down to the sea. This is a remnant of one of the last surviving royal groves planted for Prince Lot, who ruled Hawai'i as King Kamehameha V from 1863 until his death in 1872. The park, which once boasted over 1,000 trees, is now closed for renovations

> **BE PREPARED**
>
> Since Moloka'i is not oriented to the visitor industry you won't find much around to cater to your needs. Pick up a disposable cooler in Kaunakakai town, then visit the local markets and fill it with road supplies. Don't forget water, sunscreen, and mosquito repellent.

but you can park on the side of the road and walk in to the beach. Watch for falling coconuts. ⊠ *Makai (toward the ocean) of Rte. 460, 5½ mi south of airport.*

Kaunakakai Wharf. Docks, once bustling with barges exporting pineapples, now host visiting boats, the ferry from Lahaina, and the weekly barge from O'ahu. The wharf is also the starting point for excursions, including fishing, sailing, snorkeling, whale-watching, and scuba diving. ⊠ *Rte. 450 at Ala Mālama St.; drive makai (toward the ocean) on Kaunakakai Pl., which dead-ends at wharf.*

EAST MOLOKA'I

On the beautifully undeveloped east end of Moloka'i, you can find ancient fishponds, a magnificent coastline, splendid ocean views, and a fertile valley that's been inhabited for 14 centuries. The eastern uplands are flanked by Mt. Kamakou, the island's highest point at 4,961 feet and home to the Nature Conservancy's Kamakou Preserve. Mist hangs over waterfall-filled valleys, and ancient lava cliffs jut out into the sea.

TOP ATTRACTIONS

Fodor'sChoice ★ **Hālawa Valley.** As far back as AD 650 a busy community lived in this valley, the oldest recorded habitation on Moloka'i. Hawaiians lived in a perfectly sustainable relationship with the valley's resources, growing taro and fishing until the 1960s, when cultural changes plus an enormous flood wiped out the taro patches and forced the old-timers to abandon their traditional lifestyle. Now a new generation of Hawaiians has returned and begun the challenging work of restoring the taro fields. Much of this work involves rerouting stream water to flow through carefully engineered level ponds called *lo'i*. The taro plants with their big dancing leaves grow in the submerged mud of the *lo'i*, where the water is always cool and flowing. Hawaiians believe that the taro plant is their ancestor and revere it both as sustenance and as a spiritual necessity. The Hālawa Valley Cooperative leads hikes through the valley, which is home to two sacrificial temples, many historic sites, and the 3-mi trail to Moa'ula Falls, a 250-foot cascade. The $75 fee ($45 for children 7–11; under 6 free with paying adult) goes to support the restoration work. ⊠ *Eastern end of Rte. 450* 📞 *808/553–9803* ⊕ *www.gomolokai.com.*

Honouliwai Taro Patch Farm. Although they are not reviving an entire valley and lifestyle like the folks in Hālawa, Jim and Lee Callahan are reviving

10

taro cultivation on their small farm watered by a year-round spring. The owners provide 1½-hour tours so visitors can experience all phases of taro farming, from planting to eating. Lee was raised in Thailand, so she uses a traditional Southeast Asian farm device—a plow-pulling water buffalo named Bigfoot. Tours are available every day, but you must call for an appointment and directions when you are on the island. ⊠ *East of mile marker 20, Rte. 450; call for directions* ☏ *808/558–8922* ⊕ *www.angelfire.com/film/chiang mai/index.html* ⊑ *$20.*

> ## GUIDED TOURS
>
> **Moloka'i Off-Road Tours and Taxi.** Visit Hālawa Valley, Kalaupapa Lookout, Maunaloa town, and other points of interest in the comfort of an air-conditioned van on four- or six-hour tours. Pat and Alex Pua'a, your personal guides, will even help you mail a coconut back home. Tours start at $98 per person, two-person minimum, and usually begin at 10 AM. Charters and four-wheel-drive tours are also available. ☏ *808/553–3369.*

★ **Kaloko'eli Fishpond.** With its narrow rock walls arching out from the shoreline, Kaloko'eli is typical of the numerous fishponds that define southern Moloka'i. Many of them were built around the 13th century under the direction of powerful chiefs. This early type of aquaculture, particular to Hawai'i, exemplifies the ingenuity of precontact Hawaiians. One or more openings were left in the wall, where gates called *makaha* were installed. These gates allowed seawater and tiny fish to enter the enclosed pond but kept larger predators out. The tiny fish would then grow too big to get out. At one time there were 62 fishponds around Moloka'i's coast. ⊠ *Rte. 450, about 6 mi east of Kaunakakai.*

OFF THE BEATEN PATH

★ **Kamakou Preserve.** Tucked away on the slopes of Mt. Kamakou, Moloka'i's highest peak, the 2,774-acre preserve is a dazzling wonderland full of wet *'ōhi'a* (hardwood trees of the myrtle family, with red blossoms called *lehua* flowers) forests, rare bogs, and native trees and wildlife. Guided hikes, limited to eight people, are held one Saturday each month; reserve well in advance. You can visit the park without a tour, but you need a good four-wheel-drive vehicle (which is hard to find on the island), and the Nature Conservancy requests that you sign in at the office and get directions first. ⊠ *The Nature Conservancy, 23 Pueo Pl., Kualapu'u* ☏ *808/553–5236* ⊕ *www.nature.org* ⊑ *Free; donation for guided hike, $10 members, $25 nonmembers, includes 1-yr membership.*

WORTH NOTING

Kamalō. A natural harbor used by small cargo ships during the 19th century and a favorite fishing spot for locals, this is also the site of the **Church of St. Joseph's**, a tiny white church built by Father Damien of the Kalaupapa colony in the 1880s. The door may be locked but, if not, slip inside and sign the guest book. The congregation keeps the church in beautiful condition. ⊠ *Rte. 450, about 11 mi east of Kaunakakai, makai (toward the ocean) .*

NEED A BREAK?

The best place to grab a snack or picnic supplies is **Mana'e Goods & Grinds** (⊠ *Rte. 450, 16 mi east of Kaunakakai, Puko'o* ☏ *808/558–8498 or 808/558–8186*). It's the only place on the east end where you can find essentials such as ice and bread, and not-so-essentials such as burgers and shakes. Try a refreshing smoothie while here.

Pu'u O Hoku Ranch. A 14,000-acre private spread in the highlands of East Moloka'i, Pu'u O Hoku was developed in the 1930s by wealthy industrialist Paul Fagan. Route 450 cuts right through this rural gem with its pastures and grazing horses and cattle. As you drive slowly along, enjoy the splendid views of Maui and Lāna'i. The small island off the coast is Mokuho'oniki, a favorite spot among visiting humpback whales, where the military practiced bombing techniques during World War II. The ranch offers two guest cottages and a retreat facility for groups. If you love seclusion you will love it here. ⊠ *Rte. 450 about 25 mi east of Kaunakakai* ☎ *808/558–8109* ⊕ *www.puuohoku.com.*

BEACHES

Moloka'i's unique geography gives the island plenty of drama and spectacle along the shorelines but not so many places for seaside basking and bathing. The long north shore consists mostly of towering cliffs that plunge directly into the sea and is inaccessible except by boat, and even then only in summer. Much of the south shore is enclosed by a huge reef that stands as far as a mile offshore and blunts the action of the waves. Within this reef you will find a thin strip of sand, but the water here is flat, shallow, and at times clouded with silt. This reef area is best suited to wading, pole fishing, kayaking, or learning how to windsurf.

The big, fat, sandy beaches lie along the west end. The largest of these—one of the largest in the Islands—is Pāpōhaku Beach, which fronts a grassy park shaded by a grove of *kiawe* (mesquite) trees. These stretches of west-end sand are generally unpopulated. ■ TIP→ **The solitude can be a delight, but it should also be a caution; the sea here can be treacherous.** At the east end, where the road hugs the sinuous shoreline, you encounter a number of pocket-size beaches in rocky coves, good for snorkeling. Don't venture too far out however, or you may find yourself caught in dangerous currents. The road ends at Hālawa Valley with its unique double bay, which is not recommended for swimming.

If you need beach gear, head to Moloka'i Fish and Dive at the west end of Kaunakakai's only commercial strip or rent kayaks from Moloka'i Outdoors at Kaunakakai Wharf.

All of Hawai'i's beaches are free and public. Camping, by permit (fee varies), is permitted at Pāpōhaku and One Ali'i beach parks. None of the beaches on Moloka'i have telephones or lifeguards, and they're all under the jurisdiction of the **Department of Parks, Land and Natural Resources** ⌂ *Box 1055, 90 Ainoa St., Kaunakakai 96748* ☎ *808/553–3204* ⊕ *www. hawaiistateparks.org.*

WEST MOLOKA'I

Moloka'i's west end looks across a wide channel to the island of O'ahu. Crescent shape, this cup of coastline holds the island's best sandy beaches as well as the most arid and sunny weather. This side of the island is largely uninhabited and few signs of development mark the coast besides a few condos, the Kaluako'i Resort (now closed), and a handful of ocean-view homes. Remember: all beaches are public property, even those that front developments, and most have public access roads. Beaches below are listed from north to south.

Kawākiu Beach. Seclusion is the reason to come to this remote beach, accessible only through a gate (that is sometimes locked) by four-wheel drive or a 45-minute walk. The white-sand beach is beautiful. △**Rocks and undertow can make swimming extremely dangerous at times, so use caution.** ⊠*Past Ke Nani Kai condos on Kaluako'i Rd., look for dirt road off to right. Park here and hike in or, with 4WD, drive along dirt road to beach* ⌖ *No facilities.*

Kepuhi Beach. Kaluako'i Hotel is closed, but it does have this half mile of ivory white sand. The beach shines beautifully against the turquoise sea, black outcroppings of lava, and magenta bougainvillea flowers of the resort's landscaping. When the sea is perfectly calm, lava ridges in the water make good snorkeling spots. With any surf at all, however, the water around these rocky places churns and foams, wiping out visibility and making it difficult to avoid being slammed into the jagged rocks. ⊠ *Kaluako'i Rd., at Kaluako'i Hotel and Golf Club (which is now closed)* ⌖ *Toilets, showers.*

FodorśChoice
★
Pāpōhaku Beach. One of the most sensational beaches in Hawai'i, Pāpōhaku is a 3-mi-long strip of light golden sand, the longest of its kind on the island. ■ TIP→ **Some places are too rocky for swimming, so look carefully before entering the water and go in only when the waves are small (generally in summer).** There's so much sand here that Honolulu once purchased barge loads in order to replenish Waīkīkī Beach. A shady beach park just inland is the site of the Ka Hula Piko Festival of Hawaiian Music and Dance, held each year in May. The park is also a great sunset-facing spot for a rustic afternoon barbecue. Camping is allowed with a permit, available from the Department of Parks, Land and Natural Resources in Kaunakakai. ⊠*Kaluako'i Rd.; 2 mi south of Kaluako'i Hotel and Golf Club (which is now closed)* ⌖ *Toilets, showers, picnic tables, grills/firepits.*

Kapukahehu Bay. Locals like to surf just out from this bay in a break called Dixie's or Dixie Maru. The sandy protected cove is usually completely deserted on weekdays but can fill up when the surf is up. The water in the cove is clear and shallow with plenty of well-worn rocky areas. These conditions make for excellent snorkeling, swimming, and boogie boarding on calm days. ⊠*Drive about 3½ mi south of Pāpōhaku Beach to end of Kaluako'i Rd.; beach-access sign points to parking* ⌖ *No facilities.*

CENTRAL MOLOKA'I

The south shore is mostly a huge, reef-walled expanse of flat saltwater edged with a thin strip of gritty sand and stones, mangrove swamps, and the amazing system of fishponds constructed by the chiefs of ancient Moloka'i. From this shore you can look out across glassy water to see people standing on top of the sea—actually, way out on top of the reef—casting fishing lines into the distant waves. This is not a great

DID YOU KNOW?

Long, sandy, and golden, Pāpōhaku Beach on the west end is one of Hawai'i's most spectacular for sunning and sunsets. The ocean is generally calmer in summer and in the morning.

area for beaches, but is interesting in its own right.

One Ali'i Beach Park. Clear, close views of Maui and Lāna'i across the Pailolo Channel dominate One Ali'i Beach Park (*One* is pronounced *o-nay*, not *won*), the only well-maintained beach park on the island's south-central shore. Moloka'i folks gather here for family reunions and community celebrations; the park's tightly trimmed expanse of lawn could almost accommodate the entire island population. Swimming within the reef is perfectly safe, but don't expect to catch any waves. Nearby is the restored One Ali'i fishpond. ⊠*Rte. 450, east of Hotel Moloka'i* ☞*Toilets, showers, picnic tables.*

BEACH SAFETY

Unlike protected shorelines such as Kā'anapali on Maui, the coasts of Moloka'i are exposed to rough sea channels and dangerous rip currents. The ocean tends to be calmer in the morning and in summer. No matter what the time, however, always study the sea before entering. Unless the water is placid and the wave action minimal, it's best to simply stay on shore. Don't underestimate the power of the ocean. Protect yourself with sunblock. Cool breezes make it easy to underestimate the power of the sun as well.

EAST MOLOKA'I

The east end unfolds as a coastal drive with turnouts for tiny cove beaches—good places for snorkeling, shore-fishing, or scuba exploring. Rocky little Mokuho'oniki Island marks the eastern point of the island and serves as a playground for humpback whales in winter. The road loops around the east end, then descends and ends at Hālawa Valley.

Waialua Beach Park. This arched strip of golden sand, a roadside pull-off near mile marker 20, also goes by the name Twenty Mile Beach. The water here, protected by the flanks of the little bay, is often so clear and shallow (sometimes too shallow) that even from land you can watch fish swimming among the coral heads. ■ TIP→ This is the most popular snorkeling spot on the island, a pleasant place to stop on the drive around the east end. ⊠*Drive east on Rte. 450 to mile marker 20* ☞*No facilities.*

Hālawa Beach Park. The vigorous water that gouged the steep, spectacular Hālawa Valley also carved out two bays side by side. Coarse sand and river rock has built up against the sea along the wide valley mouth, creating some protected pool areas that are good for wading or floating around. Most people come here just to hang out and absorb the beauty of this remote valley. All of the property in the valley is private, so do not wander without a guide. Sometimes you'll see people surfing, but it's not wise to entrust your safety to the turbulent open sea along this coast. ⊠*Drive east on Rte. 450 to dead-end* ☞*Toilets.*

WATER SPORTS AND TOURS

Moloka'i's shoreline topography limits opportunities for water sports. The north shore is all sea cliffs; the south shore is largely encased by a huge, taming reef. ⚠Open-sea access at west-end and east-end beaches should be used with caution because seas are rough, especially in winter.

Continued on page 273

Father Damien's Church, St. Philomena

KALAUPAPA PENINSULA: TRAGEDY & TRIUMPH

For those who crave drama, there is no better destination than Moloka'i's Kalaupapa Peninsula—but it wasn't always so. For 100 years this remote strip of land was "the loneliest place on earth," a feared place of exile for those suffering from leprosy (now known as Hansen's Disease).

The world's tallest sea cliffs, rain-chis-eled valleys, and tiny islets dropped like exclamation points along the coast emphasize the passionate history of the Kalaupapa Peninsula. Today, it's im-possible to visit this stunning National Historic Park and view the evidence of human ignorance and heroism with-out responding. You'll be tugged by emotions—awe and disbelief for start-ers. But you'll also glimpse humorous facets of everyday life in a small town. Whatever your experience here may be, chances are you'll return home feeling that the journey to present-day Kalau-papa is one you'll never forget.

THE SETTLEMENT'S EARLY DAYS

Father Damien with patients outside St. Philomena church.

IN 1865, PRESSURED BY FOREIGN RESI-DENTS, the Hawaiian Kingdom passed "An Act to Prevent the Spread of Leprosy." Anyone showing symptoms of the disease was to be permanently exiled to Kalawao, the north end of Kalaupapa Peninsula—a spot walled in on three sides by nearly impassable cliffs. The peninsula had been home to a fishing community for 900 years, but those inhabitants were evicted and the entire peninsula declared settlement land.

The first 12 patients were arrested and sent to Kalawao in 1866. People of all ages and many nationalities followed, taken from their homes and dumped on the isolated shore. Officials thought the patients could become self-sufficient, fishing and farming sweet potatoes in the stream-fed valleys. That was not the case. Settlement conditions were deplorable.

Father Damien, a Belgian missionary, was one of four priests who volunteered to serve the leprosy settlement at Kalawao on a rotating basis. There were 600 patients at the time. His turn came in 1873; when it was up, he refused to leave. He is

credited with turning the settlement from a merciless exile to a place where hope could be heard in the voices of his recruited choir. He organized the building of the St. Philomena church, nearly 300 houses, and a home for boys. A vocal advocate for his adopted community, he pestered the church for supplies, administered medicine, and oversaw the nearly daily funerals. Sixteen years after his arrival, in 1889, he died from the effects of leprosy, having contracted the disease during his service. Known around the world for his sacrifice, Father Damien was beatified by the Catholic Church in 1995, and is expected to be canonized as early as 2010.

Mother Marianne heard of the mission while working at a hospital in Syracuse, New York. Along with six other Franciscan Sisters, she volunteered to work with those with leprosy in the Islands. They sailed to the desolate Kalaupapa Peninsula in November of 1888. Like the Father, the Sisters were considered saints for their tireless work. Mother Marianne stayed at Kalaupapa until her death in 1918; she was beatified by the Catholic Church in 2005.

VISITING KALAUPAPA TODAY

Kalaupapa Peninsula

FROZEN IN TIME, Kalaupapa's one-horse town has bittersweet charm. Signs posted here and there remind residents when the bank will be open (once monthly), where to pick up lost sunglasses, and what's happening at the tiny town bar. The town has the nostalgic, almost naive ambience expected from a place almost wholly segregated from modern life.

About 30 former patients remain at Kalaupapa (by choice, as the disease is controlled by drugs and the patients are no longer carriers), but many travel frequently to other parts of the world and all are over the age of 60. Richard Marks, the town sheriff and owner of Damien Tours, will likely retire soon, as will the elderly postmistress. They haven't, however, lost their chutzpah. Having survived a lifetime of prejudice and misunderstanding, Kalaupapa's residents aren't willing to be pushed around any longer—several recently made the journey to Honolulu to ask for the removal of a "rude and insensitive" superintendent.

To get a feel for what their lives were like, visit the National Park Service Web site (⊕ www.nps.gov/kala/docs/start.htm) or buy one of several heartbreaking memoirs at the park's library-turned-bookstore.

THE TRUTH ABOUT HANSEN'S DISEASE

■ A cure for leprosy has been available since 1941. Multi-drug therapy, a rapid cure, has been available since 1981.

■ With treatment, none of the disabilities traditionally associated with leprosy need occur.

■ Most people have a natural immunity to leprosy. Only 5% of the world's population is even susceptible to the disease.

■ There are still about 500,000 new cases of leprosy each year; at least two-thirds are in India.

■ All new cases of leprosy are treated on an outpatient basis.

■ The term "leper" is offensive and should not be used. It is appropriate to say "a person is affected by leprosy" or "by Hansen's Disease."

GETTING HERE

The Kalaupapa Trail and Peninsula are all part of Kalaupapa National Historic Park (☎ 808/567–6802 ⊕ www.nps. gov/kala/), which is open every day but Sunday for tours only. Keep in mind, there are no public facilities (except an occasional restroom) anywhere in the park. Pack your own food and water, as well as light rain gear, sunscreen, and bug repellent.

TO HIKE OR TO RIDE?

There are two ways to get down the Kalaupapa Trail: in your hiking boots, or on a mule.

Hiking: Hiking allows you to travel at your own pace and stop frequently for photos—not an option on the mule ride. The hike takes about 1 hour down and 1½ hours up. You must book a tour in order to access the trail. **Damien Tours** ☎ *808/567–6171.*

Kalaupapa Beach & Peninsula

THE KALAUPAPA TRAIL

Unless you fly (flights are available through Pacific Wings [☎ 808/873–0877 or 888/575–4546 ⊕ www.pacificwings. com]), the only way into Kalaupapa National Historic Park is on a dizzying switchback trail. The switchbacks are numbered—26 in all—and descend 1,700 feet to sea level in just under 3 mi. The steep trail is more of a staircase, and most of the trail is shaded. Keep in mind, however, that footing is uneven and there is little to keep you from pitching over the side. If you don't mind heights, you can stare straight down to the ocean for most of the way. *Access Kalaupapa Trail off Hwy. 470 near the Kalaupapa Overlook. There is ample parking near end of Hwy. 470.*

Mule-Skinning: You'll be amazed as your mule trots up to the edge of the switchback, swivels on two legs, and completes a sharp-angled turn—26 times. The guides tell you the mules can do this in their sleep, but that doesn't take the fear out of the first few switchbacks. Make reservations well in advance. **Moloka'i Mule Ride** ☎ *808/567–6088 or 808/567–7550* ⊕*www.muleride.com.*

IMPORTANT INFORMATION

Daily tours are offered Monday through Saturday through Damien Tours or Moloka'i Mule Ride. Be sure to reserve in advance. Visitors ages 16 and under are not allowed at Kalaupapa, and photographing patients without their written permission is forbidden.

Generally speaking, there's no one around—certainly not lifeguards—if you get into trouble. For this reason alone, guided excursions are recommended. At least be sure to ask for advice from outfitters or residents. Two kinds of water activities predominate: kayaking within the reef area, and open-sea excursions on charter boats, most of which tie up at Kaunakakai Wharf.

BOOGIE BOARDING AND BODYSURFING

You rarely see people boogie boarding or bodysurfing on Moloka'i, and the only surfing is for advanced wave riders. The best spots for boogie boarding, when conditions are safe (occasional summer mornings), are the west-end beaches. Another option is to seek out waves at the east end around mile marker 20.

DEEP-SEA FISHING

For Moloka'i people, as in days of yore, the ocean is more of a larder than a playground. It's common to see residents fishing along the shoreline or atop South Shore Reef, using poles or lines. If you'd like to try your hand at this form of local industry, you can rent or buy fishing equipment and ask for advice at **Moloka'i Fish and Dive** (*61 Ala Mālama St., Kaunakakai* ☎*808/553–5926* ⊕*molokaifishanddive.com*).

Deep-sea fishing by charter boat is a great Moloka'i adventure. The sea channels here, though often rough and windy, provide gorgeous views of several islands. The big sport fish are plentiful in these waters, especially mahimahi, small marlin, and various kinds of tuna. Generally speaking, boat captains will customize the outing to your interests, share a lot of information about the island, and let you keep some or all of your catch. That's Moloka'i style—personal and friendly.

BOATS AND CHARTERS

Alyce C. The six-passenger, 31-foot cruiser runs excellent sportfishing excursions in the capable hands of Captain Joe. The cost for the boat is $550 for a full-day trip, $500 for six to seven hours, and $450 for four to five hours. Shared charters are available for six passengers maximum. Gear is provided. It's a rare day when you don't snag at least one memorable fish. ⊠*Kaunakakai Wharf, Kaunakakai* ☎*808/558–8377* ⊕*www. alycecsportfishing.com*.

Fun Hogs Sportfishing. Trim and speedy, the 27-foot flybridge sportfishing boat named *Ahi* offers half-day ($428), six-hour ($535), and full-day ($642) sportfishing excursions. Skipper Mike Holmes also provides one-way or round-trip journeys to Lāna'i, as well as (in winter only) sunset cruises. ⊠*Kaunakakai Wharf, Kaunakakai* ☎*808/567–6789.*

Moloka'i Action Adventures. Walter Naki's Moloka'i roots go back forever, and he knows the island intimately. What's more, he has traveled (and fished) all over the globe, and he's a great talker. He will create customized fishing and hunting expeditions and gladly share his wealth of experience. He will also take you to remote beaches for a day of swimming. If you want to explore the north side under the great sea cliffs,

10

this is the way to go. His 21-foot *Boston Whaler* is usually seen at the mouth of Hālawa Valley, in the east end. ☎808/558–8184.

KAYAKING

Moloka'i's south shore is enclosed by the largest reef system in the United States—an area of shallow, protected sea that stretches over 30 mi. This reef gives inexperienced kayakers an unusually safe, calm environment for shoreline exploring. ⚠**Outside the reef, Moloka'i waters are often rough and treacherous. Kayakers out here should be strong, experienced, and cautious.**

BEST SPOTS

The **South Shore Reef** area is superb for flat-water kayaking any day of the year. It's best to rent a kayak from Moloka'i Outdoors in Kaunakakai and slide into the water from Kaunakakai Wharf, on either side. Get out in the morning before the wind picks up and paddle east, exploring the ancient Hawaiian fishponds. When you turn around to return, you'll usually get a push home by the wind, which blows strong and westerly along this shore in the afternoon.

Independent kayakers who are confident about testing their skills in rougher seas can launch at the west end of the island from **Hale O Lono Harbor** (at the end of a long, bumpy, private dirt road from Maunaloa town). At the east end of the island, enter the water near mile marker 20 or beyond and explore in the direction of Mokuho'oniki Island. ⚠**Kayaking anywhere outside the South Shore Reef is safe only on calm days in summer.**

EQUIPMENT, LESSONS, AND TOURS

Moloka'i Fish and Dive. At the west end of Kaunakakai's commercial strip, this all-around outfitter provides guided kayak excursions inside the South Shore Reef. One excursion paddles through a dense mangrove forest and explores a huge, hidden ancient fishpond. A bonus of going with guides: if the wind starts blowing hard, they tow you back with their boat. The fee is $89 for the half-day trip. Check at the store (61 Ala Mālama Street) for numerous other outdoor activities. ✉*61 Ala Mālama St., Kaunakakai* ☎*808/553–5926* ⊕*molokaifishanddive.com.*

Moloka'i Outdoors. This is the place to rent a kayak for exploring on your own. Kayaks rent for $26–$39 per day (weekly rates offered), and extra paddles are available. ✉*Kaunakakai Wharf, Kaunakakai* ☎*808/553–4227 or 877/553–4477* ⊕*www.molokai-outdoors.com.*

SAILING

Moloka'i is a place of strong predictable winds that make for good and sometimes rowdy sailing. The island views in every direction are stunning. Kaunakakai Wharf is the home base for all of the island's charter sailboats.

SCUBA DIVING

Moloka'i Fish and Dive is the only PADI-certified purveyor of scuba gear, training, and dive trips on Moloka'i. Shoreline access for divers is extremely limited, even nonexistent in winter. Boat diving is the way

to go. Without guidance, visiting divers can easily find themselves in risky situations with wicked currents. Proper guidance, though, opens an undersea world rarely seen.

Moloka'i Fish and Dive. Owners Tim and Susan Forsberg can fill you in on how to find dive sites, rent you the gear, or hook you up with one of their PADI-certified dive guides to take you to the island's best underwater spots. Their 32-foot dive boat, the *Ama Lua,* is certified for 18 passengers and can take eight divers and gear. Two tank dives lasting about five hours cost $155 with gear, $135 if you bring your own. They know the best blue holes and underwater-cave systems, and they can take you swimming with hammerhead sharks. ⊠ *61 Ala Mālama St., Kaunakakai* ☎ *808/553–5926* ⊕ *molokaifishanddive.com.*

SNORKELING

During the times when swimming is safe—mainly in summer—just about every beach on Moloka'i offers good snorkeling along the lava outcroppings in the island's clean and pristine waters. Certain spots inside the South Shore Reef are also worth checking out.

BEST SPOTS

Kepuhi Beach. In winter, the sea here is deadly. But in summer, this ½-mi-long west-end beach offers plenty of rocky nooks that swirl with sea life. The presence of outdoor showers is a bonus. Take Kaluako'i Road all the way to the west end. Park at Kaluako'i Resort (it's closed) and walk to the beach.

Waialua Beach Park. A thin curve of sand rims a sheltered little bay loaded with coral heads and aquatic life. The water here is shallow—sometimes so shallow that you bump into the underwater landscape—and it's crystal clear. To find this spot, head to the east end on Route 450, and pull off near mile marker 20. When the sea is calm, you'll find several other good snorkeling spots along this stretch of road.

EQUIPMENT AND TOURS

Rent snorkel sets from either Moloka'i Outdoors or Moloka'i Fish and Dive in Kaunakakai. Rental fees are nominal—$6 to $10 a day. All the charter boats carry snorkel gear and include dive stops.

Fun Hog Sportfishing. Mike Holmes, captain of the 27-foot powerboat *Ahi,* knows the island waters intimately, likes to have fun, and is willing to arrange any type of excursion—for example, one dedicated entirely to snorkeling. His 2½-hour snorkel trips leave early in the morning and explore rarely seen fish and turtle posts outside the reef west of the wharf. Bring your own food and drinks; the trips cost $65 per person. ⊠ *Kaunakakai Wharf, Kaunakakai* ☎ *808/567–6789.*

> ### ACTIVITY SPECIALISTS
>
> There are basically two activity vendors on the island who book everything: **Moloka'i Fish and Dive** (⊠ *61 Ala Mālama St., Kaunakakai* ☎ *808/553–5926* ⊕ *molokaifishand-dive.com*) and **Moloka'i Outdoors** (⊠ *Kaunakakai WharfKaunakakai* ☎ *808/553–4227* or *877/553–4477* ⊕ *www.molokai-outdoors.com*). Be sure to book well in advance because not all activities are offered daily.

Moloka'i Fish and Dive. Climb aboard their 27-foot cabin cruiser or 31-foot twin hull Power Cat for a snorkel trip to Moloka'i's pristine barrier reef. Trips cost $69 per person and include equipment, water, and soft drinks. ⊠ *61 Ala Mālama St., Kaunakakai* ☎ *808/553–5926.*

WHALE-WATCHING

Maui gets all the credit for the local wintering humpback-whale population. Most people don't realize that the big cetaceans also come to Moloka'i. Mokuho'oniki Island at the east end serves as a whale playground, and the whales pass back and forth along the south shore. This being Moloka'i, whale-watching here will never involve floating amid a group of boats all ogling the same whale.

BOATS AND CHARTERS

Alyce C. Although this six-passenger sportfishing boat is usually busy hooking mahimahi and marlin, the captain gladly takes three-hour excursions to admire the humpback whales. The price is $75 per person, depending on the number of passengers in the group. ⊠ *Kaunakakai Wharf, Kaunakakai* ☎ *808/558–8377* ⊕ *www.alycecsportfishing.com.*

Ama Lua. This 32-foot dive boat, certified for up to 18 passengers, is respectful of whales' privacy and the laws that protect them. A 2½-hour whale-watching trip is $70 per person; they depart from Kaunakakai Wharf at 7 AM during whale season, roughly from December to April. Call Moloka'i Fish and Dive for reservations or information. ⊠ *91 Ala Mālama St., Kaunakakai* ☎ *808/553–5926 or 808/552–0184* ⊕ *molokaifishanddive.com.*

Fun Hogs Sportfishing. The *Ahi*, a flybridge sportfishing boat, takes 2½-hour whale-watching trips in the morning from December to April. The cost is $70 per person. Bring your own snacks and drinks. You can print your ticket on-line ahead of time and arrive ready to go. ⊠ *Kaunakakai Wharf, Kaunakakai* ☎ *808/567–6789* ⊕ *www.molokaifishing.com.*

GOLF, HIKING, AND OUTDOOR ACTIVITIES 10

BIKING

Street biking on this island is a dream for pedalers who like to eat up the miles. Moloka'i's few roads are long, straight, and extremely rural. You can really stretch out and go for it—no traffic lights and most of the time no traffic. If you don't happen to be one of those athletes who always travels with your own customized cycling tool, you can rent something from **Moloka'i Bicycle** (⊠ *80 Mohala St. Kaunakakai96748* ☎ *808/553–3931*) in Kaunakakai.

GOLF

Ironwood Hills Golf Course. Like the other 9-hole plantation-era courses with which it shares lineage, Ironwood Hills is not for everyone. It helps if you like to play laid-back golf with locals and can handle occasionally rugged conditions. On the plus side, most holes here offer lovely views of the ocean. Fairways are *kukuya* grass and run through pine, ironwood, and eucalyptus trees. Carts are rented, but there's not always someone there to rent you a cart—in which case, there's a wooden box for your green fee (honor system), and happy walking. ⊠ *Kala'e Hwy. Kualapu'u* ⌕ *9 holes. 3088 yds. Par 35. Green Fee: $20* ⌕ *Facilities: Putting green, golf carts, pull carts.*

HIKING

Rural and rugged, Moloka'i is an excellent place for hiking. Roads and developments are few, so the outdoors is always beckoning. The island is steep, so hikes often combine spectacular views with hearty physical exertion. Because the island is small, you can traverse quite a bit of it on foot and come away with the feeling of really knowing the place. And you won't see many other people around. Just remember that much of what may look like deserted land is private property, so be careful not to trespass without permission or an authorized guide.

BEST SPOTS

Kalaupapa Trail. You can make a day of hiking down to Kalaupapa Peninsula and back by means of a 3-mi, 26-switchback trail. The trail is nearly vertical, traversing the face of some of the highest sea cliffs in the world. Only those in excellent condition should attempt this hike. You must book with Damien Tours to access the trail and see the peninsula. *See A Tale of Tragedy & Triumph earlier in this chapter.*

★ **Kamakou Preserve.** Four-wheel drive is essential for this half-day (minimum) journey into the Moloka'i highlands. The Nature Conservancy of Hawai'i manages the 2,774-acre Kamakou Preserve, one of the last stands of Hawai'i's native plants and birds. A long, rough dirt road, which begins not far from Kaunakakai town, leads to the preserve. The road is not marked, so you must check in with the **Nature Conservancy's Moloka'i office** (⊠ *At Moloka'i Industrial Park about 3 mi west of Kaunakakai, 23 Pueo Pl.* ☎ *808/553–5236* ⊕ *www.nature.org*), for directions. Let them know that you plan to visit the preserve, and pick up the informative 24-page brochure with trail maps.

On your way up to the preserve, be sure to stop at Waikolu Overlook, which gives a view into a precipitous north-shore canyon. Once inside the preserve, various trails are clearly marked. The trail of choice—and you can drive right to it—is the 1.5-mi boardwalk trail through Pēpē'ōpae Bog, an ecological treasure. Organic deposits here date back at least 10,000 years, and the plants are undisturbed natives. This is the landscape of prediscovery Hawai'i and can be a mean trek. ■ TIP→ **Wear long pants and bring rain gear. Your shoes ought to provide good traction on the slippery, narrow boardwalk and muddy trails.**

Kawela Cul-de-Sacs. Just east of Kaunakakai, three streets—Kawela One, Two, and Three—jut up the mountainside from the Kamehameha V Highway. These roads end in cul-de-sacs that are also informal trailheads. Rough dirt roads work their way from here to the top of the mountain. The lower slopes are dry, rocky, steep, and austere. (It's good to start in the cool of the early morning.) A hiker in good condition can get all the

DID YOU KNOW?

A hike through the Kamakou Preserve in East Moloka'i, on the slopes of the island's highest peak, reveals a lush world of forest, bogs, and native wildlife. Sign up in advance for a guided hike.

way up into the high forest in two or three hours. There's no park ranger and no water fountain. These are not for the casual stroller. But you will be well rewarded.

GOING WITH A GUIDE

Fodor'sChoice ★   **Hālawa Valley Cultural Waterfall Hike.** Hālawa is a gorgeous, steep-walled valley carved by two rivers and rich in history. Site of the earliest Polynesian settlement on Moloka'i, Hālawa sustained island culture with its ingeniously designed *lo'i*, or taro fields. In the 1960s, because of changing cultural conditions and a great flood, the valley became derelict. Now Hawaiian families are restoring the *lo'i* and taking visitors on guided walks through the valley, which includes two of Moloka'i's *luakini heiau* (sacred temples). Half-day visits, starting at 9:30 AM or 2 PM cost $75 (less for children) and support the work of restoration. Call ahead to book your visit. Bring water, food, and insect repellent, and wear shoes that are stable and can get wet. ☎808/553–9803 ⊕www.gomolokai. com ⤳$75.

Historical Hikes of West Moloka'i. This company has six guided hikes, ranging from two to six hours. The outings focus on Moloka'i's cultural past, and take you to sites such as an ancient quarry, an early fishing village, or high sea cliffs where Hawaiian chiefs played games during the traditional *Makahiki* (harvest festival) season. Backpacks are provided, as is lunch on intermediate and advanced hikes. Guides Lawrence and Catherine Aki are knowledgeable and passionate about Hawaiian culture. ☎808/552–0184, 808/553–5926, or 800/274–9303 ⊕www.gomolokai. com ⤳$45–$125.

SHOPPING

Moloka'i has one main commercial area: Ala Mālama Street in Kaunakakai. There are no department stores or shopping malls, and the clothing available is typical island wear. A handful of family-run businesses line the main drag of Maunaloa, a rural former plantation town. Most stores in Kaunakakai are open Monday through Saturday between 9 and 6. In Maunaloa most shops close by 4 in the afternoon and all day Sunday.

ARTS AND CRAFTS

Big Wind Kite Factory and Plantation Gallery. The factory has custom-made appliquéd kites you can fly or display. Designs range from hula girls to tropical fish. Also in stock are kite-making kits, paper kites, minikites, and wind socks. Ask to go on the factory tour, or take a free kite-flying lesson. The gallery is adjacent to and part of the kite shop and carries locally made crafts, Hawaiian books and CDs, Asian import jewelry and fabrics, and an elegant line of women's linen clothing. ⊠120 Maunaloa Hwy., Maunaloa ☎808/552–2364.

Moloka'i Artists & Crafters Guild. A small shop above the American Savings Bank downtown, the guild has locally made folk art like dolls, clay flowers, hula skirts, aloha-print visors, and children's wear. They also carry original art by Moloka'i artists and Giclée prints, jewelry, locally produced music, and Father Damien keepsakes. ⊠*40 Ala Mālama St., Suite 201, Kaunakakai* ☎*808/553–8018.*

CLOTHING AND SHOES

Imports Gift Shop. Both fancy and casual island-style wear is sold here, across from Kanemitsu Bakery. ⊠*82 Ala Mālama St., Kaunakakai* ☎*808/553–5734.*

Moloka'i Island Creations. Try this shop for exclusive swimwear, beach cover-ups, sun hats, and tank tops. ⊠*61 Ala Mālama St., Kaunakakai* ☎*808/553–5926.*

Moloka'i Surf. This surf shop is known for its wide selection of Moloka'i T-shirts and sportswear. They also sell boogie boards. ⊠*130 Kamehameha V Hwy., Kaunakakai* ☎*808/553–5093.*

FOOD

Friendly Market Center. The best-stocked supermarket on the island has a slogan—"Your family store on Moloka'i"—that is truly credible. Hats, T-shirts, and sun-and-surf essentials keep company with fresh produce, meat, groceries, liquor, and sundries. Locals say the food is fresher here than at the other major supermarket. It's open weekdays 8:30 AM to 8:30 PM and Saturday 8:30 AM to 6:30 PM. ⊠*90 Ala Mālama St., Kaunakakai* ☎*808/553–5595.*

Maunaloa General Store. Victuals and travel essentials, like meat, produce, dry goods, and drinks—and even fresh doughnuts on Sunday morning—are available here. It's convenient for guests staying at the nearby condos and for those wishing to picnic at one of the west-end beaches. It's open Monday through Saturday 8 AM to 6 PM. ⊠*200 Maunaloa Hwy., Maunaloa* ☎*808/552–2346.*

Misaki's Inc. In business since 1922, Misaki's has authentic island allure. Pick up housewares and beverages here, as well as your food staples, Monday through Saturday 8:30 AM to 8:30 PM, and Sunday 9 AM to noon. ⊠*78 Ala Mālama St., Kaunakakai* ☎*808/553–5505.*

Moloka'i Wines 'n' Spirits. Don't let the name fool you; along with a surprisingly good selection of fine wines and liquors, the store also carries cheeses and snacks. It's open Sunday through Thursday 9 AM to 8 PM, Friday and Saturday until 9. ⊠*77 Ala Mālama St., Kaunakakai* ☎*808/553–5009.*

JEWELRY

Imports Gift Shop. You'll find a small collection of 14-karat-gold chains, rings, earrings, and bracelets, plus a jumble of Hawaiian quilts, pillows, books, and postcards here. The shop also carries stunning Hawaiian heirloom jewelry, a unique style of gold jewelry inspired by popular Victorian pieces, that has been crafted in Hawai'i since the late 1800s. It's made to order. ⊠*82 Ala Mālama St., Kaunakakai* ☎*808/553–5734.*

Moloka'i Island Creations. This store features its own unique line of jewelry, including sea opal, coral, and silver, as well as other gifts and resort wear. ⊠*61 Ala Mālama St., Kaunakakai* ☎*808/553–5926.*

10

SPORTING GOODS

Moloka'i Bicycle. This bike shop rents and sells mountain and road bikes as well as jogging strollers, kids' trailers, helmets, and racks. It supplies maps and information on biking and hiking and will drop off and pick up equipment for a fee nearly anywhere on the island. Call or stop by Wednesday from 3 PM to 6 PM or Saturday from 9 AM to 2 PM to arrange what you need. ✉ *80 Mohala St., Kaunakakai* ☎ *808/553–3931 or 800/709–2453* ⊕ *www.bikehawaii.com/molokaibicycle.*

Moloka'i Fish and Dive. This is *the* source for your sporting needs, from snorkel rentals to free and friendly advice. This is also a good place to pick up original-design Moloka'i T-shirts, water sandals, books, and gifts. ✉ *61 Ala Mālama St., Kaunakakai* ☎ *808/553–5926* ⊕ *molokaifishanddive.com.*

ENTERTAINMENT AND NIGHTLIFE

Local nightlife consists mainly of gathering with friends and family, sipping a few cold ones, strumming 'ukuleles and guitars, singing old songs, and talking story. Still, there are a few ways to kick up your heels. Pick up a copy of the weekly *Moloka'i Dispatch* and see if there's a concert, church supper, or dance. The bar at the Hotel Moloka'i is always a good place to drink. It has live music by island performers every night, and Moloka'i may be the best place to hear authentic, old-time, nonprofessional Hawaiian music. Don't be afraid to get up and dance should the music move you. The "Aloha Friday" weekly gathering here, from 4 to 6 PM, features Na Ohana Aloha, a group of accomplished *kupuna* (old-timers) with guitars and 'ukuleles. This scheduled, feel-good event is a peak experience for any Moloka'i trip. The group also performs on Sunday afternoons at Coffees of Hawai'i. The Paddlers Inn in Kaunakakai has live music on Wednesday, Friday, and Saturday nights. It's informal and can get lively, especially on weekends when it's open until 1 AM. For something truly casual, stop in at Kanimitsu Bakery on Ala Mālama Street in Kaunakakai for their nightly hot bread sale (Tuesday through Sunday, until 10 PM or they sell out of bread); it's fresh from the ovens. You'll meet everyone in town and can take some hot bread home to your condo for a late-night treat.

WHERE TO EAT

During a week's stay, you might easily hit all the dining spots worth a visit and then return to your favorites for a second round. The dining scene is fun because it's a microcosm of Hawai'i's diverse cultures. You can find locally grown vegetarian foods, spicy Filipino cuisine, and Hawaiian fish with a Japanese influence—such as *'ahi* or *aku* (types of tuna), mullet, and moonfish grilled, sautéed, or mixed with seaweed and eaten raw as *poke* (marinated raw fish). Most eating establishments are on Ala Mālama Street in Kaunakakai, with pizza, pasta, and ribs all within a block or two. If you're heading to East or West Moloka'i for the day, be sure to stock up on provisions before you go as there is no place to eat in these areas. You can buy a disposable cooler and groceries at the Friendly Market Center in Kaunakakai. A more limited selection of snacks and groceries is also available in Maunaloa at the Maunaloa General Store.

WHAT IT COSTS					
	¢	$	$$	$$$	$$$$
RESTAURANTS	under $10	$10–$17	$18–$26	$27–$35	over $35

Restaurant prices are for a main course at dinner.

CENTRAL MOLOKA'I

$$
HAWAIIAN
✕**Hula Shores.** This is *the* place to hang out on Moloka'i. Locals relax at the bar listening to live music every night, or they come in for theme-night dinners. Service is brisk and friendly, the food is good, and the atmosphere casual. Prime rib specials on Friday and Saturday nights draw a crowd. Try the *kālua* pork and cabbage or the hibachi chicken. Every Friday from 4 to 6 PM Moloka'i's *kūpuna* (old-timers) bring their instruments here for a lively Hawaiian jam session, a wonderful experience of grassroots aloha spirit. ⊠*Hotel Moloka'i, 1300 Kamehameha V Hwy., Kaunakakai* ☎*808/553–5347* ▤*AE, DC, MC, V.*

¢
Fodor'sChoice
★
CAFÉ
✕**Kanemitsu Bakery and Restaurant.** Stop for morning coffee with fresh-baked bread or a taste of *lavosh,* a pricey flat bread flavored with sesame, taro, Maui onion, Parmesan cheese, or jalapeño. Or try the round Moloka'i bread—a sweet, pan-style white loaf that makes excellent cinnamon toast. Be prepared to wait, and settle down into Moloka'i time. ⊠*79 Ala Mālama St., Kaunakakai* ☎*808/553–5855* ▤*No credit cards* ☉*Closed Tues.*

$
HAWAIIAN
✕ **Kualapu'u Cookhouse.** The only restaurant in rural Kualapu'u and a local favorite, this laid-back diner is a classic refurbished green-and-white plantation house. Inside, paintings of hula dancers and island scenes enhance the simple furnishings. Typical fare is a plate of chicken or pork *katsu* served with rice. Try their mahi burger or chicken stir-fry with fresh vegetables. It's across the street from the Kualapu'u Market. ⊠*Farrington Hwy., 1 block west of Rte. 470, Kualapu'u* ☎*808/567–9655* ▤*No credit cards* ☉*Closed Sun. No dinner Mon.*

¢
HAWAIIAN
✕**Moloka'i Drive Inn.** Fast food Moloka'i-style is served at a walk-up counter. Hot dogs, fries, and sundaes are on the menu, but residents usually choose the foods they grew up on, such as *saimin* (thin noodles and vegetables in broth), plate lunches, shave ice (snow cone), and the beloved *loco moco* (rice topped with a hamburger and a fried egg, covered in gravy). ⊠*15 Kamoi St., Kaunakakai* ☎*808/553–5655* ▤*No credit cards.*

$
AMERICAN
✕**Moloka'i Pizza Cafe.** Cheerful and busy, Moloka'i Pizza is a popular gathering spot for families. Pizza, sandwiches, salads, pasta, and fresh fish are simply prepared and served without fuss. Eat in or take out. Kids keep busy on a few little coin-operated rides and their art decorates the walls. ⊠*Kaunakakai Pl. at Wharf Rd., Kaunakakai* ☎*808/553–3288* ▤*No credit cards.*

¢
VEGETARIAN
✕**Outpost Natural Foods.** Outpost is Moloka'i's only health-food store. It's a good place to pick up local produce, a few organic items, and a selection of ingredients for a healthful picnic lunch. ⊠*70 Makaena St., Kaunakakai* ☎*808/553–3377* ▤*AE, D, MC, V* ☉*Closed Sat. No dinner.*

10

$ ✕**Oviedo's.** Don't let the sagging front door fool you. This modest and spot-
PHILIPPINE less lunch counter specializes in delicious *adobos* (stews) with traditional
Filipino spices and sauces. Try the tripe, pork, or beef *adobo* for a taste of
tradition. Locals say that Oviedo's makes the best crispy roast pork in the
state. You can eat in at one of the four tables or take out. ⊠*145 Puali St.,
Kaunakakai* ☎*808/553–5014* ⊟*No credit cards* ☉*Closed Sun.*

$ ✕**Paddlers Inn.** Roomy and comfortable, this restaurant with an extensive
ECLECTIC menu is right in Kaunakakai town but on the ocean side of Kamemeha
V Highway. There are three eating areas—standard restaurant seating, a
shady cool bar, and an open-air courtyard where you can sit at a counter
eating *poke* (raw, marinated cubes of fish) and drinking beer while getting
cooled with spray—on hot days—from an overhead misting system. The
food is a blend of island-style and standard American fare (fresh poke
every day; a prime rib special every Friday night). It's a popular hangout
for the younger set and has live entertainment every Wednesday and Friday. ⊠*10 Mohala St., Kaunakakai* ☎*808/553–5256* ⊟*MC, V.*

¢   ✕**Sundown Deli.** This clean little rose-color deli focuses on freshly made
DELI takeout food. Sandwiches come on a half dozen types of bread, and
the Portuguese bean soup and chowders are rich and filling. ⊠*145
Ala Mālama St., Kaunakakai* ☎*808/553–3713* ⊟*No credit cards*
☉*Closed Sun. No dinner.*

WHERE TO STAY

The coastline along Moloka'i's west end has ocean-view condominium units and luxury homes available as vacation rentals. If you are
familiar with the high-end Lodge at Moloka'i Ranch, please note
that it is currently closed and future plans for the property remain
unknown. Central Moloka'i offers seaside condominiums and the
icon of the island—Hotel Moloka'i. The only lodgings on the east
end are some guest cottages in magical settings and the ranch house
at Pu'u O Hoku. The **Moloka'i Visitors Association** (☎*800/800–6367*)
has a brochure with an up-to-date listing of vacation rentals operated by their members.

WHAT IT COSTS				
¢	$	$$	$$$	$$$$
HOTELS under $100	$100–$180	$181–$260	$261–$340	over $340

Hotel prices are for two people in a double room in high season, including tax and service.
Condo price categories reflect studio and one-bedroom rates. Prices do not include 11.41% tax.

Moloka'i Vacation Properties (☎*800/367–2984 or 808/553–8334* ⊕*www.
molokai-vacation-rental.net*)handles upgraded condo rentals that
include initial bathroom amenities, cleaning supplies, maps, and complimentary coffee. The company can act as an informal concierge during
your stay. There is a three-night minimum on all properties.
Note: Maui County has regulations concerning vacation rentals; to
avoid disappointment, always contact the property manager or the

owner and ask if the accommodation has the proper permits and is in compliance with local ordinances.

WEST MOLOKA'I

If you are considering renting a condo unit fronting the Kaula Koi golf course, keep in mind that the course has been abandoned, and at this writing, presents a bit of a dismal view.

$

RENTAL

Ke Nani Kai. These pleasant one- and two-bedroom condo units have ocean views and nicely maintained tropical landscaping. Furnished lānai have flower-laden trellises and the spacious interiors are decorated with rattans and pastels. Each unit has a washer-dryer unit and a fully equipped kitchen. The beach is across the road. **Pros:** located on island's secluded west end; Internet; uncrowded pool. **Cons:** amenities vary as each unit is individually owned; far from commercial center; golf course units overlook abandoned course. ⊠ *Kaluako'i Rd., Maunaloa* ☎ *808/553–8334 or 800/367–2984* ⊕ *www.molokai-vacation-rental.net* ↘ *120 units* ⏁ *In-room: no a/c, kitchen, Internet. In-hotel: tennis courts, pool, laundry facilities* ⊟ *AE, MC, V.*

$–$$

RENTAL

Paniolo Hale. Perched high on a ridge overlooking a favored local surfing spot, Paniolo Hale is Moloka'i's best condominium property. Architecturally elegant studios and one- or two-bedroom units all have beautiful screened lānai, well-equipped kitchens, and washers and dryers; some have spectacular ocean views. Rooms are tidy and simple and many are beautifully furnished with ample lounging areas. The property boasts mature tropical landscaping and a private serene setting. **Pros:** close to beach; quiet surroundings;, perfect if you are an expert surfer. **Cons:** amenities vary; far from shopping; golf course units front abandoned course; three-night minimum. ⊠ *Lio Pl., Kaunakakai* ☎ *808/553–8334 or 800/367–2984* ⊕ *www.molokai-vacation-rental.net* ↘ *77 units* ⏁ *In-room: kitchen. In-hotel: pool* ⊟ *AE, MC, V.*

CENTRAL MOLOKA'I

$–$$

HOTEL

Hotel Moloka'i. Staff members are helpful and friendly at this local favorite, where the two-story, semi-A-frame buildings are arranged in a landscaped tropical setting. Some units overlook the reef and distant Lana'i. The rooms were renovated in late 2007 and are bright and comfortably furnished. The airy Hula Shores restaurant overlooks the ocean and serves breakfast, lunch, dinner, and libations—with local entertainment nightly. Ask about deals in conjunction with airlines and rental-car companies when you make your reservation. There is an activities desk in the lobby. **Pros:** five minutes to shopping and town; some kitchenettes; authentic Hawaiian entertainment. **Cons:** no-frills; can be difficult to secure a reservation on weekends; lower-priced rooms are small and plain. ⊠ *Kamehameha V Hwy., Box 1020, Kaunakakai* ☎ *808/553–5347 or 800/535–0085* ⊕ *www.hotelmolokai.com* ↘ *40 rooms* ⏁ *In-room: no a/c, Internet. In-hotel: restaurant, room service, pool, laundry facilities, public Internet* ⊟ *AE, D, MC, V.*

10

a/c, Internet. In-hotel: restaurant, room service, pool, laundry facilities, public Internet =AE, D, MC, V.

$$ RENTAL **Moloka'i Shores.** Some of the units in this oceanfront, three-story condominium complex have a view of the water. One-bedroom, one-bath units or two-bedroom, two-bath units all have full kitchens and furnished lānai, which look out on 4 acres of lawn. There's a great view of Lāna'i in the distance and a chance to see whales in season. **Pros:** convenient location; some units upgraded; near water. **Cons:** uninspiring basic accommodations; fussy cancellation policy ⊠*1000 Kamehameha V Hwy., Kaunakakai* ☎*808/553–5954 or 800/535–0085* ⊕*www.marcresorts.com* ◄*100 units* ⌂*In-room: no a/c, kitchen. In-hotel: pool, laundry facilities* =AE, D, MC, V.

$ RENTAL **Wavecrest.** This oceanfront condominium complex is convenient if you want to explore the east side of the island—it's 13 mi east of Kaunakakai. Individually decorated one- and two-bedroom units have full kitchens. Each has a furnished lānai, some with views of Maui and Lāna'i. Be sure to ask for an updated unit when you reserve. The 5-acre oceanfront property has access to a beautiful reef, excellent snorkeling and kayaking, and an oceanfront pool with covered barbecue. **Pros:** convenient location for divers; good value; nicely maintained grounds. **Cons:** amenities vary as each unit is individually owned; far from shopping; overlooks channel and can get windy. ⊠*Rte. 450 near mile marker 13* ⌂*Moloka'i Vacation Rentals, Box 1979, Kaunakakai 96748* ☎*800/367–2984 or 808/553–8334* ⊕*www.molokai-vacation-rental.net* ◄*126 units* ⌂*In-room: no a/c, kitchen. In-hotel: tennis courts, pool, beachfront* =AE, MC, V.

EAST MOLOKA'I

$ RENTAL **Pu'u O Hoku Ranch.** At the east end of Moloka'i, near mile marker 25, lie these three ocean-view accommodations, on 14,000 isolated acres of pastures and forest. This is a remote and serene location for people who want to get away or meet in a retreat atmosphere. One country cottage has two bedrooms, basic wicker furnishings, and *lau hala* (natural fiber) woven matting on the floors. An airy four-bedroom cottage has a small deck and a somewhat Balinese air. For large groups—family reunions, for example—the Ranch has a lodge with 11 rooms, 9 bathrooms, and a large kitchen. The full lodge goes for $1,250 nightly (rooms are not available on an individual basis). **Pros:** ideal for large groups; authentic working organic ranch; great hiking. **Cons:** on remote east end of island; rooms in the main lodge cannot be individually rented; road to property is narrow and winding. ⊠*Rte. 450, Kaunakakai* ☎*808/558–8109* ⊕*www.*

puuohoku.com ⏎1 2-bedroom cottage, 1 4-bedroom cottage, 11 rooms *in lodge* ⚿*In-room: no a/c, kitchen. In-hotel: pool* ▭MC, V.

MOLOKA'I ESSENTIALS

TRANSPORTATION

AIR TRAVEL

If you're flying in from the mainland United States or one of the neighbor islands, you must first make a stop in Honolulu. From there, it's a 25-minute trip to Moloka'i.

AIRPORTS Moloka'i's transportation hub is Ho'olehua Airport, a tiny airstrip 8 mi west of Kaunakakai and about 18 mi east of Maunaloa. An even smaller airstrip serves the little community of Kalaupapa on the north shore.

Information Ho'olehua Airport (☎*808/567–6140*). **Kalaupapa Airfield** (☎*808/567–6331*).

CARRIERS Three commercial airlines provide daily flights between Moloka'i and O'ahu in turboprop aircraft. If you fly into the airstrip at Kalaupapa, you must book a ground tour with Damien Tours before you depart. Island Air and go! Airlines fly from Honolulu to Ho'olehua and Pacific Wings flies from Honolulu to Kalaupapa, and from Ho'olehua to Kalaupapa.

Contacts Damien Tours (☎*808/567–6171*). **go! Airlines** (☎*888/435–9462* ⊕*www.iflygo.com*). **Island Air** (☎*800/652–6541* ⊕*www.islandair.com*). **Pacific Wings** (☎*808/873–0877 or 888/575–4546* ⊕*www.pacificwings.com*).

GROUND TRANSPOR-TATION From Ho'olehua Airport, it takes about 10 minutes to reach Kaunakakai and 25 minutes to reach the west end of the island by car. There's no public bus.

A taxi will cost about $28 from the airport to Kaunakakai with Hele Mai Taxi.

Shuttle service for two passengers costs about $18 from Ho'olehua Airport to Kaunakakai. For shuttle service, call Moloka'i Off-Road Tours and Taxi or Moloka'i Outdoors. Keep in mind, however, that it's difficult to visit the island without a rental car.

Contacts Hele Mai Taxi(☎*808/336–0967 or 808/553–5700*). **Moloka'i Off-Road Tours and Taxi** (☎*808/553–3369*). **Moloka'i Outdoors** (☎*808/553–4477 or 877/553–4477* ⊕*www.molokai-outdoors.com*).

CAR TRAVEL

If you want to explore Moloka'i from one end to the other, you must rent a car. With just a few main roads to choose from, it's a snap to drive around here.

The gas stations are in Kaunakakai. When you park your car, be sure to lock it—thefts do occur. All front-seat occupants and back-seat passengers under the age of 18 must wear seat belts; violators risk a $92 fine. Children under eight must ride in a federally approved child passenger-restraint device, easily leased at the rental agency. Ask your rental agent for a free *Moloka'i Drive Guide.*

10

Alamo maintains a counter at Ho'olehua Airport. Expect to pay $40 to $50 per day for a standard compact and $50 to $60 for a midsize car. Rates are seasonal and may run higher during the peak winter months. ■ TIP→ **Make arrangements in advance because there may not be cars available when you walk in.** If you're flying on a commercial airliner, see whether fly-drive package deals are available—you might luck out and find a less-expensive rate. Hotels and outfitters might also offer packages.

Locally owned Island Kine Rent-a-Car offers airport or hotel pickup and sticks to one rate year-round for vehicles in a broad spectrum from two- and four-wheel drives to 11-passenger vans. Be sure to check the vehicle before departing the agency; there is a $75 surcharge for taking a four-wheel-drive vehicle off-road.

Major Agencies Alamo (☎877/222–9075 ⊕ www.alamo.com).

Local Agency Island Kine Rent-a-Car (☎808/553–5242 or 866/527–7368 ⊕ www.molokai-car-rental.com).

FERRY TRAVEL

The Moloka'i Ferry crosses the channel every day between Lahaina (Maui) and Kaunakakai, making it easy for West Maui visitors to put Moloka'i on their itineraries. Keep in mind that the ferry is an older vessel that has had some mechanical difficulties in the past, and the crossing can be very rough in strong trade-wind weather, especially on the return trip. The 1½-hour trip takes passengers but not cars, so arrange ahead of time for a car rental or tour at the arrival point.

Contact Moloka'i Ferry (☎808/661–3392 or 800/275–6969 ⊕ www.molokai ferry.com).

CONTACTS AND RESOURCES

EMERGENCIES

Round-the-clock medical attention is available at Moloka'i General Hospital. Severe cases or emergencies are often airlifted to Honolulu.

Emergency Services Ambulance and general emergencies (☎911). **Coast Guard** (☎808/552–6458 on O'ahu). **Fire** (☎808/553–5601 in Kaunakakai, 808/567–6525 at Ho'olehua Airport). **Police** (☎808/553–5355).

Hospital Moloka'i General Hospital (✉280A Puali St., Kaunakakai ☎808/ 553–5331).

VISITOR INFORMATION

There's tourist information in kiosks and stands at the airport in Ho'olehua or at the Moloka'i Visitors Association. The association has a brochure that lists a number of activity vendors, accommodations, and places to eat. Call them for a copy before you leave home; they are very helpful and can also advise you about specific locations and sites. Be sure to book all activities well in advance because not every activity is available every day. Plan ahead and you will have a happier visit.

Information Maui Visitors Bureau (⊕ On Maui: 1727 Wili Pa Loop, Wailuku 96793 ☎808/244–3530 ⊕ www.visitmaui.com). **Moloka'i Visitors Association** (✉12 Kamo'i St., Suite 200, Kaunakakai 96748 ☎808/553–3876 or 800/800–6367 ⊕ molokai-hawaii.com).

Lāna'i

WORD OF MOUTH

"The island is full of charm—away from any type of commercialism. If you need to relax this is your place. The beaches on Lāna'i are wonderful. If you end up on the northwest side of the island you can have a pristine couple of miles of beach for yourself. Quite a feeling you won't get anywhere else."

—ARIC

WELCOME TO LĀNA'I

TOP REASONS TO GO

★ **Seclusion and Serenity:** Lāna'i is small: local motion is slow motion. Get into the spirit and go home rested instead of exhausted.

★ **Garden of the Gods:** Walk amid the eerie red-rock spires that ancient Hawaiians believed to be a sacred spot. The ocean views are magnificent, too; sunset is a good time to visit.

★ **A Dive at Cathedrals:** Explore underwater pinnacle formations and mysterious caverns lighted by shimmering rays of light.

★ **Dole Park:** Hang out in the shade of the Cook pines in Lāna'i City and talk story with the locals for a taste of old-time Hawai'i.

★ **Hit the water at Hulopo'e Beach:** This beach may have it all; good swimming, a shady park for perfect picnicking, great reefs for snorkeling, and sometimes plenty of spinner dolphins.

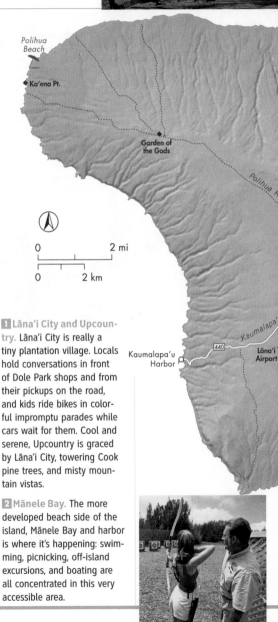

1 **Lāna'i City and Upcountry.** Lāna'i City is really a tiny plantation village. Locals hold conversations in front of Dole Park shops and from their pickups on the road, and kids ride bikes in colorful impromptu parades while cars wait for them. Cool and serene, Upcountry is graced by Lāna'i City, towering Cook pine trees, and misty mountain vistas.

2 **Mānele Bay.** The more developed beach side of the island, Mānele Bay and harbor is where it's happening: swimming, picnicking, off-island excursions, and boating are all concentrated in this very accessible area.

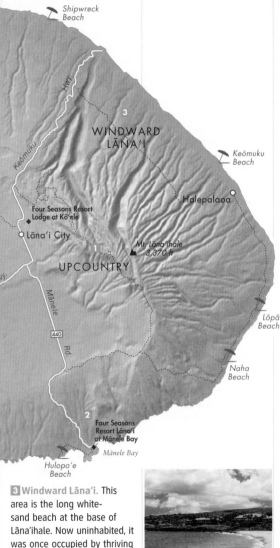

GETTING ORIENTED

Unlike the other Hawaiian islands with their tropical splendors, Lānaʻi looks like a desert: kiawe trees right out of Africa, red-dirt roads that glow molten at sunset, and a deep blue sea that literally leads to Tahiti. Lānaʻihale (house of Lānaʻi), the mountain that bisects the island, is carved into deep canyons by rain and wind on the windward side, and the drier leeward side slopes gently to the sea, where waves pound against surf-carved cliffs.

3 Windward Lānaʻi. This area is the long white-sand beach at the base of Lānaʻihale. Now uninhabited, it was once occupied by thriving Hawaiian fishing villages and a sugarcane plantation.

LĀNA'I PLANNER

Navigating Without Signs

Lāna'i has no traffic, no traffic lights, and only three paved roads. Bring along a good topographical map, study it, and keep in mind your directions. Stop from time to time and refind landmarks and gauge your progress. Distance is better measured in the condition of the road than in miles. Watch out for other jeep drivers who also don't know where they are. Never drive to the edge of lava cliffs, as rock can give way under you. ■TIP➔ Directions on the island are often given as mauka (toward the mountains) and makai (toward the ocean).

Renting a Car

Renting a four-wheel-drive vehicle is expensive but almost essential to get beyond the resorts. There are only 30 mi of paved road on the island. The rest of your driving takes place on bumpy, muddy, secondary roads, which generally aren't marked. Make reservations far in advance, because Lāna'i's fleet of vehicles is limited. If you're staying at the island's hotels, a convenient shuttle bus can take you from the beach to Upcountry.

Timing Is Everything

Whales are seen off Lāna'i's shores from December through April. A Pineapple Festival on the July 4 Saturday in Dole Park features local food, Hawaiian entertainment, a pineapple-eating and -cooking contest, and fireworks. Buddhists hold their annual outdoor Obon Festival honoring departed ancestors with joyous dancing, food booths, and taiko drumming in early July. Lāna'i celebrates the statewide Aloha Festivals in mid-October with a hometown parade, car contests, more food, and more music. Beware hunting season weekends—from mid-February through mid-May, and mid-July through mid-October.

Dining and Lodging on Lāna'i

Although Lāna'i has a somewhat wide range of choices for dining, from simple plate-lunch local eateries to fancy upscale gourmet resort restaurants, the range of lodgings is limited. Essentially there are only three options to choose from: the two Four Seasons Resorts Lāna'i (at Mānele Bay and Upcountry at the Lodge at Kō'ele), and the older Hotel Lāna'i. Camping at Hulopo'e Bay is another option for stays of three nights or less but is not practical for most travelers.

Will It Rain?

As higher mountains on Maui capture the trade-wind clouds, Lāna'i receives little rainfall and has a desert ecology. It's always warmer at the beach and can get cool or even cold (by Hawaiian standards) Upcountry. Consider the wind direction when planning your day. If it's blowing a gale on the windward beaches, head for the beach at Hulopo'e or check out Garden of the Gods. Overcast days, when the wind stops or comes lightly from the southwest, are common in whale season. Try a whale-watching trip or the windward beaches.

By Joana
Varawa

With no traffic or traffic lights and miles of open space, Lāna'i seems lost in time, and that can be a good thing. Small (141 square mi) and sparsely populated, it is the smallest inhabited Hawaiian Island and has just 3,500 residents, most of them living Upcountry.

Though it may seem a world away, Lāna'i is separated from Maui and Moloka'i by two narrow channels, and is easily accessed by boat from either island. The two resorts on the island are run by the Four Seasons. If you yearn for a beach with amenities, a luxury resort, and golf course, the Four Seasons Resort Lāna'i at Mānele Bay beckons from the shoreline. Upcountry, the luxurious Four Seasons Resort Lodge at Kō'ele provides cooler pleasures. This leaves the rest of the 100,000-acre island open to explore.

FLORA AND FAUNA

Lāna'i bucks the "tropical" trend of the other Hawaiian Islands with African kiawe trees, Cook pines, and eucalyptus in place of palm trees, and deep blue sea where you might expect shallow turquoise bays. Abandoned pineapple fields are overgrown with drought-resistant grasses, Christmas berry, and lantana; native plants, a'ali'i and 'ilima, are found in uncultivated areas. Axis deer from India dominate the ridges, and wild turkeys lumber around the resorts. Whales can be seen December through April, and a family of resident spinner dolphins drops in regularly at Hulopo'e Bay.

ON LĀNA'I TODAY

Despite its fancy resorts, Lāna'i still has that sleepy old Hawai'i feel. Residents are a mix of just about everything—Hawaiian/Chinese/German/Portuguese/Filipino/Japanese/French/Puerto Rican/English/Norwegian, you name it. The plantation was divided into ethnic camps, which helped retain cultural cuisines. Potluck dinners feature sashimi, Portuguese bean soup, *laulau* (morsels of pork, chicken, butterfish, or other ingredients wrapped with young taro shoots in tī leaves), potato salad, teriyaki steak, chicken *hekka* (a gingery Japanese chicken stir-fry), and Jell-O. The local language is pidgin, a mix of words as complicated and rich as the food. In recent years, David Murdock's plan to pay for the resorts by selling expensive homes next to them has met with opposition from locals.

THE GHOSTS OF LĀNA'I

Lāna'i has a reputation for being haunted (at one time by "cannibal spirits") and evidence abounds: a mysterious purple *lehua* (an evergreen tree that normally produces red flowers) at Keahialoa; the crying of a ghost chicken at Kamoa; Pohaku O, a rock that calls at twilight; and remote spots where cars mysteriously stall, and lights are seen at night. Tradition has it that Pu'u Pehe (an offshore sea stack) was a child who spoke from the womb, demanding *awa* root. A later story claims it is the grave of a woman drowned in a cave at the nearby cliffs. Hawaiians believe that places have *mana* (spiritual power), and Lāna'i is far from an exception.

EXPLORING LĀNA'I

Lāna'i has an ideal climate year-round, hot and sunny at the sea and a few delicious degrees cooler Upcountry. In Lāna'i City, the nights and mornings can be almost chilly when a mystic fog or harsh trade winds settle in. Winter months are known for *slightly* rougher weather—periodic rain showers and higher surf.

You can easily explore Lāna'i City and the island's two resorts without a car; just hop on the hourly shuttle. To access the rest of this untamed island, you'll need to rent a four-wheel-drive vehicle. Take a map, be sure you have a full tank, and bring a snack and plenty of water. Ask the rental agency or your hotel's concierge about road conditions before you set out. If the roads are impassable (as they often are after heavy rains), you may be able to negotiate a refund for your rental car. The main road on Lāna'i, Route 440, refers to both Kaumalapau Highway and Mānele Road.

LĀNA'I CITY, GARDEN OF THE GODS, AND MĀNELE BAY

Pineapples once blanketed the Pālāwai, the great basin south of Lāna'i City. Before that it was a vast dryland forest; now most of it is fenced-in pasture or a game-bird reserve, and can only be viewed from the Mānele Road. Although it looks like a volcanic crater, it isn't. Some say that the name Pālāwai is descriptive of the mist that sometimes fills the basin at dawn and looks like a huge shining lake.

The area northwest of Lāna'i City is wild; the Garden of the Gods is one of its highlights.

TOP ATTRACTIONS

Fodor'sChoice
★ **Garden of the Gods.** This preternatural plateau is scattered with boulders of different sizes, shapes, and colors, the products of a million years of wind erosion. Time your visit for sunset, when the rocks begin to glow—from rich red to purple—and the fiery globe sinks to the horizon. Magnificent views of the Pacific Ocean, Moloka'i, and, on clear days, O'ahu provide the perfect backdrop for photographs.

> **WORD OF MOUTH**
>
> "On Lāna'i, we found the dirt road to the Garden of the Gods, with further journey on to the isolated Polihua Beach, to be quite scenic and the most extreme legal off-roading experience in Hawai'i." –JohnD

The ancient Hawaiians shunned Lāna'i for hundreds of years, believing the island was the inviolable home of spirits. Standing beside the oxide-red rock spires of this strange, raw landscape, you might be tempted to believe the same. This lunar savanna still has a decidedly eerie edge, but the shadows disappearing on the horizon are those of mouflon sheep and axis deer, not the fearsome spirits of lore. According to tradition, Kawelo, a Hawaiian priest, kept a perpetual fire burning on an altar

You need a four-wheel-drive to explore the eroded rocks of the Garden of the Gods.

at the Garden of the Gods, in sight of the island of Moloka'i. As long as the fire burned, prosperity was assured for the people of Lāna'i. Kawelo was killed by a rival priest on Moloka'i and the fire went out. Keahikawelo, the fire of kawelo, is the presumed site of the altar. ⊠6 *mi north of Lāna'i City* ✛ *From Stables at Kō'ele, follow dirt road through pasture, turn right at crossroad marked by carved boulder, head through abandoned fields and ironwood forest to open red-dirt area marked by a carved boulder.*

Ka Lokahi o Ka Mālamalama Church. This picturesque church was built in 1938 to provide services for Lāna'i's growing population—for many people, the only other Hawaiian church, in coastal Keōmuku, was too far away. A classic structure of preplantation days, the church had to be moved from its original Lāna'i Ranch location when the Lodge at Kō'ele was built. Sunday services are still held, in Hawaiian and English; visitors are welcome, but are requested to attend quietly. ⊠*Left of entrance to Four Seasons Resort Lodge at Kō'ele.*

Kānepu'u Preserve. Kānepu'u is the largest example in Hawai'i of a rare native dryland forest characterized by Hawaiian sandalwood, olive, and ebony trees. Thanks to landowners Castle & Cooke Resorts, the 590-acre remnant forest is protected from the axis deer and mouflon sheep that graze on the landscape beyond its fence. More than 45 native plant species, including *na'u*, the endangered Hawaiian gardenia, can be seen here. A short self-guided loop trail, with eight signs illustrated by local artist Wendell Kaho'ohalahala, reveals this ecosystem's beauty and the challenges it faces. ⊠*Polihua Rd., 4.8 mi north of Lāna'i City.*

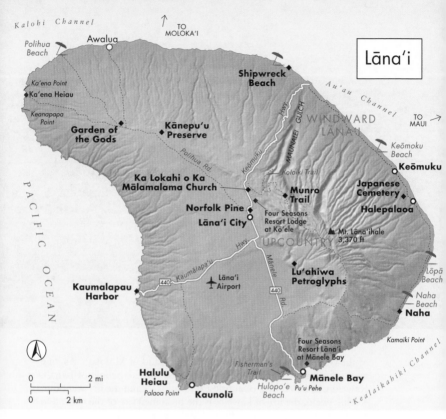

Lāna'i

Kaumalapau Harbor. Built in 1926 by the Hawaiian Pineapple Company, which later became Dole, this is Lāna'i's principal commercial seaport. The cliffs that flank the western shore are as much as 1,000 feet tall. Water activities aren't allowed here, but it's a dramatic sunset spot. The harbor is closed to visitors on barge days: Wednesday, Thursday, and Friday. ⊠ *Western terminus of Hwy. 440 (Kaumalapau Hwy.). From Lāna'i City turn right and follow Kaumalapau Hwy. west as far as it goes.*

Lāna'i City. This tidy plantation town, built in 1924 by Jim Dole, is home to old-time residents, recently arrived resort workers, and second-home owners, and is slowly changing from a quiet rural village to a busy little town. A simple grid of roads here is lined with stately Cook pines and all the basic services a person might need. The pace is slow and the people are friendly. **Dole Park,** in the center of Lāna'i City, is surrounded by small shops and restaurants and is a favorite spot among locals for sitting, strolling, and talking story. Visit the **Lāna'i Arts & Cultural Center** to get a glimpse of this island's creative abundance. ⊠ *339 7th Ave.*

Lu'ahiwa Petroglyphs. On a steep slope overlooking the Pālāwai Basin are 34 boulders with carvings. Drawn in a mixture of styles dating to the late 1700s and early 1800s, the simple stick figures depict animals, people, and mythic beings. A nearby *heiau,* or temple, no longer visible, was used to summon the rains and was dedicated to the god Kāne. Do not draw on or deface the carvings, and do not add to the collection. ✉ *From Lāna'i City turn left on Hwy. 440 (Mānele Rd.) and continue to first dirt road on your left. Follow dirt road along fields 1.2 mi; do not go left uphill but continue straight and when you see boulders on hillside, park and walk up to petroglyphs.*

Mānele Bay. The site of a Hawaiian village dating from AD 900, Mānele Bay is flanked by lava cliffs hundreds of feet high. Though included in a Marine Life Conservation District, it's the island's only public boat harbor and was the location of most postcontact shipping until Kaumalapau Harbor was built in 1926. The ferries to and from Maui and Ma'alea pull in here. Public restrooms, a small café, water, and picnic tables make it a busy pit stop—you can watch the boating activity as you rest and refuel.

Just offshore to the west is **Pu'u Pehe.** Often called Sweetheart Rock, the isolated 80-foot-high islet carries a sad Hawaiian legend that is probably not true. The rock is said to be named after Pehe, a woman so beautiful that her husband, afraid that others would steal her away, kept her hidden in a sea cave. One day, while Pehe was alone, the surf surged into the cave and she drowned. Her grief-stricken husband buried her on the summit of this rock and then jumped to his own death. A more authentic, if less romantic, story is that the enclosure on the summit is a shrine to birds, built by bird-catchers. Archaeological investigation has revealed that the enclosure was not a burial place. ✉ *From Lāna'i City follow Hwy. 440 (Mānele Rd.) 9 mi south to bottom of hill and look for large sign marking harbor on your left.*

WORTH NOTING

Halulu Heiau. The well-preserved remains of an impressive *heiau* (temple) at Kaunolū village, which was actively used by Lāna'i's earliest residents, attest to this spot's sacred history. As late as 1810, this hilltop temple was considered a place of refuge, where those who had broken *kapu* (taboos) were forgiven and where women and children could find safety in times of war. If you explore the area, be respectful; take nothing with you and leave nothing behind. This place is hard to find, so get someone to mark a map for you. The road is alternately rocky, sandy, and soft at the bottom. ✉ *From Lāna'i City follow Hwy. 440 (Kaumalapau Hwy.) west toward Kaumalapau Harbor. Pass airport, then look for carved boulder on hill on your left. Turn left on dirt road, follow it 3 mi to another carved boulder, turn right then head downhill.*

Kaunolū. Close to the island's highest cliffs, Kaunolū was once a prosperous fishing village. This important archaeological site includes a major *heiau* (temple), terraces, stone floors, and house platforms. The impressive 90-foot drop to the ocean through a gap in the lava rock is called **Kahekili's Leap.** Warriors would make the dangerous jump into the shallow 12 feet of water below to show their courage. The road is very rocky then gets sandy at the bottom. ✉ *From Lāna'i City follow Hwy. 440 (Kaumalapau Hwy.) west past the airport turnoff; at carved boulder on your left on hill, turn left onto an unmarked dirt road; continue 3 mi until you reach the second carved boulder and then go right (makai [toward the ocean]) 3 mi to village.*

Lāna'i Culture & Heritage Center. This small, carefully arranged, historical museum features artifacts and photographs from Lāna'i's varied and rich history. Plantation-era clothing and tools, precious feather lei, stone adzes and poi pounders, ranch memorabilia, old maps, and family portraits combine to give you a good idea of the history of the island and its people. Postcards,

maps, books, and pamphlets for sale. The friendly staff can orient you to the island's historical sites and provide directions. ⊠ *730 Lana'i Ave., Lāna'i City* ☎ *808/565–7177* ⊕ *www.lanaichc.org.*

Norfolk pine. More than 160 feet high, this majestic pine tree was planted here, at the former site of the manager's house, in 1875. Almost 30 years later, George Munro, then the ranch manager, would observe how, in foggy weather, water collected on its foliage, forming a natural rain. This fog drip led Munro to supervise the planting of Cook pines along the ridge of Lāna'ihale and throughout the town in order to add to the island's water supply. ⊠ *Entrance of Four Seasons Resort Lodge at Kō'ele, 1 Keōmuku Hwy., Lāna'i City.*

WINDWARD LĀNA'I

The eastern section of Lāna'i is wild and untouched. An inaccessible *heiau,* or temple, is the only trace of human habitation, with the exception of rocks and boulders marking old shrines, and trails. Four-wheel drive is a must to explore this side of the isle, and be prepared for hot, rough conditions. Hawaiians request that you not stack or disturb rocks. Pack a picnic lunch and bring plenty of drinking water.

TOP ATTRACTIONS

★ **Munro Trail.** This 12.8-mi jeep trail along a fern- and pine-clad narrow ridge was named after George Munro, manager of the Lāna'i Ranch Co., who began a reforestation program in the 1950s to restore the island's much-needed watershed. The trail climbs **Lāna'ihale** (House of Lāna'i), which, at 3,370 feet, is the island's highest point; on clear days you'll be treated to a panorama of canyons and almost all of the Hawaiian Islands. ■ TIP➔ The one-way road gets very muddy, and trade winds can be strong. A sheer drop-off in some sections requires an attentive driver. Keep an eye out for hikers along the way. You can also hike the Munro Trail *(see Golf, Hiking & Outdoor Activities later in this chapter),* though it's a difficult trek: it's steep, the ground is uneven, and there's no water. ⊠ *From Four Seasons Resort Lodge at Kō'ele head north on Hwy. 440 (Keōmuku Hwy.) for 1¼ mi, then turn right onto Cemetery Rd. and continue straight, passing cemetery on right.*

★ **Shipwreck Beach.** The rusting World War II tanker off this 8-mi stretch of sand adds just the right touch to an already photogenic beach. Maui is visible in the distance, and Moloka'i lies just across beautiful but unrelenting Kalohi Channel. Strong trade winds have propelled innocent vessels onto the reef since at least 1824, when the first shipwreck was recorded. Some believe that the unknown Navy oiler you see stranded today, however, was intentionally scuttled. To see petroglyphs of warriors and dogs decorating dark-red boulders, follow the painted rocks and signs at the end of the road south about 200 yards. ■TIP→ **The water is unsafe for swimming; stick to beachcombing.** ⊠ *Take Hwy. 440 (Keōmuku Hwy.) to its eastern terminus, then turn left on dirt road and continue north for 2 mi.*

WORTH NOTING

Halepalaoa. Named for the whale bones that once washed ashore here, Halepalaoa, or house of whale ivory, was the site of the wharf used by the short-lived Maunalei Sugar Company to ship cane in 1899. Some say the sugar company failed because the sacred stones of nearby **Kahe'a Heiau** were used for the construction of the cane railroad. Angry gods turned the drinking water salty, forcing the sugar company to close after just two years in 1901. The remains of the *heiau* (temple), once an important place of worship for the people of Lāna'i, are now difficult to find through the *kiawe* (mesquite) overgrowth. There's good public beach access here and clear shallow water for swimming, but no other facilities. ⊠ *Take Hwy. 440 (Keōmuku Hwy.) to its eastern terminus, then turn right on dirt road and continue south for 5½ mi.*

Japanese Cemetery. In 1899 sugar came to this side of Lāna'i. A plantation took up about 2,400 acres and seemed a profitable proposition, but that same year, disease wiped out the labor force. This authentic Buddhist shrine commemorates the Japanese workers who died. ⊠ *Take Hwy. 440 (Keōmuku Hwy.) to its eastern terminus, then turn right on dirt road and continue south for 6½ mi.*

Keōmuku. There's an eerie beauty about Keōmuku, with its faded memories and forgotten homesteads. During the late 19th century, this busy Lāna'i community of some 900 to 2,000 residents served as the headquarters of Maunalei Sugar Company. After the company failed, the land was used for ranching, but by 1954 the area lay abandoned. Its church, **Ka Lanakila O Ka Mālamalama,** was built in 1903. It has been partially restored by volunteers, and visitors often leave some small token, a shell or faded lei, as an offering. ⊠ *Take Hwy. 440 (Keōmuku Hwy.) to its eastern terminus, then turn right on dirt road and continue south for 5 mi.*

Naha. An ancient rock-walled fishpond—visible at low tide—lies here, where the sandy shoreline ends and the cliffs begin their rise along the island's shores. The beach is a frequent resource for local fisherfolk. ■TIP→ **Treacherous currents make this a dangerous place for swimming.** ⊠ *Take Hwy. 440 (Keōmuku Hwy.) to its eastern terminus, then turn right on dirt road and continue south for 11 mi. The shoreline dirt road ends here.*

The calm crescent of Hulopo'e Beach is perfect for swimming, snorkeling, or just relaxing.

BEACHES

Lāna'i offers miles of secluded white-sand beaches on its windward side, plus the moderately developed Hulopo'e Beach, which is adjacent to the Four Seasons Resort Lāna'i at Mānele Bay. Hulopo'e is accessible by car or hotel shuttle bus; to reach the windward beaches you'll need a four-wheel-drive vehicle. Offshore reef, rocks, and coral make swimming on the windward side problematic, but it's fun to splash around in the shallow water. Driving on the beach itself is illegal and can be dangerous. Beaches in this chapter are listed alphabetically.

Fodor's Choice ★ **Hulopo'e Beach.** A short stroll from the Four Seasons Resort Lāna'i at Mānele Bay, Hulopo'e is considered one of the best beaches in Hawai'i. The sparkling crescent of this Marine Life Conservation District beckons with calm waters safe for swimming almost year-round, great snorkeling reefs, tide pools, and, sometimes, spinner dolphins. A shady, grassy beach park is perfect for picnics. If the shore break is pounding, or if you see surfers riding big waves, stay out of the water. In the afternoons, watch Lāna'i High School students heave outrigger canoes down the steep shore break and race one another just offshore. ⊠ *From Lāna'i City turn left on Hwy. 440 (Mānele Rd.) and go 9 mi south to bottom of hill; turn right, road dead-ends at beach's parking lot* ☞ *Toilets, showers, picnic tables, grills, parking lot.*

Lōpā Beach. A popular surfing spot for locals, Lōpā is also an ancient fishpond. With majestic views of West Maui and Kaho'olawe, this remote, white-sand beach is a great place for a picnic. △ **Don't let the sight of surfers fool you: the channel's currents are too strong for swimming.**

⊠*East side of Lāna'i; take Hwy. 440 (Keōmuku Hwy.) to its eastern terminus, then turn right on dirt road and continue south for 7 mi* ☞*No facilities.*

★ **Polihua Beach.** This often-deserted beach gets a star for beauty with its long, wide stretch of white sand and clear views of Moloka'i. However, the dirt road to get here can be bad with deep, sandy places (when it rains it's impassable), and frequent high winds whip up sand and waves. ■TIP→ In addition, strong currents and a sudden drop in the ocean floor make swimming dangerous. On the more positive side, the northern end of the beach ends at a rocky lava cliff with some inter-

THE COASTAL ROAD

11

Road conditions can change overnight and become impassable due to rain in the uplands. Car-rental agencies should be able to give you updates before you hit the road. Many of the spur roads leading to the windward beaches from the coastal dirt road cross private property and are closed off by chains. Look for open spur roads with recent tire marks (a fairly good sign that they are safe to drive on). It's best to park on firm ground and walk in to avoid getting your car mired in the sand.

esting tide pools. Polihua is named after the sea turtles that lay their eggs in the sand. (Do not drive on the beach and endanger their nests.) Curiously, wild bees sometimes gather around your car for water at this beach. To get rid of them, put out water some place away from the car and wait a bit. ⊠*Windward Lāna'i, 11 mi north of Lāna'i City. Turn right on marked dirt road past Garden of the Gods* ☞*No facilities.*

Shipwreck Beach. Beachcombers come to this fairly accessible beach for shells and washed-up treasures; photographers for great shots of Moloka'i, just across the 9-mi-wide Kalohi Channel; and walkers for the long stretch of sand. It may still be possible to find glass-ball fishing floats but more common is waterborne debris from the Moloka'i channel. Kaiolohia, its Hawaiian name, is a favorite local diving spot. ■TIP→ An offshore reef and rocks in the water mean that it's not for swimmers, though you can play in the shallow water on the shoreline. ⊠*North shore, take Hwy. 440 (Keōmuku Hwy.) to its eastern terminus, then turn left on dirt road and continue north for 3 mi* ☞*No facilities.*

WATER SPORTS AND TOURS

DEEP-SEA FISHING

Some of the best sportfishing grounds in Maui County are off the southwest shoreline of Lāna'i. Pry your eyes open and go deep-sea fishing in the early morning, with departures at 6 or 6:30 AM from Mānele Harbor. Console yourself with the knowledge that Maui fishers have to leave an hour earlier to get to the same prime locations. Peak seasons are spring and summer, although good catches have been landed year-round. Mahimahi, *ono* (a mackerel-like fish; the word means "delicious" in Hawaiian), *'ahi* tuna, and marlin are prized catches and preferred eating.

BOATS AND CHARTERS

Fish-N-Tips. This roomy 36-foot Twin-Vee with tuna tower will get you and your family to the fishing grounds in comfort, and Captain Jason will do everything except reel in the big one for you. Plan on trolling along the south coast for *ono* (a mackerel-like fish) and around the point at Kaunolū for mahimahi or marlin. A trip to the offshore buoy often yields skipjack tuna or big *'ahi* (yellowfin tuna), and the captain and crew are always open to a bit of bottom fishing. Fishing gear, sodas, and water are included. A four-hour charter (six-passenger maximum) is $850; each additional hour costs $150. Guests can keep up to a third of all fish caught. Shared charters on Sunday are $200 per person. Book with the concierge at your resort or call directly. ☎808/565–7676.

KAYAKING

Lāna'i's southeast coast offers leisurely paddling and miles of scenic coastline with deserted beaches to haul up on inside the windward reef. Curious sea turtles and friendly manta rays may tag along your kayak for company. When the wind comes from the southwest, the windward coast is tranquil. Kayaking along the leeward cliffs is more demanding with rougher seas and strong currents. No kayaking is permitted in the Marine Conservation District at Hulopo'e Bay.

Early mornings tend to be calmer. The wind picks up as the day advances. Expect strong currents along all of the coasts. Experience on the water is advised, and knowing how to swim is essential. There is one other glitch: there are no kayak rentals on the island, so you need to book a tour or bring your own.

TOURS

Trilogy Oceansports Lāna'i. Join Trilogy's experienced ocean kayak guide for a full morning of kayaking inside the reef of Lāna'i's unspoiled coastline. This six-hour adventure costs $170 for adults and $85 for *keiki*, or kids (ages 3 to 5). Lunch, sodas, bottled water, and snacks are served. Reservations are required at least 24 hours in advance. Book with your hotel concierge or online. ☎888/628–4800 ⊕*www.sailtrilogy.com.*

RAFTING

If you're looking to get out on the water without fishing, Trilogy Oceansports Lāna'i offers comfortable marine mammal tours on a 32-foot, hard-bottom inflatable raft.

TOURS

Trilogy Oceansports Lāna'i. Trilogy offers a 1½-hour marine mammal watch on the *Manele Kai*, a 32-foot, jet-drive, hard-bottom inflatable raft. Cruise the coast and search for protected whales, dolphins, and monk seals. Sodas and bottled water provided. Cost is $80 for adults, $40 for *keiki* (kids) under 15. You can book trips through your hotel concierge, but try online first, where discounts are often available. ☎888/628–4800 ⊕*www.scubalanai.com.*

SCUBA DIVING

11

When you have a dive site such as Cathedrals—with eerie pinnacle formations and luminous caverns—it's no wonder that scuba-diving buffs consider exploring the waters off Lāna'i akin to having a religious experience.

BEST SPOTS

Just outside of Hulop'oe Bay, the boat dive site **Cathedrals** was named the best cavern dive site in the Pacific by *Skin Diver* magazine. Shimmering light makes the many openings in the caves look like stained-glass windows. A current generally keeps the water crystal clear, even if it's turbid outside. In these unearthly chambers, large *ulua* and small reef shark add to the adventure. **Sergeant Major Reef,** off Kamaiki Point, is named for big schools of yellow- and black-striped *manini* (sergeant major fish) that turn the rocks silvery as they feed. The site is made up of three parallel lava ridges, a cave, and an archway, with rippled sand valleys between the ridges. Depths range 15 to 50 feet.

EQUIPMENT, LESSONS, AND TOURS

Trilogy Oceansports Lāna'i. Serious divers should go for Trilogy's two-tank dive; location depends on the weather. You must be certified, so don't forget your documentation. The $213 fee includes a light breakfast of cinnamon rolls and coffee. Equipment, wet suits, accessories are included. Beginners (minimum age 12) can try a one-tank introductory dive for $101. You'll wade into Hulopo'e Bay with an instructor at your side; actual dive time is 20 to 30 minutes. Certified divers can choose a 35- to 40-minute wade-in dive at Hulopo'e, also for $101. ☎888/628–4800 ⊕*www.scubalanai.com.*

SNORKELING

Snorkeling is the easiest ocean sport available on the island, requiring nothing but a snorkel, mask, fins, and good sense. Borrow equipment from your hotel or purchase some in Lāna'i City if you didn't bring your own. Wait to enter the water until you are sure no big sets of waves are coming; and observe the activity of locals on the beach. If little kids are playing in the shore break, it's usually safe to enter. ■TIP→ **To get into the water safely, always swim in past the breakers, and in the comparative calm put on your fins, then mask and snorkel.**

BEST SPOTS

Hulopo'e Beach is an outstanding snorkeling destination. The bay is a State of Hawai'i Marine Conservation District and no spearfishing or diving is allowed. Schools of *manini* (sergeant major fish) feeding on the coral coat the rocks with flashing silver, and you can view *kala* (unicorn fish), *uhu* (parrot fish), and *papio* (*small* trevally) in all their rainbow colors. As you wade in from the sandy beach, the best snorkeling is toward the left. Beware of rocks and surging waves. When the resident spinner dolphins are in the bay, it's courteous to watch them from the shore. If swimmers and snorkelers go out, the dolphins may leave and be deprived of their necessary resting place. Another wade-in snorkel spot is just beyond the break wall at **Mānele Small Boat Harbor.** Enter over the rocks, just past the boat ramp. ■TIP→ **It's dangerous to enter if waves are breaking.**

EQUIPMENT, LESSONS, AND TOURS

Trilogy Oceansports Lāna'i. A 4½-hour blue-water snorkeling and adventure catamaran trip explores Lāna'i's pristine coastline with Trilogy's experienced captain and crew. The trip includes lessons, equipment, and deluxe lunch served onboard. Tours are offered Monday, Wednesday, Friday, and Saturday; cost is $181 for adults and $90 for kids 15 and under. You can book trips through your hotel concierge, but try online first, where discounts are often available. ☎888/628–4800 ⊕*www. sailtrilogy.com.*

SURFING

Surfing on Lāna'i can be truly enjoyable. Quality, not quantity, characterizes this isle's few breaks. Be considerate of the locals and they will be considerate of you—surfing takes the place of megaplex theaters and pool halls here, serving as one of the island's few recreational luxuries.

BEST SPOTS

Don't try to hang 10 at **Hulopo'e Bay** without watching the conditions for a while. When it "goes off," it's a tricky left-handed shore break that requires some skill. Huge summer south swells are for experts only. The southeast-facing breaks at **Lōpā Beach** are inviting for beginners. Give them a try in summer, when the swells roll in nice and easy.

EQUIPMENT AND LESSONS

Lāna'i Surf School. Nick and his wife Alex offer the only surf instruction on the island. Sign up for their "4X4 Safari"—a four-hour adventure that includes hard- or soft-top boards, snacks, and transportation to "secret spots." Nick, who was born on Lāna'i, is a former Hawai'i State Surfing Champion. Group lessons are $175 per person (minimum of two); private lessons are $200. Experienced riders can rent short- or long-boards overnight for $58 with a $125 deposit; stand-up paddles are available for an additional $25. ☎808/306–9837 ⊕*www.lanai surfsafari.com.*

GOLF, HIKING, AND OUTDOOR ACTIVITIES

BIKING

Many of the same red-dirt roads that invite hikers are excellent for biking, offering easy flat terrain and long clear views. There's only one hitch: you may have to bring your own bike, as there are no rentals or tours available for nonresort guests.

BEST SPOTS

A favorite biking route is along the fairly flat red-dirt road northward from Lāna'i City through the old pineapple fields to Garden of the Gods. Start your trip on Keōmuku Highway in town. Take a left just before the Lodge at Kō'ele's tennis courts, and then a right where the road ends at the fenced pasture, and continue on to the north end and the start of Polihua and Awalua dirt roads. If you're really hardy you could bike down to Polihua Beach and back, but it would be a serious all-day trip. In wet weather these roads turn to mud and are not advisable. Go in the early morning or late afternoon because the sun gets hot in the middle of the day. Take plenty of water, spare parts, and snacks.

For the exceptionally fit, it's possible to bike from town down the Keōmuku Highway to the windward beaches and back, or to bike the Munro Trail *(see Hiking)*. Experienced bikers also bike up and down the Mānele Highway from Mānele Bay to town.

CAMPING

Camping isn't encouraged outside Lāna'i's one official campground at Hulopo'e: the island is privately owned; islanders are keen on privacy; and, unless you know about local conditions, camping on the beach can be hazardous.

★ **Castle & Cooke Resorts Campground.** The inviting, grassy campground at Hulopo'e Beach has shade trees, clean restrooms, barbecue grills, beachside showers, and a big grass lawn, perfect for Frisbee. All of that *and* it happens to be a stone's throw from one of the best beaches in the state. (Camping on the beach itself is reserved for residents only.) Buy charcoal in Lāna'i City, as well as basic camping supplies and food. Cutting firewood is not allowed. It is possible to walk from Mānele Harbor to the campground. Call in advance; it's $20 for a permit, plus a $5 fee per person per night (three-night limit). ☎*808/565–3273 for permits and advance reservations.*

GOLF

Lāna'i has two resort courses that offer very different environments and challenges. They are so diverse that it's hard to believe they're on the same island, let alone just 20 minutes apart by resort shuttle.

The Challenge at Mānele. Designed by Jack Nicklaus (1993), this course sits right over the water of Hulopo'e Bay. Built on lava outcroppings, the course features three holes on cliffs that use the Pacific Ocean as a water hazard. The five-tee concept challenges the best golfers—tee shots over natural gorges and ravines must be precise. This unspoiled natural terrain is a stunning backdrop, and every hole offers ocean views. ⊠*Four Seasons Resort Lāna'i at Mānele Bay, Challenge Dr., Lāna'i City* ☎*808/565–2222* ⊕*www.fourseasons.com/manelebay/golf* ⚑*18 holes. 6310 yds. Par 72, slope 126. Green Fee: hotel guests $210, nonguests $225* ⚐*Facilities: Driving range, putting green, golf carts, rental clubs, pro-shop, lessons, restaurant, bar.*

The Experience at Kō'ele. This challenging Greg Norman (1991) layout begins at an elevation of 2,000 feet. The front 9 move dramatically through ravines wooded with pine, koa, and eucalyptus trees; seven lakes and streams with cascading waterfalls dot the course. No other course in Hawai'i offers a more incredible combination of highland terrain, inspired landscape architecture, and range of play challenges. ⊠ *Four Seasons Resort Lodge at Kō'ele, 1 Keōmuku Hwy., Lāna'i City* ☎*808/565–4653* ⊕*www.fourseasons.com/koele/golf* ⅄ *18 holes. 6310 yds. Par 72, slope 134. Green Fee: hotel guests $210, nonguests $225* ☞*Facilities: Driving range, putting green, golf carts, rental clubs, pro-shop, lessons, restaurant, bar.*

HIKING

Only 30 mi of Lāna'i's roads are paved. But red-dirt roads and trails, ideal for hiking, will take you to sweeping overlooks, isolated beaches, and shady forests. Don't be afraid to leave the road to follow deer trails, but make sure to keep your landmarks in clear sight so you can always retrace your steps. Or take a self-guided walk through Kāne Pu'u, Hawai'i's largest native dryland forest. You can explore the Munro Trail over Lāna'ihale with views of plunging canyons, or hike along an old, coastal fisherman trail or across Koloiki Ridge. Wear hiking shoes, a hat, and sunscreen, and carry plenty of water.

BEST SPOTS

Koloiki Ridge. This marked, moderate trail starts behind the Lodge at Kō'ele and takes you along the cool and shady Munro Trail to overlook the windward side, with impressive views of Maui, Moloka'i, Maunalei Valley, and Naio Gulch. The average time for the 5-mi round-trip is two hours. Bring snacks and water, and take your time. A map is available at Four Seasons Resort Lodge at Kō'ele.

Lāna'i Fisherman Trail. Local fishermen still use the Lāna'i Fisherman Trail to get to their favorite fishing spots. The trail takes about 1½ hours to hike and follows the rocky shoreline below the Four Seasons Resort at Lāna'i Mānele Bay, along cliffs bordering the golf course. Caves and tide pools beckon beneath you, but be careful climbing down. The marked trail entrance begins at the west end of Hulopo'e Beach. Keep your eyes open for spinner dolphins cavorting offshore and the silvery flash of fish feeding in the pools below you. The condition of the trail varies with weather and frequency of maintenance and can be slippery and rocky. Wear shoes, not flip-flops.

Munro Trail. This is the real thing: a strenuous 12.8-mi trek that begins behind the Four Seasons Resort Lodge at Kō'ele and follows the ridge of Lāna'ihale through the rain forest. The island's most demanding hike, it has an elevation gain of 1,400 feet and leads to a lookout at the island's highest point, Lāna'ihale. It's also a narrow dirt road; watch out for careening jeeps. The trail is named after George Munro, who supervised the planting of Cook pine trees and eucalyptus windbreaks. Mules used to wend their way up the mountain carrying the pine seedlings. Unless you arrange for someone to pick you up at the trail's end, you have a long boring hike back through the Pālāwai Basin to return to your starting point. The top is often cloud-shrouded and can be windy and muddy, so check conditions before you start.

Pu'u Pehe Trail. Beginning to the left (facing the ocean) of Hulopo'e Beach, this trail travels a short distance around the coastline, and then climbs up a sharp, rocky rise. At the top, you're level with the offshore stack of Puʻu Pehe and can overlook miles of coastline in both directions. The trail is not difficult, but it's hot and steep. Be aware of nesting endangered seabirds and don't approach their nests. ⚠ **Never approach the edge, as the cliff can easily give way.** The hiking is best in the early morning or late afternoon, and it's a perfect place to look for whales in season (December–April). Wear shoes; this is not a hike for sandals or slip-ons.

HORSEBACK RIDING

Stables at Kōʻele. The subtle beauty of the high country slowly reveals itself to horseback riders on the backcountry Paniolo rides. Two-hour adventures traverse leafy trails with scenic overlooks. Well-trained horses take riders of all skill levels (under 225 pounds, 9 years and older). Prices start at $95 for a two-hour group ride and go to $160 for a two-hour private ride. Lessons are also available. Book rides at the Four Seasons Resort Lodge at Kōʻele. ☏*808/565–4424.*

SPORTING CLAYS AND ARCHERY

★ **Lānaʻi Pine Sporting Clays and Archery Range.** Outstanding rustic terrain, challenging targets, and a well-stocked pro shop make this sporting-clays course top-flight in the expert's eyes. Sharpshooters can complete the meandering 14-station course, with the help of a golf cart, in 1½ hours. There are group tournaments, and even kids can enjoy skilled instruction at the archery range and compressed-air rifle gallery. The $50 archery introduction includes an amusing "pineapple challenge"— contestants are given five arrows with which to hit a paper pineapple target. The winner takes home a crystal pineapple as a nostalgic souvenir of the old Dole Plantation days. Guns and ammunition are provided with the lessons. Prices range from $80 to $150 depending on amount of ammunition and activity. ✉*Just past Cemetery Rd. on windward side of island, first left at sign on Hwy. 440 (Keōmuku Hwy.)* ☏*808/559–4600.*

SHOPPING

A miniforest of Cook pine trees in the center of Lānaʻi City surrounded by small shops and restaurants, Dole Park is the closest thing to a mall on Lānaʻi. Except for the high-end resort boutiques and pro-shops, it provides the island's only shopping. A morning or afternoon stroll around the park offers an eclectic selection of gifts and clothing, plus a chance to chat with residents. Friendly general stores are reminiscent of the 1920s, and new galleries and a boutique have original art and fashions for men, women, and children. The shops close Sunday and after 5 PM, except for the general stores, which are open a bit later.

ARTS AND CRAFTS

Dis ʻn Dat. This tiny, jungle-green shop packs in thousands of art, gift, and jewelry items in a minuscule space enlivened by a glittering crystal ceiling. Fanciful garden ornaments, serene Buddhas, and Asian antiques add to the charm. ⊠*418 8th St., Lāna'i City* ☎*808/565–9170* ⊕*www. disndatshop.com.*

Gifts with Aloha. Casual resort wear is sold alongside a great collection of Hawaiiana books and the work of local artists, including ceramic ware, *raku* (Japanese-style lead-glazed pottery), fine handblown glass, and watercolor prints. Look for a complete selection of Hawaiian music CDs and Lāna'i-designed Stone Shack shirts. ⊠*363 7th St., Lāna'i City* ☎*808/565–6589* ⊕*www.giftswithaloha.com.*

CLOTHING

Lāna'i Beach Walk. This small shop is crammed with a wide variety of styles and colors of the now indispensable "crocs," as well as colorful resort clothing, logo tee shirts, swimwear, and classy skirts and dresses. Tropical knickknacks and souvenirs complete the inventory. ⊠*850 Fraser Ave., Lāna'i City* ☎*808/565–9249.*

Local Gentry. This tiny, classy store has clothing for every need, from casual men's and women's beachwear to evening resort wear, shoes, jewelry, and hats. A selection of Lāna'i logo-wear is also available. Proprietor Jenna Gentry Majkus will mail your purchases for the cost of the postage, and can put you on her e-mail list for future fashion offerings. ⊠*363 7th St., Lāna'i City* ☎*808/565–9130.*

FOOD

Pine Isle Market. This is one of Lāna'i City's two markets, stocking everything from beach toys to cosmetics to canned vegetables. Staff is friendly and it's a great place to buy fresh fish. Look at the photos of famous local fish and fishermen opposite the beer case. Closed Sunday and during lunch hours from noon to 1:30 PM, Monday through Thursday. ⊠*356 8th St., Lāna'i City* ☎*808/565–6488.*

Richard's. Castle & Cooke Resorts has taken over this store from Richard Tamashiro, who founded it in 1946. Along with groceries, Richard's has camping gear, common household items, a good array of fine wines, and a few gourmet food items. ⊠*434 8th St., Lāna'i City* ☎*808/565–3780.*

Sergio's Oriental Store. Sergio's, the closest thing to a mini Costco on Lāna'i, has Filipino sweets and pastries; case-loads of sodas, water, and juices; family-size containers of condiments; and frozen fish and meat. Open 8 to 8 daily. ⊠*831-D Houston St., Lāna'i City* ☎*808/565–6900.*

GALLERIES

Jordanne Fine Art Studio. Take a piece of historic Lāna'i home: Jordanne Weinstein's affordable, whimsical portraits of rural island life and gold-leaf pineapple paintings make terrific souvenirs. Greeting cards and small prints complete the offerings. Stop into her bright studio just off of Dole Park, where she paints on-site. ⊠*850 Fraser Ave., Lāna'i City* ☎*808/563–0088* ⊕*www.jordannefineart.com.*

Lāna'i Art Center. Local artists practice and display their crafts at this dynamic center. Workshops in the pottery, photography, woodworking, and painting studios welcome visitors, and individual instruction may be arranged. The center's gift shop sells original art and unique

Lāna'i handicrafts. The art center sponsors occasional concerts and cultural events. Check with them for the schedule or visit the Web site. It's closed Sunday. ✉ *339 7th St., Lāna'i City* ☎ *808/565–7503* ⊕ *www.lanaiart.org.*

Mike Carroll Gallery. The dreamy, soft-focus oil paintings of resident painter Mike Carroll are showcased along with wood bowls and koa 'ukulele by Warren Osako, and fish-print paper tapestries by Joana Varawa. Local photographer Ron Gingerich, island artists Cheryl McElfresh and Billy O'Connell, and jeweler Susan Hunter are also featured. ✉ *443 7th St., Lāna'i City* ☎ *808/565–7122* ⊕ *www.mikecarroll gallery.com.*

GENERAL STORES

International Food and Clothing Center. You may not find everything the name implies, but this old-fashioned emporium does stock items for your everyday needs, from fishing gear to beer. It's a good place for last-minute camping supplies. It's closed Saturday. ✉ *833 'Ilima Ave., Lāna'i City* ☎ *808/565–6433.*

Lāna'i City Service. In addition to being Lāna'i's only gas station, auto-parts store, and car-rental operation, this outfit sells Hawaiian gift items, sundries, hot dogs and *manapua* (steamed buns with pork filling), T-shirts, beer, sodas, and bottled water in the **Plantation Store.** Open 6:30 AM to 8:30 PM daily for gas and sundries; auto-parts store open weekdays 7 AM to 4 PM. It's closed from noon to 1 PM. ✉ *1036 Lāna'i Ave., Lāna'i City* ☎ *808/565–7227.*

SPAS

If you're looking for rejuvenation, the whole island could be considered a spa, though the only spa facilities are at the Mānele Bay hotel or the Lodge at Kō'ele. For a quick polish in Lāna'i City, try one of the following spots. **Island Images** (☎ *808/565–7870*) offers hair care for men and women, pedicures, manicures, waxing, and threading. **Nita's In Style** (☎ *808/565–8082*) features hair-care services for men, women, and children.

Lodge at Kō'ele's Banyan Suite Spa. Located on the mezzanine of the Great Hall, this simple, serene spa offers a varied menu of massage treatments, including the new hot-shell treatment, Hawaiian Lomi Lomi, sports massage, and the Hehi Lani Royal Foot Treatment. Relax after your massage with herbal tea on the adjacent balcony, which offers great sunset views, or return to your room in a fluffy spa robe. Two tables accommodate couples and all massages are private. Open to non–resort guests with advance reservations. Massage services can also be enjoyed in the privacy of your room. ✉ *Four Seasons Resort Lodge at Kō'ele, 1 Keōmuku Hwy., Lāna'i City* ☎ *808/565–7300* ⊕ *www.fourseasons. com/koele/spa* ♒ *$150 50-min massage. Gym with: cardiovascular machines, free weights. Services: aromatherapy, hot-rock massage, guided stretching, reflexology.*

The Spa at Mānele. State-of-the-art pampering enlists a panoply of oils and unguents that would have pleased Cleopatra. The Spa After Hours

Experience relaxes you with private services including a neck and shoulder massage and a 50-minute treatment of your choice. Then melt down in the sauna or steam room, finish off with a scalp massage and light *pūpū* (snacks), and ooze out to your room. The *Ali'i* banana-coconut scrub and pineapple-citrus polish treatments have inspired their own cosmetic line. Massages in private *hale* (houses) in the courtyard gardens are available for singles or couples. A tropical fantasy mural, granite stone floors, eucalyptus steam rooms, and private cabanas set the scene for indulgence. ⊠*Four Seasons Resort Lāna'i at Mānele Bay, 1 Mānele Rd., Lāna'i City* ☎*808/565–2000* ⊕*www.fourseasons.com/manelebay/spa* ⌕*$145 50-min massage; $340 per person 2-hr Spa After Hours Experience (2-person minimum). Gym with: cardiovascular equipment, free weights. Services: aromatherapy, body wraps, facials, hair salon, hair care, mani/pedicures, reflexology, waxing. Classes and programs: aquaerobics, guided hikes, hula classes, personal training, tai chi, yoga.*

ENTERTAINMENT AND NIGHTLIFE

Lāna'i is certainly not known for its nightlife. Fewer than a handful of places stay open past 9 PM. At the resorts, excellent piano music or light live entertainment makes for a quiet, romantic evening. Another romantic alternative is star-watching from the beaches or watching the full moon rise in all its glory.

Four Seasons Resort Lāna'i at Mānele Bay. Hale Aheahe (House of Gentle Breezes), the classy open-air lounge with upscale *pūpū* (snacks) and complete bar, offers musical entertainment nightly from 5:30 to 9:30. Local musicians invite you to try your hula skills, and darts, pool, and shuffleboard are riotous fun. ☎*808/565–2000.*

Four Seasons Resort Lodge at Kō'ele. The cozy cocktail bar stays open until 11 PM. The lodge also features quiet piano music in its Great Hall every evening from 7 to 10, as well as special performances by well-known Hawaiian entertainers and local hula dancers. Sit fireside and enjoy a late-night cocktail and plan your next day's activities. ☎*808/565–4000.*

Hotel Lāna'i. A visit to the small, lively bar here is an opportunity to visit with locals and find out more about the island. Enjoy entertainment by Lāna'i musicians in the big green tent Saturday and Sunday nights. Last call is at 9:30. ☎*808/565–7211.*

Lāna'i Theater and Playhouse. This 153-seat, 1930s landmark theater was closed at this writing; call to check, however. ⊠*465 7th St., Lāna'i City* ☎*808/565–7500.*

SUNSET CRUISES

Trilogy Oceansports Lāna'i. On Tuesday, Thursday, and Saturday, Trilogy offers a Sunset Sail on a large catamaran, departing at either 3:45 (April–September), or 4:45 (October–March). This trip is perfect if you want to get out on the ocean and experience a relaxing time on the water. The two-hour sail includes hot and cold appetizers, soft drinks, and filtered water. You are encouraged to bring your own beer and wine and the crew will keep it cold for you. The sunset sail costs $106 for adults; $53 for children 15 and under. You can book trips through your hotel concierge, but try online first, where discounts are often available. ☎888/628–4800 ⊕ *www.scubalanai.com.*

WHERE TO EAT

Lāna'i's own version of Hawai'i regional cuisine (modern Hawaiian food) draws on the fresh bounty provided by local hunters and fishermen, combined with the skills of well-trained chefs. The upscale menus at the Lodge at Kō'ele and the Four Seasons Resort at Lāna'i Mānele Bay encompass European-inspired cuisine as well as innovative preparations of 'ahi, wild deer, and boar. Lāna'i City's eclectic ethnic fare runs from construction-worker-size local plate lunches to pizza and pesto pasta. ■TIP→ **Keep in mind that Lāna'i "City" is really just a small town; restaurants sometimes choose to close the kitchen early.**

WHAT IT COSTS					
	¢	$	$$	$$$	$$$$
RESTAURANTS	under $10	$10–$17	$18–$26	$27–$35	Over $35

Prices are for a main course at dinner.

MĀNELE BAY

$$
AMERICAN
✕ **The Challenge at Mānele Clubhouse.** This terraced restaurant has a stunning view of the legendary Pu'u Pehe offshore island, which only enhances its imaginative fare. Tuck into a Hulopo'e Bay prawn BLT, or the crispy battered fish-and-chips with Meyer lemon tartar sauce. The fish tacos are splendid and specialty drinks add to the informal fun. ⊠ *Four Seasons Resort Lāna'i at Mānele Bay, 1 Mānele Bay Rd., Lāna'i City* ☎808/565–2230 ▤ *AE, DC, MC, V* ⊗ *No dinner.*

> **FOOD WITH A VIEW**
>
> Don't miss lunch at the Challenge at Mānele clubhouse, overlooking Hulopo'e Bay. The view is spectacular. Palm trees frame a vista of the white-sand beach with the rocky headland of Pu'u Pehe (Sweetheart Rock) punctuating the luminous sky. You may also be rewarded with a perfect view of a visiting family of spinner dolphins resting in the transparent waters below.

$$$$
PACIFIC RIM
✕ **Four Seasons Hulopo'e Court.** Hulopo'e Court offers dinner and an extensive breakfast buffet in airy comfort. Retractable awnings shade the terrace, which overlooks the wide sweep of the bay. Inside, comfy upholstered chairs, cream walls, wood paneling, and modernized Hawaiian decor create an almost equally inviting backdrop. At breakfast, fresh-baked pastries and made-to-order omelets ensure your day will start well. For dinner, the selection of fresh local fish includes the catch of the day, miso-marinated mahimahi, and crispy whole Pacific snapper with stir-fry vegetables. Meat-eaters can try the grilled beef fillet or Kurobuta pork loin with

bok choy and kimchi fried rice; both are local favorites. The chocolate cake is near perfect and their coffee is excellent. ✉*Four Seasons Resort Lāna'i at Mānele Bay, 1 Mānele Bay Rd.,Lāna'i City* ☎*808/565–2290* ⏲*Reservations essential* ⊟*AE, DC, MC, V* ⊙*No lunch.*

$$$$ ✕**'Ihilani.** The fine dining room at the Four Seasons Resort Lāna'i at
ITALIAN Mānele Bay shimmers with crystal chandeliers and gleaming silver in a serene setting illuminated by floor-to-ceiling etched-glass doors. Executive chef Oliver Beckert offers an upscale version of Italian comfort food designed around classic meat and fish dishes. Homemade spinach gnocchi with marinara sauce, and *onaga* (red snapper) served alla puttanesca with artichoke puree and a spicy tomato and caper sauce, are good choices. Slow-braised osso buco with risotto Milanese, or chicken marsala with creamy goat cheese polenta will satisfy the most discriminating palates. Service is nonintrusive but attentive. ✉*Four Seasons Resort Lāna'i at Mānele Bay, 1 Mānele Bay Rd., Lāna'i City* ☎*808/565–2296* ⏲*Reservations essential* ⊟*AE, DC, MC, V* ⊙*No lunch.*

$$$$ ✕**The Ocean Grill Bar & Restaurant.** Poolside at the Four Seasons Resort
SEAFOOD Lāna'i at Mānele Bay, the Ocean Grill offers informal lunch and dinner in a splendid setting. The big umbrellas are cool and cheerful, and bamboo-inspired upholstered chairs in yellow and green are deliciously comfortable. If you're a coffee drinker, a Kona Cappuccino Freeze by the pool is a must. Favorite lunch items include the *kālua* (pit-roasted) pork and cheese quesadilla, or the 'ahi tuna *salade Niçoise* with fresh island greens. The dinner menu includes a combination of small and large plates that lean toward the healthy side. Try the wok-fried buckwheat noodles with plump tiger shrimp or lemongrass steamed *onaga* (red snapper) served with a refreshing carrot-miso vinaigrette. The view of Hulopo'e Bay is stunning and the service is Four Seasons' brand of cool aloha. ✉*Four Seasons Resort Lāna'i at Mānele Bay, 1 Mānele Bay Rd., Lāna'i City* ☎*808/565–2092* ⊟*AE, DC, MC, V.*

LĀNA'I CITY AND UPCOUNTRY

$ ✕**Blue Ginger Café.** Owners Joe and Georgia Abilay have made this
HAWAIIAN cheery place into a Lāna'i City institution with consistent, albeit simple, food. Locally inspired paintings and photos line the walls inside, while the town passes the outdoor tables in parade. For breakfast, try the Portuguese sausage omelet with rice or fresh pastries. Lunch selections range from burgers and pizza to Hawaiian staples such as saimin noodles or *musubi* (fried Spam wrapped in rice and seaweed). Try a shrimp stir-fry for dinner. ✉*409 7th St., Lāna'i City* ☎*808/565–6363* ⊟*No credit cards.*

$$$$ ✕**The Dining Room.** Reflecting the lodge's country-manor elegance, this
Fodor'sChoice peaceful and romantic octagonal restaurant is one of the best in the
★ state. Terra-cotta walls and soft peach lighting flatter everyone and inti-
HAWAIIAN mate tables are well spaced to allow for private conversations. Expanding on Hawaiian regional cuisine, the changing menu includes lava rock seared venison prepared table-side, succulent crispy *onaga* (red snapper) with Kona crab and leek fondue, and oven roasted Colorado lamb crusted with Provencale herbs and served with roasted baby artichokes. Start with a Big Island lobster savory crepe or a salad of organic island

greens with Meyer lemon vinaigrette, and finish with a warm raspberry soufflé (ordered in advance). A master sommelier provides exclusive wine pairings and the service is flawless. ⊠*Four Seasons Resort Lodge at Kōʻele, 1 Keōmuku Hwy., Lānaʻi City* ⌂*Box 631380, Lānaʻi City 96763* ☎*808/565–4580* ⚘*Reservations essential* ▤*AE, DC, MC, V* ☾*No lunch.*

$$
AMERICAN
✕**The Experience at Koʻele Clubhouse.** The clubhouse overlooks the emerald greens of the golf course, making this a pleasant spot for casual fare. Sit inside and watch sports on the TV, or on the terrace to enjoy the antics of lumbering wild turkey families. The grilled fresh-catch sandwich is accompanied by fries; the succulent hamburgers are the best on the island. Salads and sandwiches, beer and wine, soft drinks, and some not very inspiring desserts complete the menu. ⊠*Four Seasons Resort Lodge at Kōʻele, 1 Keōmuku Hwy.Lānaʻi City* ☎*808/565–4605* ▤*AE, DC, MC, V* ☾*No dinner.*

¢
HAWAIIAN
✕**565 Café.** Named after the oldest telephone prefix on Lānaʻi, this is a convenient stop for anything from pizza to a Pālāwai chicken-breast sandwich on fresh-baked focaccia. Make a quick stop for plate lunches or try a picnic *pūpū* (appetizer) platter of chicken *katsu* (Japanese-style breaded and fried chicken) to take along for the ride. If you need a helium balloon for a party, you can find that here, too. The patio and outdoor tables are kid-friendly, and an outdoor Saturday afternoon flea market adds to the quirkiness. ⊠*408 8th St., Lānaʻi City* ☎*808/565–6622* ▤*D, MC, V* ☾*Closed Sun.*

$$$$
AMERICAN
✕**Lānaʻi City Grille.** Simple white walls, local art, ceiling fans, and unobtrusive service provide the setting for a menu designed and supervised by celebrity chef Beverly Gannon. Try the pecan-crusted catch of the day, or the always-popular rotisserie chicken. The pan-seared Lānaʻi-caught venison has not traveled far from the wild. Although the menu is a bit on the heavy side for Hawaiʻi, the Grille is a pleasant alternative to the Four Seasons, and a lively gathering place for friends and family. ⊠*Hotel Lānaʻi, 828 Lānaʻi Ave., Lānaʻi City* ☎*808/565–4700* ⚘*Reservations essential* ▤*AE, MC, V.*

¢
CAFÉ
✕**Lānaʻi Coffee.** A block off Dole Park, this café offers a nice spot to sit outside, sip cappuccinos, and watch the slow-pace life of the town slip by. Bagels with lox, deli sandwiches, and pastries add to the caloric content, while blended espresso shakes and gourmet ice cream complete the old-world illusion. Local kids pile in after school. Caffeine-inspired specialty items make good gifts and souvenirs. ⊠*604 ʻIlima St., Lānaʻi City* ☎*808/565–6962* ☾*Closed Sun.*

$$
ITALIAN
✕**Pele's Other Garden.** This colorful little eatery is a deli and bistro all in one. For lunch, deli sandwiches or daily hot specials satisfy hearty appetites. At night the restaurant turns into an intimate tablecloth-dining bistro, complete with soft jazz music. A nice wine list enhances an Italian-inspired menu. Start with bruschetta, then choose from a selection of pasta dishes or pizzas. Designer beers and a mini sports bar add to the liveliness. ⊠*811 Houston St., at 8th St., Lānaʻi City* ☎*808/565–9628 or 888/764–3354* ⊕*www.pelesothergarden.com* ▤*AE, DC, MC, V.*

$$$$ ╳ **The Terrace.** Floor-to-ceiling glass doors open onto formal gardens
AMERICAN   and lovely vistas of the mist-clad mountains. Breakfast, lunch, and
dinner are served in an informal atmosphere with attentive service.
Try poached eggs on crab cakes to start the day and a grilled beef fillet
with Parmesan whipped potatoes to finish it. The soothing sounds of
the grand piano in the Great Hall in the evening complete the ambience. ⊠ *Four Seasons Resort Lodge at Kō'ele, 1 Keōmuku Hwy., Lāna'i
City* ☏ *808/565–4580* ⊟ *AE, DC, MC, V.*

WHERE TO STAY

Though Lāna'i has few properties, it does have a range of price options.
Four Seasons manages both the Lodge at Kō'ele and Four Seasons
Resort Lāna'i at Mānele Bay. Although the room rates are different,
guests can partake of all the resort amenities at both properties. If you're
on a budget, consider the Hotel Lāna'i.

House rentals give you a feel for everyday life on the island; ⊕www.
gohawaii.com has information. In hunting seasons, from mid-February through mid-May, and from mid-July through mid-October, most
private properties are booked way in advance. **Note:** Maui County
has regulations concerning vacation rentals; to avoid disappointment,
always contact the property manager or owner and ask if the accommodation has the proper permits and is in compliance with local laws.
You can also log onto the Maui County Web site (⊕www.co.maui.
hi.us), click on "Planning Department," and search for updated information on legal rentals.

WHAT IT COSTS					
	¢	$	$$	$$$	$$$$
HOTELS	under $100	$100–$180	$181–$260	$261–$340	over $340

Hotel prices are for two people in a double room in high season, including tax and service.
Condo price categories reflect studio and one-bedroom rates. Prices do not include 11.41%
tax.

$$$$ ⊡ **Four Seasons Resort Lāna'i at Mānele Bay.** This ornate resort overlook-
☾   ing Hulopo'e Bay combines Mediterranean and Asian architectural
Fodor'sChoice   elements: elaborate life-size paintings of Chinese court officials, gold
★   brocade warrior robes, and artifacts decorate the open-air lobbies.
RESORT   Courtyard gardens separate two-story guest-room buildings. Ground-
floor rooms are best—many open right up onto a lawn overlooking
Hulopo'e Beach—though spectacular coastline vantages are had just
about anywhere on the property. Adults can indulge in Evian spritzers
and massage by the pool while *keiki* (children) hunt for crabs and play
'ukulele. At night, everyone can meet for shuffleboard and darts in
Hale Ahe Ahe, the swank game room. A shuttle runs from the resort
to other destinations on Lāna'i every half hour during high season,
and every hour during low season. **Pros:** fitness center with ocean
views and daily classes; teens have their own center; friendly pool bar.
Cons: 20 minutes to town for shopping and restaurants; must rely on

Four Seasons Resort Lāna'i at Mānele Bay

Four Seasons Resort Lodge at Kō'ele

shuttle or rental car to leave property; ambience may seem stiff and formal to some. ⌂*Box 631380, 1 Mānele Bay Rd., Lāna'i City 96763* ☎*808/565–2000 or 800/321–4666* ⊕*www.fourseasons.com/manelebaya 215 rooms, 21 suites* ☐*In-room: safe, refrigerator, DVD, Internet. In-hotel: 4 restaurants, room service, bars, golf course, tennis courts, pool, gym, spa, children's programs (ages 5–12), laundry service, public Internet, no-smoking rooms* ☐*AE, DC, MC, V.*

$$$$
Fodor's Choice
★
RESORT
🏨 **Four Seasons Resort Lodge at Kō'ele.** In the highlands edging Lāna'i City, this grand country estate exudes luxury and quiet romance. Secluded by old pines, 1.5 mi of paths meander through formal gardens with a huge reflecting pond, a wedding gazebo, and an orchid greenhouse. Afternoon tea is served in front of the immense stone fireplaces beneath the high-beamed ceilings of the magnificent Great Hall for a fee of $29. The music room lounge is a relaxing haven after a day on the lodge's golf course or sporting-clays range. A long veranda, furnished with wicker lounge chairs, looks out over rolling green pastures toward spectacular sunsets. **Pros:** beautiful surroundings; impeccable service; walking distance to shops and restaurants in Lāna'i City. **Cons:** doesn't feel like Hawai'I; can get chilly at 1,700-foot elevation (especially in winter); not much to do in rainy weather. ⌂*Box 631380, 1 Keōmuku Hwy.Lāna'i City 96763* ☎*808/565–4000 or 800/321–4666* ⊕*www.fourseasons.com/koele* ☞*94 rooms, 8 suites* ☐*In-room: safe, refrigerator, Internet. In-hotel: 4 restaurants, room service, bar, golf course, tennis courts, pool, gym, bicycles, children's programs (ages 5–12), laundry service, no-smoking rooms* ☐*AE, DC, MC, V.*

$–$$
HOTEL
🏨 **Hotel Lāna'i.** Built in 1923 to house visiting pineapple executives, this 10-room inn was once the only accommodation on the island. The South Pacific–style rooms, with country quilts, white walls, ceiling fans, and bamboo shades make it seem like you're staying in someone's guest room. The two end rooms offer great views with porches overlooking the pine trees and Lāna'i City. The restaurant, the Lāna'i City Grille, has an intimate and well-stocked bar. A self-serve Continental breakfast with fresh-baked breads is served in the foyer and is included in the rate. **Pros:** friendly service; walking distance to town. **Cons:** rooms are a bit stark; noisy at times; no room phones; no activities. ✉*828 Lāna'i Ave., Lāna'i City* ☎*808/565–7211 or 800/795–7211* ⊕*www.hotellanai.com* ☞*10 rooms, 1 cottage* ☐*In-room: no a/c, no phone, no TV (some). In-hotel: restaurant, no-smoking rooms* ☐*AE, MC, V.*

LĀNA'I ESSENTIALS

TRANSPORTATION

AIR TRAVEL

Island Air is the only commercial airline serving Lāna'i City. Nonstop flights from O'ahu's Honolulu International Airport begin at $44 one-way, depending on availability. Traveling from other islands requires a stop in Honolulu.

The airport has a federal agricultural inspection station, so guests departing to the mainland can check luggage directly.

Information Island Air (☎ 800/652-6541 ⊕ www.islandair.com). **Lāna'i Airport** (☎ 808/565-6757).

GROUND TRANSPOR-TATION Lāna'i Airport is a 10-minute drive from Lāna'i City. If you're staying at the Hotel Lāna'i, the Four Seasons Resort Lodge at Kō'ele, or the Four Seasons Resort Lāna'i at Mānele Bay, you'll be met by a shuttle, which serves as transportation between the resorts and Lāna'i City. The one-time $36 per person fee buys you unlimited use of the shuttle for the length of your stay. See the resort receptionist at the airport. Dollar will arrange to pick you up if you're renting a jeep or minivan. Cost is $5 per person round-trip, and one person in your party rides for free. Call from the red courtesy phone at the airport.

CAR TRAVEL

There are only 30 mi of paved road on the island. Keōmuku Highway starts just past the Lodge at Kō'ele and runs north to Shipwreck Beach. Mānele Road (Highway 440) runs south down to Mānele Bay and Hulopo'e Beach. Kaumalapau Highway (also Highway 440) heads west to Kaumalapau Harbor. The rest of your driving takes place on bumpy, muddy, secondary roads, which generally aren't marked.

You'll never find yourself in a traffic jam, but it's easy to get lost on the unmarked dirt roads. Before heading out, ask for a map at your hotel desk. Always remember *mauka* (toward the mountains) and *makai* (toward the ocean) for basic directions. People drive slowly, wave, and give each other lots of room. The only gas station on the island is in Lāna'i City, at Lāna'i City Service.

CAR RENTAL Renting a four-wheel-drive vehicle is expensive but almost essential if you'd like to explore beyond the resorts and Lāna'i City. Make reservations far in advance of your trip, because Lāna'i's fleet of vehicles is limited. Lāna'i City Service, a subsidiary of Dollar Rent A Car, is open daily 7 to 7. Jeep Wranglers go for $139 a day, and minivans are $129 a day.

Information Lāna'i City Service (⊠ Lāna'i Ave. at 11th St.96763 ☎ 808/565-7227 or 800/533-7808).

FERRY TRAVEL

Expeditions' ferries cross the channel seven times daily, departing from Lahaina and Mā'alaea on Maui, to Mānele Bay Harbor on Lāna'i. Expeditions also arranges golf and land tours for passengers. The crossing takes 45 minutes from Lahaina, and 75 minutes from Mā`alaea, and costs $30 each way. Be warned: passage can be rough, especially in winter. On the flip side, you might see whales along the way during the season.

Information Expeditions (☎ *808/661–3756 or 800/695–2624* ⊕ *www.go-lanai. com*).

If you are staying at the Four Seasons Resort Lāna'i at Mānele Bay or the Lodge at Kō'ele, transportation from the harbor is almost effortless; the resort staff accompanies you on the boat, and shuttles stand ready to deliver you and your belongings to either resort. If you aren't staying with the Four Seasons, it's pretty much the same drill—the bus drivers will herd you onto the appropriate bus and take you into town for $10 per person. Advance reservations aren't necessary (or even possible), but be prepared for a little confusion on the dock.

Information Lāna'i City Service (✉ *Lāna'i Ave. at 11th St.* ☎ *808/565–7227 or 800/533–7808*).

SHUTTLE TRAVEL

A shuttle transports hotel guests between the Hotel Lāna'i, the Four Seasons Resort Lodge at Kō'ele, the Four Seasons Resort Lāna'i at Mānele Bay, and the airport. A $36 fee added to the room fee covers all transportation during the length of stay.

CONTACTS AND RESOURCES

EMERGENCIES

In an emergency, dial **911** to reach an ambulance, the police, or the fire department. The Lāna'i Family Clinic, part of the Straub Clinic & Hospital, is the island's health-care center. It's open weekdays from 8 to 5 and closed on weekends. There is no pharmacy so be sure to bring needed medications.

Information Straub Clinic & Hospital (✉ *628 7th St., Lāna'i City* ☎ *808/565–6423 clinic, 808/565–6411 hospital*).

VISITOR INFORMATION

Lāna'i Visitor's Bureau is open between 8 AM and 4 PM and is your best bet for general information and maps. The Lāna'i Culture & Heritage Center in the old Dole Administration Building also has information and maps.

Information Lāna'i Visitor's Bureau (✉ *431 7th St., Suite A, Lāna'i City* ☎ *808/ 565–7600* ⊕ *www.visitlanai.net*).**Maui Visitors Bureau** (☎ *808/244–3530* ⊕ *www. visitmaui.com*).

HAWAIIAN VOCABULARY

Although an understanding of Hawaiian is by no means required on a trip to the Aloha State, a *malihini*, or newcomer, will find plenty of opportunities to pick up a few of the local words and phrases. Traditional names and expressions are widely used in the Islands. You're likely to read or hear at least a few words each day of your stay.

With a basic understanding and some uninhibited practice, anyone can have enough command of the local tongue to ask for directions and to order from a restaurant menu. One visitor announced she would not leave until she could pronounce the name of the state fish, the *humuhumunukunukuāpua'a*.

Simplifying the learning process is the fact that the Hawaiian language contains only eight consonants—H, K, L, M, N, P, W, and the silent *'okina*, or glottal stop, written '—plus one or more of the five vowels. All syllables, and therefore all words, end in a vowel. Each vowel, with the exception of a few diphthongized double vowels such as *au* (pronounced "ow") or *ai* (pronounced "eye"), is pronounced separately. Thus *'Iolani* is four syllables (ee-oh-la-nee), not three (yo-la-nee). Although some Hawaiian words have only vowels, most also contain some consonants, but consonants are never doubled.

Pronunciation is simple. Pronounce *A* "ah" as father; *E* "ay" as in weigh; *I* "ee" as in marine; *O* "oh" as in no; *U* "oo" as in true.

Consonants mirror their English equivalents, with the exception of *W*. When the letter begins any syllable other than the first one in a word, it is usually pronounced as a *V*. *'Awa*, the Polynesian drink, is pronounced "ava," *'ewa* is pronounced "eva."

Almost all long Hawaiian words are combinations of shorter words; they are not difficult to pronounce if you segment them. *Kalaniana'ole*, the highway running east from Honolulu, is easily understood as *Kalani ana 'ole*. Apply the standard pronunciation rules—the stress falls on the next-to-last syllable of most two- or three-syllable Hawaiian words—and Kalaniana'ole Highway is as easy to say as Main Street.

Now about that fish. Try *humu-humu nuku-nuku āpu a'a*.

The other unusual element in Hawaiian language is the *kahakō*, or macron, written as a short line (¯) placed over a vowel. Like the accent (´) in Spanish, the kahakō puts emphasis on a syllable that would normally not be stressed. The most familiar example is probably *Waikīkī*. With no macrons, the stress would fall on the middle syllable; with only one macron, on the last syllable, the stress would fall on the first and last syllables. Some words become plural with the addition of a macron, often on a syllable that would have been stressed anyway. No Hawaiian word becomes plural with the addition of an *S*, since that letter does not exist in the language.

What follows is a glossary of some of the most commonly used Hawaiian words. Hawaiian residents appreciate visitors who at least try to pick up the local language.

'a'ā: rough, crumbling lava, contrasting with *pāhoehoe*, which is smooth.

'ae: yes.

aikane: friend.

āina: land.

akamai: smart, clever, possessing savoir faire.

akua: god.

ala: a road, path, or trail.

ali'i: a Hawaiian chief, a member of the chiefly class.

aloha: love, affection, kindness; also a salutation meaning both greetings and farewell.

'ānuenue: rainbow.

'a'ole: no.

'apōpō: tomorrow.

'auwai: a ditch.

auwē: alas, woe is me!

'ehu: a red-haired Hawaiian.

'ewa: in the direction of 'Ewa plantation, west of Honolulu.

hala: the pandanus tree, whose leaves (*lau hala*) are used to make baskets and plaited mats.

hālau: school.

hale: a house.

hale pule: church, house of worship.

ha mea iki or **ha mea 'ole:** you're welcome.

hana: to work.

haole: ghost. Since the first foreigners were Caucasian, *haole* now means a Caucasian person.

hapa: a part, sometimes a half; often used as a short form of *hapa haole,* to mean a person who is part-Caucasian.

hau'oli: to rejoice. *Hau'oli Makahiki Hou* means Happy New Year. *Hau'oli lā hānau* means Happy Birthday.

heiau: an outdoor stone platform; an ancient Hawaiian place of worship.

holo: to run.

holoholo: to go for a walk, ride, or sail.

holokū: a long Hawaiian dress, somewhat fitted, with a yoke and a train. Influenced by European fashion, it was worn at court, and at least one local translates the word as "expensive mu'umu'u."

holomū: a post–World War II cross between a *holokū* and a mu'umu'u, less fitted than the former but less voluminous than the latter, and having no train.

honi: to kiss; a kiss. A phrase that some tourists may find useful, quoted from a popular hula, is *Honi Ka'ua Wikiwiki:* Kiss me quick!

honu: turtle.

ho'omalimali: flattery, a deceptive "line," bunk, baloney, hooey.

huhū: angry.

hui: a group, club, or assembly. A church may refer to its congregation as a *hui* and a social club may be called a *hui.*

hukilau: a seine; a communal fishing party in which everyone helps to drive the fish into a huge net, pull it in, and divide the catch.

hula: the dance of Hawai'i.

iki: little.

ipo: sweetheart.

ka: the. This is the definite article for most singular words; for plural nouns, the definite article is usually *nā.* Since there is no *S* in Hawaiian, the article may be your only clue that a noun is plural.

kahuna: a priest, doctor, or other trained person of old Hawai'i, endowed with special professional skills that often included prophecy or other supernatural powers; the plural form is kāhuna.

kai: the sea, saltwater.

kalo: the taro plant from whose root *poi* (paste) is made.

kamā'aina: literally, a child of the soil; it refers to people who were born in the Islands or have lived there for a long time.

kanaka: originally a man or humanity, it is now used to denote a male Hawaiian or part-Hawaiian, but is occasionally taken as a slur when used by non-Hawaiians. *Kanaka maoli,* originally a full-blooded Hawaiian person, is used by some native Hawaiian rights activists to embrace part-Hawaiians as well.

kāne: a man, a husband. If you see this word on a door, it's the men's room. If you see *kane* on a door, it's probably a misspelling; that is the Hawaiian name for the skin fungus tinea.

kapa: also called by its Tahitian name, *tapa,* a cloth made of beaten bark and usually dyed and stamped with a repeat design.

kapakahi: crooked, cockeyed, uneven. You've got your hat on *kapakahi.*

kapu: keep out, prohibited. This is the Hawaiian version of the more widely known Tongan word *tabu* (taboo).

kapuna: grandparent; elder.

kēia lā: today.

keiki: a child; *keikikāne* is a boy, *keikiwahine* a girl.

kona: the leeward side of the Islands, the direction (south) from which the *kona* wind and *kona* rain come.

kula: upland.

kuleana: a homestead or small plot of ground on which a family has been installed for some generations without necessarily owning it. By extension, *kuleana* is used to denote any area or department in which one has a special interest or prerogative. You'll hear it used this way: If you want to hire a surfboard, see Moki; that's his *kuleana*.

lā: sun.

lamalama: to fish with a torch.

lānai: a porch, a balcony, an outdoor living room. Almost every house in Hawai'i has one. Don't confuse this two-syllable word with the three-syllable name of the island, Lāna'i.

lani: heaven, the sky.

lau hala: the leaf of the *hala,* or pandanus tree, widely used in handicrafts.

lei: a garland of flowers.

limu: sun.

lolo: stupid.

luna: a plantation overseer or foreman.

mahalo: thank you.

makai: toward the ocean.

malihini: a newcomer to the Islands.

mana: the spiritual power that the Hawaiian believed inhabited all things and creatures.

manō: shark.

manuwahi: free, gratis.

mauka: toward the mountains.

mauna: mountain.

mele: a Hawaiian song or chant, often of epic proportions.

Mele Kalikimaka: Merry Christmas (a transliteration from the English phrase).

Menehune: a Hawaiian pixie. The *Menehune* were a legendary race of little people who accomplished prodigious work, such as building fishponds and temples in the course of a single night.

moana: the ocean.

mu'umu'u: the voluminous dress in which the missionaries enveloped Hawaiian women. Now made in bright printed cottons and silks, it is an indispensable garment. Culturally sensitive locals have embraced the Hawaiian spelling but often shorten the spoken word to "mu'u." Most English dictionaries include the spelling "muumuu."

nani: beautiful.

nui: big.

ohana: family.

'ono: delicious.

pāhoehoe: smooth, unbroken, satiny lava.

Pākē: Chinese. This *Pākē* carver makes beautiful things.

palapala: document, printed matter.

pali: a cliff, precipice.

pānini: prickly pear cactus.

paniolo: a Hawaiian cowboy, a rough transliteration of *español,* the language of the Islands' earliest cowboys.

pau: finished, done.

pilikia: trouble. The Hawaiian word is much more widely used here than its English equivalent.

puka: a hole.

pupule: crazy, like the celebrated Princess Pupule. This word has replaced its English equivalent in local usage.

pu'u: volcanic cinder cone.

waha: mouth.

wahine: a female, a woman, a wife, and a sign on the ladies' room door; the plural form is *wāhine.*

wai: freshwater, as opposed to saltwater, which is *kai.*

wailele: waterfall.

wikiwiki: to hurry, hurry up (since this is a reduplication of *wiki,* quick, neither W is pronounced as a V).

Note: Pidgin is the unofficial language of Hawai'i. It is a Creole language, with its own grammar, evolved from the mixture of English, Hawaiian, Japanese, Portuguese, and other languages spoken in 19th-century Hawai'i, and it is heard everywhere.

Travel Smart Maui

"Why not just rent a car? That's what we did at every port on our Hawai'i cruise. Used our travel guides and saw what we wanted. Most of the rental car agencies have a pickup service at the ports."

—patandhank

"I am a Hawai'i resident so it cracks me up when I see tourists arrive here with several pieces of luggage each. What are they packing? All you need here are slippers (flip-flops), T-shirts, a pair of shorts, long pants (jeans), and swim trunks. For 'dressy' occasions, an aloha shirt (Hawaiian shirt) is fine. If you wear anything more than that, you are advertising that you are a tourist."

—Dewd

GETTING HERE & AROUND

▌ AIR TRAVEL

Flying time is about 10 hours from New York, 8 hours from Chicago, and 5 hours from Los Angeles.

Hawai'i is a major destination link for flights traveling to and from the U.S. mainland, Asia, Australia, New Zealand, and the South Pacific. Island-hopping is easy, with several daily interisland flights connecting all of the major islands. International travelers also have options: O'ahu and the Big Island are gateways to the United States.

Although Maui's airports are smaller and more casual than Honolulu International, during peak times they can also be quite busy. Allow extra travel time to either airport during morning and afternoon rush-hour traffic periods, and allow time if you are returning a rental car. Plan to arrive at the airport 60 to 90 minutes before departure for interisland flights.

Plants and plant products are subject to regulation by the Department of Agriculture, both when entering and leaving Hawai'i. Upon leaving the Islands, you're required to have your bags X-rayed and tagged at one of the airport's agricultural-inspection stations before you proceed to check-in. Pineapples and coconuts with the packer's agricultural-inspection stamp pass freely; papayas must be treated, inspected, and stamped. All other fruits are banned for export to the U.S. mainland. Flowers pass except for gardenia, rose leaves, jade vine, and mauna loa. Also banned are insects, snails, soil, cotton, cacti, sugarcane, and all berry plants.

You'll have to leave dogs and other pets at home. A 120-day quarantine is imposed to keep out rabies, which is nonexistent in Hawai'i. If specific pre- and postarrival requirements are met, animals may qualify for 30-day or 5-day-or-less quarantine.

▌ TIP → If you travel frequently, look into the TSA's Registered Traveler program (⊕ www.

tsa.gov). The program, which is still being tested in several U.S. airports, is designed to cut down on gridlock at security checkpoints by allowing prescreened travelers to pass quickly through kiosks that scan an iris and/or a fingerprint.

Airline-Security Issues Transportation Security Administration (⊕ www.tsa.gov) has answers for almost every question that might come up.

Air-Travel Resources in Maui State of Hawai'i Airports Division Offices (☎ 808/836–6417 ⊕ www.hawaii.gov/dot/airports).

AIRPORTS

All of Hawai'i's major islands have their own airports, but Honolulu's International Airport on O'ahu is the main stopover for most U.S.–mainland and international flights. From Honolulu, there are daily flights to Maui leaving almost every hour from early morning until evening. To travel interisland from Honolulu, you can depart from either the interisland terminal or the commuter-airline terminal, located in two separate structures adjacent to the main overseas terminal building. A free bus service, the Wiki Wiki Shuttle, operates between terminals. In addition, some carriers now offer nonstop service directly from the U.S. mainland to Maui on a limited basis. Flights from Honolulu into Lāna'i and Moloka'i are offered several times a day.

Maui has two major airports. Kahului Airport handles major airlines and interisland flights; it's the only airport on Maui that has direct service from the mainland. Kapalua–West Maui Airport is served by go! Express and Hawaiian Airlines. If you're staying in West Maui and you're flying in from another island, you can avoid the hour drive from the Kahului Airport by flying into Kapalua–West Maui Airport. Hāna Airport is very small.

Moloka'i's Ho'olehua Airport is small and centrally located, as is Lāna'i Airport. Both rural airports handle a limited number of flights per day. Visitors coming from the U.S. mainland to these islands must first stop in O'ahu or Maui and change to an interisland flight.

Airport Information Hāna Airport (HNM) (☎ 808/248–8208). Honolulu International Airport (HNL) (☎ 808/836–6413 ⊕ www.hawaii.gov/dot/airports). Ho'olehua Airport (MKK) (☎ 808/567–6361). Kahului Airport (OGG) (☎ 808/872–3893). Kapalua–West Maui Airport (JHM) (☎ 808/669–0623). Lāna'i Airport (LNY) (☎ 808/565–6757).

GROUND TRANSPORTATION
If you're not renting a car, you'll need to take a taxi. Maui Airport Taxi serves the Kahului Airport and charges $3.50, plus $3 for every mile, with a 30¢ surcharge per bag. Cab fares to locations around the island are estimated as follows: Kā'anapali $87, Kahului town $13 to $18, Kapalua $105, Kīhei town $33 to $53, Lahaina $74 to $79, Mākena $65, Wailea $57, and Wailuku $20 to $27.

SpeediShuttle offers transportation between the Kahului Airport and hotels, resorts, and condominium complexes throughout the island. There is an online reservation and fare-quote system for information and bookings.

Information Maui Airport Taxi (☎ 808/877–0907). SpeediShuttle Hawai'i (☎ 877/242–5777 ⊕ www.speedishuttle.com).

FLIGHTS
American has daily nonstop flights into Maui from Los Angeles, Chicago, and Dallas-Fort Worth; and also serves O'ahu, Kaua'i, and the Big Island. Continental flies into Honolulu from Houston, Los Angeles, New York/Newark, and Seattle. Delta serves Maui and O'ahu from Atlanta, Los Angeles, and Salt Lake City. Hawaiian Airlines serves Maui and Honolulu from Las Vegas, Los Angeles, Oakland, Phoenix, Portland, Sacramento, San Diego, San Francisco, San Jose, and Seattle. Northwest serves Maui and O'ahu

from Los Angeles, Minneapolis/St. Paul, Portland, San Francisco, and Seattle.

In addition to offering very competitive rates and online specials, all have frequent-flyer programs that will entitle you to rewards and upgrades the more you fly.

Airline Contacts American Airlines (☎ 800/433–7300 ⊕ www.aa.com). Continental Airlines (☎ 800/523–3273 for U.S. and Mexico reservations, 800/231–0856 for international destinations ⊕ www.continental.com). Delta Airlines (☎ 800/221–1212 for U.S. reservations, 800/241–4141 for international reservations ⊕ www.delta.com). Hawaiian Airlines (☎ 800/367–5320 ⊕ www.hawaiianair.com). Northwest Airlines (☎ 800/225–2525 ⊕ www.nwa.com).

INTERISLAND FLIGHTS
Hawaiian offers regular interisland service to Maui's Kahului and Kapalua airports, as well as the Moloka'i Ho'olehua and Lāna'i City airports. go! Airlines/go! Express, Island Air, and Mokulele Airlines provide interisland service between Maui (Kahului and Kapalua), Lāna'i, Moloka'i (Ho'olehua), O'ahu, Kaua'i, and the Big Island. PWExpress serves Maui's Kahului and Hāna airports, Moloka'i's Ho'olehua and Kalaupapa airports and Lāna'i City, and also flies into O'ahu and the Big Island. Pacific Wings has regular and charter service between Honolulu and Maui (all three airports), Moloka'i (both airports), Lāna'i, and the Big Island.

Be sure to compare prices offered by all of the interisland carriers. If you are somewhat flexible with your dates and times for island-hopping, you should have no problem getting an affordable round-trip ticket.

Airline Contacts go! Airlines/go! Express (☎ 888/434–5946 ⊕ www.iflygo.com). Hawaiian Airlines (☎ 800/367–5320 ⊕ www.hawaiianair.com). Island Air (☎ 800/652–6541 ⊕ www.islandair.com).Mokulele Airlines (☎ 808/326–7070 ⊕ www.mokuleleairlines.com).Pacific Wings (☎ 888/575–4546 ⊕ www.pacificwings.com). PWExpress (☎ 888/866–5022 ⊕ www.flypwx.com).

CHARTER FLIGHTS

Mokulele Airlines provides charter service between Maui and the Big Island, and between Oʻahu and Molokaʻi. The company has been in business since 1998.

In addition to its regular service between Honolulu, Lānaʻi, Maui, Molokaʻi, and the Big Island, Pacific Wings offers a variety of charter options including premier (same-day departures on short notice), premium (24-hour notice), priority (48-hour notice), group, and cargo/courier. The company also has a frequent-flyer program.

Paragon Air offers 24-hour private charter service from any airport in Hawaiʻi. In business since 1980, the company prides itself on its perfect safety record. Charter prices start at $575. Should you want to explore Kaluapapa or other sites on Molokaʻi and Maui from the air and ground, you can book tours through Paragon that depart from either the Kahului or Kapalua-West Maui airports.

Charter Companies Mokulele Airlines (☎ 808/326–7070 ⊕ www.mokuleleairlines. com). **Pacific Wings** (☎ 888/575–4546 ⊕ www.pacificwings.com). **Paragon Air** (☎ 800/428–1231 ⊕ www.paragon-air.com).

▮ BOAT TRAVEL

There is daily ferry service between Lahaina or Maʻalaea Harbor, Maui, and Mānele Bay, Lānaʻi, with Expeditions Lānaʻi Ferry. The 9-mi crossing costs $60 round-trip, per person, and takes about 45 minutes or so, depending on ocean conditions (which can make this trip a rough one).

Molokaʻi Ferry offers twice-daily ferry service between Lahaina, Maui, and Kaunakakai, Molokaʻi. Travel time is about 90 minutes each way and the one-way fare is $66.40 per person (including taxes and fees); a book of six one-way tickets costs $307.10 (including taxes and fees). Reservations are recommended.

At this writing, Hawaiʻi Superferry, a high-speed interisland ferry with routes between Honolulu and Kahului, Maui, has suspended service. Consult the Superferry Web site for updates, or go to ⊕ www.gwohawaii.com.

Ferry Contacts Expeditions Lānaʻi Ferry (☎ 800/695–2624 ⊕ www.go-lanai.com). **Hawaiʻi Superferry** (☎ 877/443–3779 ⊕ www.hawaiisuperferry.com).**Molokaʻi Ferry** (☎ 866/307–6524 ⊕ www.molokaiferry.com).

CRUISES

For information about cruises, see Chapter 1, Experience Maui.

▮ BUS TRAVEL

Maui Bus, operated by Roberts Hawaiʻi, offers 12 routes in and between various Central, South, and West Maui communities, seven days a week, including all holidays. Passengers can travel in and around Wailuku, Kahului, Lahaina, Kāʻanapali, Kapalua, Kīhei, Wailea, Māʻalaea, and Upcountry (including Pukalani, Hāliʻimaile, Haʻikū, and Pāʻia). The Upcountry and Haʻikū Islander routes include a stop at Kahului Airport. The Kahului and Wailuku loops and Lahaina Villager are free; other routes are $1.

For travelers who prefer not to rent a car, Maui Bus is a great way to go. It runs from early morning to late evening daily, and stops at most of the major towns and sightseeing destinations. And, you can't beat the price.

Bus Contact Roberts Hawaiʻi (☎ 808/871–4838 ⊕ mauicounty.gov/bus).

▮ CAR TRAVEL

Should you plan to do any sightseeing on Maui, it is best to rent a car. Even if all you want to do is relax at your resort, you may want to hop in the car to check out one of the island's popular restaurants.

Since many of Maui's roads are mostly two lanes, be sure to allow plenty of time to return your vehicle so that you can make your flight. Traffic can be bad during morning and afternoon rush hour, especially between Kahului and Pā'ia, Kīhei, and Lahaina Give yourself about 3½ hours before departure time to return your vehicle.

On Lāna'i and Moloka'i, four-wheel-drive vehicles are recommended for exploring off the beaten path. Neither island has traffic or traffic lights, and there are only a handful of paved roads. Make sure you've got a good map. Free visitor publications containing quality road maps can be found at airports, hotels, and shops.

Asking for directions will almost always produce a helpful explanation from the locals, but you should be prepared for an island term or two. Hawai'i residents refer to places as being either *mauka* (toward the mountains) or *makai* (toward the ocean) from one another.

Hawai'i has a strict seat-belt law. Those riding in the front seat must wear a seat belt and children under the age of 17 in the backseat must be belted. The fine for not wearing a seat belt is $92. Jaywalking is also very common, so please pay careful attention to the roads. In Hawai'i, your unexpired mainland driver's license is valid for rental cars for up to 90 days.

GASOLINE

You can pretty much count on having to pay more for gasoline on Maui than on the U.S. mainland. At the time of this writing, the average price of a gallon of gas is about $2.50.

PARKING

With a population of more than 119,000 and nearly 30,000 visitors on any given day, Maui has parking challenges. Lots sprinkled throughout West Maui charge by the hour. There are about 700 parking spaces in the Lahaina Center; shoppers can get validated parking. *This Week Maui* often has coupons for free parking at this lot, as well as at Whalers Village.

Parking along many streets is curtailed during rush hours, and towing is widely practiced. Read curbside parking signs before leaving your vehicle.

RENTALS

While on Maui, you can rent anything from an econobox to a Ferrari. Rates are usually better if you reserve though a rental agency's Web site. All of the big national rental-car agencies have locations on Maui, but Dollar (⊕ *www.dollar.com*) is the only company that has offices on all of the major Hawaiian Islands. There also are several local rental-car companies so be sure to compare prices before you book. It's wise to make reservations far in advance and make sure that a confirmed reservation guarantees you a car, especially if you're visiting during peak seasons or for major conventions or sporting events.

Rates begin at about $25 to $35 a day for an economy car with air-conditioning, automatic transmission, and unlimited mileage, depending on your pickup location. This does not include the airport concession fee, general excise tax, rental-vehicle surcharge, or vehicle license fee. When you reserve a car, ask about cancellation penalties and drop-off charges should you plan to pick up the car in one location and return it to another. Many rental companies in Hawai'i offer coupons for discounts at attractions that could save you money later in your trip.

How about seeing the island in your own VW camper? Aloha Campers rents older VW Westfalia Campers for $115 per day that accommodate up to four adults. And if exploring the island on two wheels is more your speed, Maui Harley-Davidson and Island Rental Cars both rent motorcycles; Island Rental Cars also rents exotic cars. Want to drive an earth-friendly automobile that gets 30 to 45 mi to the gallon? Bio-Beetle Eco Rental Cars run on clean-burning diesel fuel that comes from renewable sources like recycled vegetable oil.

In Hawai'i you must be 21 years of age to rent a car and you must have a valid driver's license and a major credit card. Those under 25 will pay a daily surcharge of $15 to $25. Request car seats and extras such as a GPS when you make your reservation.

Car Rental Resources

Local Agencies		
AA Aloha Cars-R-Us	800/655-7989	www.hawaiicarrental.com
Adventure Lāna'I EcoCentre (Lāna'i)	808/565-7373	www.adventurelanai.com
Aloha Campers (Maui)	808/281-8020	www.alohacampers.com
Bio-Beetle Eco Rental Cars	877/873-6121	www.bio-beetle.com
Discount Hawai'i	888/292-3307	www.discounthawaiicarrental.com
Hawaiian Discount Car Rentals	800/591-8605	www.hawaiidrive-o.com
Island Kine Auto Rental (Moloka'i)	866/527-7368	www.molokai-car-rental.com
Island Rental Cars		www.hawaiianriders.com
Maui Harley Davidson	808/877-7433	www.hawaiiharleyrental.com

Hawai'i's Child Restraint Law requires that all children 3 years and younger be in an approved child-safety seat in the backseat of a vehicle. Children ages 4 to 7 must be seated in a rear booster seat or child restraint such as a lap and shoulder belt. Car seats and boosters range from $5 to $8 per day.

ROAD CONDITIONS

Getting around Maui is relatively easy as there are really only a few major roads leading to and from the must-see towns and sights. Honoapi'ilani Highway will get you from the central Maui towns of Wailuku and Kahului to the leeward coast and the towns and resorts of Lahaina, Kā'anapali, Kahana, and Kapalua. Depending on traffic, it should take about 30 to 45 minutes to travel this route. Those gorgeous mountains that hug Honoapi'ilani Highway are the West Maui Mountains.

North and South Kīhei Road will take you to the town of Kīhei and the resort area of Wailea on the South Shore. The drive from Kahului to Wailea should take about 30 minutes, and the drive from Kā'anapali to Wailea will take about 45 to 60 minutes.

Your vacation to Maui must include a visit to Haleakalā National Park and you should plan on 2 to 2½ hours driving time from Kā'anapali or Wailea. Ho'okipa

and Baldwin beaches are on the Island's North Shore, just a stone's throw from Kahului, and could easily be combined with a day in Upcountry Maui. The drive from Kā'anapali or Wailea to the charming towns of Makawao and Kula will take about 45 to 60 minutes. And you must not miss the Road to Hāna, a 55-mi stretch with one-lane bridges, hairpin turns, and some of the most breathtaking views you will ever see. The Hawai'i Visitors and Convention Bureau's red-caped King Kamehameha signs mark major attractions and scenic spots. There are only two roads on Maui that require four-wheel-drive vehicles: Kahekili Highway between Waihe'e Point and Keawalua on the island's northeast coast, and the southern stretch of Pi'ilani Hwy. (HI 31) between 'Ulupalakua and Kīpahulu.

In rural areas, it's not unusual for gas stations to close early. In Hawai'i, turning right on a red light is legal, except where noted. Use caution during heavy downpours, especially if you see signs warning of falling rocks. If you're enjoying views from the road or need to study a map, pull over to the side. Remember the aloha spirit; allow other cars to merge, don't honk (it's considered rude); use your headlights and turn signals.

Emergency Services AAA Help (☎ 800/222-4357).

ESSENTIALS

▌ COMMUNICATIONS

INTERNET

If you've brought your laptop with you to Maui, you should have no problem checking e-mail or connecting to the Internet. Most of the major hotels and resorts offer high-speed access in rooms and/or lobbies. If you're staying at a small inn or bed-and-breakfast without Internet access, ask the proprietor for the nearest café or coffee shop with wireless access.

Contacts Cybercafes (⊕ *www.cybercafes. com*) lists more than 4,000 Internet cafés worldwide. **JiWire** (⊕ *www.jiwire.com*) features a directory of Wi-Fi hot spots around the world.

▌ HEALTH

Hawai'i is known as the Health State. The life expectancy here is 79 years, one of the longest in the nation. Balmy weather makes it easy to remain active year-round, and the low-stress aloha attitude certainly contributes to general well-being. When visiting the Islands, however, there are a few health issues to keep in mind.

The Hawai'i State Department of Health recommends that you drink 16 ounces of water per hour to avoid dehydration when hiking or spending time in the sun. Use sunblock, wear UV-reflective sunglasses, and protect your head with a visor or hat for shade. If you're not acclimated to warm, humid weather, allow plenty of time for rest stops and refreshments.

When visiting freshwater streams, be aware of the tropical disease leptospirosis, which is spread by animal urine and carried into streams and mud. Symptoms include fever, headache, nausea, and red eyes. If left untreated it can cause liver and kidney damage, respiratory failure, internal bleeding, and even death. To avoid this, don't swim or wade in freshwater streams or ponds if you have open sores and don't drink from any freshwater streams or ponds.

On the Islands, fog is a rare occurrence, but there can often be "vog," an airborne haze of gases released from volcanic vents on the Big Island. During certain weather conditions such as "Kona Winds," the vog can settle over the Islands and wreak havoc with respiratory and other health conditions, especially asthma or emphysema. If susceptible, stay indoors and get emergency assistance if needed.

The Islands have their share of bugs and insects. Most are harmless but annoying. When planning to spend time outdoors in hiking areas, wear long-sleeved clothing and pants and use mosquito repellent containing deet. In very damp places you may encounter the dreaded local centipede. On the Islands they usually come in two colors, brown and blue, and they range from the size of a worm to an 8-inch cigar. Their sting is very painful, and the reaction is similar to bee- and wasp-sting reactions. When camping, shake out your sleeping bag before climbing in, and check your shoes in the morning, as the centipedes like cozy places. If planning on hiking or traveling in remote areas, always carry a first-aid kit and appropriate medications for sting reactions.

▌ HOURS OF OPERATION

Even people in paradise have to work. Generally, local business hours are weekdays 8 to 5. Banks are usually open Monday through Thursday 8:30 to 3 and until 6 on Friday. Some banks have Saturday-morning hours.

Many self-serve gas stations stay open around-the-clock, with full-service stations usually open from around 7 AM until 9 PM. U.S. post offices are generally open weekdays 8:30 AM to 4:30 PM and Saturday 8:30 to noon.

Most museums generally open their doors between 9 AM and 10 AM and stay open until 5 PM, Tuesday through Saturday. Many museums operate with afternoon hours only on Sunday and close on Monday. Visitor-attraction hours vary throughout the state, but most sights are open daily with the exception of major holidays such as Christmas. Check local newspapers or visitor publications upon arrival for attraction hours and schedules if visiting over holiday periods. The local dailies carry a listing of "What's Open/What's Not" for those time periods.

Stores in resort areas sometimes open as early as 8, with shopping-center opening hours varying from 9:30 to 10 on weekdays and Saturday, a bit later on Sunday. Bigger malls stay open until 9 weekdays and Saturday and close at 5 on Sunday. Boutiques in resort areas may stay open as late as 11.

▍MONEY

Prices throughout this guide are given for adults. Substantially reduced fees are almost always available for children, students, and senior citizens.

CREDIT CARDS

Throughout this guide, the following abbreviations are used: **AE**, American Express; **D**, Discover; **DC**, Diners Club; **MC**, MasterCard; and **V**, Visa.

It's a good idea to inform your credit-card company before you travel, especially if you're going abroad and don't travel internationally very often. Otherwise, the credit-card company might put a hold on your card owing to unusual activity—not a good thing halfway through your trip. Record all your credit-card numbers—as well as the phone numbers to call if your cards are lost or stolen—in a safe place, so you're prepared should something go wrong. Both MasterCard and Visa have general numbers you can call (collect if you're abroad) if your card is lost, but you're better off calling the number of your issuing bank, since MasterCard and

Visa usually just transfer you to your bank; your bank's number is usually printed on your card.

Reporting Lost Cards American Express (☎ *800/528-4800* ⊕ *www.americanexpress. com*). **Diners Club** (☎ *800/234-6377* ⊕ *www. dinersclub.com*). **Discover** (☎ *800/347-2683* ⊕ *www.discovercard.com*). **MasterCard** (☎ *800/627-8372* ⊕ *www.mastercard.com*). **Visa** (☎ *800/847-2911* ⊕ *www.visa.com*).

▍PACKING

Probably the most important thing to tuck into your suitcase is sunscreen. There are many tanning oils on the market in Hawai'i, including coconut and *kukui* (the nut from a local tree) oils, but they can cause severe burns. Hats and sunglasses offer important sun protection, too. All major hotels in Hawai'i provide beach towels.

Hawai'i is casual: sandals, bathing suits, and comfortable, informal cotton clothing are the norm. In summer, synthetic slacks and shirts, although easy to care for, can be uncomfortably warm. The aloha shirt is accepted dress in Hawai'i for business and most social occasions.

Shorts are acceptable daytime attire, along with a T-shirt or polo shirt. There's no need to buy expensive sandals on the mainland—here you can get flip-flops for a couple of dollars and off-brand sandals for $20. Many golf courses have dress codes requiring a collared shirt; call courses for details. If you're visiting in winter or planning to visit a high-altitude area, bring a sweater, a light- to medium-weight jacket, or a polar-fleece pullover.

If your vacation plans include an exploration of Maui's northeastern coast, including Hāna and Upcountry Maui, you'll want to pack a light raincoat. And if you'll be exploring Haleakalā National Park, make sure you pack appropriately as weather at the summit can be very cold and windy. Bring good boots for hiking.

FOR INTERNATIONAL TRAVELERS

CURRENCY

The dollar is the basic unit of U.S. currency. It has 100 cents. Coins are the penny (1¢); the nickel (5¢), dime (10¢), quarter (25¢), half-dollar (50¢), and the very rare golden $1 coin and even rarer silver $1. Bills are denominated $1, $5, $10, $20, $50, and $100, all mostly green and identical in size; designs and background tints vary. You may come across a $2 bill, but the chances are slim.

CUSTOMS

Information U.S. Customs and Border Protection (⊕ www.cbp.gov).

DRIVING

Driving in the United States is on the right. Speed limits are posted in miles per hour, between 25 and 55 MPH on the island of Maui. Watch for lower limits near schools (usually 20 MPH). Hawai'i has a strict seat-belt law. Passengers in the front seats must be belted. Children under the age of 3 must be in approved safety seats in the backseat and those ages 4 to 7 must be in a rear booster seat or child restraint such as a lap and shoulder belt. Morning (between 6:30 and 9:30 AM) and afternoon (between 3:30 and 6:30 PM) rush-hour traffic around Kahului, Pā'ia, Kīhei, and Lahaina can be bad, so use caution. In rural areas, it's not unusual for gas stations to close early. If you see that your tank is getting low, don't take any chances; fill up when you see a station.

If your car breaks down, pull onto the shoulder and wait for help, or have your passengers wait while you walk to an emergency phone. If you have a cell phone with you, call the roadside assistance number on your rental car agreement.

ELECTRICITY

The U.S. standard is AC, 110 volts/60 cycles. Plugs have two flat pins set parallel to each other.

EMERGENCIES

For police, fire, or ambulance, dial 911 (0 in rural areas).

EMBASSIES

Contacts Australia (☎ 202/797–3000 ⊕ www.austemb.org). **Canada** (☎ 202/682–1740 ⊕ www.canadianembassy.org). **United Kingdom** (☎ 202/588–7800 ⊕ www. britainusa.com).

HOLIDAYS

New Year's Day (Jan. 1); Martin Luther King Day (3rd Mon. in Jan.); Presidents' Day (3rd Mon. in Feb.); Memorial Day (last Mon. in May); Independence Day (July 4); Labor Day (1st Mon. in Sept.); Columbus Day (2nd Mon. in Oct.); Thanksgiving Day (4th Thurs. in Nov.); Christmas Eve and Christmas Day (Dec. 24 and 25); and New Year's Eve (Dec. 31).

MAIL

You can buy stamps and aerograms and send letters and parcels in post offices. Stamp-dispensing machines can occasionally be found in airports, bus and train stations, office buildings, drugstores, and convenience stores. U.S. mailboxes are stout, dark-blue steel bins; pickup schedules are posted inside the bin (pull down the handle to see them). Parcels weighing more than a pound must be mailed at a post office or at a private mailing center.

Within the United States a first-class letter weighing 1 ounce or less costs 42¢; each additional ounce costs 17¢. Postcards cost 27¢ to send. Postcards or 1-ounce airmail letters to most countries cost 94¢; postcards or 1-ounce letters to Canada or Mexico costs 72¢.

To receive mail on the road, have it sent c/o GENERAL DELIVERY at your destination's main post office (use the correct five-digit ZIP code). You must pick up mail in person within 30 days, with a driver's license or passport for identification.

Contacts DHL (☎ 800/225–5345 ⊕ www.dhl.com). **Federal Express** (☎ 800/463–3339 ⊕ www.fedex. com). **Mail Boxes, Etc./The UPS Store** (☎ 800/789–4623 ⊕ www.mbe.com). **United States Postal Service** (⊕ www.usps.com).

PASSPORTS AND VISAS

Visitor visas aren't necessary for citizens of Australia, Canada, the United Kingdom, or most citizens of EU countries coming for tourism and staying for fewer than 90 days. If you require a visa, the cost is $131, and waiting time can be substantial, depending on where you live. Apply for a visa at the U.S. consulate in your place of residence; check the U.S. State Department's special Visa Web site for further information.

Visa Information Destination USA (⊕ www.unitedstatesvisas.gov).

PHONES

Numbers consist of a three-digit area code and a seven-digit local number. The area code for Hawai'i is 808. For local calls on Maui, you only need to dial the seven-digit number (not the 808 area code). If you are calling businesses on other neighboring islands while on Maui, you will need to use "1–808," followed by the number. Calls to numbers prefixed by "800," "888," "866," and "877" are toll free and require that you first dial a "1." For calls to numbers prefixed by "900" you must pay—usually dearly.

For international calls, dial "011" followed by the country code and the local number. For help, dial "0" and ask for an overseas operator. Most phone books list country codes and U.S. area codes. The country code for Australia is 61, for New Zealand 64, for the United Kingdom 44. Calling Canada is the same as calling within the United States; the country code for both is 1.

For operator assistance, dial "0." For directory assistance, call 555–1212 or occasionally 411 (free at many public phones). You can reverse long-distance charges by calling "collect"; dial "0" instead of "1" before the 10-digit number.

Instructions are generally posted on pay phones. Usually you insert coins in a slot (usually 25¢ to 50¢ for local calls) and wait for a steady tone before dialing. On long-distance calls the operator tells you how much to insert; prepaid phone cards, widely available in various denominations, can be used from any phone. Follow the directions to activate the card (there's usually an access number, then an activation code), then dial your number.

CELL PHONES

The United States has several GSM (Global System for Mobile Communications) networks, so multiband mobiles from most countries (except for Japan) work here. Unfortunately, it's almost impossible to buy a pay-as-you-go mobile SIM card in the U.S.—which allows you to avoid roaming charges—without also buying a phone. That said, cell phones with pay-as-you-go plans are available for well under $100. AT&T, T-Mobile, and Virgin Mobile offer affordable, pay-as-you-go service.

Contacts AT&T (☎ 800/331–0500 ⊕ www.att.com). **T-Mobile** (☎ 800/937–8997 ⊕ www.t-mobile.com). **Virgin Mobile** (☎ 888/322–1122 ⊕ www.virginmobileusa.com).

▌ SAFETY

Hawai'i is generally a safe tourist destination, but it's still wise to follow common-sense safety precautions. Rental cars are magnets for break-ins, so don't leave any valuables in the car, not even in a locked trunk. Avoid poorly lighted areas, beach parks, and isolated areas after dark as a precaution. When hiking, stay on marked trails, no matter how alluring the temptation might be to stray. Weather conditions can cause landscapes to become muddy, slippery, and tenuous, so staying on marked trails will lessen the possibility of a fall or getting lost.

Women traveling alone are generally safe on the Islands, but always follow the safety precautions you would use in any major destination. When booking hotels, request rooms closest to the elevator and always keep your hotel-room door and balcony doors locked. Stay away from isolated areas after dark; camping and hiking solo are not advised. If you stay out late visiting nightclubs and bars, use caution when returning to your lodging.

Contact Transportation Security Administration (TSA) (⊕ www.tsa.gov).

▌ TAXES

There's a 4.16% state sales tax on all purchases, including food. A hotel room tax of 7.25%, combined with the sales tax of 4.16%, equals an 11.41% rate added onto your hotel bill. A $3-per-day road tax is also assessed on each rental vehicle.

▌ TIME

Hawai'i is on Hawaiian standard time, 5 hours behind New York, 2 hours behind Los Angeles, and 10 hours behind London.

When the U.S. mainland is on daylight saving time, Hawai'i is not, so add an extra hour of time difference between the Islands and U.S. mainland destinations. You may find that things generally move more slowly here. That has nothing to do with your watch—it's just the laid-back way called Hawaiian time.

▌ TIPPING

As this is a major vacation destination and many of the people who work at the hotels and resorts rely on tips to supplement their wages, tipping is not only common but expected.

TIPPING GUIDELINES FOR MAUI	
Bartender	$1 to $5 per round of drinks, depending on the number of drinks
Bellhop	$1 to $5 per bag, depending on the level of the hotel and whether you have bulky items like golf clubs, surfboards, etc.
Hotel Concierge	$5 or more, depending on the service
Hotel Doorman	$1 to $5 if he helps you get a cab or helps with bags, golf clubs, etc.
Hotel Maid	$1 to $3 a day (either daily or at the end of your stay, in cash)
Hotel Room-Service Waiter	$1 to $2 per delivery, even if a service charge has been added
Porter at Airport	$1 per bag
Skycap at Airport	$1 to $3 per bag checked
Spa Personnel	15% to 20% of the cost of your service
Taxi Driver	15% to 20%, but round up the fare to the next dollar amount
Tour Guide	10% of the cost of the tour
Valet-Parking Attendant	$2 to $5, each time your car is brought to you
Waiter	15% to 20%, with 20% being the norm at high-end restaurants; nothing additional if a service charge is added to the bill

▌ TOURS

Guided tours are a good option when you don't want to do it all yourself. You travel along with a group (sometimes large, sometimes small), stay in prebooked hotels, eat with your fellow travelers (the cost of meals sometimes included in the price of your tour, sometimes not), and follow a schedule.

A knowledgeable guide can take you places that you might never discover on your own, and you may be pushed to see more than you would have otherwise. Tours aren't for everyone, but they can be just the thing for first-time travelers to Maui or those who enjoy the group-traveling experience. None of the companies offering general-interest tours in the Hawaiian Islands include Moloka'i or Lāna'i.

Whenever you book a guided tour, find out what's included and what isn't. A "land-only" tour includes all your travel (by bus, in most cases) in the destination, but not necessarily your flights to and from or even within it. Also, in most cases prices in tour brochures don't include fees and taxes. And remember that you'll be expected to tip your guide (in cash) at the end of the tour.

GENERAL-INTEREST TOURS

Globus has seven Hawai'i itineraries that include Maui, one of which is an escorted cruise on a Norwegian Cruise Line ship that includes two days on the island. Tauck Travel and Trafalgar offer several land-based Hawai'i itineraries that include three nights on Maui. Both companies offer similar itineraries with plenty of free time to explore the island. Tauck offers 7- and 11-night multi-island tours, including a "Magical Hawai'i" trip for families. Trafalgar has 7-, 9-, 10-, and 12-night multi-island tours. With the Tauck tours, participants will discover the majesty of Mt. Haleakalā, while the Trafalgar tours all include visits to verdant 'Īao Valley.

EscortedHawaiiTours.com, owned and operated by Atlas Cruises & Tours, sells more than a dozen Hawai'i trips ranging from 7 to 12 nights. These are operated by various tour companies including Globus, Tauck, and Trafalgar.

Tour Contacts Atlas Cruises & Tours (☏ 800/942–3301 ⊕ www.escortedhawaii tours.com). **Globus** (☏ 866/755–8581 ⊕ www.globusjourneys.com). **Tauck Travel** (☏ 800/788–7885 ⊕ www.tauck.com). **Trafalgar** (☏ 866/544–4434 ⊕ www.trafalgar.com).

SPECIAL-INTEREST TOURS

CULTURE

Elderhostel, a nonprofit educational travel organization, offers several guided Hawai'i tours for older adults that provide in-depth looks into the culture, history, and beauty of the Islands. For all Elderhostel programs, travelers must purchase their own airfare if coming from outside of Hawai'i. Below are a few typical trips; the Web site shows more options.

Presented in association with Volcano Arts Center, Moloka'i Museum & Cultural Center, and Hawai'i Pacific University, "Islands of Life in the Pacific" is a 15-night, five-island, Elderhostel tour that includes three nights each on Maui and Moloka'i. Prices start at around $4,120 per person and include accommodations, meals, ground transportation, and interisland air and ferry transportation between the islands and all activities.

"Tall Ship Sail Training: Sailing the Hawaiian Islands" is a six-night sailing adventure through the Hawaiian Islands aboard the SSV *Makani Olu,* a 96-foot, three-masted schooner. Prices for this tour start at about $1,510 per person and include accommodations and meals on board the schooner.

"The Entire Island Is a Classroom" is a six-night tour to Moloka'i that examines the island's historical and cultural significance to Hawai'i. Offered in conjunction with the Moloka'i Museum & Cultural Center, travelers will learn traditional Hawaiian fishing practices,

LOCAL DO'S AND TABOOS

Hawai'i was admitted to the Union in 1959, so residents can be pretty sensitive when visitors refer to their own hometowns as "back in the States." Remember, when in Hawai'i, refer to the contiguous 48 states as "the mainland" and not as the United States. When you do, you won't appear to be such a *malahini* (newcomer).

GREETINGS

Hawai'i is a very friendly place, and this is reflected in the day-to-day encounters with friends, family, and even business associates. Women will often hug and kiss one another on the cheek and men will shake hands and sometimes combine that with a friendly hug. When a man and woman are greeting each other and are good friends, it is not unusual for them to hug and kiss on the cheek. Children are taught to call any elders "auntie" or "uncle," even if they aren't related. It's a way to show respect.

When you walk off a long flight, nothing quite compares with a Hawaiian lei greeting. The casual ceremony ranks as one of the fastest ways to make the transition from the worries of home to the joys of your vacation. Though the tradition has created an expectation that everyone receives this floral garland when they step off the plane, the state of Hawai'i cannot greet each of its nearly 7 million annual visitors.

If you've booked a vacation with a wholesaler or tour company, a lei greeting might be included in your package. If not, it's easy to arrange a lei greeting before you arrive at Kahului International Airport with Kama'aina Leis, Flowers & Greeters. To be really wowed by the experience, request a lei of plumeria, some of the most divine-smelling blossoms on the planet. A plumeria or dendrobium orchid lei is considered standard and costs about $22 per person.

Information Kama'aina Leis, Flowers & Greeters (☎808/836–3246 or

800/367–5183 ⊕ www.alohaleigreetings.com).

LANGUAGE

English is the primary language on the Islands. Making the effort to learn some Hawaiian words can be rewarding, however. Hawaiian words you are most likely to encounter during your visit to the Islands are *aloha* (hello), *mahalo* (thank you), *keiki* (child), *haole* (Caucasian or foreigner), *mauka* (toward the mountains), *makai* (toward the ocean), and *pau* (finished, all done). If you'd like to learn even more Hawaiian words, check out ⊕ www.geocities.com/~olelo, a Hawaiian-language Web site.

Hawaiian history includes waves of immigrants, each bringing their own language. To communicate with each other, they developed a language known as pidgin. If you listen closely, you will know what is being said by the inflections and by the body language. For an informative and somewhat-hilarious view of things Hawaiian, check out Jerry Hopkins's books titled *Pidgin to the Max* and *Fax to the Max*, available at most local bookstores in the Hawaiiana sections.

VISITING AND ALOHA

If you've been invited to the home of friends living in Hawai'i (an ultimate compliment), bring a small gift and don't forget to take off your shoes when you enter their house. Try to take part in a cultural festival during your stay in the Islands; there is no better way to get a glimpse of Hawai'i's ethnic mosiac.

And finally, remember that "aloha" is not only the word for hello, good-bye, and love, but it also stands for the spirit that is all around the Islands. Take your time (after all you're on "Hawaiian time"). Respect the *aina* (land) that is not only a precious commodity here but also stands at the core of the Polynesian belief system. "Living aloha" will transform your vacation, fill you with a warmth unique to Hawai'i, and have you planning your return.

dances, songs, and crafts. A highlight is a day trip to Kalaupapa National Historic Park. Prices start at about $1,220 per person and include accommodations, meals, activities, and ground transportation.

Contacts Elderhostel (☎ *800/454-5768* ⊕ *www.elderhostel.org*).

ECOTOURS

"Hawai'i's Humpback Whales and Marine Environment" is a six-night Elderhostel tour that provides visitors with an in-depth study of these gentle giants that migrate to Hawaiian waters every year. You'll participate in whale-watch cruises and snorkel trips with research and conservation groups. Prices start at around $1,200 per person and include accommodations, meals, ground transportation, and activities.

Want to participate in a service project and observe the migrating humpbacks? "Sun, Service, and Whales" is the theme of a 10-night trip organized by Sierra Club Outings. Participants explore the dramatic coastline and the Kīpahulu area of Haleakalā National Park and work at an ancient Hawaiian farming community being preserved by Maui Cultural Lands, Inc. The trip costs about $1,980 per person and includes lodging, most meals, and ground transportation. Travelers must purchase their own air between Maui and their gateway city.

Contacts Elderhostel (☎ *800/454-5768* ⊕ *www.elderhostel.org*). **Sierra Club Outings** (☎ *415/977-5522* ⊕ *www.sierraclub.org/ outings*).

HIKING

"Hawai'i Three Island Hiker" is a seven-night hiking tour to Maui, the Big Island, and Kaua'i. Included in the per-person price of about $3,700 are accommodations, meals, interisland airfare between the three islands, shuttle transportation, support vehicles, and professional guides. Hikers will spend two nights on Maui exploring Hāna's Wai'ānapanapa State Park, Kīpahulu Valley, and Hāmoa Beach; plus the 7-mi Sliding Sand Trail

within Haleakalā Crater. The trip is rated moderately easy to moderate. The World Outdoors has been organizing and leading adventure trips for 20 years.

Contacts The World Outdoors (☎ *800/488-8483* ⊕ *www.theworldoutdoors. com*).

LUXURY

Included in Pure Maui's high-end adventure and spa vacations are private accommodations at elegant estates and villas, all meals prepared by a personal chef, activities, and on-island transportation. Among the options are "Adventure Boot Camp," "Family Adventure," "Learn to Surf/ Yoga," "Romantic Getaway," and "Ultimate Golf" programs. The company can also create customized vacations. Vacationers must purchase their own air travel between Maui and their gateway city.

Contacts Pure Maui (☎ *866/787-6284* ⊕ *www.puremaui.com*).

SPORTS AND WELLNESS

Certified yoga instructor Laurel White, founder of Light Journey Hawai'i, has been running yoga rejuvenation retreats on Maui for more than 10 years. Light Journey has 2- to 12-night "Yoga Cleansing Retreats" and 5-day "Yoga Surf Maui" vacations. Both programs are designed for two people at a time, either a couple or friends. Included in the cleansing retreats are raw nutrition and/or juicing, cleansing herbs, yoga and meditation, infrared sauna, massage and sound therapies, and island adventures. Rates for the retreat vary based on number of nights and inclusions selected.

Imagine learning how to "hang 10" on the perfect wave on Maui. SwellWomen offers six-night "Surf & Yoga" vacations that include accommodations, daily yoga and surf sessions, activities such as hikes and snorkel trips, one-hour massages, meals, and snacks prepared by a private chef. SwellWomen was founded by Me-Shell Barnas, a certified yoga instructor and former professional snowboarder. There are programs for women only, as well as for both men and women. Rates vary depending on the type of house and room category you choose.

You must purchase your own air between Maui and your gateway city for these sports and wellness vacations.

Contacts Light Journey Hawai'i (☎ 808/870-8573 ⊕ www.lightjourney. net). **SwellWomen** (☎ 800/399-6284 or 808/579-8211 ⊕ www.swellwomen.com).

❚ VISITOR INFORMATION

Before you go, contact the Hawai'i Visitors & Convention Bureau (HVCB) for general information on Maui, Lāna'i, or Moloka'i, and to request a free official vacation planner with information on accommodations, transportation, sports and activities, dining, arts and entertainment, and culture.

The Hawai'i Tourism Authority's Travel Smart Hawai'i site offers tips on everything from packing to flying. Also visit the Hawai'i State Vacation Planner for personalized Hawai'i vacation planning help and to sign up for a free Best Places Hawa'i Discount Card, which provides discounts on accommodations, activities, and wedding services on Maui, O'ahu, Kaua'i, and the Big Island. There also are special monthly deals and discounts offered by various hotels, condominiums, and vacation management companies.

Contacts Hawai'i State Vacation Planner (⊕ www.bestplaceshawaii.com). **Hawai'i Tourism Authority** (⊕ www.travelsmarthawaii. com). **Hawai'i Visitors & Convention Bureau** (✉ 2270 Kalakaua Ave., Suite 801, Honolulu, ☎ 808/923-1811, 800/464-2924 for brochures ⊕ www.gohawaii.com).

ALL ABOUT MAUI

Hawai'i Beach Safety has the latest updates on Maui's beaches, including surf forecasts and safety tips. The Hawai'i Department of Land and Natural Resources has information on hiking, fishing, and camping permits and licenses; online brochures on hiking safety and mountain and ocean preservation; and details on volunteer programs. Check with the Kā'anapali Beach Resort Association for detailed information about the resorts, condominiums, attractions, activities, and special events at this 1,200-acre resort in West Maui. Nā Ala Hele, the state's trail and access program, has online maps and directions for hikes on Maui, Moloka'i, and Lāna'i.

Lāna'i Visitors Bureau has good introductory information about the island. The Maui Visitors Bureau has special-interest sections on wellness and honeymoons, among other topics. Moloka'i Visitors Association includes information on golf, transportation, and special events.

Contacts Hawai'i Beach Safety (⊕ www. hawaiibeachsafety.org). **Hawai'i Department of Land and Natural Resources** (⊕ www. state.hi.us/dlnr). **Kā'anapali Beach Resort Association** (⊕ www.kaanapaliresort.com). **Lāna'i Visitors Bureau** (⊕ www.visitlanai. net). **Maui Visitors Bureau** (⊕ www.visitmaui. com). **Moloka'i Visitors Association** (⊕ www. molokai-hawaii.com). **Nā Ala Hele** (⊕ www. hawaiitrails.org)

INDEX

Photo credits: 1-2, Douglas Peebles/eStock Photo. 5, Photodisc. Chapter 1: Experience Maui: 8-9, Pacific Stock/SuperStock. 10 (top), Photodisc. 10 (bottom left), Douglas Peebles/age fotostock. 11 (top left), Walter Bibikow/viestiphoto.com. 11 (top right), Ron Dahlquist/Maui Visitors Bureau. 11 (bottom left), Walter Bibikow/viestiphoto.com. 11 (bottom right), Chris Hammond/viestiphoto.com. 14 (left), Danita Delimont/Alamy. 14 (top center), David Schrichre/Photo Resource Hawaii. 14 (bottom center), David Fleetham/Alamy. 14 (right), Andy Jackson/Alamy. 15 (top left), David Fleetham/Alamy. 15 (bottom left), Mitch Diamond/Alamy. 15 (bottom center), Jim Cazel/Photo Resource Hawaii/Alamy. 15 (right), Starwood Hotels & Resorts. 16 (top left), Jim Cazel/Photo Resource Hawaii/Alamy. 16 (bottom left), Robert Holmes/Alamy. 16 (right), SuperStock/age fotostock. 17 (left), Jim Cazel/Photo Resource Hawaii/Alamy. 17 (top right), Andre Jenny/Alamy. 17 (bottom center and bottom right), Douglas Peebles Photography/Alamy. 19, SuperStock/age fotostock. 20-21, Dana Edmunds/Starwood Hotels and Resorts. 22, Douglas Peebles/age fotostock. 24, Joe Solem/HVCB. 25, Danita Delimont/ Alamy. 27, SuperStock/age fotostock. Chapter 2: Exploring Maui: 31, Maui Visitors Bureau. 33, Pacific Stock/age fotostock. 40, Giovanni Simeone/SIME/eStock Photo. 42, Walter Bibikow/age fotostock. 45, Ron Dahlquist/SuperStock. 46, Douglas Peebles/eStock Photo. 57, National Park Service. 60, Maui Visitors Bureau. 61, Photodisc. 62, Maui Visitors Bureau. 65, Chris Hammond/viestiphoto.com. 67, Ron Dahlquist/Maui Visitors Bureau. 68, Chris Hammond/viestiphoto.com. 71, Richard Genova/viestiphoto.com. 72, SuperStock/age fotostock. 73, Chris Hammond/viestiphoto.com. Chapter 3: Beaches: 75, Brent Bergherm/age fotostock. 79, David Olsen/Aurora Photos. 83, Robert Simon/iStockphoto. 85, Tomas del Amo/Alamy. 88, Richard Genova/viestiphoto.com. Chapter 4: Water Sports & Tours: 91, Eric Sanford/age fotostock. 93, Pacific Stock/SuperStock. 104, SUNNYphotography.com/Alamy. 109, Ron Dahlquist/HVCB. 110, Pacific Stock/SuperStock. 111 (all), William Wu. 119, Michael S. Nolan/age fotostock. 120, SuperStock/age fotostock. Chapter 5: Golf, Hiking & Outdoor Activities: 123, SuperStock/age fotostock. 125, Douglas Peebles/eStock Photo. 129, Pacific Stock/SuperStock. 136, Phil Degginger/Alamy. 139, Luca Tettoni/viestiphoto.com. 140, Kauai Visitors Bureau. 141 (top illustrations), William Wu. 141 (bottom), Jack Jeffrey. 143, Ken Ross/viestiphoto.com. 145, SuperStock/ age fotostock. Chapter 6: Shops & Spas: 149, Douglas Peebles Photography/Alamy. 155 (top), Linda Ching/HVCB. 155 (bottom), Sri Maiava Rusden/HVCB. 156, Michael Soo/Alamy. 157 (top), leisofhawaii.com. 157 (2nd from top), kellyalexanderphotography.com. 157 (3rd, 4th, and 5th from top), leisofhawaii.com. 157 (bottom), kellyalexanderphotography.com. 163 (all), Hotel Hana Maui. 165 (top), Grand Wailea Resort. 165 (bottom left), John C. Russell/Four Seasons Maui at Wailea. Chapter 7: Entertainment & Nightlife: 167, Gaetano Images Inc./Alamy. 169, David Olsen/Photo Resource Hawaii/Alamy. 172, Chad Ehlers/Stock Connection Distribution/Alamy. 176, Hawaii Convention & Visitors Bureau. 177, Thinkstock LLC. 179-80, Hawaii Convention & Visitors Bureau. Chapter 8: Where to Eat: 185, Douglas Peebles Photography/Alamy. 195, Polynesian Cultural Center. 196 (top), Douglas Peebles Photography. 196 (top center), Douglas Peebles Photography/Alamy. 196 (center), Dana Edmunds/Polynesian Cultural Center. 196 (bottom center), Douglas Peebles Photography/Alamy. 196 (bottom), Purcell Team/Alamy. 197 (top, top center, and bottom center), HTJ/HVCB. Chapter 9: Where to Stay: 217, Renaissance Wailea Beach Resort. 232 (top and bottom), Ritz Carlton Kapalua. 240 (top and bottom), Peter Vitale/Four Seasons Maui at Wailea. 245 (top), Old Wailuku Inn at Ulupono. 245 (bottom), Rough Guides/Alamy. 251 (all), Hotel Hana Maui. Chapter 10: Molokai: 253, Greg Vaughn/Alamy. 254 (top), Walter Bibikow/viestiphoto.com. 254 (bottom), Molokai Visitors Association. 255 (top left), Douglas Peebles/age fotostock. 255 (center and right), Walter Bibikow/viestiphoto.com. 255 (bottom), Molokai Visitors Association. 259, David R. Frazier Photolibrary, Inc./Alamy. 267, Tony Reed/Alamy. 269, Walter Bibikow/viestiphoto.com. 270, IDEA. 271-72, Walter Bibikow/viestiphoto.com. 275, Douglas Peebles/eStock Photo. 279, Greg Vaughn/Alamy. Chapter 11: Lanai: 289 and 290 (top), Walter Bibikow/viestiphoto.com. 290 (bottom), Lanai Image Library. 291 (top left), Michael S. Nolan/age fotostock. 291 (top center), Lanai Image Library. 291 (top right), Ron Dahlquist/ SuperStock. 291 (bottom), Lanai Visitors Bureau. 295, Ron Dahlquist/SuperStock. 300, Pacific Stock/ SuperStock. 315 (both), Peter Vitale/Four Seasons Lanai at Koele.

ABOUT OUR WRITERS

Eliza Escaño-Vasquez was raised in Manila, Philippines, and lived in California before falling in aloha with Maui four years ago. She is a contributing writer for *Maui Concierge* and *Modern Luxury Hawai'i*. For this edition Eliza updated the Water Sports and Tours, Shops and Spas, and Entertainment and Nightlife chapters.

Bonnie Friedman, a native New Yorker, has made her home on Maui for more than 25 years. A well-published and well-traveled freelance writer, she also owns and operates Grapevine Productions. She traveled around Maui to get the latest news for the Exploring Maui, Beaches, and Where to Stay chapters, adding some of her favorite places.

Heidi Pool moved to Maui in 2003 after having been a frequent visitor for the previous two decades. She works in the visitor publications industry as a writer and production assistant. An outdoor enthusiast, Heidi enjoys playing "tour guide" when friends or family members come to visit. She updated the Golf, Hiking, and Outdoor Activities chapter.

Cathy Sharpe, our Travel Smart Maui updater, was born and reared on O'ahu.

For 13 years she worked at a Honolu public-relations agency representing major travel-industry clients. Now livi in Maryland, she is a marketing cons tant. She returns home to visit family a friends, relax at her favorite beaches, a enjoy island cuisine—and to keep her e on the latest tips for travlers.

Carla Tracy hails from the mainland (s was born in Ohio), but she has call Maui home for the past 30 years. Sh been with the *Maui News* for more th 25 years, and for much of that time I served as the dining editor. The Where Eat chapter was her Fodor's beat. Ca is also a James Beard Awards panel and writes freelance articles for num ous island magazines.

Joana Varawa has lived on Lān for more than 30 years and is e tor of the *Lāna'i Times Communi Email,* an online newspaper. She ha authored three books and many maga zine and newspaper stories, and con tinues to explore her island. For thi edition, Joana updated Lāna'i and als sailed across the Pailolo Channel t update the Moloka'i chapter.